The Church in the Republic

The Church in the Republic

Gallicanism & Political Ideology in Renaissance France

Jotham Parsons

The Catholic University of America Press
Washington, D.C.

Copyright © 2004
The Catholic University of America Press
All rights reserved
The paper used in this publication meets the minimum requirements of American National Standards for Information Science—Permanence of Paper for Printed Library materials, ANSI Z39.48-1984.
∞

Library of Congress Cataloging-in-Publication Data
Parsons, Jotham
The church in the republic : Gallicanism and political ideology in Renaissance France / by Jotham Parsons. —1st ed.
p. cm.
Includes bibliographical references.
ISBN 978-0-8132-3365-9 (pbk : alk. paper)
1. Gallicanism I. Title
BX1529 .P37 2004
282′.44′09032-dc22
2003024906

To my parents

Contents

Acknowledgments ix

Abbreviations xi

Introduction 1

1. Gallicanism from Reform to History 14

2. Custom, History, and Law 52

3. Gallicanism in the Wars of Religion 96

4. The Problem of Jurisdiction 137

5. Gallicanism as a Political Ideology 185

6. Assemblies of the Clergy and Absolute Monarchy 227

Conclusion 274

Bibliography 285

Index 315

Acknowledgments

The research and writing of this book were funded in part by grants from The Johns Hopkins University, the Ministère des Affaires Etrangères of the Republic of France, the Mellon Foundation, Roosevelt University, and the National Endowment for the Humanities. The research was carried out at a number of libraries and archives, all of which provided highly professional service, in one case within the constraints of severely limited resources. I therefore offer heartfelt thanks to the staffs of the Milton S. Eisenhower Library, the Peabody Institute of The Johns Hopkins University, the Bibliothèque Nationale de France, the Archives Nationales de France and the Bibliothèque Mazarine, the Harvard College and Harvard Law School Libraries, the Library of Congress and its Law Library, the Morris Library of the University of Delaware, and the Newberry Library.

I have received support and encouragement from many individuals. In the first place must stand Orest Ranum, who has amply fulfilled all the highest traditions of academic mentorship. At various stages, I have received valuable comments from Thomas Izbicki, David Bell, Joseph Bergin, Gérard Defaux, Jacques Grès-Gayer, James Hankins, Mack Holt, John Hurt, J. G. A. Pocock, Michel Reulos, Mack Walker, many faculty members and students in the Department of History at The Johns Hopkins University, and other colleagues at the University of Delaware and Roosevelt University. I owe a particular debt of gratitude to Mme. Simone Pautrat for an extraordinary *accueil* in France which not only made my stay pleasant but also contributed no small amount to my understanding of that country. Finally, I have had the good fortune to work closely with a small group of scholars who share my interest in the political implications of sixteenth-century French Catholicism. I owe a great deal to advice and information generously shared by, and conversations with, Megan Armstrong, Alain Tallon, and particularly Eric Nelson.

My most profound debt, however, is to my family. My mother, father, and sister, Marjorie, Charles, and Sylvia, have not only provided me with a truly exceptional level of practical, intellectual, and emotional support, but have also set for me an example of intelligence and erudition as inspiring as it is challenging. My wife, Elaine, has been their equal in both of these things, in addition to providing cogent critiques of even my most incoherent prose, tolerating with great patience the year-long absence of her fiancé during my research and the sundry other indignities that attend the spouse of a writer. It goes without saying that without them this book would never have been completed, and moreover that this is only the smallest part of what I owe to them. Without my daughter, Charlotte, on the other hand, this book would have been completed sooner, but it would have meant much less to me.

Portions of Chapter 2 appeared previously in *The Sixteenth Century Journal* and are reprinted with its kind permission.

This enumeration of my indebtedness, together with much else that I have doubtless omitted, is more than sufficient to account for any virtues this study may possess. For the faults that nevertheless remain, I blame society.

Abbreviations

AN: Archives Nationales (France)

BN: Bibliothèque Nationale de France

    500 Colb.: collection des cinq cents de Colbert

    Duchesne: collection Duchesne

    Dupuy: collection Dupuy

    fr.: manuscrits français

    lat.: manuscrits latins

Gallia Christiana: Denis de Sainte-Marthe et al., eds. *Gallia Christiana, in provincias ecclesiasticas distributa; qua series & historia archiepiscoporum, episcoporum & abbatum Franciae vicinarumque ditionum ab origine ecclesiarum ad nostra tempora deducitur, et probatur ex authenticis instrumentis,* 16 vols. Paris: Jean-Baptiste Coignard, 1715–1865.

Mémoires du Clergé: Recueil des actes, titres et mémoires concernant les affaires du clergé de France, 14 vols. Paris: G. Desprez, 1768–71.

Procès-verbaux: Collection des procès-verbaux des Assemblées-Générales du Clergé de France, 8 vols. (Paris: Guillaume Desprez, 1767).

The Roman Law is cited as I. *(Institutes);* D. *(Digest);* or C. *(Codex Justiniani).*

All translations are my own unless otherwise indicated.

The Church in the Republic

Introduction

The French have always confronted most energetically the great problems of the state and of the church, and with a unique talent of expression have brought them home to all others; they have always had the knack of, so to speak, concentrating the free speculations of thinkers and giving passionate theories a practical orientation.[1]

SO, OVER A CENTURY AND A HALF AGO, the father of modern historiography summarized the world-historical importance of French political culture. While the very idea of the world-historical has fallen into disuse, and even Marxists no longer speak in terms of a dialectic of theory and practice, Ranke's analysis remains convincing in its outlines. From the time of Philip Augustus to that of Napoleon, France was at the forefront of European state building and the French of necessity confronted the secular and religious problems this process raised with an unmatched vigor and consistency. The charge that French thought on political, let alone on ecclesiastical matters, was derivative would be hard to sustain: thinkers from Thomas Aquinas to Rousseau testify against such an interpretation. Still, wherever in Europe an idea originated, it was quite likely that the French would develop its relationship to centralized political power first or most importantly. As Ranke recognized clearly, this was preeminently the case with some of the great social and intellectual movements of the six-

---

1. Leopold von Ranke, *Französische Geschichte vornehmlich in sechszenten und siebzehnten Jahrhunderts*, vol. 1 (Stuttgart, Germany: J. G. Cotta'scher Verlag, 1852), iv–v.

teenth century, including Calvinism, Catholic Reform, and the later stages of humanism.

If it was in France that religious and political ideas confronted the practice of state power, in the early modern period those who undertook to reconcile the two were most likely to be jurists. Men concerned by their training and daily practice with the law were leaders in such matters everywhere in Europe on account of their systematic habits of thought and their affinity for the bureaucratic state, but their numbers, prestige, and influence were particularly striking in France.[2] Ever since William Farr Church published his classic study of sixteenth-century French constitutional thought in 1941, historians have been very deeply concerned with the contribution of jurists to French political thought and political culture, and hence to the development of the Western state.[3] Other scholars have examined the bureaucratic, financial, and family details of how this class of men rose in power and influence.[4] Such inquiries have been productive, greatly increasing our understanding of the origins, limits, and nature of government in early modern Europe. Despite this intensive work, however, several lacunæ remain in the picture historians have thus far reconstructed. This study seeks to fill one of the most important of them.

Living in an era when political life in general and the law in particular are essentially secular, we have a strong tendency to underestimate or misinterpret the religious half of the "great problems of the state and of the church." The sixteenth century is often cited as the point when these fields became separated from the religious, and in many ways this picture is a correct one. Certainly, French humanist jurists devoted an enormous amount of effort to the development of an idea of the state largely—in some cases radically—independent of religious considerations and institutions. This

---

2. William Bouwsma, "Lawyers in Early Modern Culture," *American Historical Review* 78 (1973): 303–27.

3. William Farr Church, *Constitutional Thought in Sixteenth-Century France: A Study in the Evolution of Ideas* (Cambridge, Mass.: Harvard University Press, 1941). Roland Mousnier's parallel though largely independent investigation of the juridical structure of the old regime has had a not dissimilar influence. See, for one synthetic statement, *La plume, la faucille et le marteau: Institutions et société en France, du Moyen Age à la Révolution* (Paris: Presses Universitaires de France, 1970).

4. The pioneering work was that of Denis Richet on the Séguier clan, reprinted in *De la réforme à la Révolution: Études sur la France moderne* (Paris: Aubier, 1991). A fine recent example is Olivier Poncet, *Pomponne de Bellièvre (1529–1607): Un homme d'état au temps des Guerres de religion* (Paris: Editions de l'Ecole des Chartes, 1998).

very process, however, entailed an extraordinarily intimate relationship between political thought and religious life. The fact that the realm of secular politics had to be differentiated from religious ideas and institutions in particular meant that those ideas and institutions had a defining influence on the way that contemporaries conceived and practiced politics. This influence, moreover, was reciprocal. The process of differentiation deeply marked the ideological and political stance of the Catholic clergy in particular, but also the thought of all those who looked with suspicion on the secularization of the political.

In old-regime France, this abstract and involved conflict took a concrete form, particularly though by no means exclusively in the last years of the sixteenth and the first years of the seventeenth centuries. This was the quarrel undertaken by a group of well-placed lawyers and magistrates against all comers on behalf of the so-called liberties of the Gallican church. It gave rise to endless litigation, to diplomatic imbroglios and political showdowns and, as a climax, to a dispute that wrecked the already shaky Estates General of 1614–1615.[5] It then continued in a less acute form for at least the next century and a half. Significant as this quarrel was on the level of pure politics— and to contemporaries it was one of the great issues of the day—it was even more important on the level of ideology, for this was the only context in which a sustained and continuous debate took place over the nature of the French monarchy and of French Catholicism. It produced a voluminous literature, probably the largest and certainly the most coherent on any political issue in the late sixteenth and early seventeenth centuries, which historians of French political thought have mined episodically but not yet examined as a whole. What is more, an understanding of this political context sheds light on the question of how sixteenth-century theoretical speculations became integrated into the practice of seventeenth-century government: a process in which, among other things, the clergy turns out to have played a far more considerable role than has generally been recognized.

This study, then, places religion at the center of the early modern state.

5. The only extensive treatment of this political crisis is the very old one by François-Tommy Perrens, *L'Eglise et l'Etat en France sous le règne de Henri IV et la régence de Marie de Medicis*, 2 vols. (Paris: A. Durand et Pedone-Lauriel, 1872), though there are many interesting insights in a more essayistic work by Salvo Mastellone, *La reggenza di Maria de' Medici* (Messina, Italy: Casa Editrice G. D'Anna, 1962). The best recent study of politics in early-seventeenth-century France, J. Michael Hayden's *France and the Estates General of 1614* (Cambridge, U.K.: Cambridge University Press, 1974), leaves religious conflict among Catholics in the background as a structural or motivating factor.

The theoretical and political contest over the "liberties of the Gallican church" amounted to a fight over how to partition control of the Catholic Church in France among the papacy, the French clergy, and the various organs of the government. After the conversion of Henri IV definitively fixed France on a Catholic path, this contest shaped the way Catholic magistrates, laypeople, and clergy understood the French state and their own places within it. In so doing, it lay at the root of much of the old regime's future politics. It also revealed the assumptions underlying the political thought of two of its most influential participants: the lawyers and judges of the sovereign courts, and the bishops and other prelates of the Catholic clergy. Without a proper understanding of "Gallicanism," its politics and its ideologies, it is impossible to understand how and why the early modern French church and government adopted many of their most important policies and positions. Examining how this conflict played out in France also provides a model of how Renaissance humanism and the Catholic and Protestant Reformations interacted to create the modern state. By the end of the sixteenth century the republic had overtaken the church as the organizing unit of Western society but, like a snake swallowing an elephant, it was profoundly shaped by what it had engulfed.

What, then, were these Gallican liberties, and what was the quarrel that they provoked? It is hard to say, not least because their defenders were reluctant to define them.[6] If they did, they worried, and "if Rome wanted to attempt something against the Gallican church, or those of the church against the king, it would be a sufficient basis for saying that it was not against the authority of the Gallican church or the king, to have recourse to the extensive list."[7] One influential tract even claimed that such a definition was impossible in principal.[8] Nominally at least, the liberties were the guarantees

---

6. The most comprehensive attempt at a global definition of Gallicanism in the sixteenth century is Alain Tallon, *Conscience nationale et sentiment religieux en France au XVIe siècle: Essai sur la vision gallicane du monde* (Paris: Presses Universitaires de France, 2002), 137–62, a chapter with the revealing title "Contradictions et cohérence des gallicanismes." One could not write a chapter on the "coherence and contradictions of Gallicanism."

7. Eugène Halphen, ed., *Lettres inédites de Jacques Faye et de Charles Faye, publiées d'après le manuscrit de la Bibliothèque nationale* (Paris: Champion, 1880), no. 42 (letter dated 20 July 1588). This is a fine example, incidentally, of how much Gallicanism had by then become an essentially *political* movement.

8. Jacques Leschassier, "Contre ceux qui disent que les Juges de ce Royaume doivent dire & compter, quelles, & combien sont les libertez de l'Eglise Gallicane, & de quelle authorité elles sont procedees," in Jacques Leschassier, *Œuvres* (Paris, 1649), 295–97.

of a relative French ecclesiastical autonomy. According to the lawyer Pierre Pithou, who gave them their most influential formulation, they were reducible to two principles: first, that the pope had no temporal authority in France, and second, that the pope was subject to the authority of a general Church council.[9] All formulations of the Gallican liberties also included restrictions on the rights of the pope to raise revenues from and to exercise legal jurisdiction over French subjects. Beyond this level of generality, it is very difficult to find a distinct and permanent set of these liberties. In many ways, in fact, the details of the liberties were less important than were the history and the mind-set they represented and that lay at the heart of the controversies they aroused, not only *between* France and Rome but also *within* France itself. This attitude among the defenders of the Gallican liberties is what modern historians call "Gallicanism." However, as is usually the case with such things, this attitude took very different forms at different times and in different historical contexts.

While the term *Gallicanism* refers to this tradition in general, it is otherwise poorly defined. The word itself is first attested in 1810, under the regime of the Napoleonic Concordat; hence its direct applicability to the *ancien régime* is far from self-evident.[10] That is not to say that the term is illegitimate, but it does suggest that precision in its use will not come easily. It seems in practice to have both a broader and a narrower usage. In the former, it may designate any line of thought that, while remaining within the Catholic Church, valorized a particularly French (usually as opposed to Italian or Roman) religious organization or sensibility. Alain Tallon has recently analyzed it as a "national consciousness" in religious feeling: as such, it was shared almost universally among French Catholics.[11] In its narrower form, Gallicanism designates any one of a large number of doctrines of canon or public law defining the liberties of the Gallican church. "Papalism" or "curialism" would be the most appropriate antonym in this usage. One can sometimes discern an intermediate stage, in which "Gallicanism" designates a purely political position, generally supportive of the policies of the French monarchy as opposed to those of the papacy. This terminologi-

9. Pierre Pithou, *Les Libertez de l'Eglise gallicane* (Paris: Mamet Patisson, 1594), 1.
10. The date of 1810 is from Ferdinand Brunot, *Histoire de la langue française des origines à 1900*, vol. 9.1 (Paris: Armand Colin, 1937), 915–16. He does not cite his source, nor is it clear that he even has one. The earliest firm attestation dates to 1827; see Paul Imbs, *Trésor de la langue française: Dictionnaire de la langue du XIXe et du XXe siècle (1789–1960)*, 16 vols. (Paris: Editions du C. N. R. S., 1971–1994), s.v. "gallicanisme."
11. Tallon, *Conscience nationale*.

cal confusion creates two potentially serious illusions. The first is a possible confusion of affective, political, and legal stances. The second is that it may come to seem that there was one particular and coherent Gallican party or ideology either across time or across social and political groups. Even the traditional distinction among royal, ecclesiastical, and legal Gallicanisms, while helpful, is far from exhaustive.[12] Clarity and precision are all the more important now that the term has become important for analysis of eighteenth-, as well as of sixteenth- and seventeenth-, century French public life.[13] Much the same could be said of "ultramontanism" and equivalent terms as well. These, however, have lately begun to receive some of the analytical attention they deserve, as recent work has begun to reveal some of the complexity in thought and attitude within what has often been portrayed as a monolithic Roman or Tridentine Reformation.[14] Neither Gallicanism nor ultramontanism can be understood apart from each other, for they owed their existence mainly to their conflict.

While this implies that the conflict over the Gallican liberties played an immensely important role in shaping government and culture in early modern France, it also suggests one of the reasons why this importance has not always been recognized. For the stakes in this contest were largely *ideological*. It was a conflict between (at least) two different visions of how the emerging reality of the centralized state should be conceived in relation to both new and traditional intellectual and religious frameworks. It was the kind of

---

12. For these distinctions, see Aimé-Georges Martimort, *Le gallicanisme de Bossuet* (Paris: Editions du Cerf, 1953), pt. 1.

13. See most recently Dale van Kley, *The Religious Origins of the French Revolution: From Calvin to the Civil Constitution, 1560–1791* (New Haven, Conn.: Yale University Press, 1996). Very roughly, the conventional wisdom is now that the ideology of the French Revolution emerged first in the conflicts between Louis XV and the parlements, and that these conflicts in their turn were based at least initially on a Gallican ideology of the type that I investigate in this book.

14. For discussions of what we are to make of sixteenth-century Catholicism, see William Hudon, "Religion and Society in Early Modern Italy: Old Questions, New Insights," *American Historical Review* 101 (1996): 783–804; and the passionate and influential book by John O'Malley, *Trent and All That: Renaming Catholicism in the Early Modern Era* (Cambridge, Mass.: Harvard University Press, 2000). Recent work has also suggested new complexities behind a distinction generally thought to be more or less homologous with that between Gallicans and ultramontanists: the seventeenth-century parties of *dévots* and *bons français*. One of the major findings of Joseph Bergin's *The Making of the French Episcopacy, 1589–1641* (New Haven, Conn.: Yale University Press, 1996), for example, is that the two parties coexisted and intermingled quite comfortably in the episcopal nomination process under Richelieu and Mazarin.

conflict that our media refers to as a "culture war," that is, one in which the stakes of individual incidents—in this case, things like the wording of legislation or jurisdiction over minor court cases—were often not as important as the chance they gave the parties to debate much larger and more nebulous issues. In order to make sense of the many individual skirmishes and major battles this war, then, it is necessary to begin with some model of what the overall conflict was. What were the theories, institutions, and events, examined or unexamined, to which the debate over the Gallican liberties gave a practical application?

In practice, Gallicanism arose out of two particular medieval movements. The first was a series of conflicts between the papacy and secular rulers over who had ultimate authority in political affairs. Popes and their ideological defenders claimed that the transcendent significance of the religious community, over which they held the plenitude of power, gave them directly or indirectly the right to regulate secular affairs and to correct or even depose rulers who interfered with the Church's salvific mission. France enjoyed generally good relations with the papacy, and these debates were correspondingly less critical there than in the Holy Roman Empire. Indeed, France had an equally long tradition of support for the papacy, from Pepin the Short's intervention in Italy to the refuge of Avignon. It was the coexistence and often the tension of these two traditions that shaped French Catholic ecclesiology. Still, particularly in the bitter conflict between Philip the Fair and Boniface VIII, they were fully aired in the French context. From the beginning of the fourteenth century, therefore, any form of Gallicanism necessarily included recognition of the king's right to tax his clergy (with its consent), to control the implementation of new papal legislation within France, and above all to be immune to deposition by the pope. By an obscure corollary, French jurists held that the king could and should minimize the amount of money transferred to the papacy in the form of taxes, fees, and bribes.

A more complex set of ideas had their origin in the period of the Great Schism, and particularly in France's policy, starting in 1395, of withdrawing obedience from both contending popes.[15] At this time, out of practical ne-

---

15. On this period, see the classic study by Noël Valois, *La France et le grand schisme d'occident*, 4 vols. (Paris: Alphonse Picard et fils, 1896–1902), and also his *Histoire de la Pragmatique Sanction de Bourges sous Charles VII* (Paris: Alphonse Picard et fils, 1906); Victor Martin, *Les origines du Gallicanisme*, 2 vols. (Paris: Bloud & Gay, 1939); and most recently Howard Kaminsky, *Simon de Cramaud and the Great Schism* (New Brunswick, N.J.: Rutgers University Press, 1983).

cessity, the prelates and the government organized the Gallican church on a self-administrating basis. They did so, however, in a radical way, declaring that the new system was based on the ancient common law of the Church. This doctrine, associated with but distinct from contemporary theories on the supremacy of Church councils, became the second pillar of Gallicanism. The two had in common at least a verbal commitment to the general reform of a corrupt and overweening Church, a reform to be based on ancient customs and mores and strongly supported, if not led, by the French king.

Taken together, and insofar as they cooperated, these two tendencies constituted a classic Gallicanism, already in place by the second quarter of the fifteenth century. It was directed outward, against the legal, political, and fiscal claims of the papacy. It depended as much on assertions of France's moral superiority to the ambitious and avaricious curia as on concrete legal or philosophical arguments, and such assertions never lacked resonance with the French. In one way, this was its strength, since it could thus command a strong national consensus. On the other hand, though, it was a serious weakness, for it meant that the development and implementation of any Gallican program was liable to be subordinated to broader foreign policy goals. More often than not, that involved cultivating relations with Rome or Avignon. In fact, from the later fifteenth century onward, the ideal of a largely autonomous, self-legislating Gallican church became increasingly irrelevant. It was with this not entirely promising legacy that political thinkers in the sixteenth century set out to build a new Gallican ideology that would respond to a new international landscape and, above all, to the reality of political and social cleavages within France itself. In effect, they did so by ceasing to consider the Church in and of itself and taking instead as their unit of analysis, in the terms of a favorite patristic tag, "the church in the republic."[16] (The term "republic," by the way, was used in the Renaissance to refer to any legally governed polity. For lack of a better modern equivalent, I employ it in that sense throughout the present study.)

This book follows a generally chronological organization, alternating between narrative chapters that describe important stages in the development of Gallican politics and thought and analytical chapters that explore the in-

16. Optatus Milevitanus, "De schismate Donatistarum adversus Parmenium," in J. P. Migne, ed., *Patriologia latina*, vol. 11 (Paris: Vrayet, 1845), cols. 883–1104, col. 999: "Non enim respublica est in Ecclesia, sed Ecclesia in respublica est, id est, in imperio Romano."

tellectual background of these events. The first half explores how the simultaneous development of Reformation religious conflict and Renaissance humanism transformed French magistrates' understanding of the French church's place and role in the "republic." The second half traces some of this transformation's practical and ideological consequences. The first step is to describe the Gallicanism of the fourteenth and fifteenth centuries in somewhat greater detail, and to see what remained of it after its crushing defeat in the struggle over the 1516 Concordat of Bologna. In particular, it is important to understand how Gallicanism fit into larger ideas of ecclesiastical reform, and how it transformed or abandoned those ideas after the Concordat closed the door on many of them. Chapter 1 makes no claim to cover such a vast, and generally well-studied, area of inquiry comprehensively. Its aim is simply to point out some of the more important elements of medieval Gallicanism that would either inform or be radically altered by the influence of humanism and Protestantism.

Since it was humanist magistrates who ultimately took up and reshaped the legacy of Gallicanism, Chapter 2 will investigate in detail their changing political philosophy over the second half of the sixteenth century. We will then see how they applied this philosophy to the problem of the Gallican church and its liberties. The new Gallicanism was not primarily a theological or even a religious theory; instead, it was a theory of how to maintain stability and authority within a state. In the context of the seemingly endless civil war that dominated this period, this was an overriding concern, and in many cases the events of those wars dictated the particular forms that what I will call "erudite Gallicanism" eventually took. Since these were *religious* civil wars, wars (at least in their later stages) fought to a considerable extent *among* Roman Catholics, the relations of church and state necessarily formed the first and most urgent area of application of the humanist magistrates' political thought. Thus, not the least benefit of studying the development of Gallican ideology is that in so doing this important and influential strain of political thought appears far more clearly than it has previously.

Perhaps the most practically important aspect of the new erudite Gallicanism was that it sought to stabilize the French state, as opposed to the Catholic Church or even the Gallican church. Thus, it was not directed in the first instance against Rome, but against what it saw as destabilizing elements within France itself. This made it at least potentially, and increasingly in actuality, into the ideology of a political party, a development traced in Chapter 3. It also inevitably brought it into conflict with powerful forces in

French politics and society. In large part, the erudite Gallican jurists picked this fight deliberately. One of the foundations on which they built their theory was "jurisdictionalism," the long tradition of opposition to ecclesiatical courts and to the extended influence of canon law. The new Gallicanism took this opposition to lengths seldom before seen within orthodox Catholicism, and Chapter 4 shows how the near-complete negation of visible ecclesiastical jurisdiction became a characteristic of erudite Gallicanism. At the same time, both within France and throughout the Christian world, the Catholic Church was promoting a powerful new ideology, or set of ideologies, of its own, collectively known as "the Tridentine Reformation." Chapter 5 investigates the issues and personalities that brought Gallicanism and Tridentinism into conflict. Chapter 6 finally continues this investigation, focusing on the French church's most powerful institutional body, the Assemblies of the Clergy. These assemblies deliberately presented the monarchy with a choice between their more personalized and transcendent view of kingship and the erudite Gallicans' institutional and historical one. Henri IV's and Louis XIII's tilt toward the latter, confirmed in the rise of Cardinal Richelieu, set the tone of French politics for a century to come.

The debate over the Gallican liberties left a deep imprint on the political culture of old-regime France. By the beginning of the seventeenth century, it had become one of the defining features of French political culture, and in one form or another remained so until the middle of the eighteenth century. While it survived, it worked powerfully in favor of the royal government, for the hostility it engendered between prelates and magistrates led each to rely on the king for support, and to glorify the role of the monarchy for their own ends. In the century of Enlightenment, cut off at last from the entire bedrock of ideological presuppositions that had been its origin and foundation, the Gallican quarrel lost its political relevance and fell into abeyance. At the time, this must have seemed merely the passing of an antiquarian curiosity, but the significance of its disappearance was deeper than that. The issue of the Gallican liberties had aroused such passions precisely because it formed and was formed out of the very stuff of early modern politics. Its progressive irrelevance was a major symptom of the increasing irrelevance of the old regime itself, and, for those who could read the signs, a harbinger of the storm that was to break in 1789.

The first task, though, is not to peer so far into the future, but to clarify what Gallicanism was in the sixteenth century. Perhaps it is best to start with the words of an actual early modern Gallican. Introducing his remarks on an important 1565 court case between the Jesuits and the University of Paris, the *avocat général* (attorney general) Baptiste du Mesnil had this to say about the nature of French Catholicism:

> Not all that other nations have received in religion, as long as it is in its administration [*police*], nor even all that has pleased the Holy Father . . . has been admitted in France and its church. . . . She has retained the liberty to submit uniquely and sovereignly to the holy precepts of the sacred Bibles [*sic*] and of holy general and universal councils, without necessarily constraining herself by other laws, fashions, and habits, specifically foreign ones, except insofar as the assembly of this church and the will of the kings have found it expedient or advisable to do so for the good and utility of the said church and of the kingdom of France. And when someone has attempted to do or undertake something to the prejudice of this liberty, . . . one has made use of . . . opportune remedies, which the said Holy Fathers have tolerated and looked on favorably, so that such things have passed, by their patience or tacit consent, into the form of a kind of contract.[17]

Such a statement, fairly typical of mid-sixteenth-century Gallicanism, does tell us a few important things. The Gallican liberties are apparently matters of administration, *police*, as opposed to some more central element of religious life. They involve, in particular, restrictions on the administrative power of the papacy, though they may extend beyond that. They exist within the constraints of Scripture and of the ecumenical councils. The king and the French clergy defend and perhaps define them, and the papacy has more-or-less tacitly recognized them.

Beyond that, however, all is vague. What, exactly, has the Gallican church avoided adopting? Why, indeed, should practices that seem good to the rest of the world not be good for France as well? Specifically, what is wrong with papal administration? Who decides what the Scriptures and the general councils say, or even what they are? How do the French clergy and the monarchy come to decisions, and what happens if they disagree internally or with each other? What makes this system legal and orthodox? Is it its conformity with Scripture (but, then, why not adopt the Protestant Reform?)? Is it Rome's dubious approval (but how would this constitute liberty)? Indeed, du Mesnil immediately added that France held these distinctions "not so much by a privilege as by maintaining and conserving her first liberty."

17. Baptiste du Mesnil, *Plaidoié de feu M. l'advocat du Mesnil, en la cause de l'Université de Paris & des Jesuites* (Paris: Abel L'Angelier, 1594), 13–14.

We will address all of these questions in the following pages, but the last-quoted passage raises some of the most fundamental issues, ones that will be our first concern. It clearly suggests that the Gallican liberties should be somehow defined by their relation to time, by their antiquity and originality. Even here, however, there are some major ambiguities. First of all, where was that "first liberty" to be found? On the one hand, it would be logical to seek it in the origins of the Christian Church, perhaps in apostolic times, according to the tradition of Christian reform thought. On the other hand, though, a Gallican might just as easily seek it somewhere in the early history of French Christianity; and there would be no a priori reason to expect to find the same conditions in both places. As a matter of fact, while both of these possibilities remained open throughout the history of Gallicanism, the sixteenth century saw a distinct shift in emphasis from the first to the second. Moreover, it might not be clear whether it was the fact that the Gallican liberties had existed in ancient times, or that they had been preserved into the present, that gave them their authority. This may seem like a picayune matter, but we shall see that it had considerable implications, and again that there was a tendency in the Renaissance to move from the first to the second alternative. Finally, of course, du Mesnil's final statement does no more than those that came before it to resolve the question of what, specifically, the Gallican liberties liberated the French *from*.

For the sake of orienting ourselves, let us postulate two more specific answers to that question. The first might have been current at the accession of François I: "Rome, corrupted by wealth, greed, and luxury, has consistently attempted to drain France of its wealth, to appoint favorites to its benefices, and to make war on its kings. This threatens to destroy the spiritual and economic life of the kingdom, and to thwart attempts to assert our rights in Italy and elsewhere. The Gallican liberties are our bulwark against this peril. They are the divine law of the Church, revealed in Scripture and in the decisions of the councils, and the expression of divinely instituted justice as it is practiced in secular government." A century later—say, on the accession of Louis XIII—the same question would have elicited a quite different reply. "The Gallican liberties," the seventeenth-century jurist might have said, "are the ancient order of the church in this kingdom and in the world. They guard us today against a restless and ambitious faction, supported by Spain, that seeks to destroy the authority and even the lives of our kings. If we do not stand firm against innovations such as the so-called Society of Jesus, the Council of Trent, and their powerful supporters within the French church itself, we are likely to slip back into chaos." The specific measures proposed by the Gallican jurists (subjecting papal legislation, diplomacy, and legal action to royal control; reservation of French benefices to French subjects; restriction of the ecclesiastical jurisdiction within France) might not have changed radically from the fifteenth century. The ways in which they were justified, however, the modes of their implementation, and their political repercussions had altered drastically. Let us turn now to the first phase of that process.

CHAPTER 1

Gallicanism from Reform to History

THE GALLICANISM of the fourteenth and fifteenth centuries formed an organic part of the great tradition of medieval ecclesiastical reform. From the eleventh century onward, Western Christendom was swept by wave after wave of enthusiasm for the project of purifying the Church: of removing it from the corrupting influence of secular power, ambition, and avarice and reviving an earlier, more innocent state. In particular, at least from the time of Saint Augustine, reformers dreamed of returning to an apostolic ideal of discipline, poverty, and communal harmony.[1] This movement embraced all shades of doctrine from the most orthodox to the most heretical, and was shared by the most absolutist popes and their staunchest adversaries. Thus, it was certainly not surprising that it

---

1. The basic introduction to Christian reform thought remains Gerhard Ladner, *The Idea of Reform: Its Impact on Christian Thought and Action in the Age of the Fathers* (New York: Harper Torchbooks, 1967). The literature on reform in the Middle Ages and early sixteenth century is now very large. There is no really complete survey, but see Gerald Strauss, "Ideas of *Reformatio* and *Renovatio* from the Middle Ages to the Reformation," in Thomas A. Brady Jr., Heiko Oberman, and James Tracy, eds., *Handbook of European History, 1400–1600*, 2 vols. (Leiden, The Netherlands: E. J. Brill, 1994–1995), 2:1–30; and Steven Ozment, *The Age of Reform (1250–1550): An Intellectual and Religious History of Late Medieval and Reformation Europe* (New Haven, Conn.: Yale University Press, 1980). Three specialized studies of particular relevance to the issues discussed here are John O'Malley, *Giles of Viterbo on Church and Reform: A Study in Renaissance Thought* (Leiden, The Netherlands: E. J. Brill, 1968); Louis Pascoe, *Jean Gerson: Principles of Church Reform* (Leiden, The Netherlands: E. J. Brill, 1973); and Thomas Izbicki, *Protec-*

was the common vocabulary for defenses of the liberties of the Gallican church, but the implications of this fact are deeper than they might at first appear. It focused the attention of the Gallican reformers on the specific question of the appointment and personal morality of ecclesiastical officials, and particularly their corruption through avarice. It also tended to mitigate the "nationalistic" edge of medieval Gallicanism, since connection to the general reform tradition automatically made the revival of France's church part of the revival of the Catholic Church in the broad sense.

This is especially important when one considers the relationship between Gallicanism and the French monarchical state. A Gallicanism essentially tied to the tradition of ecclesiastical reform could never be wholly identical with the royal interest, though the two might easily coincide in particular instances. At the same time, while deep divisions could and did develop among medieval Gallicans, between clergy and laity, or between secular and regular clergy, for example, the common vocabulary and, generally speaking, the common aims of ecclesiastical reform lent an overall coherence to the movement. To put the matter a bit more strongly, medieval Gallicanism was a religious movement in a sense in which its early modern successor was not. It placed the French republic, like the rest of Christendom, firmly within the universal Church, or rather, placed both within a fully sacralized vision of human society.

"It sometimes happens that, wishing to avoid a certain error, one falls into its contrary." This is how the theologian Jean de Paris described the landscape of thought in his day concerning the relations of the Church and the world. He was writing around 1300, in the middle of the conflict between Pope Boniface VIII and King Philip the Fair of France.[2] His "two errors" define the limits of reforming thought on relations between church and state. The first,

---

tor of the Faith: Cardinal Johhanes de Turrecremata and the Defense of the Institutional Church (Washington, D.C.: The Catholic University of America Press, 1981).

2. On the context of this tract, see the introductions to John of Paris, *On Royal and Papal Power*, ed. J. A. Watt (Toronto: Pontifical Institute for Medieval Studies, 1971), and the book of the same title, ed. Arthur P. Monahan (New York: Columbia University Press, 1974). Janet Coleman, in "The Dominican Political Theory of John of Paris in Its Context," in Diana Wood, ed., *The Church and Sovereignty c. 590–1918: Essays in Honour of Michael Wilks*, Studies in Church History Subsidia 9 (Oxford, U.K.: Basil Blackwell, 1991), 187–223, dates this tract a few years earlier than Watt, and argues that its political context is not as important as the context of Dominican-Franciscan polemic.

the error of the Waldensians, was that the successors of the apostles, namely, the pope and the prelates of the Church, were not compatible with temporal lordship, nor was it permissible for them to have temporal wealth. Thus they claimed that the Church of God and the successors of the apostles and the true prelates of the Church of God had endured up to Pope Sylvester, from which time, Emperor Constantine having made his donation to the Church, they say that the Roman church began, in such a way that, according to them, God is not in the Church.[3]

This statement of the situation became a classic of the ecclesiological literature, repeated down through the fifteenth century and in some ways becoming more relevant as time went on.[4]

Jean de Paris's mention of the Waldensians was actually a red herring. He was a Dominican, and, as with any good Dominican, his main target was the Franciscans. Suspicion of ecclesiastical wealth had had a long and powerful history in medieval Europe, culminating in some sense a century before with the foundation of the mendicant orders.[5] The more radical strain, which concerned Jean, though, had not merely survived but grown in influence and virulence since that time. The conflict between the "conventual" and the "spiritual" tendencies of the Franciscan order in the latter half of the thirteenth century made the nature of apostolic poverty and its implied contrast with the realities of the medieval clergy a major topic of ecclesiological controversy.[6] Spiritualist extremists, finding little support within the institutional Church, showed a strong tendency to combine their doctrines with the chiliastic speculations of Joachim of Fiore and other prophetic thinkers.

---

3. Jean de Paris, "Tractatus de potestate regie et papale," in Simon Schard, ed., *De jurisdictione, et praeeminentia imperiali, ac potestati ecclesiasticam* (Basel, Switzerland: n.p., 1566), 142–224, p. 142.

4. See Izbicki, *Protector of the Faith*, 109–16.

5. See the classic study by Lester K. Little, *Religious Poverty and the Profit Economy in Medieval Europe* (Ithaca, N.Y.: Cornell University Press, 1978). On the early history of apostolic poverty and community of property in Christian reform, see Ladner, *Idea of Reform*, 319–424; for a more recent overview of the problem as it related to medieval political life, see Janet Coleman, "Property and Poverty," in J. H. Burns, ed., *The Cambridge History of Medieval Political Thought* (Cambridge, U.K.: Cambridge University Press, 1988), 607–48.

6. See Malcolm Lambert, *Franciscan Poverty: The Doctrine of the Absolute Poverty of Christ and the Apostles in the Franciscan Order, 1210–1323*, 2nd ed. (St. Bonaventure, N.Y.: Franciscan Institute, 1998); and, most recently, David Burr, *The Spiritual Franciscans: From Protest to Persecution in the Century after Saint Francis* (University Park: Pennsylvania State University Press, 2002), who particularly stresses the importance of millenialist thought in Peter John Olivi and his followers in the south of France.

Gallicanism from Reform to History 17

They and above all their lay followers equated his coming "Age of the Spirit" with the movement for radical poverty, while radically condemning the "carnal" Church of their own day for precisely the reasons that Jean attributed to the Waldensians.[7] The brutal conflict between Pope John XXII (reigned 1316–1334), on the one hand, and, serially, the spiritual Franciscans, the conventual Franciscan defenders of the doctrine of Christ's absolute poverty, and finally those Franciscans (notably William of Ockham) who aligned themselves with the Emperor Ludwig of Bavaria, on the other hand, gave much wider circulation to these issues. While many of the enthusiasts of poverty were willing to admit the theoretical legitimacy of the post-Constantinian Church, they were united in believing that a return to apostolic poverty would be part and parcel of any true renovation and of the new Age of the Spirit. Particularly in the final stages of this conflict, the question of apostolic and ecclesiastical poverty was enmeshed in the most fundamental questions of papal, conciliar, and secular authority.[8]

Even very moderate (and reasonably well-off) members of the Church hierarchy, while by no means defending apostolic poverty, saw wealth in general and the Donation of Constantine in particular as the source of much corruption in the Church and in Christendom in general. The fact that in the High Middle Ages, Avarice generally replaced Pride at the head of the list of the Seven Deadly Sins gives the measure of how deep this sentiment went.[9] In northern Europe, from the late eleventh century on, a widespread and influential tradition of satirical and moralistic verse attributed to Rome and the curia an especially flagrant devotion to that vice, at least implying that reform of the Church should start with an attack on Roman wealth.[10] It is particularly noteworthy that Jean Gerson, the most prominent reforming theologian of the early fifteenth century, made the due subordination of Church property and all the legal and bureaucratic ap-

---

7. See Marjorie Reeves, *The Influence of Prophecy in the Later Middle Ages: A Study in Joachimism* (Oxford, U.K.: Clarendon Press, 1969), 190–228, 242–50, and passim; and Malcolm Lambert, *Medieval Heresy: Popular Movements from Bogomil to Hus* (New York: Holmes & Meier, 1976), 182–208.

8. On the ecclesiological implications of these issues, see Brian Tierney, *The Origins of Papal Infallibility*, 2nd ed. (Leiden, The Netherlands: E. J. Brill, 1988).

9. See Lester K. Little, "Pride Goes before Avarice: Social Change and the Vices in Latin Christendom," *American Historical Review* 76 (1971): 16–49.

10. See John A. Yunck, *The Lineage of Lady Meed: The Development of Mediaeval Venality Satire* (South Bend, Ind.: University of Notre Dame Press, 1963), esp. pp. 82–132 and, on France, 189–226.

paratus it entailed a centerpiece of his reform program.[11] Given how widespread the mistrust of clerical wealth was even among the clergy, it is no surprise to discover it at the very heart of reform theory among the French laity. One of the causes of the dispute between Philip and Boniface had been the former's assertion of a right to tax his clergy, and one of the steps the king took to bring the pope to heel was to forbid any transfer of funds to Rome.[12] The resultant syllogism was defective, but psychologically compelling: if cutting off the papacy's wealth was the solution, then the wealth of the papacy must have been the problem in the first place. The courts and royal administrators who were charged with implementing these policies, and who were often engaged in battles of their own to wrest jurisdiction over various kinds of property disputes from ecclesiastical courts, were particularly attracted to such thinking.

Restricting ourselves to more-or-less official French expressions of this economically based antipapalism, we find its first clear expression in the reign of Louis IX. While the royal saint was generally friendly toward Rome, he was strongly influenced by the mendicant orders; he also faced unprecedented fiscal demands from a papacy locked in bitter military struggle with Emperor Frederick II.[13] Thus, it is not surprising to find the king's ambassador in 1247 criticizing the rapacity of papal tax collectors, but it is perhaps somewhat startling to find in that critique most of the elements that would form the core of medieval Gallicanism.[14] By imposing arbitrary taxes on ecclesiastics under penalty of excommunication, and by recklessly disposing of French benefices, Louis complained, the papacy "caused infinite amounts of money to be carried out of the kingdom." Not only did this damage the Gallican church itself and the king as its overlord and principle

11. See Pascoe, *Jean Gerson*, 49–58. As we shall see, such sentiments could be found even among enthusastic papalists.

12. See Jeffrey Denton, *Philip the Fair and the Ecclesiastical Assemblies of 1294–1295*, Proceedings of the American Philosophical Society 81, no. 1 (Philadelphia: American Philosophical Society, 1991), and "Taxation and the Conflict between Philip the Fair and Boniface VIII," *French History* 11 (1997): 241–64.

13. On mendicant influence, see Jacques le Goff, *Saint Louis* (Paris: Gallimard, 1996), 745–50 and passim. On papal fiscal pressures, see Giuseppe Martini, "La politica finanziaria dei Papi in Francia intorno alla metà del secolo XIII," *Nuova rivista storica* 65 (1981): 209–82, esp. 229–37.

14. This text, generally known as the "Protest of St. Louis," is preserved in a sort of documentary appendix that the English monk Matthew Paris attached to his *Chronica majora*. Despite some objections, there can be little question as to its authenticity; see Gerard J. Campbell, "The Protest of Saint Louis," *Traditio* 15 (1959): 401–18.

endower, but "by the impoverishment of the church the kingdom is impoverished, since when the church's goods are thus taken from the realm, the realm is despoiled and from its spoils outsiders are enriched." Such actions exceeded the reasonable powers of the papacy, which could not be exercised "for one's own pleasure rather than for the benefit of the subjects." Such exactions brought hatred and disobedience on the popes, not only because they violated others' interests, but because of their manifest discordance with the life of the apostles, who "in humility and poverty of spirit planted the Christian religion."[15]

This combination of fiscal self-interest and idealism was to reappear repeatedly in the history of medieval Franco-papal relations. Philip the Fair began his public relations offensive against Boniface VIII in 1302 by accusing the pope of abusive collations and taxation, "from which comes the diminution of the divine cult, ... the impoverishment of the realm follows, and the churches incur the damage of deformation."[16] Philip's victory in this struggle and the papacy's subsequent relocation to Avignon instituted an era of good feelings. In the fifteenth century, however, during and after the Great Schism, the various popes were simultaneously desperate for funds and (given their many opponents within the Church) poorly positioned to resist pressure from secular governments.[17] At the same time, deflation meant that the fiscal burden of the papacy became a more serious drain on France's straitened money supply.[18] In response, royal advisors dug the old weapons out of the closet and put them to much more intensive use. Thus, for example, in 1406 Charles VI complained that because of the fiscal exactions of the papacy "the divine cult and works of charity, which he [king or pope?] should cause to multiply, are defrauded and cease, the intent of founders is not served; by these means, too, the kingdom is stripped and impoverished of enormous sums of money and wealth, and infinite and al-

---

15. Matthew Paris, *Chronica majora*, Vol. 6: *Additamenta*, ed. Henry Luard (London: Longman, 1882), 102, 111, 101. The last passage cites the *Decretum*, q. 11 c. 3 *Sæpe amborum*.

16. Georges Picot, ed., *Documents relatifs aux Etats Généraux et assemblées réunis sous Phillipe le Bel* (Paris: Imprimerie Nationale, 1901), 7–8. This is from the French prelates' account of a (lost) royal harangue in a letter to Boniface.

17. On papal fiscality and related politics during the Great Schism, see Jean Favier, *Les finances pontificales à l'époque du grand schisme d'Occident, 1378–1409* (Paris: E. Boccard, 1966); on the subsequent period, see John A. F. Thomson, *Popes and Princes, 1417–1517: Politics and Polity in the Late Medieval Church* (London: George Allen & Unwin, 1980).

18. See Harry A. Miskimin, *Money and Power in Fifteenth-Century France* (New Haven, Conn.: Yale University Press, 1984), 73–90. Miskimin does, however, ignore that fact that money going to Avignon, in particular, must have flowed back into France quite promptly.

most uncountable scandals erupt daily. That all is permitted should be sufficiently evident, and the pope is clearly seen to stray from the ends to which his power is ordained."[19] Like Philip the Fair before him, and in what was to be a standard Gallican maneuver, Charles therefore cut off the flow of any funds to Rome.

From this point on, such declarations become too frequent to follow in any detail. The climax of fifteenth-century Franco-papal relations was the Pragmatic Sanction of Bourges (1438), the French response to the Council of Basel. Among both the clergy and the judiciary, it remained the touchstone of French resistance to papal pretensions well into the sixteenth century, and its preamble set forth the classic version of the "filthy lucre" narrative.[20] As long as the Church had kept the ancient canons of the Fathers, its work had prospered in virtue:

> But alas! damned ambition, depravity, and detestable, insatiable cupidity, the root of all evil, violating the laws of humanity, one began little by little to abandon and even contemn this salutary order of the holy ancient fathers and gradually to slip into vice. From whence have followed the corruption and depravity of morals, dishonorings and discolorations of the ecclesiastical state, very grave usurpations and intolerable enterprises.[21]

The glossator of this text waxed eloquent on the corrupting power of avarice, which "like an evil poison feminizes the infected manly body and spirit: it is always infinitely insatiable." If this powerful force truly was the downfall of the Christian Church, it made every kind of sense to react, as the French kings did, by restricting the papacy's ability to draw funds from France.

When they defended the Pragmatic Sanction to Louis XI, the officers of the Parlement of Paris sounded more like economists than moralists. The four evils that followed from its abrogation were, first, "the confusion of the whole ecclesiastical order"; second, "the depopulation of the kingdom's

---

19. *Ordonnances des rois de France de la troisième race, recueillies par ordre chronologique*, vol. 9 (Paris: Imprimerie Royale, 1755), 184.

20. The standard treatment of the Pragmatic Sanction's origins and nature remains Noël Valois, *Histoire de la Pragmatique Sanction de Bourges sous Charles VII* (Paris: Alphonse Picard et fils, 1906).

21. *Pragmatica sanctio cum glossis egregii, eminentisque scientiæ viri, Domini Cosmæ Guimier Parisini, in supremo Parisiensi senatu Inquestarum Præsidis. Quibus accesserunt ad cuiuslibet Decreti Parraphos summaria, suisque in locis Concordatorum concordia, & illorum dissonantia: Necnon glossæ, ac additiones, . . . Opera aut labore D. Philippi Propi Biturici . . . Secunda editio quoad additiones* (Paris: Apud Galeotum à Prato, 1555), fols. 28–31 and (Guimier's) *glossa ad* "insatiabilitas."

subjects"; third, "the emptying of the kingdom of money"; and fourth, "the ruin and total desolation of churches." They complained of the death rate on voyages to Rome, and backed up their analysis with a detailed if highly imprecise accounting of the annual flow of specie to Rome. They also bemoaned the plight of parishes where "the money that should be used for repairs will be taken out of the kingdom.... Thus church buildings will remain in ruins, and the revenues uncollectible, and consequently the divine service will remain ruined to the great detriment of the souls of the living and the dead."[22]

This rhetoric was calculated to appeal to Louis XI, the notoriously grasping "universal spider," but it had another political benefit as well. It represented a view that the clergy, or much of it, could unambiguously embrace. Thus, in the Estates General of 1484, as a canon of the cathedral of Rouen reported, the proposed ecclesiastical article of the grievances to be submitted to the king "greatly satisfied all, except a few isolated bishops. To prevent a great deal of money from leaving the kingdom for Rome and also to promote schooled and educated men, it was there stated and written that nothing should be removed by apostolic power, even in accordance with the Pragmatic Sanction. At the same time we also petitioned for the Pragmatic Sanction, which had been suspended in the reign of Louis [XI]."[23] The Estates got their way. By the late fifteenth century, France's magistrates and clergy had reached a rough but solid consensus on the fiscal independence of the Gallican church.

A similar agreement on how authority and jurisdiction should be distributed within the Church in order to avoid "the confusion of the ecclesiastical order" buttressed this ideology. One can get an idea of that second consensus by following the ways in which the French avoided Jean de Paris's other extreme,

> the opinion of certain moderns, who so flee the above-mentioned error of the Waldensians that they go over entirely to its opposite, even to the point of asserting that the lord pope, insofar as he holds Christ's place, has on earth lordship

---

22. *Les Remonstrances faictes au Roy Loys Unzieme, sur les privileges de l'Eglise Gallicane* (Paris: Jean Dallier, 1561), fol. 6r., fol. 17v.

23. Jehan Masselin, *Journal des états généraux de France tenus à Tours en 1484 sous le règne de Charles VIII*, ed. A. Bernier (Paris: Imprimerie Royale, 1835), 82. Those bishops, it was said, had been appointed by Louis XI while the Pragmatic Sanction was suspended. The article did appear in the final *cahier*; see *Journal des états généraux*, 662–65.

over the temporal goods of princes and barons, and cognition or jurisdiction [over them].[24]

As a statement of the papalist position, this was unfair, and it became more so as time went on and extravagant claims were toned down—but it clearly captured the vital issue that *opponents* of papalism considered to be at stake, namely, the freedom of temporal lordships from being disposed of in papal judgments. The view that the pope could not so dispose of temporal power was, at least apparently, a much narrower and more moderate view than the rejection of clerical possessions. As such, it was suitable as a centerpiece for royalist propaganda and ideology.

Moreover, just as the royal officials found extraneous and partially emotional reasons to support their doubts about the wealth of Rome, so the European and particularly the French clergy found their own reasons to favor a limitation of papal jurisdiction. First, a series of disputes erupted in France beginning in the 1250s over how strictly local bishops could control the activities of Dominicans and Franciscans.[25] The mendicants claimed that papal privileges gave them blanket authority to teach, preach, and administer the sacraments anywhere in Christendom. Since, according to their theory, Christ had given Saint Peter total jurisdiction over such matters, which he and his successors thence delegated to the various bishops, popes had a right to override any local jurisdiction. The bishops, naturally, had little sympathy for such reasoning. They, and the secular masters of the University of Paris whose livelihood the popular mendicant professors threatened, argued just as strongly that their jurisdictional authority, whatever its source, was inalienable within their own dioceses, and that even the pope was overstepping his bounds in seeking to infringe upon it. An episcopate afraid that the papacy might at any time extend its own jurisdiction at its expense was more likely to view extensions of papal jurisdiction in other di-

---

24. Schard, ed., *De jurisdictione*, 143. According to Coleman, in "Dominican Political Theory," Jean's immediate target is again a certain strain of Franciscan argument.

25. On this, see Christine Thouzellier, "La place du *De periculis* de Guillaume de Saint-Amour dans les polémiques universitaires du XIIIe siècle," *Revue historique* 156 (1927): 69–83; and, above all, Yves Congar, "Aspects ecclésiologiques de la querelle entre mendiants et séculiers dans la seconde moitié du XIIIe siècle et le début du XIVe," *Archives d'histoire doctrinale et littéraire du moyen âge* 28 (1961): 34–151. The most comprehensive statement of the papalist position in these disputes has been edited, with a valuable introduction, by William D. McCready under the slightly misleading title *The Theory of Papal Monarchy in the Fourteenth Century: Guillaume de Pierre Godin, Tractatus de causa immediata ecclesiastice potestatis* (Toronto: Pontifical Institute of Medieval Studies, 1982).

rections with grave suspicion, while the university developed its own habit of suspicion toward the papacy.

Finally, the Great Schism put the very institution of the papacy in practical, if not theoretical, doubt. Since the Schism coincided with a near-collapse of the French monarchy during the madness of Charles VI and the subsequent civil wars, the clergy led the way in reacting to the ecclesiastical crisis after 1394. They did so, led by the Faculty of Theology at the University of Paris and a small group of prelates, by subtracting the Gallican church from obedience to either of the claimants to the See of Peter.[26] In doing so, they were forced to develop an interim system of jurisdiction, and here they fell back explicitly and radically on the tradition of ecclesiastical reform. They claimed to revert to the ancient common law of the Church (rather than, say, instituting emergency regulations in extraordinary circumstances). Further, they claimed that these ancient canons provided the mechanism whereby the Church could be cleansed of the manifold impurities then infecting it—above all simony and avarice. This hearkened back to a reform ideal of the patristic era, and was to have a very considerable future in France.[27] A large segment of French political society backed this movement enthusiastically—most notably those jurists who had long opposed papal interference in temporal affairs and the development of canon law under papal leadership. Victor Martin, in a classic study of this period, has identified in it the "origins of gallicanism"; and it does indeed seem that in the early fifteenth century Gallicanism first emerged as a fully formed ideology.[28]

In the end, of course, and largely under French leadership, the Councils of Constance, Pisa, and Basel took it upon themselves to depose the various pretenders to the papacy and impose their own candidates. In doing so, they both implicitly and explicitly rejected the central contention of the papalist theory of jurisdiction: that the pope was in the strongest sense the man

---

26. On the formulation and pursuit of the *via cessionis*, see Howard Kaminsky, *Simon de Cramaud and the Great Schism* (New Brunswick, N.J.: Rutgers University Press, 1983); and Hélène Millet, "Du conseil au concile (1395–1408): Recherche sur la nature des Assemblées du clergé en France pendant le Grand Schisme d'occident," *Journal des savants* (1985): 137–59.

27. See Ladner, *Idea of Reform*, 298–303. From the late fourth century on, this idea had been nourished both by the history of the Ecumenical Councils and by the supposititious "Apostolic Canons," supposed to incarnate the practices of the earliest Church. On the latter, see the *Dictionnaire de droit canonique* (Paris: Letouzey, 1935–1965), s.v. "canons apostoliques."

28. Victor Martin, *Les origines du gallicanisme*, 2 vols. (Paris: Bloud & Gay, 1939).

"who judges everyone and is judged by no one."[29] The link between this assertion of conciliar power and the conciliarism that was its theoretical justification, on the one hand, and denial of papal power to adjudge temporal lordships, on the other hand, was not a strict one, but it was sufficiently plausible to become, at times, an article of faith for both lay and clerical Gallicans. Only the ignominious failure of conciliarist policies in the last part of Louis XII's reign, up to 1514, shattered this consensus. In this context, the defense of the French monarchy against papal interference became inextricably linked with the conciliar tradition, which, as we now know, was one of the most fertile sources of political theory from the Middle Ages well into the modern period.[30]

By the mid-fifteenth century, particularly after the Pragmatic Sanction had codified both the economic and the jurisdictional sides of the question, Gallicanism as an official ideology (with certain variations and much lapse in practice) was effectively unchallenged in France. By the end of the century, indeed, the Italian campaigns of Charles VIII and Louis XII had brought the French monarchy once again into close and sustained contact with the papacy, and had given new urgency to old theories of church-state relations. By the dawn of the sixteenth century, all over Europe, religious ideology was enjoying an unusual prominence in the operation of government. Dynastic ambition remained undeniably central to the real business of states, while secular national identities were beginning to emerge around the continent, but between the two there was a gap often filled by visions of the Christian community incarnated in one or the other body politic. Florence, at the height of its Renaissance glory, found an explanation for its own existence in the prophecies of Savonarola. Spain, under the Catholic monarchs and Charles V, promoted the crusading myths of the *reconquista* and the Joachite myths of the universal monarchy. France, having abandoned the illuminations of Joan of Arc as excessively dangerous, for a time built an inter-

---

29. *Corpus juris canonici editio Lipsiensis secunda*, ed. Aemilius Friedberg, 2 vols. (Leipzig, Germany: B. Tachnitz, 1879), 2: col. 1245. This is the rubric to the bull *Unam sanctam*, as it was incorporated into the *Extravagantes communes*.

30. The literature on conciliarism is now vast. Among the seminal works in the field are Brian Tierney, *Foundations of the Conciliar Theory: The Contribution of the Medieval Canonists from Gratian to the Great Schism* (Cambridge, U.K.: Cambridge University Press, 1955); Antony J. Black, *Monarchy and Community: Political Ideas in the Later Conciliar Controversy, 1430–1450* (Cambridge, U.K.: Cambridge University Press, 1970); Francis Oakley, "Almain and Major: Conciliar Theory on the Eve of the Reformation," *American Historical Review* 70 (1965): 673–90; and J. H. Burns, *Lordship, Kingship, and Empire: The Idea of Monarchy, 1400–1525* (Oxford, U.K.: Clarendon Press, 1992).

national and domestic identity around the constitutional program of (in the eyes of its adherents) reform and moderation in the Church: conciliarism, Gallicanism, and the "liberties of the Gallican church."

The first two decades of the sixteenth century were, then, the classic period of medieval Gallicanism, when the ideological tendencies that had their origins in the quarrels over the papal power of deposition and the Great Schism reached their definitive formulation. The same period, however, saw the irruption of three forces that would profoundly transform the character of Gallican thought. In 1515, immediately upon his accession to the throne, François I reversed the usual course of the French monarchy since the Great Schism and reached a negotiated settlement with the papacy on most outstanding jurisdictional issues. Embodied in the Concordat of Bologna, and forced by the king upon the deeply reluctant *corps* of French royal and clerical officials, this agreement removed much of the legal ground for jurisdictional Gallicanism as it then existed. The Protestant Reformation, beginning three years later, provided a radical alternative to Gallicanism for those disgusted by the worldliness of the Church, while encouraging less radical critics to mute their cries lest aid and comfort be given to the common enemy. Finally, the flood of the Renaissance into France, already underway in the reign of Louis XII, reached, under the patronage of his successor, the proportions of a true cultural revolution. As humanist learning became the paradigm of the French educated classes, all ideology had to be reformulated to consider it. The result, slowly and painfully over the first half of the century, was the replacement of medieval Gallicanism by a new construct, containing much old material but suitable for the new conditions.

The history of sixteenth-century Gallicanism really begins on 30 July 1510, when King Louis XII of France very deliberately opened a crisis in his relations with the papacy.[31] On that day, following precedents reaching back to Philip the Fair, he summoned his bishops to send delegations from their dioceses to a council of the national church. It was to meet at Orleans (later changed to Tours) in a month and a half, to discuss the affairs of the Galli-

31. The only recent studies of this crisis are Frederic Baumgartner's essay, "Louis XII's Gallican Crisis of 1510–13," in Adrianna Bakos, ed., *Politics, Ideology and Law in Early Modern Europe* (Rochester, N.Y.: University of Rochester Press, 1994), 55–72, and his book *Louis XII* (New York: St. Martin's Press, 1994), 169–82 and 209–28. There is a more thorough and heavily documented, though somewhat narrow, account in Pierre Imbart de la Tour, *Les origines de la réforme*, Vol. 2: *L'Eglise catholique, la crise et la renaissance* (Paris: Hachette, 1909), 127–81.

can church.[32] Louis did not further specify those affairs, but everyone knew that they involved the impending war in Italy between Louis and Pope Julius II, who was then in the process of deserting the French in the anti-Venetian War of the League of Cambrai. When the war finally broke out, Julius might well excommunicate Louis, declare him stripped of his territories, and even place France under interdict and refuse to authorize any ecclesiastical administration there. Louis, on the other hand, would certainly wish to prevent the pope from collecting any money from France with which he could sustain his war effort. On the ecclesiastical as on the military front, then, the kingdom needed to make both offensive and defensive preparations, and for this reason Louis (and his advisors) found it worthwhile to invoke one of the monarchy's more potent consultative mechanisms.

The potential benefits of calling an assembly of the clergy were double. First, it could demonstrate to the world at large that Louis had the full support of his clergy and that the pope could not hope to detach them from their obedience. Second, as during the Great Schism, the clergy could arrange to bypass the pope in the administration of the Gallican church. Such assemblies had done this as far back as the reign of Philip the Fair. The potential danger, of course, was that either the hoped-for support would not be forthcoming or that, once assembled, the clergy would make demands or impose regulations not desired by the government. History, however, suggested that Louis was quite safe in relying on his clergy. Since Carolingian times, the French clergy had consistently backed its kings in confrontations with Rome. This reliability had been firmly demonstrated a century previously during the endless crises of the Great Schism, and there were no signs that it had frayed significantly since then. As it happened, when the clergy did meet, the king was not deceived.

The assembly returned exactly the desired answers to eight questions that had been prepared for it, declaring that there was no reason the king could not fight a just war against the pope.[33] The king and the clergy, however, at least professed to believe that the ultimate issue at hand was not dynastic

---

32. There is a good account of these events in Augustin Renaudet, *Préréforme et humanisme à Paris (1494–1517)* (Paris: Honoré Champion, 1916), 524–62.

33. The questions were: (1) Is it permissible for the pope to declare war on a Christian prince, on lands subject to him, and when there is not a question of faith at issue? (2) May a prince so attacked defend his realm? (3) May an unjustly attacked prince withdraw his obedience from the pope? (4) If he does, what measures should be taken for the internal government of the Gallican church? (5) May the prince come to the aid of an ally unjustly attacked by the pope? (6) May the pope attack a prince because of a dispute over his

politics and the theological subtleties thereof, but rather the reform of both the Gallican church and the Universal Church. The assembly of Tours called for the return of the (once again widely ignored) Pragmatic Sanction, an idea that the king discouraged. He did, however, summon them to meet again in a few months' time in Lyons, to vote him a subsidy, but also to deliberate on ways to reform the Church.[34] As expected, they agreed to back the project of three dissident cardinals for a general council to be held without the pope. However, they also adopted a set of interim decrees on the discipline of the national church, underlining the seriousness of their commitment to reform.[35]

In the event, the general council was a failure. The "goodly number of prelates ... who," as Louis optimistically put it, "given this holy work have liberally taken up the charge of going there, fearing no perils or dangers," failed to materialize.[36] The self-styled Council of Pisa turned out to be, in Marx's approved manner, the Council of Constance repeated as farce, retreating gradually northward with a steadily dwindling membership to expire ingloriously in Lyons in 1513. For some time, though, the French church at least pretended not to realize this, and continued to defend the Council and the Gallican liberties against their detractors. Until Louis XII's death on New Year's Day in 1515, a steady stream of Gallican rhetoric flowed through France under the auspices of various bodies and expressing most of the current ideas on organization of the Church and its relations to secular politics.

The first important defense of the French view in this conflict came from one of Louis XII's "hired guns," the poet Jean Lemaire de Belges. In 1510 and 1511, he wrote a little collection of four pamphlets praising Louis's allies in his current war (including, improbably enough, the Safavid Persian ruler Sheik Ismail), and attacking the Venetians and the pope.[37] Lemaire was

---

patrimony, if that prince has demanded arbitration? (7) Are the censures against such a prince valid if the pope refuses arbitration? (8) Are they valid if he attacks under arms? See de la Tour, *Les origines*, 133, after BN lat. 1559, fol. 1 v.

34. See the *procès-verbal* of that assembly, BN lat. 1549^A.

35. See BN lat. 1559, fols. 20–24. The decrees are interesting for their similarity to the program later adopted (with French support) at Trent.

36. BN lat. 1559, fol. 14r (letters patent of 2 September 1511, cop. aut.).

37. Jean Lemaire de Belges, *Le Traicté intitulée: De la differance des scismes et de la preeminence et utilite des concilles de la saincte Eglise; L'entretenement de l'union des princes; L'histoire de Syach Ismail; Le blason des armes des Veneticns*, 4 vols. in 1 (Lyon, France: Estienne Baland, 1511). I quote from the more accessible modern edition.

a vehement and imaginative polemicist, and his attack on the pope was one of the fiercest to appear between Marsiglio of Padua's *Defensor minor* and Luther's *95 Theses*. Its most striking feature was that it was a historical narrative, not one of the legal or philosophical treatises typical of earlier antipapal argument. This may have had something to do with Lemaire's exposure to Italian humanism as well as those humanist movements already operating in France and the Low Countries. It certainly pointed the way to future developments in Gallican discourse, though Lemaire's direct influence is doubtful, and it would be many years before humanist historicism played an important role in French ecclesiastical politics.[38]

At any rate, even in its historical narrative, the *Traicte des scismes* did not break radically with medieval Gallicanism or with the ways of thinking that had sustained it. For Lemaire, humanist scholarship remained a foreign source, not a native way of thought. As he summed it up, his thesis was that

> the riches given to the Church, namely, by the Emperor Constantine the Great, and his successors Pepin, Charlemagne, Louis the Bold, and other good princes, though they were made under the show of sanctity, prudence, and chastity, have nevertheless given birth sinisterly to several evil children, namely, pride, pomp, arrogance, heresy, disregard of princes, tyranny over subjects, and impudence, that is to say shamelessness. After which things has come the omission of general councils.[39]

In other words, Lemaire used a modified and somewhat historicized version of the old argument against the material wealth of the Church, combined with a reverence for councils as a sovereign means of reform.

Lemaire's arguments were not an exotic transplant from Italy or the Hapsburg lands. Another of Louis's polemicists, the very French lawyer Jean Bouchet, similarly combined prophecy and a denunciation of the corrupting effects of ecclesiastical wealth in his 1512 *Déploration de l'église militante*. Though he concentrated much less on the papacy and much more on simony than did the fiercer Lemaire, Bouchet hardly strayed from his overall out-

---

38. Later writers had little respect for Lemaire de Belges's scholarship, while this particular tract was adopted early on by the Protestants; see the introductory material to a Latin translation by Ludovicus Camerarius, *Tractatus de differentiis schismatum et conciliorum in ecclesia & de utilitate ac præeminentia conciliorum sanctæ ecclesiæ Gallicanæ* (Leipzig, Germany: A. Schneider, 1572).

39. Jean Lemaire de Belges, *Œuvres*, ed. Jean Stecher, 4 vols. (Louvain, Belgium: Lefever frères et sœur, 1885), 3: 243–44. For more details on Lemaire's doctrine and sources, see Jennifer Britnell, "The Antipapalism of Jean Lemaire de Belges' *Traité de la Difference des Schismes et des Conciles*," *Sixteenth Century Journal* 24 (1993): 783–800.

look. Appropriating a Joachist commonplace, he located the Church in the third of three persecutions. After the depredations of the pagan Romans and the early heretics, now "Humility has turned to pride; / Cursed be the hour and the day / That poverty was abandoned for riches!"[40] Bouchet recommends the usual set of reforms: strict enforcement of the Pragmatic Sanction and the rules against simony, a less avaricious clergy, and Franco-papal cooperation in summoning a holy council and leading a crusade against the Turks. This was an essentially moderate program, postponing both its greatest hopes and its hardest decisions to an indefinite sacred future, and it commanded very wide support among both clergy and laity in France.

Contemporary readers would have recognized that this set of ideas pointed toward one of the prophetic views of history that was prevalent at the time. This was all the clearer in combination with the extraordinarily eclectic alliance system Lemaire promoted in his pamphlets and both poets' suggestion that the king of France was best placed to unify Christendom and overcome the infidels. In case they missed the point, Lemaire concluded the *Traicte des scismes* with a prediction of a final schism to come, followed by the triumph of a reunified Church. This type of prophetic theory had a long association with the critique of ecclesiastical wealth, being traceable to the Spiritual Franciscan movement and Joachim of Fiore. By the early sixteenth century, though, such prophecy had become largely political, bound up in particular with the idea of a millennial world emperor who would regenerate Christianity. Lemaire's usual patrons, the Hapsburgs, traded heavily in such ideas, but in France too they could be combined with existing antipapal traditions to produce an overall religious vision of the monarchy's place in history.[41]

The results could be truly startling in their concordance not just with Lemaire's tract but with the entire tenor of medieval Gallican thought. One such prophetic story, attributed to the Dominican Saint Vincent Ferrer and part of a widely circulating fifteenth-century tradition (finally published in Venice in 1516) illustrates this particularly well.[42] According to this scheme,

---

40. Jean Bouchet, *La déploration de l'église militante*, ed. Jennifer Britnell (Geneva: Droz, 1999), 81, ll. 644–46: "Humilité en orgueil est tournée; Que mauldicte soit l'eure et la journée Dont on laissa pauvreté pour richesse." Prophetic overtones abound in this poem; see also, e.g., 86–87 and notes.

41. See Frances Yates, *Astræa: The Imperial Theme in the Sixteenth Century* (London: Routledge, 1975); and Reeve, *Influence of Prophecy*, 293–392.

42. This comes from a collection put together by a fifteenth-century Venitian Domini-

an angelic pope would come to the Roman see in the wake of persecution by the emperor and a German antipope. Then, moved by tales of this paragon's virtue and miracles, "a generous king of Pepin's line, . . . a king of France will come from abroad to see the light of the glorious angelic pastor. That pastor, . . . the temporal seat then being vacant, shall sweetly bestow it on the said king," getting him elected emperor. The king/emperor would then reconquer the Holy Land and convert the Muslims. "The king of the French or new emperor, returning in glory from Jerusalem, shall prohibit all to bear arms, and there shall be peace and tranquility throughout the world, and anyone may take his way in justice. And the clergy shall hold to a most apostolic life." Meanwhile, the pope "shall be holy, as it were having nothing and possessing everything . . . he will not intervene in temporal things, but with his staff he will visit all lands and regions. . . . The city of Rome will become as nothing in temporal things, but in spiritual ones, for what little [time] remains, it shall be exceedingly great."[43] As a Gallican vision, this lacks nothing. The king of France will rule in harmony *with*, but without interference *from*, the pope, who will in fact swear off arms altogether. The two of them will enforce, apparently by both precept and example, a poor and apostolic way of life for the clergy. The result will be so appealing to humanity and pleasing to God that it will produce a unified Christian society of peace and harmony, lasting until the End Times. To crown the happiness of all, the Germans will be put in their place!

Indeed, this complex of ideas is truly omnipresent in the literature of the Pisan schism. It flourished even in the heart of Rome, where Julius II called the Fifth Lateran Council as a counterblast to the Pisans. The opening orator in Rome, the general of the Augustinian Hermits, Egidio of Viterbo, was personally steeped in the traditions of reformist and prophetic thought.[44] His speech to the conciliar fathers lamented the demoralization of Christians in general and the clergy in particular—"when was our life

---

can named Rusticianus, built around the prophetic compilations of Telesphorus of Costenza, which in turn were very widely circulated, particularly in France. See Reeves, *Influence of Prophecy*, 173, 262, and 320–46; and E. Donckel, "Die Prophezeiung des Telesforus," *Archivum franciscanum historicum* 26 (1933): 29–104.

43. *Expositio magni prophete Joachimi in libris beati Cirilii de magnis tribulationibus & statu sancte matris ecclesie: ab his nostris temporibus usque in finem seculi: una cum compilatione ex diversis prophetes novi ac veteris testamenti Theolosphori de Lusentia*, etc. (Venice, Italy: Lazaro de Soardis, 1516), fol. 5v.

44. On his background, see O'Malley, *Giles of Viterbo*, who points out in particular that Egidio was also deeply influenced by Ficinian Platonism. The Joachite tradition was very strong among the Augustinian Hermits, and it was in fact a group of them who had published the prophetic texts quoted above. See Reeves, *Influence of Prophecy*, 250–73.

softer? our ambition more naked? our greed more inflamed? licentious sin more impudent?"—and threatened the most dire divine wrath if this was not amended. More significantly, though, he placed this situation in the context of a historical decline that was exacerbated above all by a lack of councils: "just as without the nourishment of bread living beings cannot long survive, so the souls of men, so the Church cannot act well without the care of synods." "Thus," he continued, "generally, since Constantine's day, where sacred things are side by side with splendor and ornaments, so the severity of life and morals have weakened not a little; every time synods have ceased to be held, we see the divine bridegroom deserted by his bride."

While Egidio praised Julius's aggressive military policies, he took care to stress that God had not instituted the Church for warfare. Instead, as with Moses on the mountain while Joshua fought the Amalechites, the military fortunes of Christendom would prosper while the Church upheld its faith and morals. In this context, Egidio returned to the sad story of the post-Constantinian Christian community: "And when the bride who was then everywhere called for, summoned, desired in garments not ornamented with gold, exchanged the golden armor of an ardent spirit for the iron arms of mad Ajax, she let slip the empire, the office by blood of the twelve apostles, she lost Asia and Jerusalem, was forced to relinquish Africa and Egypt, she saw a great part of Europe, with Greece and the Byzantine Empire, taken from her."[45] Only a divinely inspired reformation, presumably to include some renunciation of both temporal arms and temporal wealth, could free the Church from such apocalyptic scourging. Later speakers at the council echoed similar themes, albeit less fully and forcefully.[46] Overall, it is on one level scarcely possible to distinguish between the ideals of the Church and its place in the world promoted by Louis XII and by Julius II![47]

Of course, on the level of formal ecclesiology, not to mention that of power politics, differences were far clearer. In this realm, it is possible to discern a certain tendency in France to move away from the classic, unifying vision of a Church and society to be renewed through apostolic life within sa-

---

45. Egidius Virturbensis, "Oratio prima synodi Lateranensis habita," in Joannes Dominicus Mansi et al., eds., *Sacrorum conciliorum nova et amplissima collectio*, vol. 32 (Paris and Leipzig, Germany: Hubert Welter, 1902), cols. 669–76.

46. See Nelson H. Minnich, "Concepts of Reform Proposed at the Fifth Lateran Council," *Archivum historiæ pontficiæ* 7 (1969): 163–251.

47. Indeed, a similar ideology motivated the great heterodox movements of the later Middle Ages as well; see Michael Wilks, "*Reformatio regni:* Wyclif and Hus as Leaders of Religious Protest Movements," *Studies in Church History* 9 (1972): 109–30.

cred history. Ironically, the best example came from an element in the self-proclaimed intellectual arbiter of Christendom: the University of Paris. The Paris Faculty of Theology, the most important standing body speaking for the French church, was dubious from the start about the entire project of the Council of Pisa, and dodged requests to issue a formal opinion on it.[48] But neither would the faculty allow papal attacks on the principle of conciliar superiority to go unanswered. When the Dominican theologian Tomasso de Vio Cajetanus published a blistering attack on Pisa in particular and conciliar authority in general, the faculty commissioned a rising star, Jacques Almain, to produce a reply.[49] Almain's *De auctoritate ecclesiæ* became effectively the last canonical exposition of the conciliarist doctrine, and, as such, it has attracted a fair amount of attention from recent scholars.[50] For that reason, and because much of Almain's argument simply recapitulates fifteenth-century conciliarist commonplaces, we can deal rather briefly with most aspects of this work.

Almain argued that Christ had conferred the power or jurisdiction of the Church—the right "to bind and to loose"—on the apostles as a corporate body, with Peter only *primus inter pares*. Though divinely instituted toward a spiritual end, this power acted to all intents and purposes like "a natural power of jurisdiction for a natural end."[51] In particular, it resided essentially in the Church as a community, and could be exercised most perfectly when that community came together in a corporate body: in this case, as a general council. Such a council represented the interest of the community (the final cause of the jurisdictional power), and in defending that interest it could exercise jurisdiction over any individual member, even the pope. Thus, councils could overrule, ignore, or depose popes if the common good demanded it.

The most striking thing about Almain's view of the Church was that it almost entirely avoided any implication that the Church was distinguishable from a secular government, or that God operated within it in any direct way. This outlook (which had not characterized earlier conciliarists such as Jean Gerson) left little room for a reform to apostolic purity within the clergy,

---

48. See James K. Farge, *Orthodoxy and Reform in Early Reformation France: The Faculty of Theology of Paris, 1500–1543* (Leiden, The Netherlands: E. J. Brill, 1985), 222–25.

49. The texts are now collected in English translation in J. H. Burns and Thomas M. Izbicki, eds., *Conciliarism and Papalism* (Cambridge, U.K.: Cambridge University Press, 1997).

50. See, e.g., J. H. Burns, "Conciliarism, Papalism and Power, 1511–1518," in Diana Wood, ed., *The Church and Sovereignty: Essays in Honor of Michael Wilks* (Oxford, U.K.: Basil Blackwell, 1991), 409–28; and Oakley, "Almain and Major," and "Conciliarism in the Sixteenth Century: Jacques Almain Again," *Archiv für Reformationsgeschichte* 68 (1977): 111–32.

51. Burns and Izbicki, eds., *Conciliarism and Papalism*, 160.

and still less for any kind of millennial renovation. Cajetan was quick to seize on Almain's innovation. He ended his reply to the Parisian scholar with a powerful defense of his own contention that intercessory prayer was the Church's most effective weapon against papal malfeasance. "God instituted the ecclesiastical commonwealth much better and much more excellently than the civil one, since he instituted it with an immediate and homogeneous head [Christ] . . . spiritually present to the prayers of all."[52] Cajetan was in no way a radical papal monarchist, but his vision of Christian society remained irreducibly sacred, while arguably Almain's vision, even of the Church alone, was not.

One group not called upon to speak out in support of the Council of Pisa was the secular magistrates of France. Though the Parlement of Paris, as we have seen, had long defended the policies of the Pragmatic Sanction, and were fierce defenders of their own legal jurisdiction against pope and clergy alike, they remained the junior partners of the Gallican consensus. Indeed, there was no obvious reason why they should take the lead in defending the supremacy of the council and the bishops, or in attacking the demoralizing effects of wealth and worldliness on the clergy. These were, primarily, *interior* issues for the Church. The Parlement did have one characteristic, though, that made it more suitable than any of the clergy as defenders of Gallicanism. It was in more-or-less permanent session, with its hands continuosly on the levers of judicial power. Unlike clerical assemblies, it did not need to be called together by the king. Thus, it could oppose royal policies far more effectively than the clergy, as its remonstrances to Louis XI had famously demonstrated.

When Louis XII died, the new king, François I, abruptly reversed his entire ecclesiastical program. He made peace with Pope Leo X, submitted to the Fifth Lateran Council, and finally traveled to a summit meeting at Bologna, where he and the pope negotiated a concordat to govern the administration of the French church.[53] The Concordat of Bologna was by no means a complete surrender of Gallican practice. While it abolished the election of prelates (something that hardly ever happened anyway), it left

---

52. Burns and Izbicki, eds., *Conciliarism and Papalism*, 282. This was an important theme in Cajetan's work; see Thomas M. Izbicki, "Cajetan's Attack on Parallels between Church and State," *Cristianesimo nella storia* 20 (1999): 81–89.

53. For a comprehensive, though not always fully reliable, account of the Concordat, the negotiations surrounding it, and its registration, see Jules Thomas, *Le concordat de 1516: Ses origines, son histoire au XVIe siècle*, 3 vols. (Paris: A. Picard, 1910).

the king in control of most important ecclesiastical appointments. It limited France's financial obligations to Rome, and severely restricted the circumstances and manner in which cases could be appealed from French ecclesiastical courts to the pope. Nevertheless, it had serious theoretical implications, above all because it made no concessions to church reform, to conciliar as opposed to papal governance, or to the supposed ancient common law of the Gallican church. To underline these points, Leo had demanded as a condition of his final approval that François approve Lateran V's condemnation of the Pragmatic Sanction, and that the king officially and perpetually replace that document with the new concordat. He was also to have this arrangement "within the space of six months read, published, sworn, and registered in our kingdom by all prelates and other ecclesiastical persons and the courts of parlement, like other royal constitutions."[54]

Beginning with a session on 5 February 1517, attended by the king in person, the government undertook a concerted campaign to obtain that registration, against the Parlement of Paris's bitter opposition.[55] In the end, it required more than a year and the serious threat to dissolve the Parlement and replace it with a more tractable body before it grudgingly approved the concordat. Though ultimately ineffective, this resistance demonstrated both how strongly attached many in France remained to the old Gallican ideals and the power of the Parlement as an institutional locus of that attachment. As Roger Doucet put it, "there is a particular analogy" between the Parlement's remonstrance against the concordat and their 1464 remonstrance in favor of the Pragmatic Sanction.[56] In 1517, the *parlementaires* objected above all to three of the concordat's provisions: that benefices be assessed at market value for purposes of papal taxation, that particularly important legal cases *(causæ majores)* and suits involving papal officers could be appealed to Rome, and that elections be suppressed.[57] This broadening of the issues beyond the strictly financial concerns of 1461 was, however, largely illusory,

---

54. Letters patent of François I, dated 13 August 1516, quoted in Thomas, *Le concordat*, 2:12.

55. On this process, see Thomas, *Le concordat*; and Roger Doucet, *Etude sur le gouvernement de François Ier dans ses rapports avec le Parlement de Paris*, 2 vols. (Paris: Honoré Champion, 1921), 1:77–148.

56. Doucet, *Etude*, 1:104. The *procès-verbal* of the sessions in which the Parlement registered the Concordat "de expresso mandato regis iteratis vicibus facto" was printed in the early seventeenth century; see *Proces-verbal des remonstrances faites en la Cour de Parlement au mois de mars 1517, sur la publication des Concordats* (s.l., n.d.).

57. "Raisons du Parlement de Paris pour ne pas enregistrer & faire publier les concordatz faictz entre le Pape & le Roy," BN fr. 6396, fols. 3–50, fol. 4v. This is the oldest surviving copy of the remonstrances. A later one in the hand of Pierre Dupuy, "Remonstrances de la

since all three objections actually centered around the loss of French funds. The first was obviously fiscal; from the second "there would follow another great loophole for the Court of Rome to draw money from this kingdom, and also to molest and harass its poor subjects, both because of the long journeys they would have to take to Rome for these appeals, and because of the fees and expenses that are so excessive in the said Court of Rome." The Parlement defended elections on their own merits, but they were also concerned that "if the right of election is taken from the churches, all elective dignities will necessarily have to pay annates [an accession tax payable to Rome], against the prohibition of the holy decrees, and in thus paying annates on both collated benefices ... and elective ones, in a short time the kingdom will be completely stripped of gold and silver, and left poor and desolate."[58]

Even more significantly, the Parlement continued to see the entire question of the Pragmatic Sanction and the concordat through the lens of Church reform. Thus, the problem with annates was not solely, or even primarily, that they impoverished the kingdom. Rather, "in the lands where annates are raised on collative benefices, those benefices or most of them are desolate and ruined, poorly served as to divine service, hospitality is poorly kept, and few alms distributed. For the moneys that should be used for repairs to those benefices, alms, and divine service must be used to pay the annates."[59] A set-piece speech given by a lawyer in the Parlement, Jean Bochard, earlier in the affair makes this even clearer.[60] Bochard placed the concordat within a dismal history of stymied reform. "It is most certain that the popes since the Council of Basel ... even though, by the determination of the Church, councils should be held every ten years *for the reform of the Church in head and members*, have not held a single one, fearing the reform of the simony and abuse that are more common in Rome than anywhere else."[61]

Cour de Parlement contre le Concordat," in BN Dupuy 117, fols. 81–102, differs mainly in a modernized orthography.

58. BN fr. 6396, fol. 11r, fol. 25r.

59. BN fr. 6396, fol. 6v.

60. Bochard was destined for a brilliant career, continuing to represent the University of Paris, notably against partisans of Evangelicism and the Reformation, as well as the unhappy Constable de Bourbon. See Doucet, *Etude*, passim; and C. A. Meyer, "L'avocat du roi d'Espagne, Jean Bouchard; le Parlement de Paris, Guillaume Briçonnet et Clément Marot," *Bulletin de la société de l'histoire du protestantisme français* 137 (1991): 7–24, who rather improbably makes him out to be a sworn enemy of the French monarchy.

61. "Plaidoyé de Maistre Jean Bochart sr de Noroy Champigny & la Mesnilles advocat en parlement, pour luniversité de Paris opposante et empeschante la publication du Concordat,

Bochard also placed his reformism within a more-or-less apocalyptic sacred history. "One might well be of the opinion," he mused, "that the wrath of God has descended on that holy city for the said avarice and simony, though without judging the matter and leaving all judgment to God. We can say, though, that our Lord has allowed and permitted this vessel to float, sway, and begin to sink for our salvation, and to make us return to him . . . and the tempest . . . will cease if we fear, honor, and serve him, but if we do not he will multiply our crimes and afflictions and increase his correction sevenfold."[62] The outcome of this process would obviously depend greatly on the actions of the king of France, to whom Bochard directly addressed his oration. François I thus found himself cast, *nolens volens*, in the traditional role of the millenarian good king, purifying the Church. Bochard posed to him that very question:

> Will you have on this that very title, and honor after your death before God, and in Heaven the recompense and eternal blessing promised to those who have defended and sustained on earth the honor of God, of our lord Jesus Christ, and of the Church his spouse, founded and dedicated in his precious blood? Will you help to chase the merchants and simoniacs from the house of God, will you not overturn the changers' tables that we see every day in the Church, where today more than ever and by an abusive custom they sell by the pound and by weight of gold the dignities, estates, and sacraments of the Church, the treasure and merit of the holy Passion of Jesus Christ, commonly selling bishoprics, abbeys, dignities and benefices, pardons, indulgences and dispensations . . . ? Will you permit, sire, that contrary to the determination of the Universal Church, the pope, by a manifest abuse, claims the power to open Purgatory and the prisons, and release a prisoner for a silver piece or other tax?[63]

In 1517, needless to say, he was not the only person asking that final question. As much as the concordat itself, the appearance of Martin Luther's radically new version of Church reform was destined to render Bochard's synthesis politically obsolete almost as soon as he pronounced it.

Once the concordat was firmly in place, Franco-papal relations for many years receded from the forefront of French and European politics, and Gallicanism itself seems to have gone into hibernation. Or perhaps it would be

---

sur l'abolition de la pragmatique sanction prononcé en presence du Roy seant au Parlement en son lict de Justice," in BN Dupuy 117, fols. 168–75, fol. 171r. Evidently Bochard (like most Gallicans) did not accept the validity of the Fifth Lateran Council.

62. BN Dupuy 117, fol. 173v.
63. BN Dupuy 117, fol. 169r.

better to say that it underwent a kind of pupation, for during the period of obscurity that lasted with one brief interruption up to the 1560s, it transformed itself profoundly. It is impossible to trace the process in detail, since sources are rare, but its outlines are discernible. The enormous changes in European religious life during the era of the Reformation required and shaped that transformation. At the same time, even had Luther never lived and Protestantism never existed, Gallicanism would have looked very different in 1565 than it had a half-century before. In that time, the humanist movement had largely rebuilt the foundations of French elite culture, and Gallicanism could not help but appear differently.

Nevertheless, the details of French humanist religious thought shed less light than one might expect on the development of Gallican thought in the first half of the sixteenth century. The most important strand of that thought, the "Evangelicism" that runs in various forms from Jacques Lefevre d'Etaples and Desiderius Erasmus through Guillaume Budé, Clément Marot, and François Rabelais, was notable for its resolute refusal to take a discernable stand on any ecclesiological question whatsoever.[64] Given the dangers of legal pursuit and, perhaps more importantly, of being drawn into a developing rigid and partisan confessionalization that many humanists saw as profoundly distasteful, this refusal was far from irrational.[65] Moreover, because of their rhetorical training and inclinations, and of their formative conflicts with university theology faculties, the French humanists tended to regard the emotional and devotional style of religion as more important than its institutional matrix. Thus, aside from continuing the medieval reformers' generalized distaste for the avarice and hypocrisy of Rome, the humanist Evangelicals had little direct involvement with the heritage of Gallicanism.

64. On the origins of French Evangelical reform, the standard studies remain Imbart de la Tour, *Les origines;* and Renaudet, *Préréforme.* The most detailed studies on the classic period of French Evangelicism are M. A. Screech, *L'Evangélisme de Rabelais,* Etudes rabelaisiennes 2 (Geneva: Droz, 1959), and *Clément Marot: A Renaissance Poet Discovers the Gospel. Lutheranism, Fabrism and Calvinism in the Royal Courts of France and of Navarre and in the Ducal Court of Ferrara* (Leiden, The Netherlands: E. J. Brill, 1994).

65. On humanist resistance to confessionalization in contemporary Germany, see Erika Rummel, *The Confessionalization of Humanism in Reformation Germany* (Oxford, U.K.: Oxford University Press, 2000). For various reasons, the hardening of confessions and confessional churches was rather late in coming to France. Not until Calvin and his followers consolidated the Reformed Church in the 1550s did the substantial grey area between Protestant and Catholic there disappear—and even up to the 1561 Colloquy of Poissy many did not or refused to realize that this had occurred!

Ultimately, it was not so much the religious as the historical element of humanist thought that played the key role in reviving and reshaping the Gallican tradition. Where the reformist Gallicanism of the Middle Ages, and down to the time of the Pisan Schism, had relied as we have seen on a prophetic and millenarian view of history, sixteenth-century humanism moved in a different direction.[66] It used the philological tools of textual criticism, the skills developed in the painstaking Renaissance reconstruction of classical culture, and a heightened appreciation for the historical particularity of all political communities to construct narrower, more national, and far better documented histories than its predecessors. The first person to apply some form of this method to the Gallican tradition was the first trained humanist to enter the high circles of the French judiciary. Jacques Cappel was appointed to the Parlement of Paris as a royal attorney *(avocat du roi)* in 1534 under the patronage of Cardinal Jean du Bellay on the strength, it seems, of a Neoplatonic set of commentaries on random classical texts and of a Ciceronian oration in praise of Paris. He occupied the office until his death in 1541.[67] Du Bellay played a major role in cultivating French historical and literary humanism in its early days, and Cappel's appointment no doubt fitted into that project.

The cardinal was also a leading figure in French attempts to limit the influence of the curia on any eventual reform of the Church, particularly in the context of the anticipated Council of Trent; in other words, in a certain sense, he was a Gallican.[68] Thus it may have been to further his patron's policies as much as the Crown's that Cappel, at some point during his tenure, prepared a memoir in seventy-three articles on royal authority over the Gallican church.[69] His major concern was the flow of money out of the realm to Rome, tying him to the fifteenth-century tradition, but his treatment was innovative in one important respect. His arguments were largely

---

66. On the larger context of this movement from a millenarian to a secular history, see above all J. G. A. Pocock, *The Machiavellian Moment: Florentine Political Thought and the Atlantic Republican Tradition* (Princeton, N.J.: Princeton University Press, 1975). On the new history in France, the classic study is Donald Kelley, *The Foundations of Modern Historical Scholarship* (New York: Columbia University Press, 1972).

67. On Cappel's life and career, see J. H. M. Salmon, "Protestant Jurists and Theologians in Early Modern France: The Family of Cappel," in Roman Schnur, ed., *Die Rolle der Juristen bei der Entstehung des modernen Staates* (Berlin: Dunker & Humblot, 1986), 357–79, esp. 358–61.

68. The best extended treatment of his ecclesiastical and intellectual outlook is in Gilbert Gaddofre, *Du Bellay et le sacré* (Paris: N.R.F./Gallimard, 1971). For more detail on his historical and institutional context, see Alain Tallon, *France et le concile de Trent (1518–1563)* (Rome: Ecole Française de Rome, 1997), passim.

69. "Memoires dressez par Me. Jacques Cappel Advocat du Roy au Parlement de Paris.

historical, and he supported them with a virtual dossier of original documents referred to by their shelfmarks in the king's major repository of historical titles and documents, the Trésor des Chartes. Cappel's production contrasts markedly even with a slightly later one by his immediate superior, a set of "Memoires dressez par M. Noel Brulart Procureur general du Roy, environ l'an 1548," regarding the status of the Concordat in Provence and Brittany (united to the Crown after 1516).[70] Brulart's concerns, like Cappel's, were hardy perennials: the flow of funds to Rome and a feared invasion of unqualified, nonresident Italians into French benefices, to the detriment of the laity and French university graduates. His argument, however, was terse and apodictic, owing more to medieval predecessors like the fourteenth-century jurist Pierre de Cuignières than to Renaissance theorists like Poliziano or Machiavelli.

It was only after 1550, then, that a new, historicist Gallicanism began to emerge in any systematic form. The most important immediate occasion for this phenomenon was a major crisis in Franco-papal relations, by far the worst since the Pisan Schism. The so-called Gallican Crisis of 1551 was above all a dynastic squabble between Henri II and Julius III over control of Parma.[71] However, it once again raised the specter of the pope deposing a French king. Moreover, it was also not out of the question that the king of France, like his English colleague, might abandon the Roman Church altogether; this, in the context of the Reformation, was a far more serious step than the withdrawal of obedience or the Pisan conciliabule. Of course, matters did not in the end go so far, but the incident did prompt the royal government to deliberately revive the traditions of Gallican reform and autonomy largely abandoned since 1516. To a considerable extent, this involved the pure expression of the old reformist ideology. The first major move in the conflict was the promulgation of an edict "on the reform of abuses that are

Pour le Roy et l'Eglise Gallicane," in *Traictez des droicts et libertez de l'Eglise gallicane*, 2nd ed. (Paris: Pierre Chevalier, 1612 [1609]), 23–70. The 1609 printing was the first of this treatise, and there is no discernable manuscript tradition.

70. First printed in the 1612 edition of the *Traictez*, 71–78. This memoir seems to have been related to the jockeying for position then going on over the languishing Council of Trent; see H. Outram Evennett, *The Cardinal of Lorraine and the Council of Trent: A Study in the Counter-Reformation* (Cambridge, U.K.: Cambridge University Press, 1930), 32–33. On the diplomatic context of the Concordat in Brittany and Provence, where it was extended by a series of papal indults to the constant vexation of the Crown, see Tallon, *France et le concile*, 219–23.

71. For the sordid details, see Evennett, *Cardinal of Lorraine*, 35–44; and above all Lucien Romier, "La crise gallicane de 1551," *Revue historique* 108–109 (1911): 225–50, 27–55.

committed in the collation of benefices in the Court of Rome," followed swiftly by a prohibition on the transfer of money to Rome predicated, among other things, on the pope's alleged opposition to an ecumenical council.[72]

However, the presence of a powerful humanist element in the king's service naturally led to expressions of a new, distinctively humanist, Gallicanism as well.[73] Most striking was a document produced by Jean du Tillet, secretary of the Parlement of Paris and keeper of the royal archives, the Trésor des Chartes, for the royal Council of State, of which he was a member. Entitled "Traitte des droicts et usages du Royaume de France, envers l'eglise et la sainct siege apostolique," it was essentially a history of Franco-papal relations through the Concordat of Bologna.[74] It was a history, though, of a strikingly new type, even when compared to Cappel's. For Cappel, the royal prerogatives as revealed by documentary history were not organically tied to the very nature of the French state, but had rather been acquired through papal (and, to a lesser extent, conciliar) grants and by the operation of natural law. According to him, the king "as patron and principal founder of the churches of France, and by the prerogatives, preeminences, privileges, and indults granted to himself and to his predecessors the Most Christian Kings," was entitled "to convoke and assemble the princes of his blood, prelates and churchmen of his kingdom, and in that assembly, called the Congregation of the Gallican Church, to make or have made statutes, edicts, and ordinances to remedy abuses," exactly the procedure used by monarchs from Philip the Fair to Louis XII.[75] It was the originality of Jean

72. The *ordonnances* are in M. Isambert and A. Jourdan, eds., *Recueil général des anciennes lois françaises, depuis l'an 420 jusqu'à la revolution de 1789*, 29 vols. (Paris: Belin-Leprieur, 1826–1833), 13:164–75, 211–22. The former was the "Edict of the *parvæ datæ*" commented upon by Dumoulin, though it is worth noting that it seems as much to form part of Henri II's reorganization of the judicial administration as of the Gallican Crisis.

73. Besides the works discussed here, Rabelais's *Quart livre* (in its 1552, second, version), with its series of attacks on the papacy, should doubtless be seen as part of this movement. See Gérard Defaux's introduction to his edition of François Rabelais, *Le Quart livre* (Paris: Le Livre de Poche, 1994), 38–99. To my mind, however, Rabelais's anti-papalism remains almost purely *moralizing*, centered around a call for individual regeneration as against the Seven Deadly Sins; thus, though unusually violent and built on a panoply of humanist erudition, it remains close in spirit to its medieval predecessors.

74. This was printed with later editions of his *Recueil des rois de France*, and with all the collections of Gallican treatises from 1609 on. I follow here a manuscript version, BN fr. 473, much more archaic in orthography than the printed editions, which is most likely a contemporary reference copy made for the royal library.

75. *Traictez*, 24–25. I am not aware of any other appearance of the term "Congregation de

du Tillet to move away from such an account of the Gallican liberties and to proclaim the principle that (as the very moderate Antoine Hotman would later put it) the liberties of the Gallican church "are in no way concessions of the popes, nor rights acquired against common law. For since France has preserved her liberty more than any other Catholic nation, she cannot be said to have been freed: she is truly free from her first origins."[76] This was the decisive step in the development of a Gallican tradition based on humanist and republican ideals and independent of any declared interest of a particular king.

Du Tillet's alignment with the du Bellay clan, his citation of documents from the Trésor des Chartes, and his concern with fiscal issues (which the incipient armed conflict between Henri II and the pope had rendered, for the last time, a live issue) all point to a connection with Cappel's text, while his millenarian streak is reminiscent of Lemaire de Belges and other writers associated with the Pisan Schism. What du Tillet had to offer in the way of novelty were a well-developed narrative, a much more complex vision of the ecclesiastical constitution than those of his predecessors, and a command of institutional history to support it. On his account, the decay of a certain community within the Church, and the division of power and property among its constituent groups and individuals, had opened the way to corruption and conflict. At one moment the laity was cut off from the clergy: "[Pope] Lucian ... restricted the right of election [of bishops] to the chapters, and the door was opened to simony." Here the loss of unity leads to avarice, which then feeds on itself: "the said popes divided the goods of bishops and chapters ... each had their own root and nourishment of avarice, which very soon destroyed the community and charity of the ecclesiastical estate."[77] This version of events was both sketchy and idiosyncratic, but it represented a line of thought that was to develop great importance among the erudite Gallicans. In du Tillet its most important feature is already visible: by presenting the rupture of an originary community where the sacred and the secular were in some way undivided, it opens up to the modern secular arm the possibility of action to retrieve that original purity, with or without the cooperation of the now corrupted Church.

Besides du Tillet's tract, the most significant piece of royalist apologetic produced during the 1551 crisis was a commentary on the 1550 edict of the

---

l'Eglise Gallicane," though it clearly relates to the idea of French ecclesiastical counsel as developed by monarchs from Philip the Fair through Charles VI.

76. Antoine Hotman, "Traitté des droicts Ecclesiastiques," in *Traictez*, 331–445, p. 331.
77. BN fr. 473, fol. 4r, v.

parvæ datæ written by the jurisconsult Charles Dumoulin.[78] The government had originally commissioned the commentary, but it was by no means an official document. It was a not particularly subtle warning to Rome of the king's willingness to contemplate drastic measures and, as soon as it had served its purpose, the authorities disowned it. The Faculty of Theology censured the work, and the Parlement of Paris showed very little inclination to come to its defense, launching an independent inquiry into the matter.[79] In the end, Dumoulin felt compelled to flee the kingdom to avoid punishment, and he remained in exile for a decade. He seems to have fancied himself in the role of the great medieval antipapal publicists, like those who supported Philip the Fair, but his fate demonstrated sufficiently the anachronism of such a position in the new climate of developing religious conflict and confessionalization.

Nevertheless, Dumoulin was by no means a mere throwback to the Middle Ages. Donald Kelley has even attributed to him the leading role in developing a "gallican view of history," and thence modern historicism.[80] In one respect, he was certainly an innovator: in his entire treatise, he never once mentioned that venerable fetish of the Parlement, the Pragmatic Sanction of Bourges.[81] He also included a rather full antipapal history of the Catholic Church, in an immense gloss on a single word of a parlementary decree from 1406.[82] Still, Dumoulin's narrative was more than a little unfocused. Moreover, it, like its author, could reasonably be accused of serious unorthodoxy even in matters purely of faith. This made it dangerous to cite:

78. Charles Dumoulin, *Commentarius ad edictum Henrici Secundi contra parvas datas & abusus curiae Romanae, & in antiqua edicta & senatus consulta Franciae contra Annatarum & id genus abusus, multas novas decisiones juris & praxis continens* (Paris: n.p., 1552); he later published his own translation, *Abus des petites dates, reservations, preventions, annates et autres usurpations et exactions de la Cour de Rome contre les edictz et ordonnances des roys de France* (Lyons, France: Pour le dit Du Moulin, 1564). The basic work on Dumoulin's life and thought is now Jean-Louis Thireau, *Charles du Moulin (1500–1566): Etude sur les sources, la méthode, les idées politiques et économiques d'un juriste de la Renaissance* (Geneva: Droz, 1980).

79. Some of the documents from this incident are reproduced in Kelley, "Fides Historiæ: Charles Dumoulin and the Gallican View of History," *Traditio* 22 (1966): 347–402, esp. 396–402; see also Thireau, *Charles du Moulin*, 35–38.

80. Kelley, "Fides Historiæ," and *Foundations*, 151–82.

81. This is true only of the Latin version: in 1561, while preparing the expanded French version, he unbent to the point of mentioning it twice in passing.

82. Dumoulin, *Commentarius*, 185–303, glossing the word "subtractionis." One suspects some influence here of Lemaire's "Traicte des scismes." The gloss grew much longer, and even less coherent, in the French translation of 1561. The decree in question was the basis of the edict discussed above (and also cited by the Parlement's remonstrance against the Concordat) forbidding transfer of funds to Rome.

Gallicanism from Reform to History   43

when one much later Gallican did so, a detractor accused him of "speaking of master Charles Dumoulin and citing him even in matters of religion and ecclesiastical discipline," though "one must take from [Dumoulin] what pertained to his profession, and not his errors in religion, where he showed himself learned only to mock."[83] In such matters, evidently, Dumoulin was a source to be avowed only with the greatest caution. His very radicalism, however, made him an important source for later commentators, especially those seeking powerful arguments against one or another aspect of ecclesiastical jurisdiction.[84] Thus, through Dumoulin as well as du Tillet, the more radical humanist theories of the 1551 crisis continued to echo during the remainder of the sixteenth century. At the same time, though, the crisis of 1551 seems to have opened the way to a more general reconsideration by French humanists of their relations with Rome, both religious and secular, which was to prove equally though more subtly important to the development of Gallican ideology.

Sometime shortly after 1566, Edmund Campion, soon to be the intellectual leader of the English Catholics, but then a scholar at Oxford University, set down to work out his confused thoughts on the relationship between church and state. He wrote a Virgilian mini-epic that superimposed the histories of imperial Rome and of the persecuted early Church, soon triumphant in that same city.[85] While the specific literary form he adopted was original, the idea of contrasting the imperial and the Christian Eternal Cities went back to the Middle Ages, and had been revived and popularized in the Renaissance, beginning with Flavio Biondo's topographical work *Roma instaurata*. That topos, of "Rome refounded" or "renewed," quickly became enormously popular in Italy and abroad, but it was inherently ambiguous.[86] Was the reborn Rome to be a simple copy of the ancient city, peopled by orators indistinguishable from Cicero, architects indistinguishable from

---

83. *Discours sur les meurs et humeur de Monsieur Servin Advocat General au Parlement de Paris*, reprinted in *Archives curieuses de l'histoire de France*, ser. 2, vol. 3 (Paris: Beauvais, 1840 [s.l., 1617]), 197–98.
84. On Dumoulin's ecclesiology, see Thireau, *Charles du Moulin*, 272–347.
85. Gerard Kilroy, "Eternal Glory: Edmund Campion's Virgilian Epic," *Times Literary Supplement*, 8 March 2002, pp. 13–14.
86. On the development of these ideas in their native environment, Rome during the high Renaissance, see Ingrid D. Rowland, *The Culture of the High Renaissance: Ancients and Moderns in Sixteenth-Century Rome* (Cambridge, U.K.: Cambridge University Press, 1998); on the form they took in France, see Margaret M. McGowan, *The Vision of Rome in Late Renaissance France* 90. (New Haven, Conn.: Yale University Press, 2000). There is an interesting historical overview

Vitruvius, historians indistinguishable from Livy, and so on? Or was it to be assimilated to the ideal of Christian reform and renewal, so (as Egidio of Viterbo, for example, suggested) that the revived art and learning of pagan antiquity might ornament a Rome essentially "refounded by the death of the holy apostles Peter and Paul," upon the prototype of the Heavenly Jerusalem?[87] In other words, what role would the idea of Christian reform play in the humanists' understanding of their own place in history?

Italian humanists, especially those less committed to a reforming Christianity, could look with some equanimity upon the possibility of reviving Roman antiquity rather literally. Machiavelli certainly did so on the political level, with his various calls for the renewal of Italian unity and Roman *virtù*; the largely Roman partisans of Ciceronian purity in language did so more abstractly. It was possible for a Frenchman, like Marc-Antoine Muret, simply to move to Italy and adopt this outlook wholesale, but for most French and other northern humanists, there was little appeal in the idea of abandoning political independence and national culture in a project that smacked at once of pagan impiety and rampant papal monarchism.[88] Erasmus presented one answer to this problem in his treatise on oratory, the *Ciceronianus*, in which he argued that a renewed Latin eloquence would have to take into account the social, political, and—above all—the religious differences between the ancient and the modern worlds, and could not rest on a single rigid model.[89] Any *Roma instaurata* would have to be a modern and Christian one, in line presumably with the broader program of Evangelical reform. It was not until some years later, though, that a new generation would ask how France in particular might fit into this vision.

Specifically, the man who did so was Joachim du Bellay, cousin of the Gallican cardinal. He first came to prominence by applying Erasmian rhetorical theory to the problem of French vernacular literature in the *Def-*

---

of the idea of Roman rebirth in Kenneth J. Pratt, "Rome as Eternal," *Journal of the History of Ideas* 26 (1965): 25–44.

87. John O'Malley, "Giles of Viterbo: A Reformer's Thought on Renaissance Rome," *Renaissance Quarterly* 20 (1967): 1–11, p. 10, quoting a letter of Egidio's in Biblioteca Comunale, Siena, ms. G.X.26, 60. On *instauratio* as a term in Christian reform thought, see Ladner, *Idea*, 44, 277–78.

88. Of course many Italians, particularly Tuscans, Venetians, and Ghibellines of all stripes, were equally unwilling to sacrifice their language and polity to the Roman cause.

89. Desiderius Erasmus, *De recta latini græcique sermonis pronuntiatione . . . dialogus . . . [et] Dialogus cui titulus, Ciceronianus, sive, de optimo genere dicendi* (Basel, Switzerland: Froben, 1528). On this tract and its influence, see, above all, Marc Fumaroli, *L'Age de l'éloquence: Rhétorique et «res literaria» de la Renaissance au seuil de l'époque classique* (Geneva: Droz, 1980), 77–115.

fence et illustration de la langue francoyse, which appeared on the eve of the Gallican crisis, in 1549. He, and the burgeoning movement of the Pléiade with him, adopted the view "that it is impossible to equal the ancients in their own languages." At the same time, they believed that to raise the vernacular to the same level as the classical tongues, writers must "enrich" it by the systematic *imitation* of Greco-Roman models, whether at the level of individual words, of commonplaces, or of genres. Greece and Rome could not be renewed in themselves, since "with the fall of such superb edifices, together with the fatal ruin of those two powerful monarchies, one part was reduced to powder, and the other must be in many pieces which it would be impossible to put back together."[90] However, taking into account their own and their imitators' historical specificity, those fragments could be reused or digested to form a new, comparable French literature.

Four years later, after the diplomatic crisis had passed, du Bellay found himself contemplating literally the ruins he had metaphorically evoked, having (like Rabelais in 1548) followed the cardinal on a diplomatic mission to Rome.[91] There, in the intervals of tedious administrative service, he undertook a profound poetic meditation on the relationship among Roman antiquity, the Rome of the Renaissance popes, and France as it existed or could exist in the age of humanism. Unsurprisingly, the papacy did not impress him. Where one of his contemporaries and literary influences, Janus Vitalis, saw the curia and the College of Cardinals as a monument that in itself constituted a *Roma instaurata*, du Bellay found them, his cousin excepted, risible.[92] He had clearly been reading medieval Latin satires on the venality of Rome, like those the humanist Flacius Illyricus was then collecting for purposes of Protestant polemic, though his terms were the perfectly traditional ones of relatively moderate (and in his case disillusioned) reformism.[93] In the Con-

90. Joachim du Bellay, *La deffence et illustration de la langue francoyse*, ed. Henri Chamard (Paris: Librarie Marcel Didier, 1961), 79–80; cf. the title of Bk. I, ch. 11: "Qu'il est impossible d'egaler les anciens en leurs langues." On du Bellay's idea of imitation, see Bk. I, ch. 8, "D'amplifier la langue francoys par l'immitation des anciens aucteurs grecz & romains."

91. For all details on du Bellay's Roman stay, see Gladys Dickinson, *Du Bellay in Rome* (Leiden, The Netherlands: E. J. Brill, 1960).

92. Janus Vitalis published his *Sacrosancti Romanæ Ecclesiæ elogia* in 1553, which, besides epigrams on "Roma prisca" and "Roma instaurata," consisted essentially of individual panegyrics on each of the cardinals. See George Hugo Tucker, *The Poet's Odyssey: Joachim du Bellay and the* Antiquitez de Rome (Oxford, U.K.: Clarendon Press, 1990), 105–74.

93. Marcus Flacius Illyricus, ed., *Varia doctorum piorumque virorum de corrupto ecclesiæ statu poemata* (Basel, Switzerland: Ludvicus Lucius, 1557). This work, which appropriates the medieval anti-Roman discourse for the service of the Reform, marks a stage in the confession-

clave, one sees "ten cardinals for sale for less than one gold coin"; du Bellay compares the pope himself to Jupiter on Olympus,

> From whence he often casts his lightning on us:
> The other unleashes his thunder from the Vatican
> When some king has acted to pique his spite.[94]

Each, the poet concludes, has his own Ganymede (pederasty was a frequent ground of anti-Roman innuendo), but where Jupiter hates tyrants, Julius III favors them. The only thing missing, though a very significant one, is any indication that God or man will ever do anything to reform this distressing state of affairs. At least as he presented it in his *Regrets*, du Bellay's only hope for a less corrupt world was a return to France!

Instead, as a humanist, du Bellay looked to a refounded antiquity to renew the corrupt Rome—but as the *Deffence* would lead one to expect, he did not find it. A striking poem from the *Regrets* dramatizes his itinerary:

> If I go up to the palace, I find only pride,
>   Only vice disguised and a ceremony,
>   The noise of tambourines and a strange harmony,
>   And a superb apparatus of red habits.
> If I go down to the bank, a mass and collection
>   Of news I find, an infinite usury,
>   A banished troop of rich Florentines,
>   And the sad mourning of poor Siennese:
> If I go further, wherever I arrive
>   I find the great lascivious band of Venus
>   Setting a thousand amorous dishes on every side:
> If I pass beyond them, and from the new Rome
>   Enter the old Rome, then I only find
>   A stony debris-pile of old monuments.[95]

---

alization of the critique of Rome, and thus of the narrowing possibilities of Catholic Gallicanism.

94. Joachim du Bellay, *Les regrets et autres œuvres poëtiques suivis des antiquitez de Rome, plus un songe ou vision sur le mesme subject*, ed. J. Jolliffe and M. A. Screech (Geneva: Droz, 1966), 153 (*Regrets* 81), 180 (*Regrets* 106): "pour moins d'un escu dix Cardinaux en vente"; "Les Grecz nous ont fait l'un sur Olympe habiter, Dont souvent dessus nous ses fouldres il desserre: L'autre du Vatican délasche son tonnerre, Quand quelque Roy l'a fait contre luy despiter."

95. Du Bellay, *Les regrets*, 151 (*Regrets* 80): "Si je monte au Palais, je n'y trouve qu'orgueil, Que vice desguisé, qu'une cerimonie, Qu'un bruit de tabourins, qu'une estrange armonie, Et de rouges habits un superbe appareil: Si je descens en banque, un amas & recueil De nouvelles je treuve, une usure infinie, De riches Florentins une troppe banie, Et de pauvres Sienois un lamentable dueil: Si je vais plus avant, quelque part ou j'arrive, Je treuve de Venus

In thus reversing the trajectory of Dante's *Inferno*, traveling ironically downward from corrupt prelates to virtuous, but irremediably entombed, ancients, du Bellay rejects the premises of Roman renewal through either ecclesiastical reform or classical rebirth. Given the argument of the *Deffence*, perhaps the only solution would be to build a distinctly modern society, not from the corrupt elements of the new Rome but from what little remained of the old. He explored this problem at length in his other vernacular Roman collection, the *Antiquitez de Rome* with their accompanying *Songe ou vision*.

The *Antiquitez* rejected with scorn as well the idea that Roman glory might be reborn in Roman Christianity. One poem, developing the final line of the one just quoted, pointed out that

> These stony debris-piles, these old walls that you see
>   Were first the boundaries of a grassy field,
>   And these brave palaces, which time has mastered,
>   Were formerly the huts of shepherds.

Once the Empire had risen there and fallen there, though,

> ... Heaven, opposing such growth
> Put this power in the hands of the successor of Peter,
>   Who, under the title of "shepherd," fated to this land,
>   Shows how everything returns to its beginning.[96]

This was not the kind of Roman revival the propagandists of the Renaissance papacy portrayed! A series of poems at the end of the concluding *Songe* underlined the idea that papal Rome merely recapitulated and culminated the story of Roman declension. In one, a clear flame reaching toward Heaven is extinguished by a "golden rain," while in another, a city like the New Jerusalem of the Apocalypse, but built on sand, is destroyed by a north wind. In the final sonnet of the sequence, "the sister of great Typheus," the giant who personified the Roman Empire in earlier poems, sets up an "audacious" trophy by a riverbank.

---

la grand' bande lascive Dressant de tous costez mil appas amoureux: Si je passe plus oultre, & de la Rome neufve Entre en la vieille Rome, adonques je ne treuve Que de vieux monuments un grand monceau pierreu." Note that du Bellay ironically appropriates Charles V's motto "plus ultra," redolent of pretensions to a renewed universal empire, to mark his transition from contemporary to ancient Rome.

96. Du Bellay, *Les regrets*, 291 (*Antiquitez* 18): "Ces grands monceaux pierreux, ces vieux murs que tu vois, Furent premierement le cloz d'un lieu champestre: Et ces braves palais dont le temps s'est fait maistre, Cassines de pasteurs ont esté quelquefois."; "Mais le Ciel s'opposant à tel accroissement Mist ce pouvoir es mains du successeur de Pierre, Qui sous nom de pasteur, fatal à ceste terre, Monstre que tout retourne à son commencement."

> A hundred conquered kings trembled at her feet
> Their arms tied shamefully behind their backs.[97]

This figure, probably to be identified with the secular pretensions of the papacy, goes on (like her brother) to war with heaven: the ill-omened thunder of the conflict wakes the dreamer from his vision. In the two final poems, in particular, classical and papal Rome, in both their triumphs and their destruction, seem almost to merge into one.

In the *Antiquitez/Songe*, then, du Bellay portrays all of Rome as lost, reduced to powder and shadow, exiled forever behind the "banks of the Styx, not passable to those who would return, / Surrounding you in a three times triple bend."[98] The entire sequence is an exercise in necromancy, one that seems to be driven by some burning compulsion.[99] But what is the source of that compulsion? No doubt, it is the same impulse that motivated the *Deffence et illustration de la langue françoise*: at once to demonstrate the vanity of any attempt at a literal renewal of antiquity, and to develop a renewed vernacular by an exercise of close study and imitation. At the same time, du Bellay's Roman poems placed both the Roman Empire and the papacy firmly within a finite time, in which the "grand Tout" would inevitably end, but so would each individual city, state, and culture. Even the work of the poet's own lute is not immortal:

> If there were any eternity under heaven,
> The monuments of which I have made you sing,
> Not paper, but marble and porphyry,
> Would have kept their living antiquity.

---

97. Du Bellay, *Regrets*, 321 (*Songe* XV): "Cent Roys vaincuz gemissoient à ses piedz Les bras aux doz honteusement liez." The other two poems cited are *Songe* XI and *Songe* XIV. Gaddofre, in *Du Bellay et le sacré*, 151–82, interprets the final poems of the *Songe* as a detailed (Gallican) historical allegory of the papacy in the sixteenth century. His interpretation is not implausible, but it is (and would have been for contemporaries) far from self-evident. It also, I think, ignores du Bellay's apparent intention to assimilate papal Rome to the universal historical-philosophical reflections of the *Antiquitez* as a whole. In either case the conclusion holds that a true *instauratio Romæ* is out of the question.

98. Du Bellay, *Regrets*, 288 (*Antiquitez* 15): "les tenebreuses Rives de Styx non passable au retour, Vous enlassant d'un trois fois triple tour." My general interpretation of the *Antiquitez* follows Tucker, *Poet's Odyssey*; for a summary of current critical opinion, see McGowan, *Vision of Rome*, 187–88.

99. There are echos in the *Antiquitez* of the great, eerie, necromantic episode in Lucan, *Pharsalia* 6:413–830. All commentators agree that Lucan's tragic vision of Rome's self-destruction in civil war haunts du Bellay's works.

All is inscribed within what J. G. A. Pocock has called the "Machiavellian moment," the finite life-cycle of the republic, of which the rise and fall of Rome was already the greatest emblem. Church and state alike exist in a one-way, linear history. Given that reality, du Bellay's only alternative was to accept the modest honor "Of having, first among the French, / Sung the ancient honor of the long-robed people," and return to the task of improving the homeland and the historical moment into which he had been born.[100] Such were the limits within which humanist Gallicanism would have to exist.

This, however, was easier said than done. In the 1550s, there was not yet a new way to discuss the reform and administration of the French church outside the old, universal, and millenialist categories of apostolic purity, moral reform, and prophetic vision. It is significant, perhaps, that in the short time du Bellay lived after his return from Italy he did not find a new, confident poetic voice.[101] His last work was an "ample discourse to the king on the state of the four estates of the Kingdom of France," supporting the policies of the chancellor, Michel de l'Hospital, and dedicated to the most influential prelate in the realm, the brilliant young Charles de Guise, cardinal de Lorraine.[102] The dedicatee was appropriate, since the discourse dealt prominently with religious reform. Neither du Bellay nor l'Hospital had either a new diagnosis or a new cure to offer.

> In the virtuous times of the ancient Church
> Holiness did not disdain Christian poverty,
> It was the mirror of all purity,

---

100. Du Bellay, *Regrets*, 306 (*Antiquitez* 32): "Si sous le ciel fust quelque eternité, Les monuments que je vous ay fait dire, Non en papier, mais en marbre & porphyre, Eussent gardé leur vive antiquité. . . . Vanter te peuls, quelque bas que tu sois, D'avoir chanté le premier des François, L'antique honneur du peuple à longue robbe." Commentators have perhaps not sufficiently appreciated the significance of the fact that du Bellay concludes by stressing the status of the Romans as "gens de robe" rather than as "gens d'épée." As we shall see, this aligns him with a particular element of French political culture.

101. On the discomforts of du Bellay's French identity, see Timothy Hampton, *Literature and Nation in the Sixteenth Century: Inventing Renaissance France* (Ithaca, N.Y.: Cornell University Press, 2001), 150–90.

102. "Ample discours au roy sur le faict des quatre estats du royaume de France," in Joachim du Bellay, *Œuvres poétiques*, Vol. 6: *Discours et traductions*, ed. Henri Chamard (Paris: Klincksieck, 1991), 190–237. Though written in 1559, the "Ample discours" was not published until 1567, when the Wars of Religion were already well underway.

and so on. An improvement in morals and the residence of clergy would move the Church back toward that happy state. Apparently, though, what gave the new king (François II) the hope and authority of accomplishing this reform was

> the happy prophecy
> That promises you the honor, along with long life
> Of returning the Church to its authority
> And delivering Rome from its captivity.[103]

This prophecy, reproduced in full in the poem's 1567 edition, was an only slightly modified version of the medieval standby discussed above![104] It would be a new generation's task to understand the Church in the strictly limited terms that du Bellay's Roman poems suggested.

By way of a coda, one may remark that even the 1560s did not see the immediate death of a Gallicanism based on the Pragmatic Sanction and all it stood for. As was by that time traditional, the Estates General of Orleans in 1560 placed first in its *cahier* demands for the election of prelates and the end of all payments to Rome. The subsequent Edict of Orleans granted these requests, but it remained a dead letter. It only promised a ban on transfers to Rome until the king could "confer on the matter more amply with our holy father the pope," and even so, it was suspended before it took effect.[105] Still,

---

103. du Bellay, *Œuvres*, 6:220, 235: "Du temps de la vertu que l'Eglise ancienne Saincte ne dedaignoit la pauvreté Chrestienne, Elle estoit le miroir de toute pureté."; ". . . l'heureuse prophetie Qui l'honneur vous promet, avecques longue vie, De remettre l'Eglise en son auctorité, Et Rome delivrer de sa captivité." The 1563 version of the prophecy is transcribed at 235n.

104. Specifically, it was a version of what Reeves, in *Influence*, 375–83, calls the "second Charlemagne prophecy," in this case awkwardly reworked to use the name "François" instead of "Charles" for the world monarch. Unsurprisingly, this prophecy came back in the next reign, when the king shared the name (if none of the other qualities) of Charles the Great. See Reeves, *Influence*; and the amply titled *Livre merveillieux, contenant en bref le fleur et substance de plusieurs traictez, tant des Propheties & revelations, qu'anciennes Croniques, faisant mention de tous les faicts de l'eglise universelle, comme des Scismes discords & tribulations qui doivent advenir en l'Eglise de Rome, & d'un temps auquel lon ostera & tollira aux gens d'Eglise & Clergé, leur biens temporels: tellement qu'on ne leur laissera que leur vivre & habit necessaire. Item, aussi est faicte mention des souverains Evesques & Papes, qui apres regneront & gouverneront l'Eglise: & specialement d'un Pape, qui sera appellé Pasteur Angelique, & d'un Roy de France, nommé Charles Sainct homme. Item, au temps du grand & dernier Antechrist, apres sa mort, jusques au dernier jour du jugement, & en la fin du monde & quand ce doit estre, De nouveau a esté adjousté vers la fin une Prophetie, laquelle demonstre ce qui est advenu depuis le Roy François premier jusques à present* (Paris: Pour Antoine Hoüic, n.d. [prob. 1566; first published 1565]).

105. Isambert, *Recueil*, 14:64–65 (article 2). The article, not yet even registered, was suspended by an edict of 10 January 1561.

Catherine de Medicis considered observing the forms sufficiently important that she appointed Arnault de Ferrier, a president in the Parlement of Paris, to negotiate with Rome. He left in February 1561, "armed with all the remonstrances, protests, and memoirs kept for the past century with the secret registers" of the court.[106] He achieved nothing, least of all Catherine's main objective of pacifying the party of the reform. Within two years, the conclusion of the Council of Trent and the outbreak of civil war had made the old order of the long-dead Pragmatic Sanction so patently irrelevant that even its die-hard partisans in the Parlement began to develop the new issues, new arguments, and new philosophies pioneered by the humanists of the 1550s in their quest to make Gallicanism a political reality.

106. Maugis, *Histoire*, 603, citing AN X^{1A} 1596, fol. 372v.

CHAPTER 2

Custom, History, and Law

GALLICAN THEORISTS of the later sixteenth and seventeenth centuries had a favorite motto, drawn from the Vulgate version of Proverbs 22:28. Readers glancing at the title pages of the various collections of tracts and documents published by the arch-Gallican Pierre Pithou and his successors were admonished "pass not the bounds that your ancestors have placed."[1] "The verse," according to William Bouwsma, "was more than a conservative slogan. It was an invitation to historical scholarship."[2] If so, though, it was an invitation to historical scholarship of a specifically legal kind. Jurists understood the word *termini*, "bounds," literally, as markers dividing fields; one of them translated the word as *haies*, "hedges."[3] The boundaries of ecclesiastical administration were thus to be treated like a disputed piece of real estate, which is a bit odd considering what we have just seen about the history of Gallican thought. For centuries, after all, Gallicans had idealized a Church stripped of wealth, worldly cares,

---

1. "Ne transgrediaris terminos antiquos quos posuerunt patres tui." Cf. Proverbs 22:28 and 23:10: "Remove not the old landmark; and enter not into the fields of the fatherless" (King James Version). This appeared on the title pages of Pierre Pithou, *Les libertez de l'eglise Gallicane* (Paris: M. Patisson, 1594); and of the 1609 collection *Traictez des droits et libertez de l'Eglise gallicane* (Paris: Pierre Chevalier, 1609) and all subsequent editions.

2. William Bouwsma, "Gallicanism and the Nature of Christendom," in Anthony Molho and John A. Tedeschi, eds., *Renaissance Studies in Honor of Hans Baron* (Florence, Italy: G. C. Sansoni, 1971), 811–30, p. 823.

3. *Les remonstrances de Messire Jacques de la Guesle* (Paris: Pierre Chevalier, 1611), 427.

Custom, History, and Law   53

and hence corruption. More specifically, since the fourteenth century they had held as an indisputable maxim that the Church could have no jurisdiction over real property in France.[4] The significance of this tag is therefor less than obvious.

The key to this riddle is to be found in the political theories of humanistically trained Gallicans. This becomes clearer if one examines other contexts in which similar concepts were cited. Take, for instance, a learned dinner party held in Rome in 1580 at which the essayist Michel de Montaigne found himself defending Jacques Amyot (not present at the table) against charges that his translation of Plutarch's *Lives* had travestied the original author's meaning. One piece of evidence Amyot's detractors put forward was that, in a passage describing how the Athenian legislator Solon had removed the stones marking fields as mortgaged, Amyot made the great statesman boast of having "freed Attica, and having removed the boundaries that separated heritages."[5] If Solon had done what Amyot made him do, though, he would have been exactly the opposite of a great statesman, destroying the very foundations of the society he was in fact restoring. The implication was that Amyot understood neither Greek nor that political wisdom of which Plutarch was a sage. Markers dividing fields stood for the traditional underpinnings of the social order in general, and in particular for that part of it which law and political prudence ought to preserve.

These markers also stood for the ineluctable realities of a finite political and historical order, the same realities that du Bellay had evoked in his Roman poems. Thus, in 1596, when France had narrowly escaped destruction in the frenzied climax of the Wars of Religion, a prominent magistrate opened a special court session in Lyons with this deliberate invocation of the *Antiquitez*:

Change and alteration of kingdoms, provinces, and empires is an ordinary thing, based on the natural law of created things, for God has established for them

4. See Olivier Martin, *L'Assemblée de Vincennes de 1329 et ses conséquences* (Paris: Alphonse Picard, 1909), 342–65.

5. Michel de Montaigne, "Journal de voyage en Italie," in *Œuvres complètes*, ed. Albert Thibaudet and Maurice Rat (Paris: N.R.F./Gallimard, 1962), 1223–24: "en la vie de Solon, environ sur le milieu, où il dict que Solon se vantoit d'avoir affranchi l'Attique, et d'avoir osté les bornes qui faisoint les séparations des héritages. Il a failli, car ce mot grec signifie certenes marques qui se mettoint sur les terres qui estoint engagées et obligées, afin que les acheteurs fussent avertis de ceste hypotheque. Ce qu'il a substitué des limites n'a point de sens accomodable, car se seroit faire les terres non libre, mais commune." Among the other guests at this dinner was the French expatriate Marc-Antoine Muret, greatest of the neo-Ciceronians. Montaigne, it seems, had no answer to this criticism of Amyot.

bounds that they can in no fashion pass. All former ages are faithful witnesses, for there remains of them not even their shades, but only what we read. The proud cities have been buried, and have returned to their primal state of nothingness. The ruins of Babylon, of great Troy, are certain marks of this immutable law. Even the history that, we have said, is all that remains of antiquity will perish. Time itself will perish: *the world itself collapses on itself.*[6]

The boundaries here are boundaries of time, and they have been set by God himself, not by ancestors. But Antoine Séguier's sense of the radical temporalness of political prudence is striking. A statesman, or a judge, must operate within a claustrophobic world, where even classical antiquity can offer no access to eternity and where the state may at any moment suffer its inevitable collapse into ruin. The only place Séguier even bothered to look for political lessons was written history. The Gallican proverb, it seems, was an invitation not so much to historical scholarship as to a radically historicized political theory.

Taken together, the association of boundary markers with Solon's prudence and the mortality of empires also tells us which political theory was to be historicized. As J. G. A. Pocock has shown, the struggle between a prudent legislator and the entropy that was destined eventually to destroy every state was the central drama of republican thought in the Machiavellian tradition.[7] This outlook came to prominence in the early sixteenth century as the "prophetic" vision (exemplified by Savonarola), which hoped to transcend time and history by bringing individual states directly into the Kingdom of God, lost favor. Instead, Machiavellian theorists searched for essentially secular ways in which states might be preserved as long as possible amid the flux of a purely human world. In particular, legislators and statesmen somehow needed to compensate for the fact that a state's citizens and leaders would (probably increasingly) lack virtue and disinterestedness, and would thus promote their own ambitions at the expense of the common good and the interests of the state itself.[8]

---

6. Antoine Séguier, "Remonstrance de Mr Seguier a l'ouverture des grands jours a Lion le 26. Aoust 1596," in BN Dupuy 313, fols. 70–73, fol. 70r. The Latin does not seem to be a direct quotation, but it echoes a number of passages in Lucretius, *De rerum natura*.

7. See J. G. A. Pocock, *The Machiavellian Moment: Florentine Political Thought and the Atlantic Republican Tradition* (Princeton, N.J.: Princeton University Press, 1975); as well as Quentin Skinner, *The Foundations of Modern Political Thought*, 2 vols. (Cambridge, U.K.: Cambridge University Press, 1978), esp. vol. 1.

8. Political scientists generally call "republican" any political theory that, following Aristotle, seeks first of all to create virtuous citizens. For a recent summary of such theories and their place in the history of political thought, see M. M. Goldsmith, "Republican Liberty

It is a matter of controversy to what extent this theoretical viewpoint dominated Renaissance political thought in general, but its relevance to the specific case of Gallicanism is clear.[9] Medieval Gallicanism, as we have seen, had made extensive use of the prophetic ideal of moving directly to a millennial Kingdom of God on Earth. As this project came to seem less plausible, Machiavellian republicanism, with its historicism, offered an obvious alternative. At the same time, it was easy to generalize the traditional fear that Rome sapped France's economic and military strength, and that the clergy's virtue was destroyed by luxury and avarice, into a belief that Rome's partisans were basically opposed to the French national interest and indeed that they were the prime movers in any decay of French republican virtue. Finally, Gallicans with public offices in the royal councils and courts were more than ready to cast themselves in the role of the virtuous and heroic legislator, struggling for the stability of the state against vice, interest, and bad luck. The real questions, then, were, first, what policies the jurists would recommend to preserve that stability, and, second, why anyone else should take them seriously in their pretensions.

The answers to these two questions were closely intertwined, creating the distinctively erudite Gallican form of republican political thought. The rules of the game specified that states should be preserved by a return to their origins, the *ad fontes* so dear to humanists, and that those who so preserved them should be distinguished by prudence and disinterestedness. This, however, was not terribly specific, and indeed raised some serious difficulties. First of all, there were likely to be disagreements over what, as a matter of fact, those putative origins had been. This happened in an acute form in debates between Catholics and Protestants, and gave rise to the competing historical projects of the Magdeburg Centuriators and Cardinal Baronius and his continuators. Similarly, the flowering of historical scholarship in sixteenth-century France was in large part a response to this issue on

---

Considered," *History of Political Thought* 21 (2000): 543–59. Renaissance "republicans," however, were as likely as not to seek virtue only among public officials, and even then only in the actual exercise of their office (though this is not true of Machiavelli specifically). One should thus be cautious about equating the "Machiavellian" tradition with republican thought as a whole. I develop this argument in more detail in Jotham Parsons, "The Roman Censors in the Renaissance Political Imagination," *History of Political Thought* 22 (2001): 565–86.

9. For various critiques of the republicanism of Renaissance political thought, see James Hankins, ed., *Renaissance Civic Humanism: Reappraisals and Reflections* (Cambridge, U.K.: Cambridge University Pres, 2000); and Paul A. Rahe, *Republics Ancient and Modern: Classical Republicanism and the American Revolution*, 3 vols. (Chapel Hill: University of North Carolina Press, 1994), vol. 2.

the secular level. This scholarship was concentrated in the legal profession, not only (as scholars have noted) because it drew heavily on new legal studies methodologies, but also because jurists actively adopted humanist-republican political theories to advance their own political agendas.[10] They also believed, as we shall see, that legal training and the possession of legal office gave them a unique authority both as historians and as republican statesmen.

Beyond all this, however, there was a more subtle question about the nature of political reformation within history. Return *ad fontes* could and did mean two different things. On the one hand, it could be a slightly weakened version of millennialism, seeking to resurrect an originary state that (like the Golden Age of the ancients or the Christian state of innocence) had for all practical purposes completely vanished. Only heroic, visionary, nearly miraculous action could attain this essentially revolutionary goal. The Protestant Reformation's restoration of (its idea of) the primitive Church is by far the most dramatic example of this possibility, while Machiavelli's desire to revive the *virtù* of republican Rome in modern Italy is a secular case.[11] As Séguier's and du Bellay's dramatic stress on the boundedness of historical time and the radical destruction of classical models suggests, though, Gallican thinkers were not much drawn to this line of reasoning. On the other hand, reformation could involve nothing more than nurturing a living tradition, pruning out deformations and novelties. For those who preferred this essentially conservative point of view, society should be governed by its ordinary, accessible, and continuous past practice—in other words, by custom. This was the path the erudite Gallicans took, but along the way they showed that this very conservative outlook could have genuinely radical implications, both philosophical and practical.

Medieval political thought, like medieval philosophy generally, tended to account for the particular based on the general and absolute, to locate for-

---

10. The classic works on the legal base of sixteenth-century French historical scholarship are Julian H. Franklin, *Jean Bodin and the Sixteenth-Century Revolution in the Methodology of Law and History* (New York: Columbia University Press, 1963); and Donald Kelley, *Foundations of Modern Historical Scholarship: Language, Law and History in the French Renaissance* (New York: Columbia University Press, 1970).

11. Machiavelli's and Guicciardini's contrasting views on the use of history are interesting in this context. The former, of course, believed strongly in the exemplarity of history, while the latter famously prefaced his history of Italy with a ringing attack on such exemplarity. The erudite Gallicans, in the wake of this dispute, sought new ways of explaining the political utility of historical study.

mal properties in the nature or the will of God, and to see all political authority emanating from and directly established by God.[12] In France, beside the prophetic and moralistic discourse of Gallican reform, such theories tended to cluster around the ideal of justice. From its foundation, the distribution of justice was central to the French monarchy's claim of legitimacy. It was exemplified by Joinville's famous story of Saint Louis giving judgment to all comers under an oak at Vincennes.[13] Over the course of the Middle Ages, the monarchy came to be identified with "the very idea of justice," the rule of which was guaranteed by the constitution and divine sanction of the monarchy.[14] This theory appealed to those committed to the belief that valid political organization was the direct or indirect instantiation of a preexistent ideal. There were numerous precedents for identifying that ideal with justice. It also had the advantage of identifying the political with one of the few functions that the kings of the High Middle Ages were actually in a position to perform. Almost of necessity, the idealization of justice also gave a preeminent role to technicians of the law, seen (particularly after the Bolognese revival of the Roman law) as the most visible and perfect form of justice within the political realm. After all, the opening words of Justinian's *Digest*, the foundation of Roman law, called jurists "priests of the law," a turn of phrase that did much to integrate sacerdotal and juridical ideas of monarchy.[15]

Guillaume Budé, a jurist himself in addition to being François I's librarian and minister of philology, expressed the philosophical presuppositions of this theory very clearly in the *Institution du prince* he wrote for that king. This work encapsulated the essence of medieval political theory even as it

---

12. See Walter Ullmann, *Principles of Government and Politics in the Middle Ages* (New York: Barnes & Noble, 1961), and "Juristic Obstacles to the Emergence of the Idea of the State in the Middle Ages," *Annali di storia del diritto* 13 (1969): 43–64, pp. 44–46.

13. Jean de Joinville, *Vie de saint Louis*, ed. J. Monfrin (Paris: Classiques Garnier, 1995), 30 (§59–60). On this story and its significance, see Jacques le Goff, *Saint Louis* (Paris: Gallimard, 1996), 702–4.

14. Ernst Kantorowicz, *The King's Two Bodies: A Study in Medieval Political Theology* (Princeton, N.J.: Princeton University Press, 1957), 96. On "law-centered kingship" in general, see ibid., 87–192. On this line of thought in the sixteenth century, see Kenneth Pennington, *The Prince and the Law, 1200–1600: Sovereignty and Rights in the Western Legal Tradition* (Berkeley and Los Angeles: University of California Press, 1993), esp. 276–84; Ralph Giesey, "The Juristic Basis of Dynastic Right to the French Throne," *Transactions of the American Philosophical Society* 51 (1961): 64–150; and Sarah Hanley, *The Lit de justice of the Kings of France: Constitutional Ideology in Legend, Ritual, and Discourse* (Princeton, N.J.: Princeton University Press, 1983), 14–101.

15. D.1.1.1; see also Kantorowicz, *King's Two Bodies*, 119–22, who notes that Guillaume Budé was still praising this metaphor in his commenatary on the *Digest*.

made use of the new style of humanist historical argument. The opening sections identified statecraft as the prince's grasp of "the pure and solid reason of truth." This pure and transparent knowledge of the Good, even if it could never be perfectly achieved in our fallen state, was sufficiently accessible that

from this doctrine of philosophy (in addition to the institutions of the canon law) the civil and political laws have proceeded and taken their sources and foundations: by the authority of which kings, . . . conserve their majesty and empire, and justice is retained in vigor and is observed for the preservation of truth.[16]

Thus, justice proceeded from truth, law from justice, and the authority of temporal rulers from true and just laws. Budé concentrated quite narrowly on the personal duties and education of the prince, leaving aside most questions about the institutional structure of the kingdom and its relationship to the idea of justice. Claude de Seyssel, writing a somewhat broader survey of French governance a few years earlier and also for François I, had provided some more details. He too held that the king "is elected and deputized by divine Providence . . . principally to maintain and do justice, which is the true duty of princes." He also claimed that justice "without any doubt at all has more authority in France than in any other country known, particularly because of the parlements which have been installed above all for that reason."[17] Seyssel was not mistaken in identifying the ideal of justice with the highest sovereign courts, for this was exactly how the members of those courts understood their political role.

The most complete and eloquent expressions of this metaphysical ideal of justice appear in the *remonstrances d'ouverture*—hortatory orations given at the opening sessions of the parlements.[18] They were at their apogee in the 1580s, and a quick detour through a few of them will demonstrate both the details of transcendent justice in its relation to religion and the way in

---

16. Guillaume Budé, *De L'institution du Prince*, ed. Jean de Luxembourg (L'Arrivour, France: Nicole Paris, 1547), 16, 18, reading "concervent" for "concernent."

17. Claude de Seyssel, *La monarchie de France*, ed. Jacques Poujol (Paris: Librarie d'Argences, 1961), 150, 117. On Seyssel's political thought and its importance, see William F. Church, *Constitutional Thought in Sixteenth-Century France: A Study in the History of Ideas* (Cambridge, Mass.: Harvard University Press, 1941), 22–42. Church tends to give excessive weight—as indeed I do here—to Seyssel's "medieval corporatism" and not enough to his Italian republicanism. In many ways J. H. Hexter, in *The Vision of Politics on the Eve of the Reformation* (New York: Basic Books, 1973), 213–30, is considerably closer to the mark.

18. See Marc Fumaroli, *L'age de l'éloquence: Rhétorique et «res literaria» de la renaissance au seuil de l'époque classique* (Geneva: Droz, 1980), 469–92.

which it could come to seem unsatisfactory as a foundation for the state. Take, for example, an oration given by Achille de Harlay on 23 November 1584. It began with an encomium on justice, "from which came even the first creation of kings when the passage from savagery to justice occurred." This ideal of justice should be ever before the court, especially "if we consider that we exercise the judgment not of men, but of God." Both the power of justice and the stakes involved in its preservation were as high as could be imagined, as de Harlay stressed by referring to the *Retable du parlement*, the famous painting that hung in the chamber in which he was then speaking.

We are warned by this painting that if justice is not done . . . the kingdom will be transferred from one race to another, at which we should often glance, and from which we should profit in considering two things which are depicted there. One is the figure of the passion of our Lord come for us men and for our salvation, who is shown to us perpetually to better remind us to pray to him not merely each day, but each hour. . . . The other is, below, the image of the king seated in his royal seat holding his scepter in his left hand with the right bare and closed, and this figure signifies two things. The first is that the king is a footstool for God's feet, like the sun; for however great, high, and highly exalted he may be, another is higher than the high, our refuge if he acts against right [*jus*]. For he will remedy it immediately, according to what is said in the sixth chapter of Wisdom. The other, that by means of justice he holds his scepter in his hand, and even though [justice] have no weapons, still it is the true power ordained by God from which the kings have discharged themselves and deposed entirely onto us, and which is exercised not by force and violence, but by words.[19]

It is particularly striking that this formulation gives the Parlement a much more important role in the state than the king himself. Divine Justice, after all, had created the monarch to exercise an approximation of that justice on earth. He had subsequently delegated this duty to his Parlement, which made it visible to the public at large. The public then proceeded to obey without further question.

No one expressed this vision of justice more eloquently than a lawyer named Antoine Loisel, who from 1581 to 1584 served on an extraordinary court drawn from the Parlement of Paris and operating in the Guyenne region, around Bordeaux.[20] He gave remonstrances at the opening and closing

---

19. BN fr. 4397, fol. 19v, 21r–v. The painting in question is now in the Louvre. Wisdom 6 enjoins kings to seek the divine Wisdom that has given them their thrones, and that will overthrow them if they abandon justice.

20. For the details of this story, see Jotham Parsons, "The Political Vision of Antoine Loisel," *Sixteenth Century Journal* 27 (1996): 453–67. De Harlay was almost certainly influenced directly by Loisel's Guyenne orations. This is noticeable in the remonstrance just quoted,

of each of its sessions, all of which he later published. The first pair had the fine, ringing title "Of the Eye of the King and of Justice." The "eye of the king" was a kind of roving commissar in the Persian Empire, mentioned by Xenophon, whom Loisel identified with his own itinerant court. He then discussed how he would "accommodate this phrase 'the eye of the king' to governors, magistrates, and ministers of justice," proceeding to expound a thoroughgoing Neoplatonic political vision. Among the Egyptians, he claimed, an eye represented justice.

> The eye is ... the conservator and guardian of the whole body. Now in this world, there are three principal kinds of bodies; all of which have their eyes, which serve to guide and conduct them. In the first place, we have this great world, which is a body.... We have our body, which has its proportion and correspondence with that of the great world, because of which ours is called a microcosm, or little world, and finally we have the bodies of states, empires, republics, and kingdoms, which are called bodies.[21]

The eye of the world he identified as "the sun, which is the eye of God and of his justice," while the eye of the state was, naturally, the state's own justice.

Loisel's model was something like this: as justice is to God, so is the sun to the heavens, courts of justice to the state, and the eye to the body. Each of these structures was a perfect image of the one above it in the hierarchy. If ancient jurisprudence and Aristotelian political philosophy confirmed this, so did two forms of direct divine revelation. The first and more evident was the relation of microcosm to macrocosm, whereby one could read transcendent reality directly from the natural world, in this case the body or the solar system. The second was the *prisca theologia*, that pristine knowledge of the divine that many Renaissance Platonists supposed to have been handed down from Adam (or Abraham, or Moses) through a varying chain of ancient pagan sages until it reached Plato.[22] The Iranian prophet Zoroaster

---

but even more so in one from St. Martin, 1584, which took as its subject the Persian institution of the *ophthalmos basileios* that had formed Loisel's text in 1581 (BN fr. 4397, fols. 16r–18r).

21. Loisel, *La Guyenne*, 21.

22. On the doctrine of microcosm, see, e.g., the works of Frances Yates, esp. *Giordano Bruno and the Hermetic Tradition* (Chicago: University of Chicago Press, 1964), and *The Art of Memory* (Chicago: University of Chicago Press, 1966); and also the classic, though long outdated, work of Arthur O. Lovejoy, *The Great Chain of Being: A Study of the History of an Idea* (Cambridge, Mass.: Harvard University Press, 1936). On the *prisca theologia*, see, e.g., Marc Fumaroli, "Hiéroglyphes et lettres: La «sagesse mystérieuse des anciens» au XVIIe siècle," *XVIIe siècle* 158 (1988): 7–20; James Hankins, *Plato in the Italian Renaissance*, 2 vols. (New York:

was usually included in the line of transmission, and the Egyptians were supposed to have concealed this wisdom in their hieroglyphs. Another perennial member of this company was Orpheus, "about whom," Loisel said at one point, "I cannot keep silent."[23] In this ultimate expression of the transcendent ideal of Justice, that virtue became identified with the Neoplatonic Unity from which all things derived. The courts, in turn, were not only its vehicle within the state but also, insofar as they were composed of humanistically trained scholars, capable of reading its dictates directly: not only in Christianity and the French constitution, but in nature itself.

Three years later, though, when Loisel came to deliver his final oration in 1584 in a deteriorating political environment, his view of justice had altered considerably. By then, he saw even the *Digest*'s uncontroversial definition of justice—"to give to each what belongs to him, to reward and compensate the good with praise and benefits, to punish and chastise the offenses and outrages of evildoers"—as unhelpful.[24] He then proceeded to say something startling:

In this world, we do not know well what true and interior justice is. That which we practice here below is nothing but its image, or better a shadow so frail and ruined that it is subject to diversity of opinions, changes, and variations according to places, countries, times, persons, and contingencies. And consequently the opinion of those seems best who hold that our rights are not at all according to nature, which is always one and immutable.

And a page or two later, he adds:

one can never speak particularly well about justice or its functions except broadly [*en gros*], and according to the subject at hand, and not with scientific certainty: sometimes calling right and just what, if considered separately, would seem injustice. So that true Justice having abandoned us since she has risen to the heavens, nothing remains to us but her robe: and that she consists only in opinion, in law, or in positive rights, and not in nature.[25]

This was calculated to wreak havoc with the idea that the state was founded on justice, and that the law and the courts were its conduit and guarantor.

Columbia University Press, 1990), 1:267–99 and 2:459–63; and, especially valuable for developments in France, D. P. Walker, *The Ancient Theology: Studies in Christian Platonism from the Fifteenth to the Eighteenth Century* (Ithaca, N.Y.: Cornell University Press, 1972).

23. Loisel, *La Guyenne*, 18. That he has this doctrine of transmission from Jew to pagan specifically in mind is made clear when he remarks of God's justice, on p. 19, "*& ante eam ambulit*, as David says, or at his side, as Plato says, who learned it from him."

24. Loisel, *La Guyenne*, 296.

25. Loisel, *La Guyenne*, 297, 299.

How could that continue to be the case if justice was only visible in the structure of an existing state? Loisel's claim could easily sweep away the bases of justice, or as the French said, "robe" political thought.

Another discussion of the artificiality and evanescence of justice is a dialogue written by the lawyer and historian Estienne Pasquier, apparently just around this time. Entitled "Pourparler de la Loy," it was jocular and cynical in tone, but nevertheless conveyed a more precise idea than Loisel's speech of what the issues and the stakes were in this kind of discussion. Pasquier's dialogue took place on a galley in port, beginning with a condemned criminal pleading with his captain for lenient treatment. The criminal claimed to be no ordinary cutthroat, but rather a philosopher and a citizen of "Rome, once the head of the universe and now the seat of the holy fathers."[26] He proceeded to describe how his philosophy had led him into the condition in which the captain found him. On an impulse perhaps more Paduan than Roman, he had determined to conduct his life according to the dictates of nature, "that nature, as I said, which if we believe the legists has given rise to all their laws." But the young philosopher soon became convinced that the laws governing social relations were in fact unsupported by nature, and hence not applicable to himself. The first step in the process was the rejection of private property, on the grounds that the true thief was "the one who first placed boundaries around fields."[27] Thence the philosopher's temerity descended from antinomianism into complete anomie, and his consequent antisocial behavior led him to the galleys. While Pasquier remained playful and allusive, for him as for Loisel one can detect a real anguish behind intimations that justice as it exists in political reality might be a completely artificial construct, its true essence unknowable: that nature and reason cannot provide a secure guide to human action or a secure foundation for human society.

Loisel's and Pasquier's pessimistic musings were a manifestation of the deep skeptical current that ran through all sixteenth-century thought. This tendency drew on the Christian tradition of negative theology that Nicholas of Cusa had brought to new heights in the mid-fifteenth century in his call for a "learned ignorance" in matters of faith. Taken up enthusiastically by the northern humanists in their search for a purified, nondogmatic

26. Etienne Pasquier, *Pourparlers*, ed. B. Sayhi-Périgot (Paris: Honoré Champion, 1995), 161. The echo of du Bellay is almost certainly deliberate.

27. Pasquier, *Pourparlers*, 164, 165. Traditionally, property rights were considered the most basic given of natural law; see Pennington, *The Prince and the Law*, 151–54 and passim.

religiosity, this mode of thought was enormously influential in the French Renaissance.[28] It found much that was congenial in the thought of the ancient skeptics, so that, for example, Erasmus's personification of Christian Folly could say that "human affairs are so manifold and obscure that nothing can be clearly known, as is rightly taught by my friends the Academics, the least arrogant of the philosophers."[29] Academic skepticism also appealed to the humanists because it fit well with a political philosophy that privileged rhetoric. The domain of rhetoric, that is, of persuasive speech, was the probable as opposed to the certain: certain knowledge carries its own conviction and does not need the assistance of the rhetorician. Toward the end of the sixteenth century, the reemergence of the works of Sextus Empiricus greatly enlarged the scope of moral and political skepticism.[30]

One of the differences between the Pyrrhonism of Sextus Empiricus and the Academic skepticism presented by Cicero was that, according to the latter, there is exactly one piece of certain knowledge, namely, that nothing *else* may be certainly known. Consequently when, as in moral or political affairs, some decision among contending possibilities is unavoidable, one must weigh probabilities. For the Pyrrhonist, on the other hand, all judgment is to be suspended, including judgment on the question of whether certain knowledge is possible. Even judgment about probabilities is prohibited: in the realm of practical reason one is simply to follow the prevailing custom or habit. This makes a considerable difference in political practice, leading not to the weighing and communication of probabilities through rhetorical skill but to the discovery and communication of the common custom, perhaps through historical or legal research. The person who did more than anyone else to develop and popularize this philosophical position was also the probable source for both Loisel's and Pasquier's skeptical ideas: Montaigne.[31]

---

28. On this subject, see Gérard Defaux, *Le curieux, le glorieux et la sagesse du monde dans la première moitié du XVIe siècle: L'exemple de Panurge (Ulysse, Demosthene, Empedocle)* (Lexington, Ky.: French Forum Publishers, 1982).

29. Desiderius Erasmus, *The Praise of Folly*, trans. Clarence H. Miller (New Haven, Conn.: Yale University Press, 1979), 71.

30. On skepticism and rhetoric, see Nancy Struever, *Theory as Practice: Ethical Inquiry in the Renaissance* (Chicago: University of Chicago Press, 1992). On the influence of academic skepticism in early modern Europe, see the classic account by Richard H. Popkin, *The History of Scepticism from Erasmus to Spinoza* (Berkeley and Los Angeles: University of California Press, 1979), 18–41; and José R. Maia Neto, "Academic Skepticism in Early Modern Philosophy," *Journal of the History of Ideas* 58 (1997): 199–220.

31. A very good account of the debt to and development of classical skepticism in Mon-

The idea that all true and certain knowledge is inaccessible to humans is highly characteristic of his thought. In the last of Montaigne's essays (3:13, "De l'experience") he discussed justice in terms nearly identical to, if even more disillusioned than, those Loisel had used:

> Since the laws of ethics, which concern the individual duty of each person alone are so difficult to formulate, as we see that they are, it is not surprising if those which govern so many individuals are even more so.... All this makes me remember the opinions of the ancients: that he who wishes to do justice in general [*en gros*] is forced to do injury to individuals ... and of what the Stoics believed, that nature itself proceeds against justice in most of its works, and of what the Cyrenaics held, that nothing is just in itself, but that customs and laws make justice.... Now laws maintain their credit, not because they are just, but because they are laws. This is the mystical foundation of their authority; they have no other.[32]

This one textual parallel is not the only reason to think that Montaigne strongly influenced Loisel's positivistic impulses. There are other obvious affinities between the Guyenne orations and the *Essais*, and the two men knew each other. Montaigne was mayor of Bordeaux during the special court's tenure. Loisel dedicated one of his speeches to Montaigne, who in turn inscribed a surviving copy of the 1580 edition of the *Essais* to Loisel.[33]

Loisel's most direct piece of borrowing from Montaigne also leads to a solution for the problem of how to maintain a state in a world of contingent and unstable justice. The first example Loisel chose to illustrate his claim that law "is subject to diversity of opinions, changes, and variations according to places, countries, times, persons, and contingencies" was the case of

> that king of Persia who having had some Greeks and some Indians brought before him, and having asked the latter why they wished to eat the bodies of their dead fathers, and the former [why they wished] to burn them and reduce them to

---

taigne's political philosophy may be found in John Christian Laursen, *The Politics of Skepticism in the Ancients, Montaigne, Hume, and Kant* (Leiden, The Netherlands: E. J. Brill, 1992), 94–144.

32. Michel de Montaigne, *Les Essais*, ed. Pierre Villey (Paris: Presses Universitaires de France, 1924), 1070–72. One of the passages elided is a discussion of "les officiers deputés par le Prince pour visiter l'etat de ses provinces" in China. On the debt of this essay to classical Pyrrhonism in particular, see Popkin, *History of Scepticism*, 42–65.

33. One of the speeches included in the La Guyenne collection was delivered by Loisel's close friend and colleague Pierre Pithou. The introductory letter that Loisel appended to it speaks of their friendship in terms drawn from *Essais* 1:28: "De l'amitié." On the inscribed copy of the *Essais*, see Michel Reulos, *Etude sur l'esprit, les sources et la méthode des* Institutes Coutumières *d'Antoine Loisel* (Paris: Librairie du Recueil Sirey, 1935), 33.

ashes: the ones regarded with horror and abomination what the others esteemed not only just, but also holy and pious.[34]

This was drawn almost verbatim from a passage in Montaigne's essay entitled "De la coustume et de ne changer aisement une loy receüe." It was in this essay above all that Montaigne developed what is known as his "conservatism," a portion of his political thought (and only a portion, for his range was exceptionally broad and consistency was not his first concern) that would prove particularly appealing to *parlementaire* Gallican thinkers.[35]

The essay, as its title implies, was essentially an investigation of the concept and power of custom, particularly in a legal context. Custom had a long and honorable pedigree among European lawyers. However, it was not a concept to which the transcendent ideal of justice was necessarily friendly. Custom looked altogether too much like opinion, classical philosophy's dismissive catch-all term for unfounded, unverified, and nonrational belief. Thus, Budé harshly attacked customary law as an enemy of nature and of science, the task of which was

> to extirpate and confound the errors, vices, and faults that are in us. These ... have introduced themselves into us against natural law, desiring to usurp the heart and judgment of humans as their home and seat, and to confound and prescribe their donation and domination by the law of nations, otherwise called human law by Virgil and Livy.[36]

Pasquier's galley captain, however, was considerably less skeptical about the value of custom and common sense, objecting that while he might for the sake of argument grant that there was some apparent justification in his philosophical criminal's deductions, "nevertheless there is not [any real

---

34. Loisel, *La Guyenne*, 297–98. Cf. Montaigne, *Essais*, 116.

35. On Montaigne's "conservatism," see Robert Aulotte, "'Ce ne peut estre malice, c'est pour le plus malheur': Réflexions sur l'attitude d'esprit de Montaigne face au problème de 'l'obéissance du Magistrat' et de la 'manutention des polices,'" in *Ronsard et Montaigne: Ecrivains engagés?*, ed. Michel Dassonville (Lexington, Ky.: French Forum Publishers, 1989), 117–23; Frieda S. Brown, *Religious and Political Conservatism in the* Essais *of Montaigne* (Geneva: Droz, 1963); Jean Starobinski, "'To Preserve and Continue': Remarks on Montaigne's Conservatism," trans. R. Scott Walker, *Diogenes* 118 (1982): 103–20; and André Tournon, "Le magistrat, le pouvoir et la loi," in *Les écrivains et la politique dans le sud-œust de la France autour des années 1580, Actes du Colloque de Bordeaux, 6–7 novembre 1981* (Bordeaux, France: Presses Universitaires de Bordeaux, 1981), 67–87.

36. Budé, *Linstitution*, 17. I translate the French words "usage" (Lat. *usus*) and "coustume" (Lat. *consuetudo*) indifferently as "custom." While there may be a significant semantic gap between them (presumably, the former refers primarily to the social and the latter to the legal), it must remain beyond our scope here.

one], for an infinity of reasons, which custom and common sense have taught us."[37]

❦

Montaigne aligned himself firmly with the captain's position. Montaigne built "De la coustume," like most of his essays, around the examination and manipulation of a few commonplaces. In this case, the central one was the Aristotelian topos of "custom as second nature." Never explicitly cited in the essay (it appeared in essay 3:10, in the context of Stoic doctrines concerning self-sufficiency), it nevertheless made its presence felt from the end of the essay's first paragraph: "we see [custom] force, at every turn, the rules of nature: 'custom, that most efficient master of all things.'"[38] The relation of custom to nature was not a comfortable subject for Montaigne. Custom does violence to nature, masters it, and perhaps forces it out of the way. For the essayist, nature was at once something infinitely precious and absolutely necessary, and something unavailable, defective, and dangerous—in need of supplement or replacement. In the end, Montaigne opted for a solution whereby custom would, in effect, become nature, a move seemingly modeled on the doctrine whereby the medieval nominalist philosophers derived laws of nature from God's ultimately contingent legislation, and laws of linguistic meaning from the contingencies of human usage.[39] This model could readily be and was in fact transferred from the secular to the religious sphere.

Throughout the *Essais*, Montaigne apparently held up nature as the one true guide for human action. In the final essays, it was exemplified by the fig-

37. Pasquier, *Pourparlers*, 168. In point of fact, it was more likely Pasquier who was aligning himself with Montaigne, but for the moment the matter is indifferent.

38. Montaigne, *Essais*, 109. The quotation is from Pliny, *Historia naturalis* 26:6.

39. Three studies have heavily shaped my development of this reading of Montaigne's political philosophy: André Compagnon, *Nous, Michel de Montaigne* (Paris: Seuil, 1980); Jean Céard, *La nature et les prodiges: L'insolite au XVIe siècle en France* (Geneva: Droz, 1977), 387–436; and Timothy Hampton, *Writing from History: The Rhetoric of Exemplarity in the Renaissance* (Ithaca, N.Y.: Cornell University Press, 1990), 134–197. On the other hand, I am almost diametrically opposed to the thesis put forward in the most complete recent discussion of Montaigne's poltical thought: that of David Lewis Schaefer, *The Political Philosophy of Montaigne* (Ithaca, N.Y.: Cornell University Press, 1990). This is not to say that Schaefer's reading, though fatally wounded by its Straussian hermeticism, does not point out some genuine truths about Montaigne's text, which is eminently a mansion of many rooms. For a balanced and perceptive evaluation of this book, see the review by Nannerl O. Keohane, *The Journal of Politics* 54 (1992): 296–99. Jack I. Abecassis, in "'Le Maire et Montaigne ont tousjours esté deux, d'une separation bien claire': Public Necessity and Private Freedom in Montaigne," *Modern Language Notes* 110 (1995): 1067–89, puts forward views very close to my own.

ure of Socrates, and by a "natural" death explicitly contrasted with the "philosophical" death promoted by essay 1:20 ("Que philosopher, c'est apprendre à mourir"). Yet, as Timothy Hampton, among others, has pointed out, this exemplarity, or set of exemplarities, was deeply troubled. Above all, Montaigne had great difficulty explaining how anyone might actually see and understand this natural disposition. No recognizably dialectical form of reason, a faculty in which Montaigne had little confidence, could determine it.

The philosophers, with great reason, refer us to the rules of nature; but they have nothing to do with such sublime knowledge. They falsify it and show us its face painted in too high a color, from which we get so many different portraits of such a uniform subject.... The more simply one commits oneself to nature, the more wisely one does so....

Like Montaigne himself, who claimed that "I have not corrected ... my natural complexion by the force of reason."[40]

The difficulty of locating nature, however, and the unsuitability of reason for that task, posed considerable problems to a major part of Montaigne's project: the regulation of public life. For, at least barring a major intellectual, ethical, and spiritual regeneration of the species, there was no clear way in which sufficient consensus about the dictates of nature might arise to allow them to regulate a society of any size. In fact, particularly in the third book of the *Essais*, Montaigne quite consistently confined his naturalized ethics to the private sphere and indeed to the individual human body. Other rules governed the public sphere and the body politic. These could only be the rules of custom. True, there was an ever-present possibility that those rules might offend against nature and its virtual synonym, justice, "since we call a random mixture of the first laws that we come across 'justice,' and their dispensations and practices, which are often most inept and iniquitous." "Justice in itself, natural and universal, is otherwise and more nobly regulated than is that other special, national justice constrained by the needs of our forms of administration."[41] Just as nature and its laws

---

40. Montaigne, *Essais*, 1073, 1059. On the problems posed by the possibility that Socrates had reformed himself by reason and its virtual abandonment, see Hampton, *Writing from History*, 181–88.

41. Montaigne, *Essais*, 766, 796. In fact, according to Phillipe Desan, in *Penser l'histoire à la Renaissance* (Caen, France: Paradigme, 1993), 136, Montaigne identified custom with national identity, so that "être français se résume à adopter les coutumes propres à ce pays sans y reflechir," though I would quarrel with the final phrase. Montaigne develops a very complex account of his own relationship to nationality and personality in 3:6 ("De la vanité").

were not accessible to pure reason, the justice received and administered in a given state could not be identified with, or founded on, the universal form of justice.

Still, as Montaigne made explicit in "De l'utile et l'honneste," from which the last quotation comes, the only available remedy for this situation was an at least provisional withdrawal from the public sphere. Even then, one should not hold customary usages wholesale up to the judgment of nature, for to do so might easily lead to severely antisocial behavior.

Laws take their authority from possession and usage; it is dangerous to trace them back to their birth. They grow larger and more noble as they run, like our rivers: follow them upstream to their source and they are nothing but a tiny trickle of water, hardly recognizable, which becomes strong and proud as it ages.... It is not surprising if people who take as their patron the first image of nature, in most of their opinions, stray from the common path. As, for example, few of them would have approved of the constrained conditions of our marriages.[42]

That was exactly how Pasquier's galley prisoner had started. Given time, apparently, even the most unnatural dispensations could acquire the full authority of nature. How was this possible?

The intellectual traditions available to late-sixteenth-century French jurists offered at least two possible models for such a transformation: one from political theory itself and the other, less obviously, from linguistic thought. Let us turn first to the latter. Summing up the state of the question in the early 1570s, the translator and philosopher Louis Leroy remarked that "there has at times been no small controversy among the learned as to whether words were imposed according to the pleasure and will of the speakers, or by natural art and reason." Partisans of the antinaturalist school argued that "the variety and continual mutation that is seen among languages" proved that "this imposition was casual and arbitrary, founded on the convention and custom of men."[43] There was a similarity between the problem of arbitrary variety in language and its solution by the enshrinement of customary forms, and the arbitrary variation that Montaigne found in social institutions and the resolution of that by the valorization of custom. A few pages later Leroy objected to spelling reforms on the grounds that "in grammar there is more observation than reason, and that in things

---

42. Montaigne, *Essais*, 583.

43. Louis Leroy, *De la vicissitude ou variété des choses en l'univers* (Paris: Fayard, 1988), 76. For the probable influence of this work on Montaigne, see Villey's "Catalogue des livres de Montaigne," in Montaigne, *Essais*, lxv.

like speaking, writing, and pronunciation it is better to mix with nature custom, which according to Quintilian is their sure mistress."[44] He might easily have applied the same argument to social behavior in general.

In this dispute between nominalist and realist theories of language, Montaigne explicitly and firmly sided with the former, at least in the public sphere.[45] Names, like laws, did not originate in any knowable natural mark, but at the same time their abandonment would be unthinkable. While France had no tradition strictly comparable to the English common-law ideology that held customary law, both public and private, to be immemorial, autochthonous, and virtually divine in its inviolability, the French did widely recognize the legal and constitutional importance of tradition.[46] One form this took was François Hotman's antitribonianism, an attack on the Roman law as an import unsuited to the French. Montaigne alluded at one point to this position, implying that the very irrationality of the use of Roman law demonstrated the force of custom—in this case the custom of Romanization—in the state.[47] In general, though, French thinkers took a broader view. They relied not so much on a customary jurisprudence as on the customary constitution, the "fundamental laws," of their kingdom.

Drawing on the topos of custom as second nature, theorists since the

44. Leroy, *Vicissitude*, 80. The allusion is to *Institutio oratoria* 1:6:3: "Consuetudo vero certissima loquendi magistra, utendumque plane sermone ut nummo, cui publica formata est."

45. See Compagnon, *Nous, Michel*, 17–142.

46. On the English tradition and its absence in France, see J. G. A. Pocock, *The Ancient Constitution and the Feudal Law* (Cambridge, U.K.: Cambridge University Press, 1987). For a case where Montaigne at least alludes to an English-style theory, though, see *Essais*, 270: "(C) nulle loix ne sont en leur vray credit, que celles ausquelles Dieu a donné quelque ancienne durée: de mode que personne ne sçache leur naissance, ny qu'elles ayent jamais esté autres." By the 1580s, a combination of royal reformation of customs, greater penetration of legal training, and the centralizing tendencies that had been operating in the monarchy at least since the reign of Louis XI had largely dissolved even the more cautious medieval French constitutionalism. On this process, see Church, *Constitutional Thought*, passim.

47. François Hotman, *Antitribonian* (Paris: Jeremie Perier, 1603); cf. Montaigne, *Essais*, 117: "(A) quelle chose peut estre plus estrange, que de voir un peuple obligé à suivre des loix qu'il n'entendit onques, attaché . . . à des regles qu'il ne peut sçavoir, n'estant escrites ny publiées en sa langue. . . . Je sçay bon gré à la fortune, dequoy, comme disent nos historiens, ce fut un gentil'homme Gascon et de mon pays, qui le premier s'opposa à Charlemaigne, nous voulant donner les loix Latines et Imperiales." Hotman's arguments against the Roman law, namely, that it has nothing to do with French practice, clearly do not apply to *pays de droit écrit* such as Gascony. It is worth remarking that François Hotman devoted the second chapter of the *Francogallia* to a historical account of the French language refuting essentialist accounts, like that of Henri Estienne, that derived French exclusively from Greek or some other ancient language.

Middle Ages had distinguished between newly founded states and those where the laws had acquired legitimacy through long usage. They believed that the latter were far more stable, since not only had experience proven the merit of the laws through a kind of natural selection, but also the laws and the subjects had actively shaped each other in each other's image. This concept was particularly influential in the thought of the Florentine republicans, of whom Montaigne was an attentive reader—it formed the background, for example, to the second and third chapters of Machiavelli's *Prince*.[48] English jurists claimed that through this mechanism, customary law came to form an "artificial reason," ontologically distinct from the natural reason that governed natural law, but that it functioned in an equivalent manner with respect to the conduct of the state. For Montaigne, with his strong doubts about the accessibility of natural law and his equally strong sense of the power of habit, this mode of thought was very appealing. It must have been even more appealing when he considered it in the light of nominalist linguistic theory. That philosophical school provided a model for a formal account of human behavior that did not appeal to transcendent norms.

More broadly, it allowed its followers to retain the foundations of a dogmatic philosophy in a wide range of contexts while deferring, if not completely avoiding, reference to any specific transcendent ideal. Nominalist linguistic thought accepted specific individual languages as human creations. At the same time, it resolved questions about the ultimate grounds for regularity and reference in linguistic behavior by appeal to the ineffable divine Name. Similarly, political thinkers like Montaigne could refer the ultimate grounds of law and order in the physical and moral worlds to the equally inaccessible dictates of the absolute powers of God.[49] Christian skeptics at least since Cusanus had been confident that the mere fact that the human mind could not comprehend the Divine did not mean that one should lack confidence in its effectiveness as this kind of ultimate foundation. Thus, in neither case did this sort of bracketing of the ultimate ontological ground vitiate the validity or reliability of what remained laws *in*, if

---

48. See Pocock, *Machiavellian Moment*, 3–30, 157–59.

49. On the significance of the name of God, see Compagnon, *Nous, Michel*, passim. The classic study of the distinction between the absolute and the ordained powers of God and the implications thereof is Heiko Obermann, *The Harvest of Medieval Theology: Gabriel Biel and Late Medieval Nominalism* (Cambridge, Mass.: Harvard University Press, 1963), who stresses the degree of physical and moral stability nominalist theory claimed to guarantee. It should be noted, though, that a concern for the absolute/ordained distinction is by no means diagnostic of any given set of formal philosophical beliefs.

not strictly laws *of*, nature. In fact, as Leroy's brief comment about grammar quoted above suggests, the opposite was the case. The very arbitrariness of these laws ruled out the possibility that mere mortals might dispute them. This was particularly important in the anarchic climate of France during the Wars of Religion.

When Montaigne discussed the power and uses of custom, he had in mind primarily neither private life, nor even questions of social behavior such as proper deportment in company, but rather the vital issues of law, civil order, and justice. Nothing shows this more evidently than the way in which he continually paired those discussions with considerations on the progress and causes of the French civil wars. When Montaigne wrote that childhood games "are . . . the true seeds and roots of cruelty, tyranny and treason," he was pointing out a link between custom, social conventions, and the pathologies of current public life. Moreover, he was interested above all in those customs that had the force of law and shaped entire societies. "Is there any opinion so bizarre," he asked,

(I leave aside the gross imposture of religions, by which so many great nations and so many intelligent persons have found themselves intoxicated: for, this area being beyond our human reason, it is more excusable for those not extraordinarily enlightened by divine favor to lose themselves therein), but of other opinions, are there any so strange that they have not been implanted and established by laws in whatever region [custom] has wished?[50]

The entire miscellaneous collection of examples that followed served as a negative reply to this rhetorical question.

In this passage, and the several pages that followed it, Montaigne continued to criticize custom (with the very significant exception of religious custom) in the light of reason, which it challenged but did not yet displace. His inquiry climaxed, in its final version, with the statement that "whatever is outside of the bound of custom, is believed to be outside the bounds of reason," and with a near-quote from *The Prince* that made its political relevance obvious: "Peoples raised to liberty and to rule themselves, consider any other form of government monstrous and against nature. Those who are used to monarchy act the same way."[51] In fact, Montaigne said, he had originally intended to publish just such a reasoned attack on the blind ac-

---

50. Montaigne, *Essais*, 110, 111, emphasis added.

51. Montaigne, *Essais*, 116. Cf. Niccolò Machiavelli, *The Prince*, trans. Peter Bondanella and Mark Musa (Oxford, U.K.: Oxford University Press, 1984), 19: "And anyone who becomes lord of a city used to living in liberty and does not destroy it may expect to be destroyed by it, because such a city always has as a refuge, in any rebellion, the spirit of liberty and its an-

ceptance of tyranny—the text of his friend Etienne de la Boëtie's *Discours de la servitude volontaire*—as the centerpiece of the first book of his essays. By the time that volume reached print, though, la Boëtie's work had been appropriated to the revolutionary program of the Protestant monarchomachs, and Montaigne was arguing strenuously that this kind of political critique was dangerous, irresponsible, and unfounded.

To do so, he invoked the incapacity of reason to penetrate nature:

First and universal reasons are difficult to discern, and our teachers merely skim them or, not even daring to taste them, throw themselves as soon as possible into the safety of custom, where they puff themselves up and triumph easily. Those who do not wish to leave that original source do even worse and are obliged to take up the most savage opinions.[52]

He juxtaposed this with a passage on the irrationalities and patent injustices of the French judicial system, following it in turn with a conservative credo: "These considerations, nevertheless, do not dissuade a man of understanding from following the common style; indeed, on the contrary, it seems to me that all individual and unusual fashions come more from folly or ambitious affectation than from true reason." Additions in 1588 and 1592 strengthened this assertion: "it seems to me . . . that there is great selfishness and presumption in esteeming one's own opinions so highly that, to establish them, one should destroy a public peace." Finally, he concluded, "it seem[s] to me very iniquitous to wish to submit the immobile public observances and constitutions to the instability of a private fantasy (private reason having only a private jurisdiction)." The civil laws "are sovereign judges of their judges, and the greatest capacity serves to explicate and extend received usage, not to change or innovate."[53] This was the same conclusion Loisel came to when confronted with the next round of revolutionary agitation in 1584.

The distinction between a public and a private reason was a crucial one, not least because it immediately suggested that the former might be identi-

---

cient institutions. . . . But when cities or provinces are accustomed to living under a prince and the family of that prince has been extinguished, they, being on the one hand used to obedience and, on the other, not having their old prince . . . yet not knowing how to live as free men, are as a result hesitant in taking up arms."

52. Montaigne, *Essais*, 117. Note, though, that taking "franchise" as having merely the force of "sauvegarde" (as does Villey) ignores a certain ambiguity that seems to be being played up in the final sentence: the safety of custom is also a license, surpassed only by the licentiousness of abandonment of custom and reliance on (inaccessible) first priciples.

53. Montaigne, *Essais*, 118, 120, 121.

fied with the "written" or "artificial" reason that was learned jurisprudence. However, the rhetorical path by which Montaigne arrived at this conclusion should not lead the modern reader to overestimate the perceived degree of conflict between natural and artificial, or between private and public reason. Immediately after the passage just quoted, Montaigne pointed out that "if sometimes divine Providence has passed over the rules to which it, by necessity, has constrained us, this does not mean that we are dispensed from them. These are strokes of its divine hand . . . like miracles, which it offers as a testimony to its omnipotence." The comparison was implicit, but clear. Traditional forms (here, both secular and religious) might at times have been violated or overthrown by divine command, but this had been an exercise of the absolute rather than of the ordained powers of God. As the essayist said elsewhere, God "manipulates and applies" the things of this world "according to His hidden design."[54] The absolute Providence according to which God exercises his absolute powers was entirely inaccessible, but this did not derogate from the validity or the reliability of his ordinances, or of the human customs that Montaigne assimilated to them.

At the limit, there is nothing unnatural about the second nature that is custom. This was not necessarily a comfortable thought: it appeared clearly in some very radical passages from essay 3:9 ("De la vanité"), discussing the sorry state in which France found itself at the beginning of the 1580s. At that point, the very morals and customs of society had undergone corruption even from their usual state. "I see . . . mores commonly used and received which are so monstrous in their inhumanity . . . that I have not the courage to think of them without horror." This, however, turned out to be a difference only in degree from the general case of human societies, for nature can build a society of the evil as easily as of the good.

In the end, I see from our example that the society of men holds and sticks together whatever the price. Wherever you put them down they pile up and arrange themselves, moving around and fitting together as mismatched objects that one puts in one's pocket at random find their own way of joining and arranging themselves, often better than could be contrived by art. King Philip [of Macedon] made a collection of the worst and most incorrigible men he could find, and housed them all in one city. . . . I believe that they would have made themselves, out of their very vices, a political fabric and a just and suitable society.[55]

---

54. Montaigne, *Essais*, 121, 216. The latter quote is from 1:32 ("Qu'il faut sobrement se mesler de juger des ordonnances divines").

55. Montaigne, *Essais*, 956.

Any society not composed of always already corrupted customs would be sheer utopia. "It is no mere opinion but the truth that the best and most excellent administration for each nation is that under which it has maintained itself," that is, under which it has simply survived.[56] The mere fact of continued existence in the world naturalizes a social order. *Was ist, ist Recht.* This no more vitiated the possibility of social critique for Montaigne than for Hegel, but it meant that any such critique had to be carried out with the utmost circumspection. Above all, one could never base it on any purely abstract, uninstantiated idea, like the millennium or pure justice.

In fact, Montaigne almost completely reversed the traditional schema whereby the state was built on religious truth, which in turn was based on divine nature; this is perhaps the greatest significance of his work for the history of Gallican thought. "What a marvelous example divine wisdom has left us," he exclaimed,

which, in establishing the salvation of the human race and achieving its glorious victory over sin and death, chose only to do so while sparing our political order, and submitted its progress and the achievement of so high and so salutary an effect, to the blindness and injustice of our observances and customs.[57]

Religion underwrote human justice not by revealing it as an extension of the divine nature, but by divinely exemplifying the naturalization even of injustice when it had been sanctioned by custom. This went beyond even strict nonresistance theory, which claimed merely that Christianity could not undertake to alter established polities no matter how evil or tyrannical they might be. Here Christianity actually testifies to the positive desirability of whatever polity is in place, regardless of that polity's abstract moral status.

Religion was not immune to the contingency that ruled all human political affairs, but it could at least claim to some extent to stand outside them. This depended on the very unintelligibility of the sacred. Religion dealt with things further "beyond our human understanding" than did even state-

---

56. Montaigne, *Essais*, 957.

57. Montaigne, *Essais*, 120–01. The immediately following paragraph presents "la cause de celui qui suyt les formes et les loix de son pays," who "allegue pour son excuse la simplicité, l'obeissance et l'exemple: quoy qu'il face, ce ne peut estre malice, c'est, pour le plus, malheur." Aulotte, in "'Ce ne peut estre malice,'" is correct to locate here the core of Montaigne's ideal of political conservatism, which is essentially an ethical one. It is important to note that there is a very specific "exemple" and "malheur" that the essayist has in mind: the example of Christ ("obediens usque ad mortem, mortem autem crucis") and the *malheur* of martyrdom. The new covenant's nonintervention in the Roman Empire was important to the Gallican theory of jurisdiction.

craft. It may well be fair to say that Montaigne's conservatism amounted to a moral and political fideism, but, if so, religion remained the natural habitat of such fideism.[58] Hence, among other things, the belief that Montaigne fully shared with many other Catholic jurists, that theological debate could only undermine religious stability—one must "flee all quarrels and dialectical arguments, and refer solely to the prescriptions and formulas of the ancients." Thus, Montaigne objected to the religious innovations of the reformers in exactly the same way that he objected to their political revolt, but in even more decisive terms:

It is a dangerous and consequential boldness . . . to despise what we do not understand. . . . I can say this as one who has done it, having formerly used this liberty of my choice and private selection and treating as indifferent certain points of observance of our Church which seemed to show a stranger or more vain face; when I came to speak about them with learned men, I found that those things had a massive and solid foundation, and that it was only stupidity and ignorance that make us take them with less reverence than the others.[59]

What is important about the example Montaigne drew from his own experience is that the necessity of following the customary usages of the Church rested not on the satisfactory explanation he eventually found, but on the fact that the private individual's objections to them could *never* be sufficiently well informed to justify dissent. Moreover, there is reason to believe that the religious opinions so decisively rejected were those of his friend la Boëtie, whose political thought Montaigne likewise expelled from the *Essais*.

As in this case, such arguments were most commonly advanced against the quarrelsome Protestants. Loisel in his Guyenne orations, for example, did much the same thing. At the same time, however, the arguments did almost as much to undermine the authority of Catholic theologians and the Catholic hierarchy. What had come to matter about religious doctrine was not so much revelation as sheer antiquity, of which one competent scholar could judge as well as another. This was really the heart of Gallican theory—the nexus of both its religious and its political conservatism, the philosophical link between the Gallican and *politique* parties. The entire ideological complex depended on the concept of a more-or-less fully naturalized custom as the only possible guide to public action, in the religious as well as in the secular spheres. At the same time, the possibility of treating the sacred and the secular constitution with the same intellectual tools, together

---

58. See Starobinski, "'To Preserve and Continue.'"
59. Montaigne, *Essais*, 322, 181–82.

with the greatly transformed but still potent notion that the former grounded or underwrote the latter, meant that religious issues were bound to be central to the political concerns of royalist Catholic jurists.

To conclude this survey of erudite Gallican political philosophy, let us look briefly at one important expression of it within an actual political debate. In the Parlement of Paris in 1603, the Crown's solicitor delivered a stinging attack on recent changes to the breviary of the diocese of Angers. One of his key arguments was that "novelty should be admitted only if it is necessary, otherwise not"; and, of course, in cases like the one at hand, necessity did not rear its ugly head. Quoting Cicero, the lawyer went on to explain the philosophical bases of his policy:

"Paternal or maternal blood carries great power, great obligation, great religious significance." For custom is a second nature, which we observe with as much reverence as a father or a mother. In short, [custom] can be compared . . . to a kingdom gained by succession, so that—a "reign" being called a "conclusion" in the holy tongue [Hebrew], being concluded and closed off under certain laws in imitation of nature—in the same way custom seems to transfer the rule and usage from line to line by title of hereditary succession. This is why one finds it most strange when there is a mutation in the temporal. And if that is insupportable, it is still less so in the spiritual.[60]

Religious observances naturalized by custom are of just the same kind and are just as inviolable as the very foundations of the state—if not more so. Should they be abandoned, there would be no reason why the hereditary monarchy itself should continue, and indeed (the point is implicit but not subtle) the recent events of the League had shown that enemies of traditional French religious practice were enemies of the Salic law and vice versa. What sustains both religion and kingship is the same thing that sustains property: the fact that the people have become accustomed to them, that the "fathers" have marked them out. Beyond those bounds there was nothing but chaos, crime, civil war, and irreligion.

If the erudite Gallican magistrates did reject the view that accessible, exterior reasons governed society, instead believing that one must seek the basis of social order in the engrained customs of that society itself, they still

---

60. Louis Servin, *Plaidoyez*, vol. 1 (Paris: Pierre Hennequin, 1603), 50–51. The quotation, somewhat free, is from a discussion of Œdipus's and Orestes' divine punishment in *Pro Roscio Amerino* 66: "magnam vim, magnam necessitatem, magnam possidet religionem paternus maternusque sanguis" (young Roscius was accused of parricide). My thanks to Matthew Roller for tracking down this quotation.

had a practical problem. If they were not the "priests of justice," why should anyone care what they said about political affairs? What gave anyone, and specifically magistrates and the courts, a unique insight into the custom that formed and preserved the French state? In the second half of the sixteenth century it was a matter of increasing urgency for humanist jurists to define a space within which disinterested criticism of public matters could coexist with attachment to and indeed dependence on the monarchy. Their position, unlike that either of the Church or of the semifeudal magnates, was derived almost entirely from the Crown, and as the monarchy stabilized it may have had rather less need for them. Nor did they have a solid place in the inner sancta of the royal government; indeed, from the time of Michel de l'Hospital, their access to such powerful places diminished steadily. Yet even the most modestly revolutionary agenda was ideologically unacceptable to the jurists. Politically, this dilemma may well have been irresolvable.

At a philosophical and rhetorical level, the jurists did develop an effective response, in the form of an ideology allowing them to claim prescriptive authority in maintaining the stability of the state, based on their special relationship to its past and its fundamental legal structure. In this intellectual complex the erudite jurists conceived of their main areas of activity—history, law, and counsel offered to the monarch—as each animated by the same moral qualities and located in the same institutions. In each case, their proper exercise required, on the one hand, disinterestedness—objectivity, justice, devotion to the common good—and, on the other hand, a given technique: historical science, jurisprudence, or political prudence.

The importance of history to political life in a world dominated by custom become second nature was undeniable, and no sixteenth-century thinker would have quarreled with the view that historical study both required and developed a high degree of objectivity. Lack of objectivity, to Renaissance thinkers, was the major threat to a transparent re-creation of past political reality, a transparency that in turn would allow history to live up to its high calling in public and literary life.[61] In later sixteenth-century France the major theorist of this problem was the Protestant soldier and scholar Lancelot Voisin de la Popilinière. "Truth," as he put it in *L'idée de l'histoire accomplie*, "is so natural to history, that everyone gives as its first law 'that it should not fear to tell the truth,' and as for the second, 'that it should discover the false.'" Any of these faults in the historian would obviate histo-

---

61. For a recent extensive treatment of objectivity in contemporary historiography, see Peter Novick, *That Noble Dream: The "Objectivity Question" and the American Historical Profession* (Cambridge, U.K.: Cambridge University Press, 1988).

ry's mission. "How will it be the torch of truth, if it tells only falsehood?" he asked elsewhere. "If, as the best authorities have said, history is the mirror of things, what mirror will it be, that shows figures distorted, greater or smaller?"[62] Correspondingly, la Popilinière required that the ideal historian "should thus be free, not servile nor obliged to anyone.... He should know neither hope nor fear.... He should dispense with hate, friendship, gain, and loss." Otherwise, "if he seeks favor, he will be counted among the flatterers, whom history has always so detested."[63] An acceptably objective history would seem to have entailed the complete annihilation of the author's personal interest in his or her own social position, an obvious impossibility that demanded some solution.

A historian could claim or obtain the authority of objectivity, of writing (as Tacitus had famously claimed to do in his *Annals*) without fear of favor [*sine ira et studio*], in several ways. One, well attested by the classical literature, deferred judgment, and hence personal consequences, into the indefinite future. Lucian had given as "the general principle I would have remembered ... this: do not write merely with an eye to the present, that those now living may commend and honor you; aim at eternity, compose for posterity, and from it ask your reward."[64] Such a technique, though, would deprive the historian of an authoritative voice in the present, for the act of honoring him (by heeding him) would undercut the impartiality and hence the legitimacy of his advice. The erudite jurists, intent on a real political role, would have to look elsewhere. Historians might also rely on a personal claim to virtue. Montaigne implicitly did something very much like this, claiming in the "Preface" to the *Essais* that the book displayed its author "sans estude et artifice," or as corrected in 1588, "sans *contantion* et artifice."[65] He thus collapsed the Tacitean *sine ira et studio*, stating it only allusively in each of the two versions, but with perfect clarity in their juxtaposition. Unless they wished to produce a self-justification as elaborate and exhaustive as the *Essais*, however, this strategy would probably not work for historians not of the self but of the nation.

62. Lancelot du Voisin de la Popilinière, *L'histoire des histoires, avec l'idée de l'histoire accomplie*, 2 vols. (Paris: Fayard, 1989), 2:38.

63. La Popilinière, *L'idée*, 2:41.

64. Lucian of Samosata, "The Way to Write History," in H. W. and F. G. Fowler, trans., *The Works of Lucian of Samosata* (Oxford, U.K.: Clarendon Press, 1905), 2:135. This piece was la Popilinière's major classical source.

65. *Les essais de Michel de Montaigne, publiées d'après l'exemplaire de Bordeaux, avec les variantes manuscrites & les leçons des plus anciennes impressions*, 4 vols. (Bordeaux, France: Imprimerie nouvelle F. Pech, 1906), 1:1. In his reading of "contantion" as "effort, recherche" (*Essais*, Villey ed., 3n) Villey shows a probably inevitable reductive tendency.

What they needed was something like a claim to professional expertise in indifference, allowing the work of history to justify itself. It is no coincidence that precisely at this time and in this milieu that history began to be a discipline as well as a genre.[66] Through this new vision of history, and by linking the discipline of history very closely both to the practice and the study of law, the learned jurists were able to create a self-supporting ideology capable of justifying—to themselves and perhaps even to their readers— the truth and public value simultaneously of their historical, legal, and political views. The erudite Gallicans could and did thus claim the objectivity necessary for historical authority by embracing the new science of historical method. This, however, was merely a first step in their larger ideological task. In them, the objectivity and expertise of the historian merged easily into the long-established but equally potent expertise and objectivity of the jurist.

Classical republican political theory, from Aristotle to Rousseau, was particularly concerned with preventing the private interests of citizens from undermining political life.[67] One idea advanced by the ancients and revived in the sixteenth century was that it was possible to overcome selfishness by setting up laws ahead of time to deal with contingencies that might arise. This was because, as Aristotle said in his *Rhetoric*,

> the judgment of a lawmaker is not about a particular case but about what lies in the future and in general, while the assemblyman and the juryman are actually judging present and specific cases. For them, friendliness and hostility and individual self-interest are often involved, with the result that they are no longer able to see the truth adequately.[68]

Gasparo Contarini made this mechanism the centerpiece of his enormously influential early-sixteenth-century account of the glories of the Venetian

66. On the birth of historical methods, see, besides the works cited above, Donald Kelley, "Historia integra: François Baudouin and His Conception of History," *Journal of the History of Ideas* 25 (1964): 35–57.

67. The literature on interest in political thought is extensive. See, in addition to Pocock, *Machiavellian Moment*, passim; and Albert O. Hirschman, *The Passions and the Interests: Political Arguments for Capitalism before Its Triumph* (Princeton, N.J.: Princeton University Press, 1977). This theme can be traced back to Aristotle's project of directing the individual will toward *eudaimonia*, and the will of the citizen toward its common pursuit. Significantly, in Book 3 of the *Politics* the philosopher discusses the decay of political government in terms of a lack of judicial integrity. For example, on the origins of oligarchy and mob rule: "all men cling to justice of some kind, but their conceptions are imperfect. . . . When the persons are omitted, then men judge erroneously. The reason is that they are passing judgment on themselves, and most people are bad judges in their own cases" (1280a); see *The Politics*, trans. Benjamin Jowett (Cambridge, U.K.: Cambridge University Press, 1988), 63.

68. 1:1:7 (1354b). Quoted from *On Rhetoric: A Theory of Civic Discourse*, trans. George A.

constitution. "The human race," he thought, "seems, by the invention of laws, to have obtained even this, that the position of ruling over human communities should be given entirely to the mind and reason, undisturbed by any perturbations."[69] In this way, the law became the exemplar in human society of that virtue which also, ideally, characterized history and historical research.

What was not clear from Aristotle's or Contarini's account was how this artificial disinterestedness would carry over to the guardians of the laws. Logically, there was no real reason why it *should*, but the power of association and some traditions of medieval and Roman law suggested that it *might*. Besides the old description of judges as "priests of the laws," these traditions ascribed to the jurists a particular and powerful form of the ultimate political virtue: prudence. The *Digest* defined law as "a common precept, the decision of prudent men."[70] The *vir prudens* who wished to interpret the law, however, required a special kind of prudence: *jurisprudentia*. This the *Digest* famously defined as "a knowledge of divine and human things, a science of the just and unjust."[71] The "science of the just and unjust," like the ideal science of history, could provide a guarantee of disinterestedness—*justitia*, after all, was nothing other than a fixed habit of giving to each his due. The idea of jurisprudence was thus well suited to the would-be historian. It was also well suited to the would-be royal counselor, especially when combined with the medieval concept of the *juris prudentes* as an integral part of the composite person of the Crown, the immortal body of the king. "On account of his counselors, who are part of his body," went one tag much favored by jurists seeking to reinforce their own political role, "the prince is said to have all the laws in the shrine of his breast."[72] In France, according to the erudite jurists, the sovereign courts were that shrine, and it was in them that the ideal of juristic and political science would be realized.

Kennedy (Oxford, U.K.: Oxford University Press, 1991), 31. This passage develops on Plato, *Laws* 9 (875–76). Jacques de la Guesle paraphrased this passage in an unpublished and unfinished memoir preserved in BN Dupuy 37 and (more legibly) in BN Dupuy 392, fol. 61v: "le jugement de la Loy estant des choses universelles et futures n'est subject à la corruption qui peut detraquer celuy du Juge cognoisssant des choses presentes et particulieres motifvez de la passion."

69. Gasparo Contarini, *De magistratibus et republica venetorum libri quinque* (Venice, Italy: Baldus Sabinus, 1551), 14–15.

70. D.1.3.1. The full text is: "Lex est commune præceptum, virorum prudentum consultum, delictorum quæ sponte vel ignoratia contrahuntur, coërcitio, communis reipublicæ sponsio."

71. D.1.1.10; also I.1.1.1.

72. Kantorowicz, *King's Two Bodies*, 154, quoting Mattheus de Afflictis.

The historian, the magistrate, and the counselor, then, all shared a common expertise in objective judgment and a common prudence in the affairs of state. A person or institution that combined these three parallel accomplishments would be ideally suited to guide a society subject to the regime of custom. He or it would have a direct and unmediated access to the past and to the superhuman wisdom of the laws. The laws were politically valuable insofar as they constituted stable, naturalized custom with its roots in the more-or-less distant past, and political prudence consisted of the willingness and ability to make use of that past stability to stabilize the state. The preservation of custom, precedent, and the fundamental laws ensured that stability, and the jurists' relation to these things, defined them as historians.[73] Each leg of this triad supported the other two. The looseness and circularity of this kind of argument meant that it could not be expressed effectively in formal philosophical treatises, but as a series of analogies and metaphors underlying the rhetorical culture of the erudite Gallicans it was both convincing and effective.

A few of Gallican historiography's seminal and programmatic texts illustrate the operation of this ideological complex in more detail.[74] Around the middle of the sixteenth century, humanist-trained writers thoroughly reimagined the French polity.[75] Three broad and overlapping groups participated in this project: reforming prelates, whose efforts were soon overtaken by the religious wars; persons concerned with the renovation of French vernacular literature (notably the Pléiade); and humanist jurists, the students of Jacques Cujas and Andrea Alciati. In the early days of this humanist move-

---

73. This construction of history as a special relation to the polity and its extension both backward and forward in time is, it seems to me, the basic difference between the early modern and the modern, historicist, historical discipline, pace Kelley, *Foundations*, 301–9. The taxonomic impulse that Zachary Schiffman, "Estienne Pasquier and the Problem of Historical Relativism," *Sixteenth Century Journal* 18 (1987): 505–17, has detected in Pasquier, for example, is essentially an epiphenomenon of this more basic structural datum; if history is primarily the process of reading (and writing) stability out of the past, existing models of stability will inevitably be read (and written) back into the past.

74. On the subject of the humanist character of the complex of ideas here under examination, it is worth noting that the position of advisor or counselor to a prince was the classic one of northern humanist political theory. For an account of this tendency, see Skinner, *Foundations*, 1:213–21; the classic discussion within humanist literature is to be found in Thomas More's *Utopia*.

75. For one interesting analysis of this process, see Timothy Hampton, *Literature and Nation in the Sixteenth Century: Inventing Renaissance France* (Ithaca, N.Y.: Cornell University Press, 2001).

ment, under François I and even Henri II, these three elements were very closely intertwined. This was true especially given the common role that many of its members played in promoting an ecclesiastical policy of caution or even defiance toward the papacy. The du Bellay clan was prominent in the effort, for example, as were the most accomplished of the early antiquarians, the brothers Jean du Tillet (one the clerk of the Parlement, the other a bishop). Many of these men were influential counselors of Henri II as well as intellectuals, and they were in an excellent position to consider and even to influence the nature of the French constitution.

Du Tillet's 1551 memorandum on the Gallican liberties was an early and influential example of this reexamination. Relations with the papacy had always raised the thorniest questions of international law confronting the French monarchy, but these had previously been considered largely within the framework of theology, abstract jurisprudence, and canon law. In 1551, du Tillet portrayed these questions essentially as historical ones and, if not precisely secular (it would be hard to conceive a history less secular than the one du Tillet sketched), at least not primarily a matter for men of the cloth. The tract also represented a new form of legal advice, one that could be given by someone who was not even a practicing lawyer. Although in fact the level of historical erudition in this treatise was not particularly impressive, it *presented itself* as a work of erudition. Du Tillet made frequent reference to specific documents in the royal archives, cited by shelf mark, and he claimed to reconstruct both the ecclesiastical structures of the Carolingian period and the process of historical causation that had brought them to their current sorry state.

Du Tillet, in other words, mobilized his position as a royal counselor and his command of various source collections to produce a chronological narrative of national institutions. In doing so he went well beyond the simple enumeration of precedents that had characterized earlier legal briefs on similar questions (for example, the remonstrances of the Parlement in favor of the Pragmatic Sanction, a copy of which was bound with the manuscript of du Tillet's treatise). His proposal for recapturing national stability, threatened as much by the Reformation as by an overweening papacy, looked to both the past and the future for models of sacred order. On the one hand, he argued with millenarian overtones that if the French king took his own church in hand,

> there will follow from it [the reformation] of other states, which would appease the anger of the Creator, . . . reduce to the faith those who have strayed and cover

their errors with the scandal of the ministers of the church, principally those of Rome, and open the path for other kings and potentates to imitate the said king, which would bring about universal peace among Christians.[76]

This was the familiar prophetic view of France's historical mission: under similar circumstances forty years earlier Jean Lemaire de Belges and Jean Bouchet had developed it in a much more radical vein, and Joachim du Bellay would mention it again a decade later. Beyond that point, though, this line of thought found few Gallican imitators.

But it was not merely in the future that du Tillet saw the independent governance of the Gallican church being directly useful to the Universal Church. He also wanted to show that this had been the case in the past. In this, for that matter, he did not differ from Lemaire de Belges, but he used a new political theory and a far more sophisticated historical erudition. He located a golden age of perfect concord and virtue in the French church and state, largely in the Carolingian period. "Whenever the church in France has been administered and governed under the authority of the Most Christian Kings rather than that of the popes, it has approached [the state of] the first apostolic [Church].... The evil that has since occurred came when the absolute power of those popes was tolerated in this kingdom."[77]

It was not simply the fact that the Church was under royal authority under the first two races that constituted and assured this ideal condition in du Tillet's eyes. He was above all a historian of the institutional structures of the French monarchy, and he had a much more precise idea of how this authority had been and should be organized. Specifically, he pointed to the Carolingian institutions of the *missi dominici* and the *campus martis* as the guarantors of concord within the Gallican church. The former were composed of mixed commissions of prelates and laymen who exercised their jurisdiction in perfect harmony. The annual general assembly acted as a superior instance to these commissions.

Each year, by royal command, a general assembly of the said church of France was held, in which customarily the said lord, his princes and council assisted.... Laws and constitutions for the general reformation or regulation of the two estates were considered and adopted, with the royal authority interposed on the counsel of the assembly.[78]

---

76. BN fr. 473, fol. 10r. This is the final passage of the tract.
77. BN fr. 473, fol. 1v.
78. BN fr. 473, fol. 2r. The fractured syntax is not an artefact of the elipses, but the entire responsibility of the text.

Unlike the similar claims made for the assembly of the *campis martis* in François Hotman's *Francogallia* twenty years later, this was not meant to suggest a systematic limitation on royal power: quite the opposite. It did, however, suggest that an entire consultative and administrative structure formed a necessary part of the very extensive authority of the French kings.

For, while one would hesitate to label du Tillet's vision "constitutionalist"—"royal authority," after all, must be "interposed on the counsel of the assembly"—it was deeply *institutionalist*, for it was in the very institutionalization of advice and authorization that he located the possibility of harmony between the religious and the secular powers. It is at this point that the parallel between du Tillet's past and his present become evident, for his very project was, by advising the king as to how his authority might best be exercised, to bring the disordered relation between the church and the state back into harmony. He did this as a layperson writing from a secular position, though with the support of a party of royalist prelates in the Council of State.[79] He thus re-created for himself the position and the originary harmony of the *campus martis*, but he was in a position to do so only because of his historical erudition. Documentary citations, intended to increase the authority of the text and the positions it advocated, demonstrated his erudition at several points in the text. This historical authority also inhered in du Tillet's official function as keeper of the nation's most important legal records. This treatise, however, did not spell out the relationship between the counselor and the historian in any further detail. Du Tillet's own relation to the institutions he describes remained purely implicit. Nor was it clear whether it was that relationship in particular that made him an authoritative historian, though clearly his historical erudition constructed him as a counselor to the king. Finally, and contrary to the presumed purpose of the entire exercise, du Tillet gave no clear recommendation as to the policy the Crown should follow toward either the papacy or the Gallican church!

Estienne Pasquier began to fill in these gaps a few years later in the first edition of his continually augmented collection of archivally informed reflections on French history, the *Recherches de la France*. Of particular interest is a dialogue he appended to the *Recherches* entitled "Le pourparler du prince."[80] Predating the generically similar "Pourparler de la loi," it served as a kind of theoretical apology for the historical work, and it is immediately evident that the echo of Machiavelli's great work was not unintentional. The dia-

---

79. A party that included his brother, the Cardinal du Bellay, and other figures of concern to us; see Romier, "La crise gallicane," passim.

80. Beneath its playful veneer, this is one of the most accomplished works of political

Custom, History, and Law   85

logue was in an autobiographical narrative frame, set in a period Pasquier spent in the country while ill, immediately before the publication of the *Recherches* and the plea for the University of Paris against the Jesuits that launched his legal career.[81] The interlocutors, however, were allegorical fictions and can most satisfactorily be taken as representative of impulses within the author's own work. In fact, the dialogue developed a sophisticated reflection on the various models of politics available within the humanist movement and how they related to French government.

Though Pasquier only wrote the final section of the putative conversation, he supplied a summary of its earlier part, which supposedly dealt with some of the great problems of classical political philosophy:

Which was the most secure of all republics: that which was governed by the efforts of a single person, or by the hands of several exceptional men, or yet by the common advice and deliberation of the people . . . ? Which was more profitable to the people: either to have a stupid and ignorant prince, within a council treating affairs wisely, or a depraved councilor under the conduct of a wise prince?[82]

The questions boiled down to, first, who should govern the state, and, second, with what special competency? The dialogue actually only treated the last of these points, but Pasquier's views on the others are easy to reconstruct. His first three interlocutors ("l'escolier," "le philosophe," and "le courtisan," later changed to "le curial") put forward three of the current humanist political theories, while the fourth (called "le politique" well before that word had come to denote a political party) attempted to synthesize a theory compatible at once with abstract justice and the particular, historical conditions of the French monarchy.

The *escolier* put forward a rather jejune defense of the utility of humane

---

philosophy produced in sixteenth-century France. It deserves, in my opinion, to rank with la Boëtie's *Discours de la servitude volontaire*. The only serious discussion of its political significance is in Orest Ranum, *Artisans of Glory: Writers and Historical Thought in Seventeenth Century France* (Chapel Hill: University of North Carolina Press, 1980), 75–82. But see also Béatrice Sayhi-Périgot, "A l'arrière-plan des Recherches I & II: Le Pourparler du Prince," in *Etienne Pasquier et ses Recherches de la France* (Paris: Presses de l'Ecole Normale Superieur, 1991), 61–77; and the same author's introduction to her edition of the *Pourparlers*. She notes among other things the centrality of the notion of counsel to Pasquier's project, "A l'arrière-plan," 67: "dans ces institutions [de la monarchie] l'essentiel, selon Pasquier, c'est le principe selon lequel le souverain prend 'conseil' de son entourage."

81. For these and other biographical details, see Dorothy Thickett, *Estienne Pasquier (1529–1615): The Versatile Barrister of Sixteenth-Century France* (London: Regency Press, 1979).

82. Pasquier, *Pourparlers*, 52.

letters in forming the character of a monarch—Pasquier was probably thinking in particular of Budé, who had claimed to show "how necessary it is for all princes to understand Greek as well as Latin letters, in order to command their realms well."[83] The *escolier* gave a Ciceronian account of rhetoric as the foundation of politics: "from our first being those who knew how to use the force of their eloquence more effectively have played with the will of all the rest of the people."[84] History in the first place, then law, and finally all literature act as an objective and self-deploying rhetoric that can guide the will of the prince as he guides that of the people. The *escolier* spoke of books "that discover the truth of persons without the least hypocrisy," combining the *topoi* of transparent language and disinterested counsel.[85] In short, he used a number of the concepts that went into the ideal of historicist counsel, but not in a manner satisfactory to Pasquier. Both the fallacy and the power of his account, according to the later interlocutors, was that he substituted literature for the discourse of a living council, without articulating a way in which the two might become interchangeable.

The *philosophe* presented a Stoic account of kingship, an "imitation" (as a marginal note admits) "of the beginning of Cicero's *Paradoxes*."[86] For the *philosophe*, the most important thing was that the monarch remove himself from the uncontrollable play of fortune by the practice of apathy; he had few suggestions as to how one might actually govern. The *courtisan* was a thoroughgoing Machiavellian and one who, while exaggerated, was hardly caricatured.[87] He contended that a prince should overcome rather than avoid the vagaries of fortune, and that the state was essentially a tool for the

---

83. Budé, *Linstitution*, 30; the heading to chap. 5 reads "L'Autheur veult monstrer en ce Chapitre, combien c'est chose necessaire à touts Princes, de sçavoir les bonnes lettres tant Grecques, que Latins: pour bien commander à leurs Royaulmes." Again, this is one of Jean de Luxembourg's headings, but again it does justice to Budé's text.

84. Pasquier, *Pourparlers*, 55.

85. Pasquier, *Pourparlers*, 60.

86. Pasquier, *Pourparlers*, 61. The exact wording changed slightly from edition to edition but, according to Pasquier's editor, "cette manchette est la seule qui subsiste jusqu'en 1723." It is perhaps surprising that this interlocutor does not engage seriously with Stoic political thought—e.g., Cicero's *De officiis*. Apparently, Pasquier had not developed his study of this facet of classical philosophy, which became more prominent among humanists toward the end of the century.

87. On Pasquier's complex relationship to Machiavelli's thought, see Nancy Streuver, "Pasquier's *Recherches de la France:* The Exemplarity of his Medieval Sources," *History and Theory* 27 (1988): 51–59; and John Parkin, "Machiavelism in Etienne Pasquier's *Pourparler du Prince*," *Modern Language Review* 68 (1973): 530–44, who traces the *courtisan*'s debts to Machiavelli in detail.

imposition of its leader's (private) will. Like Machiavelli, the *courtisan* tended to subordinate law and culture to armed force in the development of the state.[88] The law thus became like armed force in being an arbitrary construction and instrument of the holder of power. "From all time in all republics the law has been made with a nose of wax, each legislator pulling it to his own advantage and that of his favorites."[89] Pasquier, as we have already seen, was later inclined to accept much of this critique of a transcendental justice that could found political organization.

The *politique*, though, found none of the preceding accounts satisfactory. The *philosophe* had failed to provide a technique of politics, to demonstrate where to direct the ruler's will after it had been detached from passion and fortune. The *escolier*, on the other hand, was guilty of a different kind of oversimplification, a failure to describe the relations among study, counsel, and princely action. Law and literature, for example, though they both serve the end of preserving the republic, do so in radically different ways. Primitive republics (Sparta, Rome, Venice) have flourished greatly without any literature at all "because all their study consisted in inducing the people to obey the magistrates, and the magistrates to obey the law." If humane letters are merely a supplement to *viva voce* instruction in and by the laws of the land, they are never the less potentially a valuable one: "it is good for the prince to sometimes learn from books that which his favorites would not dare to tell him without fear of offending him."[90] Writing, insofar as it is of utility to the state, is thus placed under the sign of counsel, with the advantage that it can say what interested counselors cannot: always assuming that it is *sine ira et studio*.

Still, historical writing in particular was fraught with conflict of interest, which had to be overcome before it could offer a suitable guide to the princely will. Pasquier's critique was similar to la Popilinière's:

History ... is in itself a very prickly thing. For its principal aim is founded on the deduction of truth. Now either you discuss in it things that have come to you

---

88. In the course of his defense of guile and dissimulation by the ruler, Machiavelli says in *The Prince*, 62: "You ought to understand therefore that there are two ways of fighting, the one by the laws, the other with force. The first is proper to men, the second to beasts; but since in many instances the first is not enough, it is necessary to have recourse to the second." For an analysis of the way in which this passage subverts Ciceronian political rhetoric, see J. H. Hexter, *The Vision of Politics on the Eve of the Reformation* (New York: Basic Books, 1973), 207–9.

89. Pasquier, *Pourparlers*, 78. Note that the villains are not "conseillers."

90. Pasquier, *Pourparlers*, 83. Clearly, besides the *Republic*, Pasquier draws heavily on Plato's *Phaedrus* in the "Pourparler du prince."

88   CHAPTER 2

by hearsay, or you have actually been present at their occurrence or conduct. If by hearsay, you know how little assurance there is in relying on the reports of others, and how everyone speaks to his own party's advantage. If you were present . . . it is impossible to be everywhere at once . . . and moreover, speaking of one's own time you will flatter the prince to whom you are most bound, or whom you most fear.[91]

Pasquier's answers to this dilemma were distinctly fragmentary and allusive; he undertook a very delicate negotiation with the models available to him. He discussed the work of Phillipe Commynes, Paul Sleidan, Paulus Emilius, and Paulus Jovius in some detail—a somewhat motley collection on the face of it, but one directly connected to a historiographical debate then a decade old. The Pléiade poets (with whom Pasquier was associated) had supported an antirhetorical and evangelically pure historiography—which, Sleidan had claimed, Commynes exemplified—against the rhetorical and official history of the two Pauli and of Pierre Paschal.[92] Pasquier found both value and bias in both schools, clearing ground for his own project; but he did ultimately come down in favor of Commynes who, he said, was the favored reading of Emperor Charles V (thus, a viable political advisor). In so doing, he aligned himself once more against the views represented by the *escolier* and in favor of an independent, technical historiography.

Rather than developing this theme, though, Pasquier (like du Tillet, on whose work he certainly drew) turned to the institutional structure through which the king received counsel in the particular French case. In this way, he replied to the *curial*, whom he accused of portraying a tyrannical regime, where the will of the prince was misdirected to his personal profit rather than to the common good.[93] It was the place of counselors, presumably noted for their disinterestedness, to redirect that will correctly. Again like du Tillet, but much more explicitly, Pasquier set himself and his work in the position of just such counsel. On the one hand, this was because he presented the *Recherches* as the kind of historical work that, as he had suggested,

91. Pasquier, *Pourparlers*, 84–85.

92. See Marc Fumaroli, "Les mémoires, ou l'historiographie royale en procès," in his *La diplomatie de l'ésprit: De Montaigne à la Fontaine* (Paris: Hermann, 1994), 217–46; and Gilbert Gaddofre, *Du Bellay et le sacré* (Paris: N.R.F./Gallimard, 1971), 222–29.

93. See Pasquier, *Pourparlers*, 98: "Car tout le but, dessein, proget, & philosophie d'un bon Roy, ne doit estre que l'utilité de son peuple." It is here that Pasquier answers the question that inaugurated the discourse and, at the same time, all the questions of which the discussion was not reported. The reduction of political philosophy to the means of directing the will of citizens to their common rather than private good is, as we have mentioned, fundementally Aristotelian.

could guide princes in affairs of state. On the other hand, he identified the contemporary structures of the royal council more specifically, reducing them specifically to the Parlement. Not surprisingly, he did so with a historical argument. The Carolingian peers, the monarchy's originary council, "left to their counselors the oversight of justice, that is to say, that just as earlier in the assemblies the kings rendered themselves subject, so to speak, to what those peers advised, so from thence forth whatever the counselors ordained passed into law."[94] The courts' counsel was thus an unbroken custom itself, as well as a means of perpetuating custom in the political system. Contrast this, for example, with François Hotman's stinging attack on the parlements, in the last chapter of the *Francogallia*, as a perversion of the lost Carolingian representative constitution. Nowhere does one measure more clearly the difference between the Gallicans' program of customary reform and the possibilities of revolutionary reformism!

Pasquier's historical account of the Parlement (of which, as an *avocat*, he was a junior member) thus made a place for himself in the body politic, and at the same time virtually reconstructed, through antiquarian technique, a body capable through its counsel of harmonizing the kingdom.[95] The root of the parlements' authority was that as truly disinterested bodies—not the favorites who lead the law by its waxen nose, but men with a true knowledge of that law—they could put the general good above their own personal good, and thus guide the royal will as none of the other humanist models could. Pasquier found the solution to all the problems of political life in this arrangement:

If [the French kings] had followed, I will not say their passions, but their personal reason, even though they had each in succession been strong kings, it would have been very easy to impose on them, since they were men subject to a thousand faults. But since by a public administration their ideas were subject to the

94. Pasquier, *Pourparlers*, 100.
95. See, e.g., the opening passage of the main historical work, Etienne Pasquier, *Les Recherches de la France*, ed. M.-M. Fragonard and F. Roudaut, 3 vols. (Paris: Honoré Champion, 1996), 1:251: "Ny plus ny moins que le sage Legislateur, ou Juge, se doit bien donner garde de rendre raison, celui-là de sa loy, & cestoy-cy, de sa sentence, ains laisser penser à chacun diversement à part soy, ce qui les a peu induire de donner tels loix, ou jugements. Aussi discourant avec un stile nud & simple l'ancienneté, le lecteur en croiroit ce qu'il voudroit." Here, writing history is clearly seen as homologous to the practice both of law and of statecraft (the next chapter discusses maxims of state). Pasquier then broaches the question of what narrative technique or style is appropriate for discourse in the three fields. He eventually comes to the conclusion that the interests of posterity demand a full citation of sources, i.e., that the narrative must make visible the technique.

deliberation of a number of people, who were named neither by favor nor for money but by election for virtue, up to the present time it has been impossible that all should not go well.[96]

This answers the question with which Pasquier had begun: strong counsel is superior even to individual virtue, and in the French case the parlements supply that counsel. Their counsel exemplifies the purest republican virtue, but the context makes clear that the *parlementaires'* freedom from fear and favor is exactly the same thing as the good historian's. Indeed, Pasquier only knows that strong counsel is politically ideal because, as a historian, he can see that it has worked for many kings "each in succession," and the "public reason" that the parlements substitute for those kings' fallible private judgment is one based on custom.

There was another complication of the theoretical construction of robe historiography, one that merits a brief digression. We have already seen that claims to virtuous objectivity in various fields could reinforce each other in a circular fashion. This was even truer for claims to technical and institutional expertise. It was one of the commonplaces of classical historiography that the would-be historian must have personal experience of public affairs, since it is impossible to write effectively about things with which one is unfamiliar. This conflicts with the canon of disinterestedness—How is one to obtain such expertise while remaining detached from contemporary political passions?—but that fact seems to have bothered the commentators remarkably little.[97] According to their own account, the *parlementaire* historians satisfied the requirement for expertise: "I call a man thoroughly experienced in public affairs," said Jean Bodin, for example, "if he has shared in public counsels, executive power, or legal decisions ... for in these three are involved the gravest concerns of the state."[98]

The criterion of experience was as important for whom it excluded as for whom it included. "On this point," according to Marc Fumaroli, "the robe erudite is in perfect accord with the sword nobles against the monks and their ignorance of the *monde*."[99] Pierre Pithou made this point very strongly

---

96. Pasquier, *Pourparlers*, 101.

97. Though see a comment in Jean Bodin, *Method for the Easy Comprehension of History*, trans. Beatrice Reynolds (New York: Columbia University Press, 1945), 43: "There are ... three kinds of historian, I think: first, those very able by nature, and even more richly endowed by training, who have advanced to the control of affairs.... The best writers are equipped on all three counts, if only they could rid themselves of all emotions in writing history."

98. Bodin, *Method for the Easy Comprehension of History*, 43.

99. Fumaroli, "Les mémoires," 228. Fumaroli here analyzes a triple criterion for histori-

at the beginning of his history of the counts of Champagne, when he attributed the lack of adequate French histories to the fact that,

> for a long time all the science of Europe ... had been cloistered among those who are called clergy: who, being for the most part by profession entirely removed from the conduct of worldly things, discussed the affairs of state not merely as a clerk would speak of weapons, but even worse as one blind from birth would discuss colors.[100]

The entire panoply of Renaissance anticlericalism (and antimonasticism in particular) lurked behind Pithou's comment. He also referred to the widespread humanist belief that priestly castes had, since the earliest times, been the traditional custodians of historical memory.[101] This piece of classical tradition posed obvious problems for the claims of jurists—Gallican jurists especially—to special historiographical authority, and hence required some reply. Nor was it an accident or a particularity of the still-Protestant Pithou's that set the robe erudites and the clergy in opposition to each other. They were very real rivals for the role of royal counselor, and as we shall see, their conflict became increasingly open and bitter as erudite Gallicanism developed.

The most famous, imposing, and influential of the *parlementaire* historians was Jacques-Auguste de Thou, son of a first president and himself a president *à mortier* in the Parlement. Like du Tillet, and in contrast to Pasquier, Pithou, and Bodin, de Thou was in fact a fairly close advisor to the king, in his case Henri IV, particularly during the period leading up to his conversion.[102] Moreover, his judicial rank was much above that of a mere *avocat* like Pasquier—despite his disappointment at not rising still higher—and he was

---

cal competence according to Bodin: independence, competence, and rhetorical *mediocritas*. This is evidently a form of the schema we have been discussing, although Bodin attaches somewhat different values to the elements. For a different discussion of the same criteria in Bodin, see Paul Nelles, "The Public Library and Late Humanist Scholarship" (Ph.D. dissertation, Johns Hopkins University, 1994).

100. *Petri Pithœi opera, sacra, juridica, historica, miscellanea* (Paris: Sebastien Cramoisy, 1609), 457.

101. On priests and history, see Franklin, *Jean Bodin*, 115; and Anthony Grafton, *Defenders of the Text: The Traditions of Scholarship in an Age of Science, 1450–1800* (Cambridge, Mass.: Harvard University Press, 1991), 91–92. The identification of priests as the guardians of the past can probably be traced back to Aristotle's account of Greek archival practices at *Politics* 1321b.

102. Note, e.g., the leading role he played in the courtship of the Duc de Nevers, probably the most important of the uncommited magnates after 1589; see Michael Wolfe, "Piety and Political Allegiance: The Duc de Nevers and the Protestant Henry IV, 1589–93," *French History* 2 (1988): 1–21.

the most highly reputed historian of his day. De Thou's work was in important ways very different from that of the robe medievalists of the school of du Tillet and Pasquier. He wrote the history of his own times, and his technical armature thus differed fundamentally from that of an antiquarian historian; it depended not on control of archives and literary texts, but on personal connections and access to the centers of power.[103] Corresponding to this was a highly developed narrative mode of composition, which contrasts sharply with what were in essence commentaries produced by the antiquarians. Simultaneously, the self-conscious obscurity and "pointedness" (to use the contemporary term) of de Thou's prose placed its author within an elite segment of the international republic of letters rather detached from French antiquarian circles. It is even more striking, then, that de Thou very much shared the views of his antiquarian colleagues on historical impartiality and its role in the state.

Like Pasquier's, de Thou's history was prefaced by another composition distinct in length, genre, and method. Although labeled a "dedication" (to Henri IV), de Thou's introduction was as much a quasi-official apology for Henri IV's regime of religious toleration as it was a guide to the reader of his history.[104] While the obvious implicit purpose of this text was to provide a public defense of Henri's religious policies, its form was largely that of a plea that the United Provinces imitate the policy of toleration with respect to their own Catholic population. This was an important foreign policy initiative for Henri (though he was no doubt aware that it stood no realistic chance of success), for it allowed him to cultivate the image of an international champion of the Catholic Church without either antagonizing Huguenot sentiments or strengthening Hapsburg interests. It served as a diplomatic counterweight to French policy in the Alps and in the Holy Roman Empire, which was consistently pro-Protestant. The dedication was thus also an offer of counsel, at the very exalted level of an experienced and successful sovereign addressing an ally.

De Thou gave arguments of a conventional humanist type for toleration.

---

103. On the documentary base of the *Historia sui temporis*, see Anthony Grafton, "The Footnote from de Thou to Ranke," *History and Theory* 33 (1994): 53–76.

104. At least two contemporary French translations appeared, of which at least one was personally commissioned by Henri. See de Thou, *Histoire*, 1:311n; and Sam Kinser, *The Works of Jacques-Auguste de Thou* (The Hague, The Netherlands: Martinus Nijhoff, 1967), 297–98. The authorized translation was apparently by Hotman-Villiers. The other seems to have been printed as a polemical pamphlet in a very cheap edition: *Epistre de monsieur le president de Thou, au Roy* (Paris: Pierre Chevalier, 1614).

Mainly, he held that attempts to force conscience were doomed to failure.[105] He backed this up, however, by an examination of the ways in which the Church had dealt with heresy over the centuries, and here his style was very much that of a humanist antiquary. At the same time, the individuality of de Thou's work of necessity came into play. On the one hand, de Thou himself had played a key role in winning approval for the Edict of Nantes from that Parlement which, on Pasquier's account, was to institutionalize wise counsel within the French government. He was thus formally responsible for giving his own king the counsel now given to the leaders of other European states. On the other hand, the historical component of his argument for tolerance suggested that his recommendation was a lesson drawn directly from the *Historia sui temporis* itself. History, the Parlement, and history incarnated in the Parlement all concurred in advocating Henri IV's policy, presenting to the entire republic of letters a model of French government at its theoretical best.

De Thou began the introduction with a reply to potential attacks on his authority and, above all, his impartiality:

> I leave it to those who know me and my character to tell how far I am from dissimulation: nor have I lived obscurely, so that my candor may appear in my public actions even to the most prejudiced. Indeed from the time that we returned to favor by your [Henri's] virtue and clemency, I have so entirely forgotten private injuries, if any there were, and I have to such an extent put all sense of them away publicly and privately, that I rightfully trust that my equanimity and moderation leave nothing to be desired in these things that tend toward the memory of things gone by.... Thus when we came to write this history we did exactly as good judges ought to do when they weigh the lives and fortunes of men, diligently examining our conscience as to whether anything was treated bitterly such as to push us away from the straight path with respect to the precept of the work....
> [F]inally I have settled on a naked and simple style of writing, so that, as it were, even as by my very style I might keep free of all pretense and ostentation, so might I also [refrain] from hatred and gratitude.[106]

---

105. A very instructive discussion of this *topos* may be found in Gary Remer, "Rhetoric and the Erasmian Defence of Toleration," *History of Political Thought* 10 (1989): 377–403.

106. De Thou, *Historia*, 1:1–2. It is not easy to cultivate an unnaturally Latinate style in Latin, but de Thou did so; my thanks to Sylvia Parsons for assistance with the translation of this passage. The context of injury and return to favor that de Thou had in mind was almost certainly the schism in the Parisian courts from 1588 to 1594. The historian had to defend himself against potential charges that in writing the history of the League he was reopening the divisions that had been brought about in the French body politic during that episode.

De Thou managed to touch on almost all of the available modes of self-authorization. He started with an appeal to a purely personal integrity, followed by one based on his relationship to the king. Next, he appealed to his judicial experience and consequent expertise in detachment. Finally, he turned to the transparency of his rhetoric as a metonymic representation of his freedom from *ira et studio* (or, as it might be, *odio et gratia*).

His substantive argument on the necessity for toleration immediately began, "now we are taught well enough by experience, that the sword, flames, exile, and proscriptions irritate rather than cure this sickness of the mind."[107] In fact, like Pasquier under similar circumstances, de Thou incarnated this experience in the histories that accompanied the dedicatory letter. In fact the historical narrative to which de Thou resorted to prove his point was in roughly equal parts an account of the patristic and medieval periods in the robe-erudite vein to which we have become accustomed, and an analysis of the events of the previous century that formed his own subject. De Thou was in fact in a situation very similar to the one du Tillet had faced half a century before. He was dealing with a similar problem—religious policy in an era of religious division—and from the position of a personal advisor to the monarch.

Like du Tillet, de Thou offered as his program a reform of the Church, but one that he had almost entirely stripped of its millenarian overtones, combined with the disorders of the other estates, and reduced to an administrative program of bland republican pieties:

In my opinion, both evils—the error of the dissidents and the vices of our party—would best be cured if, removing the Church and the republic from the marketplace, the rewards of virtue were reinstated; if men outstanding for piety, doctrine, and gravity of character, who have already made experiment of their prudence and moderation, were preferred in sacred offices; if not new men, but rather those of known integrity, who fear God and hate avarice, were promoted to places of honor not for favor or price, but commended only by their virtue.[108]

To restore harmony between the ecclesiastical and the political spheres, de Thou believed, the king needed to apply to both the standards of virtue that the *parlementaires* held up as their own ideal. This was the essence of the robe historical ideology, which remained essentially religious and sought above all to stabilize the polity through the correction of religious institutions and their relations to the state. De Thou could enter his peroration

---

107. De Thou, *Historia*, 1:2 (emphasis added).
108. De Thou, *Historia*, 1:12.

with the exclamation "these are the rights, these the laws in which this realm was founded, and by which it has progressed to such greatness and power."[109] He spoke with complete confidence of the traditional, the customary, constitution of the Gallican church and the French state as it had been explicated by his predecessors. He could speak of and to the future of the French monarchy because he knew its laws as a jurist and because (which comes to the same thing) he knew its past as a historian.

109. De Thou, *Historia*, 1:16.

CHAPTER 3

Gallicanism in the Wars of Religion

In the generation of the Wars of Religion, then, Gallican jurists developed a new, humanist, ideological complex that largely replaced its medieval predecessor. This ideology provided a way for them to assert their continued importance in the political discourse in a period when they had few concrete political victories to boast of. This point of view, like any ideology, arose out of and was continually applied to specific situations. The conflict over the role of the Catholic Church in the French state was not the only arena in which it developed, but it was probably the most prominent and important. While the first signs of a Gallican revival built on the foundations of humanist historiography were visible in the 1550s, it was only after 1560 that all the elements came together to create a new tradition, distinct from the old reformist ecclesiastical nationalism and in opposition to the French clergy as often as the curia. The Council of Trent, the appearance of the Society of Jesus, and, of course, the outbreak of religious civil war made the issue of the Church's role in France all but unavoidable. Through the successive stages of endless military conflict, the St. Bartholemew's Day Massacre, and the failure of Henri III's policies, the situation continued to deteriorate. Around 1580, a genuine antiroyalist Catholic party began to appear, above all once François d'Anjou's death left Henri of Navarre heir presumptive to the throne. The erudite Gallicans expressed their reactions to this chaos in an explosion of pamphlet literature, particularly in the final stages of the religious wars. By the time Henri de Navarre triumphed in 1595, the treatise on Gallican liberties formed a recognized and healthy genre, and the Gallicans an equally well-recognized political party.¹

The development of erudite Gallicanism as a political and intellectual movement did not occur in an institutional vacuum, however. Above all, it was attached to the Parlement of Paris. It was explicitly based on that body's long tradition of supporting the Crown against the papacy and of broad opposition to ecclesiastical jurisdiction in general. This had been the case for as long as there had been a French state, and it was typical of all of Europe. From time out of mind, royal courts had clashed with the clergy, attempting to narrow the competence of the ecclesiastical courts, both local and supranational; becoming involved in local political disputes with bishops; and, when they met resistance, moving to distrain the temporal possessions of their opponents. The clergy, for its part, fought back with (usually ineffective) excommunications of the magistrates and with whatever political influence they could bring to bear, which was often a great deal.² The Parlement, as the most powerful court in the land both legally and intellectually, had always been at the forefront of this tradition. Moreover, it was strong enough to protect the friends and persecute the enemies of its brand of Gallicanism. Less obviously, the Parlement, and particularly the *gens du roi*, lawyers who represented the king's interests before it, held a strategic location between the abstract law and actual government, and between the idea of an impersonal Crown that embodied the interests of the state and the actual *royal* government. The *gens du roi* of the sovereign courts, and in particular of the Parlement of Paris, were the most important proponents of juristic Gallicanism well into the seventeenth century. The details of this issue are somewhat technical, but for men of the law in the old regime they were of vital importance because they delineated the most natural and effective means for them to form and express political opinions.

An example will make the issues at stake clearer. On 14 November 1614, the Parlement of Paris received Mathieu Molé into the office of *procureur*

---

1. This schema coincides in its general outlines with the periods of tension in *parlementaire* religiosity identified by Nancy Lyman Roelker, *One King, One Faith: The Parlement of Paris and the Religious Reformations of the Sixteenth Century* (Berkeley and Los Angeles: University of California Press, 1996), 180–88, while departing from it in several details.

2. The best summary of this long-standing situation is still to be found in Félix Aubert, *Histoire du parlement de Paris de l'origine à François Ier (1250–1515)*, 2 vols. (Paris: Picard, 1894), 1:321–46. Aubert suggests, based on impressionistic evidence, that the later fifteenth century was an era of relative good feeling between courts and clergy.

général (who with two subordinate *avocats généraux* formed the *gens du roi*, or *parquet*). Molé, who would later succeed to the highest judicial office in the realm as keeper of the seals, immediately plunged into one of the more eventful periods of the Parlement, involving himself deeply in the fights surrounding the Estates General then being convened and an abortive rebellion by the Prince de Condé. The following May, however, in the midst of all these affairs, it occurred to him that as *procureur général* he was, ex officio, custodian of the Trésor des Chartes, and that he had been neglecting this latter office.[3] Perhaps the need for documentation during the polemics surrounding the Estates General had called his attention to this matter. At any rate, he determined to undertake a complete inventory and reform of this collection of documents. Even for someone as industrious as Molé, though, combining this task with managing the Crown's interests in the Parlement did not appear practical. Thus, he delegated it to two of his contemporaries who showed an inclination for erudition: Pierre Dupuy and Théodore Godefroy, the former a councilor and the latter an *avocat* in the Parlement. In retrospect it is hard to conceive of two more qualified candidates, since each amassed and organized during his lifetime a personal collection of French historical manuscripts of the first importance. Godefroy (a former Protestant) seems to have had little concern for the liberties of the Gallican church, but he was just completing a massive work on the ceremonies of the monarchy. This carried forward a project that had been initiated by Jean du Tillet, and such work was a principal route by which erudite historical research reshaped French government, constructing a rational tradition where none had existed before.[4] Dupuy around this time was writing a lengthy treatise on the defects of the Council of Trent. In 1638 he would publish the definitive collection of treatises and documents on the Gallican liberties, and his manuscript collection remains an unparalleled source for the history of French government.[5] Together, Molé, Godefroy, and Dupuy embodied

3. On this reorganization, see E. A. R. Brown, "Jean du Tillet et les archives de France," *Histoire et archives* 2 (1997): 29–63.

4. Such, according to Hanley, *Lit de justice*, was the case with meetings of king and Parlement, though see also E. A. R. Brown and Richard C. Famiglietti, *The* Lit de Justice: *Semantics, Ceremonial and the Parlment of Paris* (Simaringen, Germany: Jan Thorbecke Verlag, 1994). For a detailed discussion of Godefroy's ceremonial treatise (*Le ceremonial de France*, 1619) and the place of the ceremonial in the historicization and textualization of French monarchical practice, see Lawrence M. Bryant, "Making History: Ceremonial Texts, Royal Space, and Political Theory in the Sixteenth Century," in Michael Wolfe, ed., *Changing Identities in Early Modern France* (Durham, N.C.: Duke University Press, 1997), 46–77.

5. Molé himself was a collector of documents, most of which found their way into the Collection des 500 de Colbert of the BN; this account is drawn essentially from the notes

the institutional practice of historical guidance for the monarchy that the sixteenth century had developed.

This episode, mundane enough in itself, illustrates the institutional structures that nourished erudite Gallicanism. Since Jacques Cappel and Jean du Tillet, custody of the Trésor des Chartes had been an important element in the authorization of Gallican history. The link between the Trésor and the Parlement (as custodian, Molé took his oath to the court) and the status of the Parlement as guardian of the Gallican liberties are self-evident. Both Dupuy and Godefroy had or soon developed many other links to the official structures of French memory and public law, and to the other highly placed Gallicans who supervised them.[6]

There were also other, more specific links among Gallicanism, historical erudition, and the offices of the *parquet*. A brief and crude prosopography of Gallican writers will serve to demonstrate how important the *parquet* was to them: more than a dozen significant writers on the Gallican liberties—by far the largest single group—served in it for a shorter or longer time.[7] Pierre Dupuy was attached to the Trésor des Chartes after it was in turn attached to the office of *procureur général*. Pasquier eventually became *avocat du roi* in the Chambre des Comptes. One finds a few presidents in the sovereign courts writing for the Gallican liberties, notably Gilles le Maistre, Claude Fauchet, and Jacques-Auguste de Thou, but of these the first was of the older school

---

on his own career published as *Mémoires de Mathieu Molé*, ed. Aimé Champollion-Figeac, 4 vols. (Paris: Jules Renouard, 1855–1857), 1:1–5, 58–62.

6. Godefroy, who specialized in the history of the French monarchy and the royal house, was appointed *historiographe du roi* by 1621; see Orest Ranum, *Artisans of Glory: Writers and Historical Thought in Seventeenth-Century France* (Chapel Hill: University of North Carolina Press, 1980), 102. The Dupuy brothers, for most of their lives, held collectively the post of *garde* of the Bibliothèque du Roi. The *maîtres de la librairie* under whom they served were J.-A. de Thou, his son, and eventually Jérôme Bignon. That this was a hotbed of Gallicanism seems sufficiently clear. See Jérôme Delatour and Thierry Sarmant, "La charge de Bibliothécaire du Roy au XVIIe et XVIIIe siècles," *Bibliothèque de l'Ecole des Chartes* 152 (1994): 462–502.

7. The names I have in mind are the following, which do not include men who served as *substituts* (the reader will doubtless find most of these characters as yet unfamiliar, but for the moment they are of only statistical interest): Jacques Cappel, Noel Brulart, Gilles Bourdin, Baptiste du Mesnil, Jacques Faye d'Espesses, Antoine Séguier, Jacques de la Guesle, Louis Servin, Simon Marion, Antoine Hotman, Pierre Pithou, Antoine Loisel, and Molé himself. The roll of those who served in the *parquet* may be found in Edouard Maugis, *Histoire du Parlement de Paris de l'avenement des rois Valois à la mort d'Henri IV*, 3 vols. in 2 (Paris: A. Picard, 1913–1916), 3:326–40. Pithou and Loisel served for only a few days in 1595, while the royalist Parlement was in transit from Tours to Paris, but both also served for several years in the *parquet* of the Chambre de justice de Guyenne, a kind of emanation of the Parlement of Paris. Hotman served in the Leaguer parlement.

and the last defended Gallican positions only incidentally, in his broader historical work, while Fauchet served in the lowly Cour des Monnaies.[8] Simple councilors are even thinner on the ground: one can offer only Charles Faye in the Parlement (the brother of an *avocat du roi*), Guy Lanier de l'Effretier in the Grand Conseil, a Burgundian named Benigne Milletot, and Pierre Dupuy, Molé's amanuensis. Indeed, the only other significant group of Gallican enthusiasts is to be found among the more prominent lawyers at the bar of the Parlement.[9] This is in fact not surprising given the close links between the *parquet* and the upper reaches of the bar in the sixteenth and early seventeenth centuries. The *gens du roi* were, of course, *avocats*, and their professional responsibilities resembled those of a working lawyer more than those of a councilor. Moreover, positions in the *parquet* were so directly tied to the royal interest that they long escaped the regime of venality (the sale of offices), and the charges of *avocats* and *procureurs généraux* were filled by practicing lawyers who might be recommended more by their skill than by their wealth and connections.[10] Even lawyers who did not rise fully into the *parquet* were frequently appointed as substitutes for the *procureur* or *avocat du roi* and took on some of the workload and dignity of the charge. To all this one may add the fact that the more successful practitioners shared with the

8. My research in the archives of the Monnaies, moreover, suggests that Fauchet was rather an outsider there. His main attachments were to the tradition of erudite royal publicists running from du Tillet to Godefroy and Dupuy.

9. In this group are Dumoulin, Pasquier, Pithou, and Loisel for much of their careers; Jacques Leschassier, Laurent Bouchel, Antoine Arnauld, and Pierre de Nancel, all of whom seem to have served as *substituts;* and Guy Coquille, a somewhat anomalous case, in that he left Paris early in his career. One might add the even more anomalous case of Pierre de l'Estoile, by profession *grand audiencier* in the Chancery but whose education, culture, and sociability were very much those of the Parisian lawyers. See Madeleine Lazard and Gilbert Schrenck's introduction to Pierre de l'Estoile, *Registre Journal du regne de Henri III* (Geneva: Droz, 1992), vol. 1. L'Estoile wrote voluminously in defense of Gallicanism, but, apparently, only for his own consumption. Bouchel was related by marriage to Servin, a fact in which he took great pride; see Jaqueline Boucher, "L'insertion sociale de Laurent Bouchel, avocat au Parlement de Paris, 1559–1629," in *Lyon et l'Europe. Hommes et sociétés: Mélanges d'histoire offerts à Richard Gascon* (Lyons, France: Presses Universitaires de Lyon, 1980), 83–99, pp. 85–86.

10. The matter is, of course, complex. In the edict of the Paulette, all offices of *gens du roi* were excluded from the regime of the *droit annuel*. In the first renewal of the edict in 1611, the *parquets* of all the sovereign courts except the Parlements were included in that regime. In practice, the posts of the *parquet* became fully venal, but it seems that this was never formalized. See Roland Mousnier, "Sully et le Conseil d'état et des finances," *Révue historique* 192 (1941): 68–86, p. 78. By the time Molé became *procureur général*, the nature of the *parquet* was changing; his own later career as a royal bulwark against the *parlementaire* Fronde demonstrates this.

parquet the responsibility of providing informal training for young lawyers, who traditionally began their careers by frequenting sessions of the Parlement and listening to the pleas. All of this explains why these two groups should have been so close in culture, interests, and ideology.[11]

What was it about the *parquet* that made it such a hotbed of erudite Gallicanism? One reason has already been mentioned in passing: it was the duty of the *gens du roi* to produce legal briefs for the Crown in any dispute that might arise over its rights and prerogatives, including disputes over religious and ecclesiastical matters. It was for this reason that the Trésor des Chartes was subordinated to the office of the *procureur général:* according to Louis XIII, the texts preserved in the Trésor were "documents important for the justification of our rights both within our realm and with the princes of neighboring states."[12] The *gens du roi* were also responsible for communicating the decisions of the parlements as needed, just as the clerks were responsible for recording them.[13] The *parquet* in fact stood at the center of the nexus of erudition, jurisprudence, and political counsel we have already discussed. In their pleas, the *gens du roi* displayed to its fullest the legal learning of the sovereign courts. In the Trésor des Chartes and the registers they oversaw the written memory of the realm, which settled custom, authenticated prerogative, and guided prudence.[14] Representing and providing learned legal counsel to the Crown, they incarnated the robe political ideal.

11. Probably the best source on the culture of Parisian *avocats* in this period is Loisel's "Dialogue des avocats," in André Dupin, ed., *Profession d'avocat: Receuil des pièces concernant l'exercise de cette profession*, 2 vols. (Paris: Alex Gobelet and B. Warré, 1832), 1:147–258; on which see also Jean-Marc Chatelain, "*Heros togatus:* Culture cicéronienne et gloire de la robe dans la France d'Henri IV," *Journal des savants* (1991): 263–87.

12. Molé, *Mémoires*, 58, quoting the letters patent authorizing the reorganization of the Trésor.

13. See François Olivier-Martin, *Les lois du Roi* (Paris: Editions Loysel, 1988), 364. An interesting document, preserved in the BN, is a minute of a 1614 *arrêt* of the Parlement of Paris against Francisco Suarez, marked up for the printer in the hand of Louis Servin: BN fr. 15734, fol. 35–37.

14. The legal theory surrounding the authentication of prerogatives was quite interesting. According to Antoine Hotman, "La longue et immemoriale possession ont cela de semblable, qu'elles doivent estre accompagnees de justice. Mais en une chose il y a difference d'autant que la longue possession . . . doit avoir un tiltre, au moins coloré, mais l'immemoriale possession, qui est la coustume de jouir, n'a besoin de faire apparoistre de tiltre, ains suffit de l'alleguer"; see *Traictez des droicts et libertez de l'Eglise gallicane* (Paris: Pierre Chevalier, 1612), 384. Moreover, at least at canon law, hierarchical superiority can be alleged as a title. This is another example of the naturalization of custom and its complex relation to justice, memory, and historical record. Further investigation of this line of legal thought would doubtless prove fruitful.

Indeed, while the *parquet* was too small and subordinate a body to have been included in any of the surveys of the institutions of the old regime, it occupied a vital place within that system.[15] The *parquet* was a genuine corporation, with all three of the elements that defined one under the old regime: written records, oaths of office, and bitter precedence disputes.[16] Since it produced an opinion on every case that came before the full body of the court, its influence was enormous. Indeed, it was probably unique in its overview of their court's legal business: only the presidents responsible for assigning cases to reporting magistrates (and the clerks) could compare. The *gens du roi*, unlike the councilors, did not rotate on the semester system, which increased their relative advantage in continuity. Moreover, they were to initiate any litigation needed for the general public interest. As one *parlementaire* memoir put it, "in this one office rest the actions and demands concerning the public."[17] In addition to the control this gave them over the court's business, it allowed them to make life miserable for people or groups of whom they disapproved, by continually hailing them up on charges. They were also responsible for conveying both routine and extraordinary royal commands to the court, and for overseeing their implementation.[18] For all this, they were generally far enough removed from the royal court and high policy that they could frequently sacrifice political realism to the demands of ideological purity.

Their discursive and ideological position, though, was even more important for our purposes than their procedural power. The writings of contemporary theorists and their own rhetorical production show how strong this was. One may begin, as in all things legal-humanistic, with Guillaume Budé,

15. The *parquet* is not included in Gaston Zeller, *Les institutions de la France au XVIe siècle* (Paris: Presses Universitaires de France, 1948); Roger Doucet, *Les institutions de France au XVIe siècle* (Paris: A. et P. Picard, 1948); or Roland Mousnier, *Institutions de la France sous la monarchie absolue, 1598–1789*, Vol. 2: *Les organes de l'état et la société* (Paris: Presses Universitaires de France, 1980); nor does it receive sustained attention in specialized treatments of the Parlement such as Maugis, *Histoire*, or Hanley, *Lit de justice*.

16. Laurent Bouchel, *La bibliotheque ou thresor du droict francois*, 2 vols. (Paris: Eustache Foucault et al., 1615), 1, s.v. "advocat"; Bernard de la Roche Flavin, *Treze livres des parlemens de France* (Bordeaux, France: Simon Millanges, 1617), 103.

17. BN fr. 6396, fol. 89r.

18. The most thorough survey of the day-to-day operations of the *parquet* concerns Pithou and Loisel's service in the Chambre de justice de Guyenne, a court whose surviving records are sufficiently modest to have received a complete monographic treatment; see Emile Brives-Cazes, *Le parlement de Bordeaux et la Chambre de Justice de Guyenne en 1582* (Bordeaux, France: G. Gounilhou, 1866), and *La Chambre de Justice de Guyenne en 1583–1584* (Bordeaux, France: G. Gounilhou, 1874).

who devoted a passage of his *Forensia* to an encomium on the "gens regia." The Latin term he chose was itself significant: a more literal translation would have been "gens regis," but he instead chose to stress the *parquet*'s subordination to the office, rather than the person, of the king. Even more than the royal office, though, it was the public interest and justice itself that the *parquet* served. The *gens regia* were "royal and public counsel in a court, a kind of machine for justice as it were, consulting in common [or, for the common good]." Their pleas in private cases were compared to the moral commentary of a Greek chorus: "[T]his chorus, intervening between acts, manfully defends justice and duty, brings up what has not been mentioned, and cleaves to the apt."[19] This account essentially gave the *parquet* a mandate to make the law what it was supposed to be, to speak for justice—for Budé, remember, justice was the central value of the state—in the same way that the tragic chorus spoke for the Hellenic moral consensus. Their position, Bernard de la Roche Flavin said, "is in a way close to that of the Roman censors."[20]

In fact, the *gens du roi* paradoxically figured as the locus of *independence from* the king within the legal system, because they were consistently in a position to appeal to higher moral authority. To continue the paradox, this was grounded legally on what is generally considered the most absolutist of legal principles. The legal theorist Laurent Bouchel pointed out that the king in person could not stand in a legal action, and thus the *gens du roi* were not his clients in anything like the way private lawyers would have been.

In Parlement only the king pleads by *procureur:* that is to say that in court records the litigating parties are always named, rather than their *procureurs*, but when the king is involved in a case only his *procureur général* is mentioned in the record.[21]

As the basis of this practice, Bouchel cited two pieces of Roman law: a text from the *Codex*—"thus one acts against the procurator of the fisc, or against the households of the prince and their procurators, for no action lies against the prince"; and what is perhaps the most notorious article of the

19. Guillaume Budé, *Forensia* (Paris: Robert Estienne, 1544), 225.

20. La Roche Flavin, *Treze livres*, 94. On this view, which stressed the role of the *parquet* in overseeing the whole class of royal officers, see Jotham Parsons, "The Roman Censors in the Renaissance Political Imagination," *History of Political Thought* 22 (2001): 565–86.

21. Bouchel, *Bibliotheque*, 2:568 [printed "586"]–69, s.v. "procureur." My translation is rather loose. See also la Roche Flavin, *Treze livres*, 13:78:879: "Que le Roy et la Royne seuls plaident au nom de leurs Procureurs generaux." The usual form in the court registers introducing the plea of a party was "N. pour le respondant [or whatever] a dit . . . ," while the plea of an *avocat du roi* was introduced by the phrase "N. pour le procureur du Roy a dit. . . ."

Digest: "the prince is loosed from the laws."[22] The very fact that the prince was above the laws meant that his legal representatives, acting *under* the laws, could only act in their own name. In effect, even more than the sovereign courts in general, the *gens du roi* were the servants of the public, the fisc (identified in turn with the corporate body of the king), and undying justice.[23]

This identification was certainly part of the *parquet*'s self-image. In his printed pleas, for example, the early-seventeenth-century *avocat du roi* Louis Servin referred to himself as "he who speaks for the king, for the public, and for the truth" (or, even more revealingly, "those who as *gens du roi* are obliged to maintain French antiquity and truth") often enough that it amounts to a verbal tic.[24] Servin in fact stands altogether as the model of the Gallican *parquet*, largely because he consciously set himself up as such, in particular through an extensive program of publishing his pleas. His name will recur frequently enough in the remainder of this study that an introduction may be in order. His most famous action was his last: in 1626, he dropped dead while inveighing before the assembled chambers of Parlement against Richelieu's financial edicts, to be hailed as a hero of republican virtue by his colleagues.[25] This fully conformed to his confrontational and histrionic temperament. It is frustrating but symptomatic that most of what is known of Servin's life is contained in a pamphlet written by his enemies; besides this there are only a few property records and his published work, which reveals almost no biographical detail.[26] His father was a client of the

---

22. Bouchel, *Bibliotheque*, 2:565: (citing C.7.37 and D.1.4.31). On the history of the latter tag in political thought, see Brian Tierney, "'The Prince is not Bound by Laws': Accursius and the Origins of the Modern State," *Comparative Studies in Society and History* 5 (1963): 378–400.

23. On the fisc as the undying corporate body, see Ernst Kantorowicz, *The King's Two Bodies: A Study in Medieval Political Theology* (Princeton, N.J.: Princeton University Press, 1957), 165–92 and passim.

24. Louis Servin, *Plaidoyez* (Paris: Jean de Heuqueville, 1603), 1:979, 123. Such phrases appear at least once per plea, sometimes more frequently.

25. See *Le Tombeau de Monsieur Servin* (Paris: Jean Bessin, 1626), e.g., p. 4: "Sa naissance... s'est trouvée dans un siecle si fertile en beaux esprits & en grands courages, que je ne m'estonne pas si son inclination, comme portée au bien naturellement, est tousjours demeurée entiere & invincible parmy les plus grands corruptions du temps." This kind of nostalgia for the *parlementaire* culture of Henri IV's day was widespread in the middle of the seventeenth century.

26. The scurrilous pamphlet is *Discours sur les meurs et humeur de Monsieur Servin Advocat General au Parlement de Paris* (s.l., 1617). It is signed "A.D.S.". *Le Tombeau de Monsieur Servin* (Paris: Jean Bessin, 1626) is not particularly helpful. For other information, see A. de Trémault, "Biographie de Louis Servin," *Extrait du Bulletin de la Société Archéologique, Littéraire et Scientifique du Vendô-*

Bourbons, while his mother, who seems to have been a scholar in her own right, came from a family of Parisian lawyers. He seems to have been chosen almost at random to fill the position of *avocat du roi* in the royalist Parlement of Tours; no doubt he was recommended as much by his fierce loyalty to Henri IV as by his not inconsiderable legal learning. At any rate, neither nepotism nor venality seem to have played a significant role in his rise. Once at his post he adopted a highly confrontational style toward all who, in his opinion, trespassed on the rights and dignity of France or of the Parlement.

In 1599, Servin earned the ire of a recently reconciled Leaguer magnate, the Duc de Mercœur, by complaining in court that he was not entitled to style himself "prince" in that forum, not being of the royal blood. Crossing paths with the insolent *avocat* later, Mercœur was with difficulty restrained from running him through on the spot. The Parlement sent its first president, Achille de Harlay, to the king to protest such unwarranted behavior toward officers of justice, where Harley delivered one of the orations for which he was famous. His major subject was the dignity of the *gens du roi*, in terms that illustrate well its ideological position:

> The *avocats du roi* may be called the tongue of the king, as the Romans spoke of the tongue of the fisc.... If you are not respected in the person of your magistrates, but only in your own, will you be king elsewhere than where you are present? ... We do not live in a popular state, but one might say that your *procureur général* and your *gens* are the tribunes who, by the necessity of their charges, are obliged to have care for the public under your authority, and who receive and embrace the complaints of your subjects, should they be just, when they are injured.[27]

Clearly the Parlement as a whole, and its top leadership, shared and were willing to defend very strongly Servin's own view of his office. The depth of Harlay's personal commitment to this exalted view of the *parquet* is revealed by a Latin preface attached to a copy of his plea, which the copyist of the

---

mois (Vendôme, France: Typographie Lemercier et fils, 1871). There is a quite comprehensive account of Servin's public career in Salvo Mastellone, *La reggenza di Maria de' Medici* (Messina, Italy: Casa Editrice G. D'Anna, 1962), 33–121.

27. "Harangue de M. le Prémier President de Harlay, faite au Roy Henri le Grand, sur une injure faite par M. le Duc de Mercœur à M. Servin Advocat général, dans sa maison," in Bibliothèque de l'Arsénal (Paris), ms. 4114, 109–19, pp. 114–15. Henri was little moved by Harlay's eloquence. He pointed out that he was marrying his natural son César de Vendôme to Mercœur's daughter, in order to secure him the title of prince among other things, and that more generally he did not want his courts to undertake conflicts with figures of key political importance without first consulting him.

manuscript claims to have taken faithfully from "the said sieur de Harlay's own book":

> An oration given to the king in his residence—not that I weighed Servin's actions toward me with respect to this duty. For a few days earlier he had reconciled with some harsh and bitter enemies of his and mine, and entered into an agreement for my violent death, because I had warned him privately to bear in mind the dignity of his office and to conduct himself more gravely and less inappropriately, and refrain from conducting the business of a certain widow Pacane. I was moved to this by the horrid injury to the *avocat du roi*, which redounded greatly to the discredit of our order.[28]

This rather lurid story cannot be taken as simple historical fact, but if the leaders of the Parlement would not be deterred from their support of the *parquet* by a blood feud, still less would any disagreement over matters of ecclesiastical politics diminish the commitment they offered the *gens du roi*.

Throughout the first half of the sixteenth century, the kings of France firmly subordinated the development of ecclesiological thought in their kingdom to their own foreign policy goals, which even in 1551 had meant suppressing the development of a new, more-or-less official, Gallican ideology. With Henri II's death in 1559, accompanied by steadily growing confessional tension, this situation changed radically. Abruptly, there was no longer any way to keep the nature of the Church and its relationship to the monarchy out of public debate. Not only did Catherine de Medicis need to discover some acceptable compromise among the religious factions tearing the kingdom apart, but the Catholic Church as an institution was beginning to demand changes in its own structure and in its relation to the secular power. The Colloquy of Poissy, held in September 1561, indecisive as it was, marked a decisive point in this process, because it made recent changes in the religious-political landscape public and undeniable. In particular, the Colloquy demonstrated the weakness of irenicist, reforming Catholic humanism; consolidated the long-visible *ralliement* of the Catholic clergy around a theologically conservative and generally pro-papal program; and began the public career of that traditionalist, historical, and jurisdictionalist tendency that would mark the future of Gallicanism.[29]

28. Arsénal ms. 4114, 109. The name of the widow is difficult to decipher, as is *a fortiori* its French form. This story is so lurid that I doubt its credibility; certainly it was unknown to Servin's anonymous biographer. The oration does not figure in the large collection of Harlay's remonstrances preserved (apparently with a view to publication) in BN fr. 4397.

29. The most important and comprehensive studies of the Colloquy are H. Outram

The Colloquy was an institutional monster, combining (in rough chronological order) an assembly of the French clergy, a kind of open advisory meeting of the royal council on religious affairs, and a theological conference. The theological debates demonstrated that irenical Catholic reform, even with strong support from the government, could neither mobilize support among the broader community of Catholic theologians nor reach a meaningful consensus with even relatively conciliatory Calvinists. Attempts to reach formulas of concord on the Eucharist and the use of images were in vain, despite being led by the ultraliberal bishop Jean de Monluc of Valence and the Erasmian theologian Claude d'Espence. In the long run, it was probably even more significant that the Colloquy, very much the creature of Queen Catherine de Medicis and of Chancellor Michel de l'Hospital, served in the end to subtly but lastingly alienate the French bishops from royal Gallicanism. The opening discourse of the Colloquy, on the Catholic side, was delivered by the Cardinal de Lorraine. Even though he did not object to the meeting, he felt compelled to remind the secular arm that religious doctrine was none of its business. In the summary of a relatively dispassionate Calvinist observer,

> He began his oration with the obedience owed by all subjects to the prince, by the command of God, who made him His minister ... as he did the Church, in which [the prince] was placed, and not above it, desiring that bishops should judge emperors, kings, and all laypeople, rather than the laity ... judging the bishops.[30]

The government's irenical policies were becoming a threat to the authority and the proper jurisdiction of the clergy. With the failure of the Colloquy, Lorraine and the prelates in general would begin their literal and figurative journey away from Gallican orthodoxy and to the Council of Trent.

The near-simultaneous conclusion of Trent and the first War of Religion ratified the new situation that Poissy had inaugurated. The Tridentine canons were received with some enthusiasm by the clergy, and with fear and loathing by a large party in the parlements, urged on by Dumoulin, now returned from exile. His enthusiasm was still judged excessive, particularly by

---

Evennett, *The Cardinal of Lorraine and the Council of Trent* (Cambridge, U.K.: Cambridge University Press, 1930), 235–394; and Donald Nugent, *Ecumenism in the Age of the Reformation: The Colloquy of Poissy* (Cambridge, Mass.: Harvard University Press, 1974).

30. *Ample discours des actes memorables de Poissy* (s.l., 1561), sig. Cii r. The summary is accurate, though slightly blunter than the original; see *L'oraison de Monseigneur le illustrissime et reverendissime Cardinal de Lorraine, faicte en l'Assemblée de Poyssi, le Roy y estant present, le XVI. Jour de Septembre, M. D. LXI* (Paris: Guillaume Morel, 1561), 2–4. Nugent, in *Ecumenism*, 105, is doubtless correct that this speech was in large part a collective statement by the assembled prelates.

Christophle de Thou, first president of the Parlement of Paris, but nevertheless the government was unable to promulgate the council officially. That story has been ably detailed by Victor Martin, and it would be superfluous to repeat its details, but it clearly signaled that relations between the emerging school of Gallican jurists and the new wave of Catholic reform would not be smooth. In the same year as his attack on Trent, moreover, Dumoulin also wrote a consultation on behalf of the University of Paris, which was suing to prevent the most important missionaries of Tridentine Catholicism, the Jesuits, from opening a college in that city.[31] Much of the resistance to the Jesuits was fiscal and old-fashioned, well represented by the *avocat général* Baptiste du Mesnil's conclusion that the Jesuits were in France "to discover and spy out what is being done on this side of the Alps, and little by little to transport the goods and money of this kingdom."[32] On the other hand, besides the defendants, at least one major new actor made his appearance in this controversy. The university's lawyer, just starting his career at the bar, was the historian and Gallican theorist Estienne Pasquier.

The opposition to both the Jesuits and Trent was also a real departure from earlier forms of *parlementaire* Gallicanism because this was the first time since the spectacularly unsuccessful opposition to the Concordat of Bologna that a party in the sovereign courts had taken a strong and coherent stand in opposition to the royal government on ecclesiastical issues. In that sense, it marked the birth of a truly new Gallicanism that would be the ideology of a lasting political party. However, the party opposed to the Jesuits never did command much political power, and quickly faded into the background before a revival under Henri IV, while opposition to the Tridentine decrees operated largely behind the scenes, without developing a larger program.[33] Thus, despite the impression that Martin's study of the reception of Trent might give of a political force sprung full-grown from the head of a *parlementaire* Zeus, the development of an erudite Gallican party was in fact still an embryonic process in the 1560s.

Though the Erasmian humanist program had demonstrated its political

---

31. This was published a number of times: e.g., *Caroli Molinæ jurisconsulti, et in supremo Parisiensi Senatu antiqui advocati consultatio, an Jesuistæ [sic] sint recipiendi in regno Franciæ, & admittendi in Universitate Parisiensi* (s.l., 1594).

32. *Plaidoié de feu M. l'advocat du Mesnil, en la cause de l'Université de Paris & des Jesuites* (Paris: Abel L'Angelier, 1594), 51.

33. On the development of the anti-Jesuit front, see Eric Nelson, *The Monarchy and the Jesuits: Political Authority and Catholic Renewal in France, 1590–1615* (Aldershot, U.K.: Ashgate, forthcoming).

impotence at Poissy, and had lost almost all of its support among the clergy at Trent, it did not vanish overnight from the hearts of Catholic humanist laymen. Michel de L'Hospital never lost his faith in it, in spite of rapidly mounting evidence of its bankruptcy. Another particularly striking instance of this style of thinking from the earliest stage of the religious wars was the "Mémoire sur l'édit de janvier 1562" composed by Montaigne's friend Estienne de la Boëtie.[34] The circulation of this piece was minuscule, but sufficiently influential to make it noteworthy.[35] Many of la Boëtie's suggestions were disciplinary, focusing on the old questions of residency and simony, but he went further, suggesting, for example, the suppression of the cult of images and relics.[36] More importantly, he trespassed on the question of the sacraments, advocating, for example, communion under both forms and the abolition of chrism in confirmation.[37] All of these ideas had been put forward by irenical Catholics before, but, of course, with no success.[38]

On the other hand, La Boëtie, not surprisingly for so deep a student of classical political theory, already displayed the most prominent characteristic of the legal Gallicans in that he was concerned above all with maintaining the stability of the state. The pernicious result of religious division was that "little by little the people becomes accustomed to irreverence toward the magistrate, and with time learns to disobey willfully, letting itself be lead by the lures of liberty or rather license, which is the sweetest and most

---

34. Montaigne mentioned the existence of this memoir in his edition of la Boëtie's works in 1571, but declined to publish it. It exists today in a single manuscript copy in Aix-en-Provence, one that was not rediscovered until 1917. It was first published by Paul Bonnefon as "Un mémoire inconnu de La Boétie: Le mémoire sur l'édit de janvier 1562," *Revue d'histoire littéraire française* 24 (1917): 1–33 and 307–19. A better edition is now available in *Œuvres complètes d'Estienne de la Boétie*, ed. Louis Desgraves, 2 vols. (s.l.: William Blake & Co., 1991), 1:99–145.

35. Montaigne certainly read it, since it is from him that we know of it in the first place. A certain thematic similarity and inherent probability make it likely that the manuscript was also read by Montaigne's friend Antoine Loisel during his tenure with the Chambre de Justice de Guyenne, charged with enforcement of the Edicts of Pacification, on which see below.

36. Though he rejects the actual *removal* of images and relics; see *Œuvres*, 122–25. Here, whether deliberately or not, la Boëtie closely follows the irenic "Advis de mess. [Jean de Monluc, evêque] de Valence, Sallignat & [Claude] d'Espences pour reformer l'abus des images," BN Dupuy 477, fol. 78. This memoir was prepared for the Colloque de St. Germain, a pendant to the Colloque de Poissy.

37. La Boëtie, *Œuvres*, 125–31. He also recommends making the sacrament of Holy Orders optional for preachers.

38. See Nugent, *Ecumenism*, passim.

delicious poison there is."[39] Moreover, he sought the solution to this problem in legislative and above all judicial action, as well as the suppression of all controversial preaching on matters of doctrine.[40] But as he wrote, his position of irenic moderation was becoming untenable even within the laity.[41] It was probably these very latitudinarian ideas that Montaigne later rejected in his essay on custom and, at least in theory, Montaigne was followed by even the most outspoken Gallicans of the seventeenth century.

It took some time for this attitude to become universal. As late as 1583 the *avocat général* Jacques Faye d'Espesses published (anonymously) a blistering attack on Trent radical in its complete refusal to accept the council's or the papacy's authority over many spiritual matters.

Most hold as doubtful or indifferent what that council commands that we accept on pain of anathema. For if we enter into our consciences, how many of us are there who would be burned for purgatory, for the invocation of saints, for the Sacrament under one species, for the feast of Corpus Christi, for the defense of images, for a million ceremonies . . . which nevertheless have passed into articles of faith necessary to salvation in the Council of Trent.[42]

Given his stress on events in the Netherlands, though, d'Espesses was almost certainly writing on behalf of the Duc d'Anjou's evanescent coalition of malcontents and Dutch Calvinists rather than any more stable French

---

39. La Boëtie, *Œuvres*, 101–2. The taste for civil disobedience shown in the *De la servitude volontaire* certainly seems to have vanished by the end of the first War of Religion!

40. His first concrete recommendation is "Soit doncques de chaque parlement envoyee une chambre pour passer par les lieux où les plus granz excez ont esté faitz, qui fasse les procès et les juge. . . . Que ceste chambre ne recerche en façon quelconque personne pour la religion, mais seulement vacque à la punition des insolences, des vols de fait et forces publiques." (*Œuvres*, 121–22). For a discussion of this program, and the spirit of anti-Tridentinism more generally, see Thierry Wanegffelen, *Une difficile fidélité: Catholiques malgré le concile en France, XVIe–XVIIe siècles* (Paris: Presses Universitaires de France, 1999), 112–14, 133–36, 150–60. Wanegffelen particularly notes the close affinity between la Boëtie and Monluc. Elements of this program were actually attempted under Henri III, probably at the initiative of Christophe de Thou.

41. For an interesting case study of this process within a French juristic milieu, see Michael Erbe, *François Bauduin (1520–1573): Biographie eines Humanisten* (Gütersloh, Germany: Gütersloher Verlagshaus Gerd Mohn, 1978), chap. 6.

42. *Advertissement sur la reception & publication du Concile de Trent* (s.l., 1583). I follow a slightly different manuscript version, which probably represents the original form of the speech d'Espesses gave: BN 500 Colbert 154, fols. 140–49, 145v. For a discussion of the speech and the circumstances surrounding it, see Martin, *Le gallicanisme*, 201–208; on Jacques Faye's life, see Eugène Halphen, ed., *Lettres inédites de Jacques Faye et de Charles Faye, publiées d'après le manuscrit de la Bibliothèque nationale* (Paris: Champion, 1880), i–xi.

Gallicanism in the Wars of Religion 111

grouping. Even during the Wars of the League in the late 1580s, the isolated jurist Guy Coquille was proposing Rube Goldberg constitutional reforms for the Church that would have had the unintended side effect of leaving the entire ecclesiastical apparatus firmly under the thumb of the Hapsburgs.[43] In his subordination of the pope, who would become a sort of spiritual *Stathouder*, he went much further even than any sixteenth-century conciliarist theologian would have been willing to countenance; he was also the last of the theological speculators.[44]

That does not mean that *parlementaire* Gallicans ceased in their hearts to doubt the adequacy of Roman doctrine: Pierre de l'Estoile, for instance, left a moving account of his ambivalent attempts to come to terms with the Roman Church during a near-fatal illness in 1610.[45] Still less did they cease to differ profoundly, if often covertly, with the clergy on issues of ecclesiology and religiosity. Rather, the erudite Gallicans began to move away from the Evangelical humanists' tendency to challenge the hierarchy directly on questions of doctrine or observance. At the political level, this was a side effect of increasing confessionalization, of the addition of the Genevan Charybdis to the Scylla of Rome. More broadly, as Nancy Roelker has demonstrated, it reflected the deep *parlementaire* commitment to an ideal whereby national religious unity would underwrite political stability. Thus, the mainstream of Gallican thought and discourse flowed more and more in the channels of a purely historical and political critique.

From the fourteenth century on, as we have seen, the mainstay of French religious nationalism had been moral condemnation of Roman ethical, spiritual, and dogmatic corruption; to this day, in the eyes of many scholars, that is the essence of Gallicanism. Over the course of the religious wars, though, Roman "corruption" came to be considered less a moral than a po-

---

43. He hoped for regular meetings of a general council, which would seat only bishops and vote by nation. He offered several different ideas on how Christendom might be divided into nations, all of which would leave an absolute majority under Hapsburg control; his ideas on this matter are thus not to be taken seriously. His model was presumably the Estates General of France (which voted by province), not unexpectedly given his general predeliction for that body. On his broader political thought, see William F. Church, *Political Thought in Sixteenth Century France: A Study in the Evolution of Ideas* (Cambridge, Mass.: Harvard University Press, 1941), 272–302.

44. On the limits of orthodox conciliarism after the Council of Constance, see Francis Oakley, "Conciliarism in the Sixteenth Century: Jacques Almain Again," *Archiv für Reformationsgeschichte* 68 (1977): 111–32, pp. 127ff.

45. See the keen analysis of this passage in Roelker, *One King*, 167–72. Even l'Estoile was of a somewhat older generation than many of the Gallican firebrands of his era.

litical matter, tending toward the domain of *raison d'état*. Meanwhile, the papacy and curia gradually abandoned some of their more flagrant violations of *gravitas*, making Rome a less tempting target for the moralist. The upshot was a considerable shift in the terms of ecclesiastical debate within the Catholic world. A good measure of this shift, outside of the purely legal domain, is a comparison of Montaigne's journal of his Italian voyage in 1579–1580 with Joachim du Bellay's Roman poems. Montaigne still found French piety and morals superior to Italian, but for him they were not incomparable. When the Bordelais set about mocking the papal court, his target was the ceremony of the bull *In cœna domini*, and the pretensions he mocked were political and ecclesiological rather than moral or spiritual.⁴⁶ Unifying all of these factors was a philosophical shift away from the idea of transcendental foundations for earthly institutions. As Montaigne recognized, this left relatively little room to critique an institution as firmly grounded in more than millennial possession as the Roman Catholic Church, if one was to avoid the danger of introducing innovation while attempting reformation.

But the erudite Gallican critique of the Church became no less stinging when it became essentially political. The probable origin and certainly the best introduction to this new critique is the work of Estienne Pasquier. While Pasquier did not publish the third book of his *Recherches* until 1595, when the French political situation had begun to stabilize, versions of the material certainly circulated in manuscript within his circle for some time before that, starting in the early 1560s. By his own account, in fact, it began in earnest with his plea against the Jesuits, and he in fact incorporated the plea bodily into it.⁴⁷ Now, since this plea first appeared in print almost thirty years after it was delivered, it is entirely possible that the surviving version differs in important ways from the original. In particular, the temptation to make it conform to the vision developed in Book 3 of the *Recherches* must

---

46. See Michel de Montaigne, "Journal du voyage," in *Œuvres complètes*, ed. Albert Thibaudet and Maurice Rat (Paris: N.R.F./Gallimard, 1962).

47. The plea actually first appeared in print a few months before the new *Recherches*: *Le plaidoyé de M. Pasquier pour l'Université de Paris deffenderesse, contre les Jesuites demandeurs en requeste* (Paris: Abel L'Angelier, 1594). In the 1596 *Recherches* it formed chap. 32; subsequent additions moved it first to chap. 36 and then to chap. 43. At the end of the previous chapter, Pasquier states that "à vray dire ce mien plaidoyé est un abbregé de mon livre" (Etienne Pasquier, *Les Recherches de la France*, ed. M.-M. Fragonard and F. Roudaut, 3 vols. [Paris: Honoré Champion, 1996], 1:806).

have been overwhelming. At the same time, though, Pasquier certainly respected the historical record, and at the very least the plea for the University of Paris gives some idea of the environment in which erudite Gallicanism emerged.

First of all, this was the environment of high forensic rhetoric. Du Mesnil remarked on this at the time, praising Pasquier and his opposite number, Pierre Versoris, for having by "their dexterity and the excellence of their spirit, doctrine, and eloquence . . . shown up so well in this case that we can plainly see that this century and this court are not . . . destitute of worthy and sufficient persons to represent the glory of their predecessors and transmit it to posterity."[48] This sense of themselves as participants in an ancient tradition of virtuous, learned, and public-spirited republican discourse, within the institutional framework of the Parlement, would continue to animate the erudite Gallicans into the seventeenth century. At the same time, the Jesuit affair involved more practical considerations. In preparing his case, Pasquier had the task of unifying the opinion and arguments of a fairly wide coalition, including Dumoulin, the old-fashioned Gallican bishop of Paris Eustache du Bellay, and the Faculty of Theology of the University of Paris.[49] In doing so, as we have already suggested, Pasquier had to engage with and synthesize the older Gallican traditions still current.

In a number of respects, though, his plea struck a new note. First of all, he concentrated on the dangers the Jesuits posed to the French state, conceived as a republican community. Their organization, he claimed, was a "seminary of party feelings between the Christian and the Jesuit." In order to demonstrate this danger, he felt that he had to provide a complex historical narrative. His showpiece was an account of the quarrel between the mendicants and the seculars at the University of Paris, which had formed a part of one of the greatest medieval ecclesiological debates. This featured (at least in the published version) the first public unveiling of his important

48. Du Mesnil, *Plaidoié*, 11. At the same time du Mesnil gave the parties some (well-deserved) criticism for "s'estre trop estandu de dire tout ce qu'il avoit amassé de matiere, sans retrancher ce qui estoit abondant, & sans polir ce qui estoit rude, & adoucir ce qui estoit aigre" and "ne s'estre espargné l'un l'autre, ny leurs parties par quelques dicacitez entremeslees, dont ilz se fussent bien passez." A publisher's note at the head of this edition of du Mesnil's plea expressed the hope that Pasquier would soon publish his own, "tant pour representer la façon de plaider du temps, dont je voy que quelques uns sont curieux, que pour ayder au restablissement & reformation de ceste Université" (3).

49. The official opinions of these figures may be found in César Egasse du Boulay, *Historia universitatis parisiensis*, 6 vols. (Paris: Petrus de Bresche and François Noël, 1665–1673), 6:570 and 572–73, respectively.

discovery that the University of Paris had come into existence under Philip Augustus rather than under Charlemagne: for those in the know, a striking proof of his erudition. To the university's (slightly abridged) antiquity and centrality to the state, Pasquier contrasted the hypocrisy, mutability, and foreignness of the Jesuits—a topos with a long future. More importantly, he presented them as a "heresy built ... on an ignorance of the antiquity of our Church."[50] Like Luther, Ignatius had proposed to return to the primitive Church of the first century, and like Luther, in so doing, he had destroyed the political balance that the Church had become over time. One reformer absolutized papal power, the other abolished it, and both destroyed the constitution of Christendom and threatened that of France. This was the danger the Parlement had to meet.

To understand the full weight of these claims, however, we must examine the larger narrative and theoretical framework in which Pasquier gradually placed them. The closest he came to defining the central question of the *Recherches* was in the first chapter of the second book, entitled "Whether Fortune or Counsel Has Done More to Maintain the Kingdom of France."[51] True to its title, this chapter considered the classic republican problem of whether prudence or luck was at the root of political stability.[52] Pasquier responded by moving the semantic weight of *conseil* away from "counsel" and toward "council": a definite institution or set of institutions that had provided advice and guidance to the king. The *Recherches*, indeed, were originally conceived as an exploration of the history of these institutions, and hence of the empirical conditions of that stability.

Pasquier proceeded to give a specifically religious valence to the stability of the realm and the institutions preserving it. Both the prudence and the councils of the French kings had been marked by a concern for the national church. Clovis, "having conquered the Gauls by his valiance and pacified them under him, had no higher priority in order to perpetuate his monarchy ... than to accommodate himself to the common justice [that is, the Roman law] and religion of the country."[53] Similarly, Pepin the Short and Hugues Capet, in order to consolidate their new dynasties, both increased

---

50. Pasquier, *Recherches*, 1:808, 832.

51. Pasquier, *Recherches*, 1:321.

52. It was a question that Claude de Seyssel, for example, had long ago answered in favor of counsel: *La monarchie de France*, ed. Jacques Poujol (Paris: Librarie d'Argences, 1961), 113–15.

53. Pasquier, *Recherches*, 1:323. The adoption of the Roman law was clearly a form of subordination of the new regime to expert and customary counsel, and the local legal experts must in Pasquier's mind have been the constitutional ancestors of the parlements.

consultation with their leading subjects. As the second and third books of the *Recherches* made clear, the forum of legal and political consultation had evolved into the parlements, and the politically essential religious accommodation into the Gallican church with its liberties. Pasquier also linked the stability of and the religious harmony instituted by the Capetian dynasty with great precision, explaining its long duration as follows:

> The first two [dynasties] produced each in its place several magnanimous and warlike kings, but not an administration [*police*] to match. And this last produced, along with force and magnanimity, an administration. Various voyages overseas displayed that magnanimity and force, [while] parlements and universities were founded, in most of which theology is cultivated—which are no small elements of *police* for our conservation.

That Parlement, "to which our kings who have succeeded St. Louis owe twice and thrice as much as to all other political orders," was what allowed them to master fortune and preserve their millennial kingdom. "And however often they depart . . . from the sage counsels and remonstrances of this great body, so often will they lose some of the ancient stock and foundation of their majesty, their fortune being bound up with that of this company."[54]

One of the items in Pasquier's dossier in his plea against the Jesuits was the conclusion by the Faculty of Theology, echoing venerable conciliarist rhetoric, that the Society of Jesus was "perilous to the conduct of the faith, disruptive of the peace of the Church, subversive of monastic observance, and more destructive than constructive."[55] As he embedded that plea in the *Recherches*, Pasquier implicitly transferred disruption of the *faith* by an overweening papacy to disruption of the *state*, whether in the case of the Jesuits or any other group. Even an internal disturbance in the monarchy quite apart from ecclesiastical interference could undermine the delicate structure of political-religious stability described in Book 2 of the *Recherches*. Pasquier explained that Pepin, who had military virtue but lacked institutionalized legitimacy, and the popes, who possessed the latter but lacked the former, formed an alliance of convenience, leading to an unbalanced and unhealthy relationship.

---

54. Pasquier, *Recherches*, 1:616–17, 675. My translation of the former passage reflects a slight conjectural emendation. The same analysis is applied to the University of Paris, "qui depuis apporta une infinité de bien à l'Eglise: Car ores qu'elle ait une perpetuel vœu & profession de vivre sous les reigles de l'Eglise Catholique Apostolique de Rome, si s'estudia-elle tousjours à l'extirpation des abus: aussi bien que des heresies: estant d'une mesme balance autant ennemie de l'une que de l'autre" (676).

55. Du Boulay, *Historia*, 573.

The grandeur of the pope being such as I have already described and infinitely respected in matters of faith because of the great religion that had always shone forth in Rome, Pepin (who had the force of France in his hands), wishing to gain the crown for his family had recourse to the pope in Rome ... by whom he was proclaimed king of France, and after his death his son Charles was also crowned emperor. In this way, the popes thenceforth began to increase their prerogatives and grandeur in this realm in another fashion than formerly. For the more authority they were given, the more the royalty newly adjudged to this second family was confirmed to the confusion of the first.[56]

Even the moral *purity* of Rome, it seems, could give rise to a dangerous extension of its influence, when combined with an overreliance by the monarchy on force and fortune rather than on learned counsel. At the heart of Pasquier's historical and political account of French religion lay an entire theory of the nature and historical contingency of ecclesiastical jurisdiction, one that in various forms can be traced through the growing Gallican literature produced in the Wars of Religion.

For many years, that literature continued to develop in an ambiguous tension with the traditional exigencies of royal policy. In 1563, for example, as part of a general campaign against the progress of Protestantism in France, the Holy Office threatened to excommunicate Jeanne d'Albret, queen of Navarre and a vassal of Charles IX.[57] Catherine de Medicis and her advisors took umbrage at this, both because they saw it as trespassing on their legal prerogatives and because it threatened their policy of accommodation with the Huguenots. They mounted a diplomatic campaign against the bull and called upon Baptiste du Mesnil to produce a legal opinion in support of this campaign.[58] Although later generations would hold this up

---

56. Pasquier, *Recherches*, 1:596.

57. On the political context of this affair, see Nancy Lyman Roelker, *Queen of Navarre: Jeanne d'Albret, 1528–1572* (Cambridge, Mass.: Harvard University Press, 1968), 221–23. A copy of the bull, "Monitorium et Citatio oficii Sanctæ Inquisitionis contra Illustrissimam & serenissimam dominam Dominam Johannam Albretiam Reginam Navarræ," may be found in BN Duchesne 47, fols. 5–12. The signatories include Cardinal Borromeo. Technically, this was a monitorial, summoning the queen to face trial within six months, "sub excommunicationis late sententie privatione Regni et principatus et cuiuslibet status et dominii vel dominiorum," etc. (fol. 11r.). A large part of the bull is devoted to a defense of a wide-ranging jurisdiction for the Holy Office. In December 1563, ignoring the stated grace period, Pius IV excommunicated Jeanne without further preamble (Roelker, *Queen of Navarre*, 223).

58. "Memoires dressez par M. Maistre Baptiste du Mesnil Conseiller & Advocat du Roy au Parlement de Paris ... sur les procedures faictes à Rome, contre la Royne de Navarre,"

as an example of firm royal action against papal excess, the facts do not bear out that interpretation.⁵⁹ Aside from the fact that the diplomatic mission was a failure, the language of the memoir was self-consciously moderate (as befitted an essentially diplomatic document), with periodic hopeful interjections of the form "which the pope will take in good part."⁶⁰ Indeed, Du Mesnil's objections to d'Albret's excommunication were essentially matters of form: mainly, that French subjects could not be judged in the first instance outside of the realm, or deprived of their temporal possessions without the consent of the secular courts. There are hints, though, that du Mesnil might have been influenced by Pasquier's new researches, or at least by du Tillet's older ones, as when he stated in his preamble that

> when the popes in Rome followed the path of Christian charity and humility, exercising their power in the spiritual realm established by God in his holy Gospel, without raising themselves to the dominion of an earthly magistrate, they received from everyone reverence and cordial obedience.⁶¹

It is impossible to say whether du Mesnil was consciously influenced by works then circulating only in manuscript if at all, but at least he shared some of their presuppositions. His legal argument on the rights of French subjects to be judged within the kingdom was backed by, and integrally related to, an erudite account of the history of French public law of the type

---

etc., *Traictez*, 193–213. There is what seems to be a draft version of this memoir in BN Duchesne 47, fols. 2–4; and a full manuscript version in BN Dupuy 313, fols. 301–11, which I follow.

    59. See J.-A. de Thou's comments on the official response to Navarre and Condé's excommunication in 1583, in *Histoire universelle de Jacques-Auguste de Thou*, 16 vols. (London: n.p., 1734), 8:374–75: "le sort de cette Bulle fut fort différent de celui qu'avoit eu celle qui 23 ans auparavant [*sic*] avoit été envoyée en France contre la reine Jenne mère du roi de Navarre, à cause de la différence des tems & du génie de ceux qui gouvernoient à la Cour. . . . Mais après la mort de ces généreux défenseurs de l'Etat [l'Hôpital and Montmorency], on vit paroître de nouveux Ministres . . . imbus des maximes de cette fausse politique, qui est aujourd'hui en vogue à la Cour, & qui par malignité, ou par défaut de sentiment, s'étoient faits des esclaves de toutes les volontés des Grands."

    60. BN Dupuy 313, fol. 311r, the *explicit* of the memoir. Both manuscript and printed versions of the memoir append the instructions of the ambassador charged with the affair, which stress dynastic considerations even more than does the legal memoir: "Memoires envoyez de la part de sa Majesté au Sieur d'Oysel son Ambassadeur à Rome, sur les procedures faictes en Cour de Rome, contre la Royne de Navarre," *Traitez*, 214–22. Legally, the memoir prepares an appeal *ad papam melior informatum*, the mildest of the forms of appeal claimed by the Gallicans (the others being appeal *ad futurum consilium* and *appel comme d'abus*; cf. Henri of Navarre's appeal of 1583: BN fr. 15733, fol. 411r).

    61. BN Dupuy 313, fol. 301v.

that du Tillet had pioneered, placed in turn into the context of an essentially political history of the Catholic Church.

This incident formed part of a broader clash between the French administration and the papacy over the final session of the Council of Trent, which also saw the attempted arrest of a number of French bishops, a walkout by the French delegation to the council, and the near collapse of the entire enterprise before the Cardinal de Lorraine intervened with successful mediation.[62] Like the more serious Gallican crises of 1511 and 1551, this faded quickly, and royal policy began at least moderately to favor the Tridentine decrees. In the later 1560s and the 1570s, even the *politiques* saw the Huguenot party as by far the greatest danger to the French state, and, while neither the government nor its supporters in the courts ever gave up on l'Hospital's project of limited religious toleration in exchange for peace, in practice both courts and government strove to exclude Protestants from as much of public life as possible, and connived at the exterminatory program of the St. Bartholemew's Day Massacre. As several scholars have pointed out, it is difficult if not impossible even to locate a continuous *politique* party between the end of the First War of Religion and the Wars of the League. Since such a party would have been the natural home of *parlementaire* Gallicanism in that period, it is equally difficult to locate that ideology. Until about 1580, with a few exceptions, the new historical and erudite Gallicanism remained as closely linked to the exigencies of royal policy as its predecessors had been, showing very few signs of an existence independent from the needs of government propaganda.[63]

Still, there were exceptions. All through the 1560s and 1570s, Pasquier was working on Book 3 of his *Recherches*. Sometime in the 1560s—perhaps during the Tridentine crisis, perhaps slightly later—the *procureur général* Gilles Bour-

---

62. See Alain Tallon, *France et le concile de Trente (1518–1563)* (Rome: Ecole Française de Rome, 1997), 337–415 and 777–81; and Martin, *Le gallicanisme*, 1–37. One of the episcopal victims of this attempted putsch, Jean de Monluc of Valence, advanced on his own behalf jurisdictional arguments similar to those produced by du Mesnil; see BN Duchesne 47, fols. 112–18.

63. See Roelker, *One King*, 313–28, on the conflicted attitude of the Parlement in the middle years of the religious wars. On the absence of an identifiable *politique* tradition, see also Christopher Bettison, "The Politiques and the Politique Party: A Reappraisal," in Keith Cameron, ed., *From Valois to Bourbon: Dynasty, State and Society in Early Modern France* (Exeter, U.K.: Exeter University Press, 1989), 35–50; and Edmond M. Beame, "The Politiques and the Historians," *Journal of the History of Ideas* 54 (1993): 355–79. Although Beame does not consider it, later Gallicans played a considerable role in retrospectively creating an illusion of continuity for a *politique* tradition.

din drew up informally a list of Gallican liberties, probably the first one ever.[64] Though never published, it circulated within the *parquet* of the Parlement, and was to serve as a model for later writers.[65] Most importantly, the question of the reception of Trent, on the one hand, and the need to counter arguments against the legitimacy of edicts of toleration in favor of the Huguenots, on the other hand, kept the issues of the Gallican liberties and the religious prerogatives of the monarchy continually on the minds of *parlementaires*. Thus, when the political situation began to alter around 1580, the new Gallican ideology that had been adumbrated in 1551 and 1561–1564 had the potential to become a viable tradition. The circumstance that brought this about was the gradual formation of a distinct royalist-Catholic tendency opposed to the extremism of the emerging League. It was centered in part around Henri III's younger brother, the fickle Duc d'Anjou, and magnates like Montmorency-Damville. We have already noted the affinity between that party and Jacques Faye d'Espesses's 1583 diatribe against Trent, but the emerging *politique* tendency was grounded most importantly on the *rapprochement* between Henri III of France and Henri of Navarre in 1579, the most concrete immediate result of which was a concerted program to stabilize royal authority in the Guyenne.

It was in pursuit of that program that Henri recalled Montaigne from Italy to become mayor of Bordeaux, prompting much of the political reflection that marks the later versions of the *Essais*. The Chamber of Justice sent to that province from the Parlement of Paris in 1581 to enforce the Edicts of Pacification united such important Gallican theorists as Pithou, J.-A. de Thou, and Antoine Loisel. The latter produced for the occasion an important statement on royal rights in the ecclesiastical sphere. This was one of his opening orations from the sessions of that court, entitled "Eusebie, ou la Religion."[66] This oration, in turn, was a kind of sequel to another pamphlet printed anonymously in 1579 but most likely authored at least in part by Loisel. That pamphlet, *De la puissance Royalle et Sacerdotale*, gave a narrative

---

64. Bourdin's list survives in two manuscript copies: BN 500 Colb. 154, fols. 17–19, and BN fr. 2760, fols. 293–96. The only indication as to the date of the piece is the fact that Bourdin died in 1570.

65. A letter of Jacques Faye d'Espesse from 1588, discussing a *hypothetical* list of the Gallican liberties, seems clearly to draw on Bourdin's; see Halphen, ed., *Lettres inédites*, 40–42. Bourdin's text appears essentially verbatim in Pierre Pithou's much more celebrated 1595 version, which is perhaps twice as long.

66. *Eusebie, ou la Religion* (Paris: Robert le Magnier, 1585); reprinted by Abel l'Angelier in 1595 and 1596; and again in *La Guyenne de M. Ant. Loisel* (Paris: Abel l'Angelier, 1605), 217–90, which collected all of the *remonstrances d'ouverture* from the Chambre de justice.

of relations between France and the Catholic Church seemingly drawn from Pasquier's work in progress, but with a different philosophical angle and a somewhat different political agenda.[67] Let us examine these works in their proper chronological order.

The treatise on royal and priestly power started from the premise that the law has a unique access to transcendental truth. It began, indeed, with an analysis of the *Digest*'s definition of jurisprudence, which it boldly identified purely and simply with philosophy, uniting theory and practice, the contemplative and the active.

Dionysius of Hallicarnasus, exhorting his readers to embrace philosophy, says that it consists not so much in contemplation as in action, which is of profit to all.... Aristedes, Lycurgus, Solon, and Epimandus all followed this wisdom... this philosophy is that virtue which the ancients called *sapience*, and it differs from prudence ... because prudence is the science of things that must be followed and those it is better to flee: *sapience* is the science of divine and human things for the maintaining of men in civil life, which is the same definition as jurisprudence. Wherefore jurisprudence, as *sapience*, is the true philosophy which consists more in action than in theory and the knowledge of precepts.[68]

The "divine things" of which the jurisprudent had knowledge included the ecclesiastical *police*, and this in turn was "for the maintenance of men in civil life." By another route, this author reached the same general view as Pasquier.

The occasion of this obviously polemical work, as far as it can be ascertained from internal evidence, bore no immediately visible relation to Loisel's later work in the Guyenne or the general development of a Catholic royalist party. The major event of ecclesiastical politics in 1579 was the Assembly of the Clergy at Mélun. Although no explicit mention of this event appears in the text, the support it could give to the clergy as a class and to

67. *De la puissance Royalle & Sacerdotale. Opuscule politique* (s.l., 1579). The only copy I have found of this work is at the Bibliothèque de l'Arsénal, 8° J 875. It bears the *ex libri* of Jacques-Auguste de Thou and of the Paris Oratory, so despite its subsequent obscurity the book might well have found some influential readers in the seventeenth century. However, the book was not included in the printed *Catalogus bibliothecæ Thuanæ*, ed. Joseph Quesnel (Paris: Impensis Directionis, 1679), which suggests that it had strayed well before the library was dispersed. I base my attribution of the opuscule to Loisel on the similarity of the legal metaphysics to that of the early orations in *La Guyenne*, and the fact that each of its chapters begins with a numbered list of points to be made, which are then noted in the margin as they are covered. Loisel followed this otherwise unknown practice in all of his published works. Besides its title, the treatise has no very marked relation to the work of Jean de Paris.

68. *De la puissance*, 7–8.

its jurisdictional interests must have been apparent to people as attuned to the workings of French political culture as were the *parlementaire* Gallicans. Moreover, the Assembly of the Clergy strongly promoted the introduction of the Tridentine canons, a reduction in royal influence over the collation of benefices, the distribution of church income, and a strengthening of ecclesiastical jurisdiction. "On 30 July," for example, "it was ordered that in all articles to be prepared concerning ecclesiastical discipline or regulation, care would be taken to attribute no jurisdiction over them to the king, as indeed his majesty claims none, but only to make a humble request to him that the execution of articles approved by the clergy should be authorized by his majesty."[69] The entire *De la puissance* can easily be read as a reply to this one passage. Furthermore, the largest section of the *De la puissance* was devoted to various implications of the royal right known as the *régale*.

For centuries the king of France had claimed the right to enjoy the revenues and to exercise some of the administrative powers of bishops during the vacancy of some poorly defined set of the dioceses of France, and from the middle of the sixteenth century royalist legists had pushed to extend this right uniformly to all the dioceses of the realm. Those sees that had formerly enjoyed a more-or-less secure exemption were distressed by this move. The issue remained before the Parlement almost continually from 1566 on. That was the year in which the canons of the Sainte Chapelle were confirmed by Charles IX in a perpetual grant of the revenues of the *régale*. The canons usually included a number of *parlementaires*, and at any rate they had merely to cross the courtyard of the *palais de justice* to file suit![70] From the Estates General of 1577 until their final defeat under Louis XIV, the clergy collectively opposed the Parlement on this issue, and the *De la puissance* was concerned to put forward a theoretical justification for the *parlementaire* position, beyond the purely legal argument that regalian rights formed part of the imprescriptable royal domain. The author of the pamphlet traced the *régale* from the authority of the Roman emperors to confirm all bishops, including that of Rome, down through the Middle Ages. Almost half the tract defended a royal right of "investiture." While this was never properly defined, it was based on a sharp distinction between the sacramental and the administrative functions of the bishop. "There is a great difference between

69. *Procès-verbaux*, 1:136A.
70. A fairly complete account of this issue, in its later stages and from the point of view of the clergy, may be found in Marc Dubruel, "La querelle de la Régale: Soixante ans de procès au Conseil du Roi (1616–1673)," *Bulletin de littérature ecclésiastique*, n.s., 18 (1917): 68–92, 119–228. On early litigation, see pp. 69–71.

the provision to the ecclesiastical benefice called collation, and ordination, consecration, and the admission of the person so provided to ecclesiastical orders and the priestly ministry."[71] It might be that "because it is part of the bishop's charge that the goods of the Church should not be abused, it has been reasonable to ordain that collations should take place by the authority of the bishop," but, if so, this merely represented a delegation on prudential grounds.[72] In principal, this was approximately the theory on which the Investiture Controversy had been settled four centuries before, but one is struck by the degree to which the erudite jurists were inclined to universalize the more radical implications of that settlement.

There were a number of continuities and discontinuities between Loisel's views in 1579 (supposing him to be the author of the *De la puissance*) and 1583. In the "Eusebie," he portrayed "religion" as something that made civil life possible in the fallen human condition, and so as something inherently political. Mystical *euphemie*, on the other hand, was a kind of spirituality that rejected the material trappings of piety, "rich and precious offerings," and the desire to "advance, maintain, and defend the Christian religion by force."[73] This last desire had manifested itself in the "ruin and demolition of our churches, temples, crosses, monasteries, convents, libraries, and archives and antiquities," while "the principal pillars and foundations of our Church, that is, its living stones, are lacking."[74] His proposed solutions were essentially juridical, consisting of adherence to the provisions of the edicts of pacification and a much closer cooperation between ecclesiastical and secular courts. In this respect, Loisel goes much farther than even la Boëtie's otherwise more radical commentary on the first edict of pacification. His desire to confine the truly spiritual to a kind of *Innerlichkeit* while bringing all the exterior facets of religious life under the purview of the state and the secular courts continued in full vigor from one pamphlet to the other. What had silently dropped (to be explicitly repudiated in the final oration of the Guyenne series) was the idea of a truly transcendent wisdom whereby the jurist could prescribe an infallible guide to action in divine and human things. As France lurched toward the most critical phase of the religious wars, the emerging party of *parlementaire politiques* was willing to leave to its

71. *De la puissance*, 153.
72. *De la puissance*, 175. In the final part of this final chapter, the author uses this position to distinguish himself from Marsilius of Padua.
73. Loisel, *La Guyenne*, 239, 241.
74. Loisel, *La Guyenne*, 248, 258.

League opponents the idea that the forms of political and religious life were revealed a priori, and that a set of public "ceremonies, sacrifices, and prayers," so revealed, was capable of appeasing divine ire, restablilizing civil life, and reinvigorating religious practice.[75]

The death of the Duc d'Anjou, the last heir to the throne in the Valois line, and the consequent near-inevitability of a Protestant succession, unleashed the conflagration that destroyed Henri III while threatening to destroy France with him. It was in this fire that erudite Gallicanism was finally forged into a well-defined ideology coherent enough to remain a political force well into the eighteenth century. By the time of Henri III's definitive break with the radical Catholics and the Guise family in 1587, the *parlementaires* had available a range of ideas and texts capable of being deployed against any attempted subordination of the historically validated monarchical order to papal fiat, the good of the ecclesiastical order, or the prophecies of religious enthusiasts. During the first phases of the Wars of the Three Henries (Henri III, Henri de Navarre [later Henri IV], and Henri, Duc de Guise, leader of the ultra-Catholics), these weapons remained largely unused. One can only speculate on the reasons for this, but they must include Henri III's hopes, up until the barricades of 1588, for some form of reconciliation with the Guise interest, and the overwhelming problem thereafter of reconstructing a royalist Parlement of Paris with that city under enemy occupation. No sooner had this been accomplished (more or less), than the assassination of Henri himself once more threw all into confusion. Thus, it was not until 1590 that the floodgates of Gallican propaganda began to creak open.

It was the Catholic League—self-proclaimed defenders, after all, of French Catholicism—who first publicly raised the issue of the Gallican liberties. An anonymous manifesto printed in 1589 had as its final plank "the maintenance of the Gallican church and its privileges, the Pragmatic Sanction, the Council of Trent. . . . Because the spirit of heresy leaves none of these blessings, there where it is the strongest."[76] Navarre's pamphleteers

---

75. Loisel, *La Guyenne*, 239. The blasphemous "pompes, sacrifices & prieres" of the Athenians are contrasted to the practice of the Lacedemonians who "remettans le tout sur Dieu, le prieoient fort simplement & en general." On the mentality behind the League practice of public relgious observance, see Denis Crouzet, *Les guerriers de Dieu: La violence au temps des troubles de réligion, vers 1525–vers 1610*, 2 vols. (Paris: Champ Vallon, 1990).

76. This was appended to Gilbert Genebrard, *Excommunication des Ecclesiastiques, principalement des Evesques, Abbez et Docteurs, qui ont assisté au divin service, sciemment & volontairement avec Henri*

were very concerned to deny such accusations, and broad programmatic statements of the royalist position did not fail to do so. Among the most interesting and influential of these were a pair of pamphlets entitled *Anti-Espagnol* and *Fleur de lys*, written (most likely) by Antoine Arnauld, and the *Satyre Menipée*, the most important section of which was written by Pierre Pithou.[77] The royalist propagandists tried in the first place to stress the merit and independence of French religiosity against the (supposed) claims of the Most Catholic king of Spain. Thus, the *Anti-Espagnol* exclaimed, "Oh poor wretches! Does our Catholic religion depend then on this old Spaniard [Philip II]? Are we then reduced to the point where if this king of Spain should now die . . . we must necessarily lose our religion?" The Spanish king was qualified as "this king of Majorca, . . . this half-Moor, half-Jew, half-Saracen," in implicit contrast to the "eldest son of the Church."[78] The *Satyre Menipée* expressed the same sentiment in much the same terms, drawing on a very vigorous if relatively recent tradition that defined the virtues of the Gallican church by contrast with its Spanish counterpart.[79]

Crude as they were, such claims were deeply rooted in the erudite project of recovering a usable, admirable, and stable French political and religious tradition amid the wreckage of the civil wars. This was a central concern for Montaigne and Bodin, of course, but Pithou was also a dedicated and subtle practitioner of that traditionalism. This took the form of a series of scholarly editions of religious texts, including one of the sixth-century churchman Salvian of Marseille's works. In his preface for this book, Pithou attacked those who, "I will not say out of malice, but out of laziness, foul up and neglect" domestic virtues, and while admitting "that this age is such that we who can hardly equal our own vices are altogether unequal to measuring the virtues of our ancestors," nevertheless hoped that by collecting

---

de Vallois, apres le massacre du Cardinal de Guyse. Traduit du Latin d'un Docteur [i.e., Genebrard] *par I. M.* (Paris: Gilles Gourbin, 1589), 60.

77. *Satyre Menipée de la vertu du Catholicon d'Espagne et de la tenue des Estats de Paris*, ed. Charles Labitte (Paris: G. Charpentier, 1880). Pithou wrote the long speech setting out Henri's position on pp. 126–221. Antoine Arnauld (attr.), *Antiespagnol autrement les Phillipiques d'un Demosthenes François touchant les menees & ruses de Phillipe Roy d'Espagne pour envahir la Couronne de France. Ensemble l'Infidelité, Rebellion & Fureur des Ligeurs Parisiens & Jesuites en faveur de l'Espagnol* (s.l., 1592); and *La Fleur de Lys. Qui est un discours d'un François retenu dans Paris, sur les impietez & desguisements contenus au Manifeste d'Espagne, publié au mois de Janvier dernier 93* (s.l., 1593). The attribution to Arnauld is from the *Memoires* of his son Arnauld d'Andilly in *Collection des mémoires relatifs à l'histoire de France*, ed. M. Petitot, 2 série, vol. 33 (Paris: Foucault, 1824), 309.

78. *Antiespagnol*, 4, 10. Very similar themes are developed in the *Fleur de lys*.

79. See Alain Tallon, *Conscience nationale et sentiment religieux en France au XVIe siècle: Essai sur la vision gallicane du monde* (Paris: Presses Universitaires de France, 2002), 213–35.

and editing old French ecclesiastical writings "there would come to be a kind of mirror of Gallican theology, in which the virtues of our ancestors, as if in a focused light, would be seen more clearly."[80] By the late 1580s, erudite Gallicans like Pithou were attempting to mobilize these ancestral virtues as a weapon for their own party.

A whole series of more specialized texts systematically developed the theory of nonresistance to (potential) religious persecution, the immunity of the French Crown from papal jurisdiction, and in general the historical relation between the secular and ecclesiastical realms in France. Many of these were not published until after the end of the wars and are difficult to date. Most prominent in this group are a number of works by the Nivernois jurisconsult Guy Coquille, and a historical treatise by the antiquary Claude Fauchet, a president in the Cour des Monnaies.[81] Pure defenses of nonresistance belong to a somewhat different intellectual tradition than that which concerns us here (though all Gallican pamphlets at least mentioned that doctrine); one of the more interesting examples was the work of the neo-Stoic philosophizer and canon Pierre Charron.[82] The Parlement of Tours (royalist exiles from Paris) published official responses to papal declarations and other diplomatic moves against Henri IV, which were the work of the *avocats généraux* Antoine Séguier and of Louis Servin.[83] Being in the first place

---

80. Pierre Pithou, ed., *Salviani Marsiliensis Pesbyteri de Gubernatione Dei, & de justo præsentique eius judicio libri VIII*, 2nd ed. (Paris: ex Officina Nivelliana, apud Sebastianum Cramoisi, 1608 [1580]), unpag. preface (dated non. Oct., 1579). Pithou was a past master of the genre of the scholarly introduction, and this particular example deserves more careful study than we can give it here. It is worth quoting the end of the preface, however: "Quanquem autem ea nunc morum labes est ut neque mala nostra, neque remedia pati posse videamur, quando tamen ægroto dum anima est spes esse dicitur, dedi & hoc spei nostræ ut Salviani de non absimili sæculo querellas nostris potissimum hominibus exponerem, quibus nullum tot tantisque malis præsentius remedium esse putavi."

81. Coquille's numerous works are to be found in the first volume of *Les œuvres de Maistre Guy Coquille Sieur de Romenay, Contenans plusieurs traictez touchant les Libertez de l'Eglise Gallicane, l'Histoire de France & le Droict François. Entre lesquels plusieurs n'ont point encore esté imprimez, & les autres ont esté exactement corrigez*, 2 vols. (Paris: Guillaume de Luyne et al., 1665). They were provoked no doubt by the fact that his patron, the duc de Nevers, was the most important of the uncommitted magnates; see Michael Wolfe, "Piety and Political Allegiance: The Duc de Nevers and the Protestant Henri IV, 1589–93," *French History* 2 (1988): 1–21. It is said of Louis XIII that he lost all taste for historical literature after being made to read Fauchet at a tender age. There is in fact something singularly deadening in Fauchet's style.

82. *Discours Chrestien, qui'il n'est permis ny loisible a un subject, pour quelque cause & raison que ce soit, de se liguer, bander & rebeller contre son Roy* (Paris: Martin Durand, 1594), signed "P.C."

83. It was Servin who opened this salvo: *Recueil des poincts principaux de la harangue faict à l'ouverture du Parlement par M. L. Servain . . . contenant exhortation aux subjects à l'obeissance envers Sa Majesté* (Tours, France: C. de Montr'œil and J. Richer, 1589); *Recueil de ce qui fut dict par monsieur Servin*

legal instruments, and propaganda only secondarily, these publications did not enter into extensive explanations of the royalist position. That task was left to another set of pamphlets, also emanating from the royalist parlements and their *gens du roi* in particular.

Prominent in that category were a brief exposition of the Gallican liberties by Servin, almost unique in that it was written in Latin; a *Discours des raisons et moyens, pour lesquelles Messieurs du Clergé . . . ont déclaré les Bulles Monitoriales decernees par Gregoire XIIII . . . nulles & injustes* by Charles Faye d'Espesses, councilor at Tours; and what was to become by far the most famous and influential statement of the legal specificities of the Gallican liberties, Pierre Pithou's *Libertez de l'eglise Gallicane*.[84] This last remained the definitive summary of the subject down to the end of the old regime. Pithou also incorporated and publicized the historicism of Cappel's and du Tillet's tracts (as yet unpublished, but with which he was evidently familiar) by publishing along with the *Libertez* a set of official documents mostly from the period of the Great Schism under the title *Ecclesiæ gallicanæ in schismate status*.[85] Those two pamphlets together generally formed the nucleus of later erudite Gallican collections.

Pithou created his list of liberties, as we have seen, by revising and expanding Gilles Bourdin's earlier collection. Comparing the two works pro-

---

Advocat General du Roy en la Cour de Parlement lors de la lecture des lettres patentes du Roy le cinquième Janvier mil cinqs cents quatre vingts dix, contenant declaration de sa Majesté à la venuë d'un des Cardinauls de la Cour de Rome envoyé par le Pape au Royaume de France (s.l., n.d.), evidently less than fully official; also *Recueil du plaidoie de Monsieur Seguier Conseiller du Roy en son Conseil d'Estat, & son Advocat en la Cour de Parlement. Contre la Bulle de Gregoire soy disant Pape 14. de ce nom. A Tours le Parlement y seant, en Aoust 1591* (Châlons-sur-Marne, France: n.p., 1595; "Jouxte la copie envoyee de Tours"); *Arrest de la Cour de Parlement contre toutes provisions de Benefices decernees par les Cardinaux Cajetan & de Plaisance eux disans Legats de nostre St. Pere le Pape mesmes à ceus de leur faction* (Paris: Jamet Mettayer and Pierre L'Huiller, 1594); the sub-Parlement at Châlons got into the act as well: *Arrest de la Cour de Parlement seant à Chaalons, sur certains libelles injurieux & scandaleux, intitulez, bulles monitoriales & imprimez à Rheims* (Châlons-sur-Marne, France: Claude Guyot, 1591). This list is not exhaustive.

84. Louis Servin, *Vindiciæ secundum libertatem ecclesiæ Gallicanæ, et defensis regii status Gallo-francorum* (Tours, France: Jamet Mettayer, 1590; rptd. 1591 and 1593); Pierre Pithou, *Les libertez de l'eglise Gallicane* (Paris: M. Patisson, 1594), published anonymously but later acknowledged and reprinted in the author's *Œuvres*; Charles Faye d'Espesses, *Discours des raisons et moyens, pour lesquelles Messieurs du Clergé . . . ont déclaré les Bulles Monitoriales decernees par Gregoire XIIII . . . nulles & injustes* (Tours, France: Jamet Mettayer, 1591). The attribution to d'Espesses is from its reproduction in Dupuy's collection, and is doubtless reliable. There is a brief analysis of Servin's pamphlet in particular, and of the Gallican pamphlet literature under Henri IV in general, in Mastellone, *La reggenza*, 38–50.

85. *Ecclesiæ gallicanæ in schismate status* (Paris: M. Patisson, 1594), with parallel French translation of Latin documents. Both pamphlets were, I believe, reprinted the following year.

vides an interesting perspective on how erudite Gallicanism had developed in the crucible of the Wars of the League. The earlier list was less than half the length of the document published by Pithou, and it had a rather different emphasis. It was meant to convey no particular theoretical position, and most of the articles dealt quite narrowly with limits on the authority of the pope. Pithou, on the other hand, imposed a kind of taxonomic order on the material by deriving it from two premises, namely, the absolute temporal supremacy of the king and the spiritual supremacy of the general council. Within this post-facto structure, the various articles were rearranged according to areas of jurisdiction, with a concluding section on the remedies available in the case of their infringement. This level of organization is in itself significant, for it shows both that the Gallican liberties had passed from a matter for internal ("secret," to use the contemporary term) notes within the government to a matter for public exposition. Simultaneously, they had achieved the dignity of a branch of juristic science with its own principles and modes of deduction. Pithou was particularly careful to define the Gallican liberties as common-law rights, that is, rights within the customary and "natural" disposition of French society. As such, they were not subject to revision by any individual (including the king), but they were accessible to historical scholarship and understanding.

In Bourdin's list, this concern was embryonic at best, but Pithou developed it into a detailed exposition of the limits on ecclesiastical jurisdiction and the rights exercised over it by the secular arm. Some of the revisions can be traced to specific events, such as the enormous extension of sections concerning the *régale*, and the item added by Pithou specifying that the bull *In cœna domini* was not received in France—an issue over which there had been a major fight in 1580.[86] The largest group of additions, though, concerned the details of jurisdiction exercised by the pope and his legates. Pithou carefully delineated the kinds of cases they could not hear, the kinds of penalties they could not impose, and the limits on their ability to derogate from established procedures and delegate authority. He also specified the procedures whereby the secular courts could override popes and other ecclesiastical authorities and how disputes between the latter and the secular authority should be resolved.[87] That matter was treated in the concluding and most

---

86. Pithou's list of liberties was divided by Pierre Dupuy into eighty-three numbered articles by which they are now customarily cited. Pithou discusses the *régale* at *Libertez*, article 66, and *Cœna domini* at article 17. On the quarrel over the latter, see Martin, *Le gallicanisem*, 173–82.

87. See Pithou, *Libertez*, articles 31–35, 58–60, and 75ff., all of which either vastly expand on Bourdin or have no equivalent at all in his list.

important section of the *Libertez*, which set forth three "methods wisely used by our ancestors, according to the times and circumstances."[88] The three (negotiations with the pope, examination of bulls before their execution, and *appel comme d'abus*, a form of appeal from ecclesiastical to secular courts) carefully tracked the ongoing process whereby the papal excommunication and deposition of Henri IV had been and was being combated, but they also underlined the role of Parlement and historians in stabilizing what was still a deeply threatened monarchy.[89] This was an important step in the development that linked history, counsel, and the Parlement's ecclesiastical jurisprudence to the viability of the state, but it also marked the full emergence of erudite Gallicanism as a tradition and of the erudite Gallicans as a party in French affairs.

This emergence was closely tied to the parlements, and particularly to the *parquet*. As early as 1589, Servin was issuing pamphlets on behalf of the Parlement of Tours, and his private efforts were almost as prompt as his official ones. On the other side of the political fence, the king's peaceful conquest of Paris in early 1594 and the consequent reunification of the Paris and Tours Parlements proved to be a critical step in the creation of Gallican tradition. While the royalist Parlement had fought against papal attempts to depose Henri IV, the Parlement at Paris, and in particular its *procureuer général* Guillaume du Vair, had in the last few months taken an official stand against attempts in the League's Estates General to set aside the Salic law, which mandated Henri IV's succession to the French throne, in favor of some new (and, potentially, Spanish) candidate.[90] This had some influence in bringing about the final checkmate of the League, but more importantly it gave the Parlement and the *gens du roi* a new claim to be the pillar of the monarchy in its hour of greatest instability.

After the surrender of Paris, Henri appointed Pithou and Loisel as tem-

---

88. Pithou, *Libertez*, article 75. Pithou also mentions appeal to a future council, which in practice had fallen into desuetude.

89. Both the examination of papal bulls and the jurisdiction of the *appel comme d'abus* in public matters were the province of the Parlement of Paris. "Conferences aimiables avec le sainct pere" (article 76)—either the negotiations over Henri's absolution or, say, the Concordat of Bologna—are prima facie removed from the competence of the juristic and humanistic counselor (*parlementaires* objected to both the cited instances). Pithou gets around this delicate problem by providing a brief but highly learned history of the correct manner and place of conducting such negotiation, with the implicit lemma that the advice of publicistic historians must be sought in order to conduct them successfully in the future.

90. See Guillaume du Vair, "Suasion de l'arrest donné au Parlement, pour la manutention de la loy Salique," in *Œuvres* (Rouen, France: Jean Osmont, 1614), pt. 1, 51–74.

porary *procureur* and *avocat du roi*, until the royalist court could return from the provinces. On that occasion, Loisel gave and published an oration stressing precisely the role of the defense of the Salic law in preserving the monarchy, while Pithou published his two pamphlets on the Gallican liberties. Simultaneously, du Tillet's 1551 memoir was printed for the first time, an action in which it is difficult not to see Pithou's hand—all the more so when one considers that when the memoir was added to the 1602 and 1607 reprints of du Tillet's *Recueil des rois de France*, Pithou's two pamphlets were included along with it.[91] It was at this point, too, that as we have noted the anti-Jesuit party began to re-create itself, leading to the publication of the various pleas from the 1565 case, beginning with the *avocat du roi* du Mesnil's, and culminating with Pasquier's. Pithou and his collaborators had thus managed to quietly construct a narrative, not of the history of the Gallican church, but of a continuous line of thought about it, running from the Great Schism, through du Tillet and (for those in the know) Bourdin, to himself and the contemporary *parquet* in general. The narrative was reinforced in the following year when Loisel republished all of his remonstrances and the third book of *Recherches* finally saw the light of day.

From this point on, compositions and publications on the liberties of the Gallican church, which had formerly been episodic and isolated, swelled to a steady stream and began to form a distinct genre. The mutation in the title of du Tillet's treatise between manuscript and print, from a "Treatise on the Rights and Customs of the Kingdom of France, with Respect to the Church and the Holy Apostolic See," to a "Memoir and Advice . . . on the Liberties of the Gallican Church," neatly summarized the transformation. It would be excessively tedious to note all of the Gallican works that flowed from French presses in the ensuing twenty years, most of which will at any rate be discussed in their place. It will suffice to mention two, already noted above: the collections published by Pierre Chevalier in 1609 and 1612 under the title *Traictez des droicts et libertez de l'Eglise gallicane*, the second being a slightly expanded version of the first. Their redaction was probably due at least in part to Pithou (who died in 1607), but is otherwise unclear. The contents included, in addition to the 1465 remonstrance for the Pragmatic Sanction and the works of Cappel and du Tillet, du Mesnil's memoir in the case of

---

91. *Memoir et advis de M. Jean du Tillet . . . faict en l'an 1551 sur les libertez de l'Eglise gallicane* (s.l., 1594); "Memoire et advis de Maistre Jean du Tillet, Protenotaire, et Secretaire du Roy tres-Chrestien, Greffier de sa Cour de Parlement, sur les libertez de l'Eglise Gallicane," in Jean du Tillet, *Recueil des Roys de France*, 2 vols. in one (Paris: Pierre Mettayer, 1607), 2:273–95, followed by Pithou's pamphlets.

Jeanne de Navarre, and pieces by Fauchet, Coquille, Charles Faye d'Espesses, Pithou, and Antoine Hotman.[92]

The sort of virtual tradition created by Pithou and the Parlement of Tours (and confirmed by du Tillet's editor) was thus solidified into a single physical volume—albeit one that gives the impression of having been set in type without alteration from a *recueil factice* of pamphlets and manuscripts— which then sold well enough to justify a second edition. The undoubted existence of individual collections such as the one detectable behind the 1609 *Traictez* is a further indication of the increased distinctiveness ascribed to legal Gallican theory. Such a collection must, for instance, have been a source for Laurent Bouchel's *Bibliotheque ou thresor du droit françois*, and in the first third of the seventeenth century Pierre Dupuy collected perhaps ten large manuscript volumes with titles mentioning the Gallican liberties. *Parlementaires* of a historical bent seem in general to have begun systematically collecting works relating to church-state relations, and this bibliographic practice quickly consolidated the newly minted Gallican tradition.[93]

The more traditional practice of collecting official documents bearing on church-state relations (dating back at least to Cappel) also gained momentum after 1594. Published examples include an *Ordre et Reglement sur les Provisions des benefices en l'Eglise Gallicane* from 1596 and *Quædam acta ecclesiæ gallicane* from 1608.[94] These, like Pithou's effort, must have been drawn from

92. Various catalogues attribute the collections to the lawyer Jacques Gillot, one of the authors of the *Satyre Menippée*. There is no reason why that should not be the case (he might have inherited the task from Pithou), but I have been unable to determine the basis for this attribution. In addition to the contents just mentioned, both collections include a pamphlet backing the Colloquy of Poissy by "Cl. G. Præt. Sen." (i.e., Claude Gousté), "Quæ regi potestas? Qui in his, cum emendanda est omnium ordinum, depravatio, Regnum, Sacerdotum, Nobilium, Procerum, Magistratuum, Populi, locus & ordo considendi," first printed at Sens by Ægidius Richebois, 1561; there was also a French translation at the time, *Traité de la puissance et authorité des roys, et de par qui doyvent estre commandez les diettes ou concils solonnels de l'Eglise* (s.l., 1561). Dupuy dropped this text. The second edition adds Bruslart's memoir and additional material by Coquille. Dupuy added (from our period) works by Lechassier and Milletot.

93. The most striking example of a Gallican collecter was certainly Pierre de L'Estoile. Roelker, in *One King*, 100–105 and 118–19, provides a careful analysis of this case, but also suggests an important if elusive nuance. L'Estoile appears largely to have ignored Pasquier, Pithou, and Loisel—in my analysis the key foundational figures in erudite Gallicanism. Pace Roelker, it seems to me inconceivable that this is anything but deliberate, but the evidence is too scanty to permit a more thorough explication.

94. *Ordre et Reglement sur les Provisions des benefices en l'Eglise Gallicane pendant les empeschemens d'aller à Rome* (Paris: Denys Duval, 1596), attributed to Jacques de la Guesle; and *Quædam acta ecclesiæ gallicanæ, pro libertatibus Ecclesiæ et Juris communis defensione* (Paris: n.p., 1608).

manuscript collections now lost or dispersed into the later-seventeenth-century erudite collections. One intriguing piece of evidence bearing on the history of this kind of collection is a manuscript catalogue of "Actes des Roys de France touschant leur puissance," probably dating to 1614, which seems to document a physical collection of documents.[95] That collection bears a strong similarity to the one published by Pierre Dupuy in 1638 under the title *Preuves des libertez de l'Eglise gallicane*, and since Dupuy was just then beginning his career as an erudite Gallican, it is hard not to suspect a direct filiation between the two.[96] Both the catalogue and the *Preuves* have tenuous but distinct connections to Matthieu Molé as well, bringing us back to the considerations with which this chapter began.

By the time Henri IV consolidated his power, then, a Gallicanism had appeared on the scene that was based on historical research and narrative, located within the sovereign courts and practiced most notably by the *parquet* of the Parlement of Paris. It was organized into a distinct set of legal, polemical, and erudite genres and possessed of a self-conscious if largely factitious tradition stretching back before the fourteenth century. As such, it was ideally suited to act as a political ideology, for it had all the characteristics such an ideology would need for success. It included a concrete program for action (though one largely confined for the moment to the negative doctrine that ecclesiastical and particularly papal influence on the law and government of the realm should be minimized); a well-developed vocabulary and rhetoric; a strong institutional base in the courts and in the sociability of late humanism; and, finally, both a visible, usable tradition—articulated by a historical method and the physical collection of documents in print and manuscript—and a philosophical position that could explain why that tradition was authoritative within the state. It comes as no surprise, then, that it functioned in just that way for the entire history of the Bour-

---

95. In BN 500 Colb. 154, fols. 200–58. This volume may well have come from the collection of Matthieu Molé, in which case it was probably prepared either on the occasion of his accession as *procureur general* or (more likely) in preparation for the Estates General. The documents run from Clovis through 1614 (hence the dating), and reference is occasionally made to "extraicts," e.g., "Parolles extraictes des Registres de Parlement qui furent entre le Roy et M. L. Servin" (fol. 252r), which militates for the existence of a physical rather than a virtual collection.

96. *Preuves des libertez de l'Eglise Gallicane* (Paris: n.p., 1638). For details on the publication of this volume (which, among other things, was republished by Dupuy and Molé at the height of the Fronde in 1651), see Gabriel Demante, "Histoire de la publication des livres de Pierre Dupuy sur les libertés de l'Eglise gallicane," *Bibliothèque de l'Ecole des Chartes* 5 (1843–1844): 585–606.

bon dynasty, alone or in combination with Frondeur, Jansenist, or Orleanist tendencies of one sort or another.[97]

From this point of view, the *parlementaire* reaction that had opposed the Jesuits and thwarted the Council of Trent earlier in the century, while undeniably continuous with seventeenth-century erudite Gallicanism both in thought and in personnel, basically formed part of the latter's prehistory. Caught up in and often pushed aside by the struggle between Catholics and Huguenots and not yet having taken the measure of the Tridentine Catholicism to which it was essentially a reaction, *parlementaire* Gallicanism under the last Valois also lacked a really stable set of doctrines and explanations for those doctrines. It also lacked a way of reproducing itself as an intellectual system for a long period and to a relatively wide public. It was that lack above all that the Gallican literature published after 1589 supplied. From that point on, what had been a basically episodic, reactionary, and undefinable political force became what in the old regime served for a party.[98]

To put the matter this way, though, is to give a false impression of complete coherence. In fact, the Gallican tradition that emerged from the Wars of the League was not monolithic, but rather split between a dominant faction and one much friendlier toward ecclesiastical and papal jurisdiction. Henri IV's supporters in the period leading up to his conversion can conveniently be divided into three groups according to the three estates of the realm.[99] The magnates (the key group, since it controlled most military power) split and vacillated as interest and conscience dictated. The clergy, on the other hand, split according to rank, with the prelates overwhelmingly supporting the Béarnais, while the lower clergy tended strongly toward the League. Finally, the more prominent and professionally successful among royal officers who led the third estate at first leaned toward the League, but

---

97. On the link between the erudite Gallican tradition and Orleanism, mainly in the person of André Dupin, see Donald Kelly, *Historians and the Law in Postrevolutionary France* (Princeton, N.J.: Princeton University Press, 1984), 57–62.

98. In this connection it is interesting to call to mind the transformation which Edouard Maugis noted years ago whereby the Parlement of Paris, under Henri IV, abandoned a longstanding moderation in ecclesiastical matters for a "nouvel esprit gallican" (*Histoire*, vol. 2, chap. 3). The explanation is partly no doubt the settlement of the Huguenot threat, which relieved the magistrates of the need for vigilance on that flank, but I would suggest that at a more basic level it reflected an intellectual and ideological shift of which the above narrative forms a considerable part.

99. I follow the account in Michael Wolfe, *The Conversion of Henri IV: Politics, Power, and Religious Belief in Early Modern France* (Cambridge, Mass.: Harvard University Press, 1993), 66–87, though the tripartite division is not original to him.

never warmly and increasingly little: the sad cases of the first president Barnabé Brisson, executed by the fanatical Paris Sixteen, and of Jean Bodin who died awaiting the failure of the cause he had been pressured into backing, are emblematic.[100] At the same time, as we have seen, a considerable, vocal, and ultimately triumphant minority within the courts backed Henri IV immediately and unreservedly. The unreservedness of that support was not matched, in general, by the other estates, and Navarrists and fence-sitters among the magnates and the clergy, together with the disillusioned robe Leaguers, combined in a moderate and potentially decisive *tiers partie* that, while never formal or openly active, pressured Henri into his conversion by the mere possibility of its existence.

From within this group came a short and imperfectly preserved, but nevertheless important, series of Gallican treatises. The most important such effort was written by Antoine Hotman, brother of the great Protestant jurisconsult and himself *avocat du roi* in the Leaguer Parlement of Paris. His work never took a definitive form. Various manuscript fragments survive, and half of a projected three-book treatise was printed in the 1609 and 1612 *Traitez*.[101] A differently arranged form of the first part of that treatise had appeared anonymously in 1608 under the title *Traicté des libertez de l'eglise Gallicane*. It apparently ran into trouble with Hotman's royalist successors: at any rate the Bibliothèque Nationale's copy bears a note on the title page in a hand suspiciously like that of Louis Servin, stating that it "has been brought to light by those who defend the authority of the Roman See against the royal dignity, who have eliminated what did not suit their purpose. Thus it has been rightly suppressed by the *procureur général*." The publication was in fact probably unauthorized, as the printer in his preface claims not to know the identity of the author and complained of "the defects of the copy, it having been impossible to restore entirely all the clauses mangled by the transcriber."[102] Either version may have been doctored to support the views of its publishers, but the basic positions put forward in the two versions are similar.

---

100. See Elie Barnavi and Robert Descimon, *La Sainte Ligue, le juge et la potence: L'assassinat du président Brisson (15 novembre 1591)* (Paris: Hachette, 1985); and Jean Bodin, *Lettre de monsieur Bodin* (Paris: Guillaume Chaudiere, 1590).

101. "Traitté des droicts Ecclesiastiques. Par M. Anthoine Hotman Advocat en la Cour de Parlement," in *Traictez*, 1612 ed., 331–445.

102. *Traicté des libertez de l'eglise Gallicane, Laquelle composition monstre la pure & sincere intelligence de ces libertez* [manuscript note in BN imp. 8° LD10-1: "selon la ligue"] (Paris: Gilles Robinot, 1608). The printed catalog of the BN erroneously attributes this piece to Lanier de l'Effreti-

Guy Lanier de L'Effretier, a councilor in the Grand Conseil (a body traditionally at odds with the Parlement of Paris and nominally charged, among other things, with most jurisdiction over beneficial matters) composed a similar treatise. Never printed, it survives in the Dupuy manuscripts.[103] We can only speculate about its influence, but it could well have reflected the jurisprudence of L'Effretier's court, which appears to have been generally less rigidly opposed to ultramontanism than the Parlement. The final tract in this group was written by a close supporter of Henri IV. In this case, though, the author was not a jurist but a churchman: Claude d'Angennes de Rambouillet, bishop of Le Mans.[104] The incompletely edited state in which these oppositional treatises are preserved testifies to their rather marginal character within erudite Gallicanism, as does the relatively muted echo they find in the rhetoric and jurisprudence of the sovereign courts. Nevertheless, they suggest some of the ways other political groupings could, and increasingly did, challenge the jurists' self-proclaimed monopoly on theorizing church-state relations.

This is all the more important when one considers the political basis of Henri's reign and of the regency that succeeded it. Besides Protestant confidants such as Sully, Henri depended on precisely the centrist group that had brought about his conversion: in particular, prelates like Rambouillet, the

---

er (see following note). The 1609 version seems the most complete and may, by default, be taken as definitive. The manuscript note reads: "Ce livre . . . a esté mis en lumiere par les deffenseurs de l'authorité du Siege de Rome contre la dignité Royale lesquels en ont retranché ce qu'ilz ont voulu a leur intention. Aussy a il esté bien supprimé par Mr le procureur general"; the printer complains of "la defectuosité de la copie, n'ayant esté possible de restituer & repargner entierement toutes les clauses viciees par le transcriptuer" (unpaged preface). Wanegffelen, in *Difficile fidélité*, 77–87, 130, 171, cites this pamphlet as typical of a certain Gallican religiosity. He is, however, unaware of its authorship and perhaps overstates its representativeness.

103. BN Dupuy 493, fols. 8–40. A colophon in Pierre Dupuy's hand states that "Monsieur maistre Guy Lanier Sieur de leffretier Angevin Conseiller du roy en son grand conseil est autheur de ce present traicté faict quelque temps apres la conversion du Roy tres Chrestien Henri 4 de ce nom—auparavant son absolution" (fol. 40r.). There is another copy in BN Dupuy 422, fols. 6–72. The latter manuscript may have come from the collection of Pierre Pithou.

104. "Discours touchant la puissance du Pape. Composé par Messire Claude d'Angenes de Rambouillet Evesque du Mans," in BN fr. 15733, fols. 9–42. The same manuscript contains another interesting piece on church-state relations written by a bishop, probably between 1615 and 1617: "Du droit des Papes sur le temporel des Roys, Par feu Mre. Daniel de la Mothe Evesque de Mande," fols. 43–88. It seeks a middle road between the Cardinal du Perron and his Anglican opponents in the quarrel over the deposition of kings.

Cardinal du Perron, and former robe Leaguers such as the secretaries of state Bellièvre and Villeroy. All three of the treatises just mentioned are located firmly within those circles. Rambouillet's position is evident, since he was one of Henri's major supporters among the prelates and a leader in the diplomacy that led to his absolution;[105] Hotman was a prototypical moderate Leaguer, and certain sentiments expressed in his treatise are sufficiently close to those one can find later in the letters of Villeroy to suggest that the two men held many opinions in common. On l'Effretier's political persuasions no direct evidence is readily available, but in one respect his theory speaks for itself.

Of all contemporary writers on Gallicanism he was, perhaps surprisingly, the only one to adopt Jean Bodin's theories and terminology at all systematically. For him, for example, the papacy was "established in monarchical and royal form, but nevertheless not a tyrannical or seigneurial one." Other elements of the apparatus developed in the *Republic* abound in l'Effretier's treatise.[106] One may argue about Bodin's personal commitment to absolutist theories, but it is certain that his work was very heavily used by proponents of a monarchy capable of overruling all other bodies in the realm, among them Henri IV's most unrestrained encomiasts.[107] Bodin himself supported the League before abandoning it on his deathbed, and his case seems to have been typical of the League's adherents within the magistracy.[108] One may thus presumptively place l'Effretier, as his disciple, in the same political camp. It is also tempting to connect the moderate Gallican position to Bodin's ideas concerning an external and natural basis for the political order, as we have attached those of the mainstream erudite Gallicans to Montaigne's theory of a historical and contingent order. Before exploring the possibilities of another Gallicanism and the identities and motivations of its adherents, however, it is first necessary to understand in greater detail what was

---

105. Rambouillet accompanied Nevers on the first mission to seek absolution from Clement VIII; see Victor Martin, "La reprise des relations diplomatiques entre la France et le Saint-Siège, en 1595," *Revue des sciences religieuses* 1–2 (1922): 338–78, 233–70, 1:347.

106. BN Dupuy 493, fol. 19r. Cf. Bodin, *République*, 2:31–67 (Bk. 2, chaps. 2–4).

107. On Bodin's influence in the development of absolutist political theory in the early seventeenth century, see Church, *Political Thought*, 303–36, but also note the cautions expressed by J. H. M. Salmon, "The Legacy of Jean Bodin: Absolutism, Populism or Constitutionalism?," *History of Political Thought* 17 (1996): 500–522.

108. A good account of Bodin's career in the League may be found in Roger Chauviré, *Jean Bodin auteur de la "République"* (Paris: Librairie ancienne Honoré Champion, 1914), 77–92. Chauviré outlines a suggestive parallel between Bodin and Brisson (p. 82); cf. Barnavie and Descimon, *La sainte Ligue*.

radical about the Gallicanism of the erudite jurists. This, in turn, requires a more detailed examination of the legal technicalities of that position, particularly its doctrines concerning secular and ecclesiastical jurisdiction. It was in that realm that mainstream erudite Gallicanism took on implications that made it uttterly unacceptable to most of the French clergy, provoking in turn a powerful political and ideological reaction, one that came precisely from the royal advisors, and above all from the prelates, closest to the emergent strain of Bourbon absolutism.

CHAPTER 4

The Problem of Jurisdiction

JULIEN PELEUS was a fairly successful *avocat* at the Paris bar near the beginning of the seventeenth century, and produced two typical and moderately successful casebooks. One, the *Questions illustres* from 1608, began with a case illustrating the following problem.

Since the royal power of princes and the sacerdotal authority of prelates are instituted by God, and each is distinct and separate, so that the one should in no way interfere with the other, it is no small knowledge in Christian jurisprudence to define and delimit the jurisdiction of the one and the other. And ignorance of this distinction has caused many honest people to stumble not only in affairs of religion, but also of state.

"This subject," Peleus added, "will serve as the entry point and frontispiece to these Illustrious Questions."[1] French law, like the state itself, could only be understood if it was first delimited, its boundaries traced and that which was foreign to it distinguished.[2] Nor was this a purely technical problem. It

---

1. *Les Œuvres de Me. Julien Peleus advocat au Parlement* (Paris: Pierre Billaine, 1638), 1. This edition was a reprint of two works, the relevant one being *Les Questions illustres de Me. Julien Peleus, advocat en Parlement*, 2nd ed. (Paris: Nicolas Buon, 1608).

2. Timothy Hampton, in *Literature and Nation in the Sixteenth Century: Inventing Renaissance France* (Ithaca, N.Y.: Cornell University Press, 2001), shows that the delimitation of Frenchness and the identification of the foreign was a central project of French literature in the sixteenth century. I argue elsewhere that French economic thought between the 1560s and the 1620s was innovative in defining France as a member of a multinational system, in com-

was a necessary prerequisite to any successful political or religious policy, to the reason of state. It was not purely technical, but it was inevitably technical. As the basic project of erudite Gallicanism, it would be carried out with that movement's tools: legal reasoning, republican political theory, and historical research.

Such problems had been central to relations between secular and ecclesiastical forces in Europe at least since the Investiture Controversy.[3] The English Reformation had begun with an Act in Restraint of Appeals, and even within Protestantism the Erastian controversy of the late sixteenth century raised the issue in an acute form.[4] Italian historians have long recognized that ecclesiastical jurisdiction was a dominant issue among political thinkers on the peninsula in the seventeenth and eighteenth centuries: secularizing and modernizing tendencies in all the early modern Italian states go under the generic title of "jurisdictionalism."[5] In France, the secular jurisdiction's victory over the ecclesiastical appeared to be relatively quick and easy, occurring essentially in the second half of the fourteenth century.[6] By the end of the fifteenth century, the royal courts had obtained a near-monopoly on serious criminal cases, cases involving real property and benefices, and all cases regarding possible infringements of royal edicts, as well as an almost unlimited right of review of the ecclesiastical courts through the *appel comme*

---

petition with its neighbors and distinct from ancient empires; see Jotham Parsons, "Money and Sovereignty in Early Modern France," *Journal of the History of Ideas* 62 (2001): 59–79.

3. The literature on this question is too extensive even to approach. Most of the major theoretical works through our period were collected in Melchior Goldast, ed., *Monarchia s. romani imperii, sive, tractatus de utriusque jurisdictione imperiali seu regia, & pontificia seu sacerdotali*, 3 vols. (Hanau, Germany: impensis Conradi Biermanni & consorti, 1612–1614).

4. The Erastian controversy has not been as extensively studied as one might expect. See the old but still valuable remarks of John Figgis, *The Divine Right of Kings* (New York: Harper & Row, 1965); Rudolf Hermann, *Die Probleme der Exkommunikation bei Luther und Thomas Erastus* (Berlin: Alfred Topelmann, 1955); and Weldon S. Crowley, "Erastianism in England to 1640," *Journal of Church and State* 32 (1990): 549–66. Erastus seems to have been unknown to the erudite Gallicans, and his doctrine (based largely on Old Testament exegesis) that the ecclesiastical constitution must differ under a godly and an ungodly magistrate would have been foreign to them.

5. See inter alia, Paolo Prodi, *The Papal Prince. One Body and Two Souls: The Papal Monarchy in Early Modern Europe*, trans. Susan Haskins (Cambridge, U.K.: Cambridge University Press, 1987); Aldo Stella, *Chiesa e stato nelle relazioni dei nunzi pontifici a Venezia: Ricerche sul giurisdizionalismo veneziano dal XVI al XVIII secolo* (Vatican City: Biblioteca Apostolica Vaticana, 1965); and Agostino Lauro, *Il giurisdizionalismo pregiannoniano nel Regno di Napoli: Problema e bibliografia (1563–1723)* (Rome: Edizioni di storia e letteratura, 1974).

6. Olivier Martin, *L'Assemblée de Vincennes de 1329 et ses conséquences: Étude sur les conflits entre la juridiction laïque et la juridiction ecclésiastique au XIVe siècle* (Paris: Alphonse Picard, 1909), provides a magisterial account of this process.

d'abus.[7] The sixteenth century thus saw little practical innovation in the reach of the secular jurisdiction, though it is important to note that in the second quarter of that century the struggle against actual and supposed Lutherans accustomed the parlements—with the support of most of the clergy—to a routine judgment of matters of doctrine.[8] What the century did see was, as Peleus implied, increased attention toward the *theory* of jurisdiction. In line with the theoretical primacy that the erudite jurists now gave to the state and its stability, it also saw increasingly radical claims to the supremacy of the secular jurisdiction. While the courts did not act systematically on such claims, their mere existence guaranteed a new level of conflict between the erudite Gallicans and the French clergy.

When one comes to examine it closely, jurisdiction turns out to be a surprisingly slippery concept, covering at one point or another almost every possible activity of government and governance. One useful way to begin investigating the way in which the erudite Gallicans understood it is to examine two concrete instances in which they raised and examined it. Both are relatively obscure, addressing the highly technical issue of how diocesan and international boundaries coexisted, but their very oddness helps to illustrate the twists and turns that the concept tended to take. While the doctrines set forth in the two cases patently contradict each other, that very fact underlines both the almost obsessive importance of jurisdictional considerations to the sovereign courts and the potential of such matters to become significant political incidents.

Physical borders, administrative boundaries existing on the ground, set the basic parameters for any system of jurisdiction. One of the unfortunate circumstances confronting those charged with delineating the boundary be-

---

7. See Robert Génestal, *Les origines de l'appel comme d'abus* (Paris: Presses Universitaires de France, 1951).

8. Pierre Imbart de la Tour, *Les origines de la Réforme* (Paris: Firmin Didot, 1905), 1:177–200, gives an extensive catalogue of late-fifteenth-century enterprises of the Parlement of Paris on ecclesiastical jurisdiction, which could be matched but not exceeded in the late sixteenth century. On the parlements' actions against heresy, see E. William Monter, *Judging the French Reformation: Heresy Trials by Sixteenth-Century Parlements* (Cambridge, Mass.: Harvard University Press, 1999); and James K. Farge, *Le parti conservateur au XVIe siècle: Université et Parlement de Paris à l'époque de la Renaissance et de la Réforme* (Paris: Collège de France, 1992). In 1525, for example, Pierre Lizet, the *avocat du roi* in the Parlement of Paris, claimed that "en maitere de foy, la court, qui est le souverain consistoire du prince treschrestien, a accoustumé et peult selon droit et raison en prendre congnoissance par plusieurs droictz et raisons" (ibid., 70, from AN X^IA 8342, fol. 262v).

tween secular and ecclesiastical jurisdiction in early modern Europe was that while the boundaries between secular powers changed continually at the whim of armies, treaties, and revolutions, ecclesiastical boundaries had largely been set in the later days of the Roman Empire and changed thereafter with glacial slowness. It was not until 1618, for example, that the hierarchy recognized the reversal in the relative importance of Paris and Sens in the millennium or so since Clovis had briefly settled on the island in the Seine by erecting an archbishopric of Paris, independent of its former metropolitan see. In that particular case, the inconveniences of the old system were not of a pressing nature, and the Church could afford to act with due deliberation, but things were not always so relaxed. For example, it was over the course of only two or three generations, through the reign of Henri II, that France and Spain hammered out much of their current border in the Pyrenees.[9]

One result of this process of demarcation was the definitive division of the Kingdom of Navarre, whose larger, southern portion was lost and eventually ceded to the Spanish monarchy. After the Treaty of Câteau-Cambresis (1559), the French government effectively recognized Hapsburg rule over Spanish Navarre, and the papacy began to consider how the ecclesiastical government of the area might be adjusted to address the new political dispensation.[10] Parts of the diocese of Bayonne (itself French) had now definitively become Spanish, making it difficult for their bishop to effectively oversee his charges. A complete realignment of the dioceses was obviously felt to be impractical, and perhaps incompatible with the dignity of the Church; thus, the proposed solution was to create a vicar who would exercise the episcopal jurisdiction in what had become Spain. Pope Pius V eventually issued an apostolic rescript to that effect. This affected the interests both of the French king and of his Navarese client (and as the case of Jeanne d'Albret demonstrated, the French Crown took a proprietary interest in the papacy's treatment of Navarre). In response, a group of at least two anonymous jurists—probably including the *procureur général* Baptiste du Mesnil—produced an "Advertissement au Pape sur son Rescript pour establir nouveaux Vicaires en la haute Navarre."[11]

---

9. Peter Sahlins, in *Boundaries: The Making of France and Spain in the Pyrenees* (Berkeley and Los Angeles: University of California Press, 1989), 10–22, gives an overview of this process.

10. See J. G. Russell, *Peacemaking in the Renaissance* (Philadelphia: University of Pennsylvania Press, 1986), 163–64.

11. BN Duchesne 47, fols. 119–24. The manuscript is in two distinct hands, one of which is that of a corrector. The latter has crossed out many references to the royal interests, and

Needless to say, they took the pope's decision vigorously to task. Aside from the "great prejudice" that his policy offered to "the ecclesiastical jurisdiction," the king of France

is manifestly and evidently injured by this act of so lightly transporting the jurisdiction of the churches of his kingdom, of which he and his royal predecessors have always been such careful protectors and preservers, into another land and clime.[12]

To support the claim that the proposed vicars were illegitimate, the jurists cited a royal privilege apparently made up on the spot:

[A]mong the many privileges, franchises, and liberties that are seen to shine among the lilies of the invincible Crown of France, this one can be justly numbered: that the jurisdiction and authority of the churches of his kingdom dilates and expands into enclaves and districts of foreign lands and kingdoms that do not have similar and so great liberties.[13]

The principal support offered for this doctrine was that Charles IX and his subjects were better Catholics than the Jews and Moors who peopled the Iberian Peninsula.

The authors of the "Advertissement" even went so far as to claim that the pope's attack on French episcopal jurisdiction would destroy any existing bonds of amity between the French and the Spanish peoples and lead them to war. They also demonstrated a connection to the emerging tradition of du Tillet and Pasquier by expressing a concern that this move, tending to undermine "the unity and jurisdiction of the Gallican church, would notoriously weaken the freedoms, preeminences and liberties of the establishments of the French Crown," and that in a period of religious war this

---

tends in general toward moderation of tone and concentration on purely canonic argument. What degree of official sanction this document had is impossible to say. The same volume includes a number of works by du Mesnil, and this might very well be attributable in part to him—most likely as the corrector. This was not the only issue of ecclesiastical boundaries raised by the peace of Cateau-Cambresis—the diocese of Thérouanne in the north was split up in a complicated agreement which had, at least, the advantage of being explicit; see Russell, *Peacemaking*, 201–2. In general, France was the loser in this process, which led to a general Gallican distaste for the reorganization of ecclesiastical territories. See Alain Tallon, "Le diocèse au Concile de Trente: Cellule close ou éspace ouverte?," in Gérald Chaix, ed., *Le diocèse: Espaces, représentations, pouvoirs (France, XVe–XXe siècle)* (Paris: Les Editions du Cerf, 2002), 17–31, pp. 17–18.

12. BN Duchesne 47, fol. 120r–v.

13. BN Duchesne 47, fol 121r. No legal or historical arguments are offered for this proposition.

was an extremely dangerous precedent.[14] What in fact became of the matter is hard to say, though those dire predictions certainly did not come to pass even after the borders of the diocese were entirely redrawn.[15] The affair did not impinge noticeably on the diplomatic relations of France, Spain, and Rome; the memoir was never published; and even the seventeenth-century jurist Jerôme Bignon, who professed deep concern for the injuries done by the papacy to the kings of Navarre, did not mention it.[16] It is easy to dismiss the arguments advanced in the "Advertissement" as special pleading, and indeed that is in all likelihood just what they were. Their importance, though, lies not so much in the details of legal doctrine as in what they demonstrate about the perceived importance of jurisdictional issues generally.

Though it was an international boundary of much longer standing than the one between French and Spanish Navarre, the border of the papal Comtat Venaissin was no less guilty of slicing through ecclesiastical territories, in this case the diocese of Cavaillon.[17] Some time in 1602 the Parlement of Provence (which was then engaged in a separate and very contentious dispute with the archbishop of Aix involving ecclesiastical jurisdiction—to be discussed in detail in the following chapter) issued a decree ordering the bishop of that diocese to appoint a vicar for his French territories to exercise his jurisdiction *in partibus*. The vice-legate of Avignon took exception to this, and since the Parlement had meanwhile recessed, it fell to the first president Guillaume du Vair personally to write a letter (on his private authority) explaining the reasoning behind the *arrêt*.[18] Du Vair was hardly known as a Gallican firebrand; indeed, he had served with Antoine Hotman in the Leaguer Parlement of Paris, and was promoted to head the (distant) Parlement of Provence for his part in leading that body's switch in time during the Estates General of the League.

His evident sympathy for conservative Catholicism, as much as a diplo-

14. BN Duchesne 47, fol. 123r–v.

15. The definitive realignment did not take place until the reign of Philip III; see Joseph Bergin, *The Making of the French Episcopate, 1589–1661* (New Haven, Conn.: Yale University Press, 1996), 33.

16. See Jerôme Bignon, *La grandeur de nos Roys, et de leur souveraine puissance* (Paris: n.p., 1615). One of the themes of the tract is that the loss of Navarre proves the danger of a persistent Spanish-papal conspiracy. Referring to that loss, Bignon ends by saying "O Clergé François, Noblesse Royale, Parlement sacré, pensez icy à cecy."

17. For a map of the offending area, see *Gallia Christiana*, vol. 1.

18. "Lettre de M. du Vair au Card[in]al Comti Vicelegate d'Avignon, sur les contentions des jurisdiction Eccles. avec les Parlemens"; BN 500 Colb. 154, fols. 73–74 (Guillaume du Vair to Cardinal Comti, 22 January 1603, copy).

matic temperament, may account for the moderate and conciliatory tone he adopted toward the papal representative, but this did not mean that he was shy about defending his court's action. He argued that French subjects could not be forced to undertake legal proceedings outside of the realm, and that French procedure required a royal officer to be present at the trial of a clerk in an ecclesiastical court, in case the matter should turn out to be a privileged case and thus justiciable in the secular courts. One thing he might have pointed out but did not was that foreigners were not allowed to exercise any jurisdiction or hold any benefice in France without royal permission. He then went on to note that despite these regulations,

> we French are exactly the opposite of the Spanish: for we seem to claim liberties, while in effect we give honor, respect, obedience, and service to the Church, while in appearance and on the face of it they show great submission and in fact make her their servant and practically appropriate her for themselves.[19]

By that argument the contradictory assertions of the two cases may be reconciled, for what it amounts to is an assertion that churches are always better off under French jurisdiction rather than Spanish! To put the matter less glibly, du Vair was arguing that the French view of ecclesiastical jurisdiction and its relation to the secular power was fundamentally more in the interests of the Church than one that was nominally less restrictive. This was one of the key elements in the Gallican view of jurisdiction.

In a way it is emblematic that du Mesnil and du Vair advanced mutually contradictory doctrines of French ecclesiastical jurisdiction, for the internal tensions of erudite Gallican ideology were most pronounced in theories of jurisdiction. In part this was because those theories were cobbled together out of disparate bits and pieces with no real attempt at system or synthesis. Our next task will be to disentangle some of those elements—in particular those derived from legal and ecclesiological theory—and suggest something about their history and relative importance.[20] Of particular interest are concepts of delegation and territoriality from the former realm, and the distinction between orders and jurisdiction from the latter. After bringing the history of these matters down to the seventeenth century, we will turn

19. BN 500 Colb. 154, fol. 74r–v.
20. Beyond what was covered in the first three chapters of this essay, William Bouwsma's analysis of Venetian republicanism in *Venice and the Defense of Republican Liberty* (Berkeley and Los Angeles: University of California Press, 1968) applies in considerable measure to the erudite Gallicans as well.

briefly to the religiosity of the *parlementaire* Gallicans and its influence on their view of jurisdictional questions. Finally, we will consider two case studies that illustrate important aspects of the way in which jurisdictional issues worked out politically and ideologically, one briefly and the other at length. The former shows a Gallican opinion strongly inclined to remove the clergy from the secular realm altogether. At the same time, however, the *parlementaires* retained their commitment to a sacramental Church and to a vision, however attenuated, of society unified in the pursuit of a Christian ideal. This left them unable, in the last analysis, to reject the reality of ecclesiastical jurisdiction even over the person of the king—though they came more than close enough to doing so to ensure the massive enmity of the clergy.

At the foundation of all theories of jurisdiction were the elements of early modern legal studies, based on the three schools of Roman, French, and canon law. Each had a distinct concept of jurisdiction and applied it to a distinct set of problems. In their writings the erudite Gallicans made implicit or explicit use of all three. As befitted "written reason," the civil law was the most explicit and straightforward, and thus offers the best place to start. Justinian's corpus itself offers no definition of the term "jurisdiction," but the medieval commentators had no hesitation in filling that gap. The Accursian gloss defined it as "a power introduced by the public, carrying with it the obligation to rule on the law and establish equity."[21] This definition was based largely on a few texts of the *Digest*, and while it includes some important aspects of those texts, it neglects others that the Gallicans found important. In particular, it makes no mention of Imperial Rome's deep concern with territoriality, largely a legacy of first the republic's and then the empire's vain attempt to prevent provincial governors from seizing power in the metropolis.[22] To the medieval commentators, these were matters of purely antiquarian interest, but the early modern jurists of the historical school had in abundance both antiquarian curiosity and a capacity for applying the products of that curiosity to contemporary issues. Thus, it is not surprising that issues of territoriality that were of little concern earlier reappear in Gallican discussions of jurisdiction.

On the other hand, the glossators did make clear that jurisdiction was an

---

21. *Glossa ad* D.2.1.1. This is supposedly a quotation from Cicero, though I have not been able to locate it.

22. The definition is based on the last few titles of D.1 and D.2.1, "De jurisdictione." Much of D.1.16–18 is devoted to territoriality, particularly to the limits on the jurisdiction of provincial governors outside their assigned provinces.

The Problem of Jurisdiction 145

emanation of what was later called "sovereignty" by referring to "a power *introduced by the public.*" This was confirmed in the *Digest* by the rules stating that only jurisdiction granted by the laws or the prince is sufficiently real to be delegated.[23] These rules were adopted in their essence by the canon law, which largely accounts for the interest they aroused among the commentators.[24] All this in turn merged with the disputes over a distinction between *jurisdictio* and *merum imperium*.[25] The Bartolists identified *imperium* with public law, criminal law, and even legislative authority. A "mixed" category covered civil law that involved either physical punishment or the public interest, while *jurisdictio simplex* dealt purely with the property of private individuals.[26] An anonymous commentator gave five cases that might be either pure *imperium* or simple jurisdiction, depending on the circumstances. One was "excommunication, which when imposed for the sake of the public against rebels or contumacious parties is pure imperium, but when granted in a private suit is simple jurisdiction," suggesting the degree to which ecclesiastical procedures were entangled in these debates.[27] Sixteenth-century legal scholars from Budé to Bodin showed an increasingly strong tendency to restrict *merum imperium* to the prince and his direct delegates, opening the possibility that its exercise by the Church might be moved under secular control. At the same time, representatives of the great French historical school of Roman law identified *imperium* more specifically as the coercive power needed to implement jurisdiction, "by the strength of which it is made effective," but separate from it.[28] This opened two further possibilities: if jurisdiction and

23. See D.2.1.5–6.

24. The fullest statement is at *Decretals* 1:29. Even a papal grant of jurisdiction, though, could only be subdelegated as specified in that grant, and all of this is an instance of the general Roman principal, applied to both public and private law, that no delegation could be subdelegated.

25. See the classic study of this dispute by Myron P. Gilmore, *Argument from Roman Law in Political Thought, 1200–1600* (Cambridge, Mass.: Harvard University Press, 1941). The distinction is drawn at D.2.1.3–4.

26. Each of these was further subdivided into either three or six levels of authority from *maximum* to *minimum*; see Gilmore, *Argument*, 36–44. For a presentation of miscellaneous Bartolist texts with a rather crude attempt to shoehorn the Scholastic trichotomies into Ramist dichotomies, see *Digestum vetus, seu pandecta*, vol. 1 (Lyons, France: n.p., 1569), cols. 159–62. The identification of *merum imperium maximum* with legislation renders the status of the entire system unclear (is this, then, the origin of the other categories rather than merely one of the set?); a more reasonable example is given, that of the papal power to convene and confirm a general council, but not to legislate per se. Bartolist jurisprudence was profoundly anti-absolutist.

27. *Digestum*, col. 162, citing Panormitan on *Decretals* 2:2, 13.

28. Jacques Cujas, quoted in Gilmore, *Argument*, 86.

coercive power were distinct, then the latter might be denied the Church while admitting its jurisdiction in principle; but, on the other hand, if they were inseparable in practice (as Jacques Cujas, for example, implied), then denying the Church coercive power might deny its jurisdiction entirely. The erudite Gallicans were to toy with both alternatives.

In native French law, the period of the sixteenth and early seventeenth centuries stands between the high points of two great debates on the question. One, which was already a live issue but would become truly explosive under the ministries of Richelieu and Mazarin, was the controversy over the proper limits of the king's so-called reserved justice: that is, jurisdiction exercised by the royal council or by appointed judicial commissions preempting the normal process of the courts.[29] An ingrained hostility to reserved justice surely reinforced the Gallican preference for the ordinary jurisdiction of bishops as opposed to papal interventions or immunities granted from Rome, while, on the other hand, the terms of discourse concerning ecclesiastical jurisdiction did much to shape the later debate over reserved justice. Still, the erudite Gallicans did not regard the constitutions of the monarchy and the Church as homologous in any degree of detail, so few direct relations were drawn between those two questions.

Much more important to the course of Gallican argument over ecclesiastical jurisdiction was the great medieval struggle to firmly establish the independence and supremacy of royal secular justice. This was fought on two fronts, on the one hand, against the feudal and ecclesiastical courts in France, and, on the other hand, against papal and imperial claims to a universal dominion. The former campaign had depended on annexing to the royal courts a growing set of royal or privileged cases (the former from the feudal and the latter from the ecclesiastical courts), and by installing a right of appeal to the king which in the case of the feudal courts became universal. The instrument of this capacity of review over the ecclesiastical courts was the *appel comme d'abus*, which was the locus of most great debates over the relation of ecclesiastical to secular jurisdiction from the sixteenth century

29. The most detailed account of debates over the proper judicial role of the royal council is in Albert Hamscher, *The conseil privé and the Parlements in the Age of Louis XIV* (Philadelphia: American Philosophical Society, 1987). On commissions, see James H. Kitchens III, "Judicial *Commissaires* and the Parlement of Paris: The Case of the Chambre de l'Arsenal," *French Historical Studies* 12 (1982): 323–50. Erudite Gallicans were no more fond of reserved justice than any other *parlementaires*. Jacques de la Guesle remarked at one point that "parmi nous les jugemens des Commissaires sont tenus si suspects, qu'ils ont donné naissance au dire commun que ce n'est pas estre jugé par Justice que d'estre jugé par Commissaires" (BN Dupuy 392, fol. 62r).

on.[30] The latter campaign turned on the assertions that the king was "emperor in his own kingdom," that the dominion granted by Christ to the Church was not a secular one, and that the secular domain was coequal with the spiritual in legitimacy and divine sanction. The most dramatic incident in that struggle was the French rejection of the bull *Unam sanctam* and the subsequent bad end of Pope Boniface VIII. Gallican writers were very fond of referring to that history; to Bignon, to take an example at random, Boniface was "the first in these extravagances" of papal jurisdiction, while his opponent, Philip the Fair, "royally resisted that pretension and with a heroic vigor cast off this yoke."[31]

What all this amounted to were parallel traditions of struggle over jurisdiction against Rome and against the French church. Neither was deeply theologically informed, since the latter was directed against (among others) the theologians, while the former relied on the University of Paris Faculty of Theology for support in that quarter. As with so much of medieval Gallicanism, the link between the jurists and the Paris theologians—still vigorous in 1512—was to a considerable extent undone by the Concordat of Bologna. The separation was not by any means final, however. An attempt by Edmond Richer, an eccentric syndic of the Faculty of Theology, to revive the old alliance after 1600, while ultimately unsuccessful, made a considerable public splash. Still, it tended to be the forms rather than the details of theological theory that influenced Gallican thought, sometimes even among theologians. Moreover, when the erudite Gallicans came into conflict with the clergy, they naturally encountered and replied to arguments drawn from theology and canon law. To understand the relation between juristic and ecclesiastical ideas of jurisdiction, then, we must turn to the canonists and theologians.

The term *jurisdictio* was imported into the canon from the Roman law during the twelfth century, at first to indicate administrative and judicial power generally.[32] Its usage soon became more restricted, however, probably

---

30. On the *cas royaux*, see Ernest Perrot, *Les cas royaux: Origine et développement de la théorie aux XIIIe et XIVe siècles* (Paris: A. Rousseau, 1910). The *appel comme d'abus* developed out of the system of privileged cases; see Génestal, *Les origines*, passim.

31. Bignon, *La grandeur*, 6, 169, with a pun on the *Extravagantes*, the canonical collection in which *Unam sanctam* was published.

32. This usage parallelled the late Roman one. On the early history of jurisdiction in canon law, see Martinien van de Kerckhove, "La notion de juridiction chez les décrétistes et les premiers décrétalistes (1140–1250)," *Etudes franciscaines* 49 (1937): 420–55; and, in somewhat greater depth, Robert L. Benson, *The Bishop-elect: A Study in Medieval Ecclesiastical Office* (Princeton, N.J.: Princeton University Press, 1968), esp. 45–71.

under the influence of theologians concerned with Donatism.³³ Thus Thomas Aquinas distinguished in priests "a double spiritual power, of which one is sacramental and the other jurisdictional." The former was "conferred by some consecration" and was ineradicable, while the latter was "conferred by a simple human injunction" and could be removed. Thus schismatic priests could perform the sacraments, though they could not licitly apply them to anyone, since "an inferior power should not become active without being moved by a superior power," but under no circumstances could they validly "either absolve or excommunicate or give indulgences or anything of the kind."³⁴ The sacramental power came to be termed *ordo*, comprehending, as the passage from Aquinas implies, a supernatural power granted directly from God by the sacrament of Holy Orders. Jurisdiction, on the other hand, remained a rather more sprawling category, which included the authority (as opposed to the power) to administer the sacraments in a given case, penance and the remission of sins with all its ramifications (except for sacramental absolution) in the internal forum, excommunication in the external forum, and the entire array of temporal or temporal-like jurisdiction carried out under canon law.³⁵ Certainly this was one of those dryly technical divisions of terms in which the Scholastics delighted, but it was one with enormous practical implications, for what it anatomized was the way in which religious authority was distributed within the Church. With that in mind, it is not surprising that soon after this distinction was made it became embroiled in two great medieval ecclesiological debates: first, the one between the mendicant orders and the secular clergy, and, second, the conciliarist controversy. These were, at least in their early stages, largely French de-

---

33. Besides the distinction between *jurisdictio* and *ordo*, thirteenth-century Scholastics developed a distinction between *jurisdictio* and *dominium*, that is, property right. See Janet Coleman, "The Two Jurisdictions: Theological and Legal Justifications of Church Property in the Thirteenth Century," *Studies in Church History* 24 (1987): 75–110.

34. Aquinas, *Summa Theologiæ* IIa IIæ q. 39 art. 3.

35. It was at this same period that excommunication became separated from penance and was converted into an essentially judicial sanction, both being part of a general distancing of the institutional Church from the direct spiritual life of the believer; see Elizabeth Vodola, *Excommunication in the Middle Ages* (Berkeley and Los Angeles: University of California Press, 1986), 42–43. It is of some importance that the definition of doctrine and the preaching of the Word remained within the realm of *jurisdictio*, in this case *non coerciva*. See the "Arbor de origine juris et legum" and "Arbor de potestate ecclesiastica," of somewhat mysterious origin but clearly late medieval and an imitation of the taxonomies of jurisdiction printed with the *Digest*, in Jean Gerson, *Opera omnia . . . tomus secundus*, ed. Louis Ellies Dupin (Antwerp, Belgium: Sumptibus Societatis, 1706), cols. 257–60.

bates, and the issues they had raised continued to be important and controversial throughout the sixteenth century.

Recall that, according to the *Digest*, true jurisdiction could be granted only by "the prince or the laws." There is an obvious ambiguity in that statement, doubtless to be accounted for by Roman history. A similar ambiguity existed in the Church, though. No orthodox thinker doubted that bishops exercised true jurisdiction, but from whence did they derive it? The medieval commentators saw two alternatives. The first, supported by the secular clergy, the conciliarists, and eventually the Gallicans was that it was distributed by divine law, having been granted immediately by Christ in his foundation of the Church. The other view was that all ecclesiastical jurisdiction came from the pope and was granted (with a greater or lesser degree of latitude) at his pleasure. This idea appealed to the curia, for obvious reasons, but especially to the mendicant orders that were sponsored by the papacy and whose members wished to preach and distribute the sacraments (and, their enemies claimed, collect fees and donations) freely throughout Christendom, regardless of the attitudes of local bishops.

The French clergy held out against this idea, particularly the Paris Faculty of Theology where, in a famous quarrel, the seculars managed to impose strong restrictions on the mendicants; the issue of Jesuit instruction in Paris kept many of the same issues alive well into the eighteenth century.[36] The episcopalist ecclesiology of John Major, Edmond Richer, and the jurists who read them descended practically unaltered from that of the thirteenth-century secular controversialists. The question of whether episcopacy, and thus episcopal jurisdiction, were *jure divino* was one of the great issues of the Council of Trent. In effect, the dispute ended with a complex settlement whereby papal claims were left intact but bishops were in practice given substantially increased jurisdictional authority within their own dioceses. Alain Tallon has suggested that this settlement rested in turn on the bishops' conception of the diocese as a spatially concrete jurisdictional network.[37] Thus, the issue of where ecclesiastical jurisdiction was ultimately located remained very much a live one in our period, with hard-line Gallicans increasingly isolated from the episcopal hierarchy.

36. On the mendicant-secular quarrel and its theological bases, see Yves Congar, "Aspects ecclésiologiques de la querelle entre mendiants et séculiers dans la seconde moitié du XIIIe siècle et le début du XIVe," *Archives d'histoire doctrinale et littéraire du moyen âge* 28 (1961): 34–151. As we shall see in the next chapter, the issue of how even non-Jesuit regular clergy should be educated in Paris remained very much alive in the sixteenth century.

37. See Tallon, "Le diocèse au Concile de Trent." Tallon puts the matter rather less pretentiously.

A related issue was the relation between the two realms of order and jurisdiction. Since it was universally admitted that the power of *ordo* came directly from God without any subordination to the extrasacramental hierarchy, papalist theologians were inclined to denigrate its relative importance, so that as one of them put it "in the prelates of the Church, the ... power of jurisdiction is superior to the priestly power, which is called the power of orders."[38] Those wishing to play down papal authority, on the other hand, were naturally inclined to take the opposite tack, subordinating what was by then a heavily papalized jurisdiction, in a greater or lesser degree, to the power of orders. Jean Gerson, at the time of the Great Schism, undertook by far the most complete and prominent attempt to do this. At the very beginning of his career, in the *resumptio* that he gave immediately after receiving his master's degree (1392), he had maintained that someone who held ecclesiastical jurisdiction should resign it if to do so would benefit the faithful. He argued that the "triple root" of pastoral duty, fraternal charity, and the obligation of service collectively constituted the raison d'être of the Church and should thus take precedence over considerations of mere form.[39] At the height of his celebrity, in the famous tract on ecclesiastical power that he wrote for the Council of Constance, he put forward a complex and difficult theory of ecclesiastical authority that maintained the same basic hierarchy.[40]

While intricate in its details, Gerson's system clearly placed *ordo* (a term he used with less precision than one might like) at the center of the Church's constitution. The final cause of all ecclesiastical power was the "edification of the Church militant, with eternal blessing to follow," and naturally the exercise of that power was subordinate to that end.[41] The means to that end

38. Jacob of Viterbo, *De regimine christiano* 2.4, quoted in Benson, *Bishop-elect*, 383. The translation is Benson's.

39. Gerson, *Opera*, 2: cols. 261–67. This was evidently put forward in defense of the *via cessionis* for the resolution of the Great Schism, which Gerson then supported. On the *resumptio* and the circumstances surrounding it, see John B. Morrall, *Gerson and the Great Schism* (Manchester, U.K.: Manchester University Press, 1960), 34–38.

40. Jean Gerson, "Tractatus de potestate ecclesiastica, et de origine juris et legum," in *Opera*, 2: cols. 225–56. In this treatise Gerson advanced four or five separate arguments in parallel, and for various reasons the relations among them are not clear. Thus, the reading I present here is not a self-evident one, though a full explication would be excessively lengthy.

41. Gerson's definition is worth quoting in full: "Potestas Ecclesiastica, est potestas quæ à Christo supernaturaliter & specialiter collata est suis Apostolis & Discipulis, ac eorum successoribus legitimis, usque in finem seculi ad ædifcationem Ecclesiæ Militantis, secundum Leges Evangelicas pro consecutione felicitatis æternæ.... Potestas Ecclesiastica secernitur prima sui divisione in potestatem Ordinis & potestatem Jurisdictionis" (cols. 227–28). Unhappily, those two species are never explicitly defined.

were the three hierarchical acts of purgation, illumination, and perfection (that is, the removal of sins, the inculcation of doctrine, and the administration of the sacraments). They were exercised by the hierarchical Church, defined in turn by its relation in the first place to the sacrament of the Eucharist—which all priests share in common—and then by other sacraments in which the power of simple priests varies from that of bishops. The role of jurisdiction was to properly regulate the application of the hierarchical acts for the edification of the Church "lest the ecclesiastical regime should be confounded, nor the hierarchical order (which, Dionysius taught, is such that the lowest is led back to the supreme by the middle) disturbed."[42]

Thus, jurisdiction was meant to operate in a system that the power of order had already put in place, for the better pastoral distribution of supernatural graces including preeminently those sacraments that define order. So far, Gerson's theory leaves open the possibility that ecclesiastical jurisdiction might be a *purely* secondary phenomenon, some kind of contingent effect of the sacramental order. As we shall see, the erudite Gallicans sometimes tended toward that position. Gerson, however, had reasons for not accepting it, reasons to which the parenthesis in the last quotation alludes; on his view, order and jurisdiction as well were direct or mediated emanations of divinity. His mode of thought was basically Neoplatonic. For Gerson, as for the pseudo-Areopagite from whom he derived his doctrine, the hierarchical acts represented a diffusion of divine grace from the highest to the lowest, the diffused grace then serving to reunite the believer in a harmonious union with God.[43] If Gerson understood *ordo* in basically Neoplatonic terms (admittedly, this is never unambiguous), as a continuous reiteration of the heavenly hierarchy through the created world, *jurisdictio* remained within a more Thomist, but equally emanationist, framework. The final section of the tract was devoted to an exposition of that model, whereby *jurisdictio* is the power to apply *jus*, which is in turn "a subordinate power or faculty belonging to something according to the dictate of original Justice," which is in turn that perfect will to give to each his due that exists in its plenitude only in the mind of God, but secondarily in human justice as well.[44] This, in

---

42. Gerson, *Opera*, 2: col 233. On the logical priority of order over jurisdictional power, see the first section of consideration 10 (col. 239).

43. On Gerson's commitment to a pseudo-Dionysian ecclesiology, see D. Catherine Brown, *Pastor and Laity in the Theology of Jean Gerson* (Cambridge, U.K.: Cambridge University Press, 1987), 39–41; and Louis Pascoe, *Jean Gerson: Principles of Church Reform* (Leiden, The Netherlands: J. E. Brill, 1973), passim.

44. Gerson, *Opera*, 2: col. 250. The full text is "Potestas Ecclesiastica, sicut & alia quæli-

turn, is a familiar enough concept: for Gerson, ecclesiastical jurisdiction was the implementation of divine justice within the divine order of salvation, in exactly the same way that the courts implemented it within the state in the traditional *parlementaire* model.

This side of Gerson's ecclesiology remained important through the end of the old regime. The dominant figure in the Paris Faculty of Theology after Henri IV's triumph was a fanatical devotee of his fifteenth-century predecessor. Until he was ignominiously expelled from his post as syndic of the Faculty in 1612, Edmond Richer did his considerable best to enforce his own vision of the university's Gallican traditions. While he was not immediately successful, he did transmit the ideal of divinely instituted jurisdiction following sacramental order through the Church hierarchy to a later generation of Parisian clergy. They drew the conclusion that the jurisdiction of curates was in fact divinely established, immediate, and inalienable, the core of an ideology (unjustly labled "Richerism") with evident revolutionary potential.[45] Before the Fronde and the rise of Jansenism, though, there was no such split between the higher and the lower clergy, and Gerson's theories were applied essentially to and by prelates.

Richer's own vision, moreover, had as much to do with the newly minted tradition of the erudite *parlementaires* as it did with high conciliarism.[46] Moreover, the temper of the times was such that even his opponents adopted a terminology much more liable to privilege the secular over the ecclesiastical than the transcendental and sacramentally ordered language Gerson had used. In 1606 Richer published a monumental edition of Gerson's works, and in 1607 he wrote a defense of Gerson's conciliarism which was printed in Italy. In 1611 he had his own brief *summa* of Gallican ecclesiology

---

bet, originatur a prima Justitia, secundum quam Jura omnia, Leges, Jurisdictiones atque Dominia pulchra Ordinis varietate fundatur. Describitur itaque Justitia, quæ est perpetua & constans voluntas, jus suum unicuique tribuens. Hæc autem descriptio competit principaliter Justitiæ divinæ in ordine ad suas creaturas. Deus nempe solus est, qui voluntate perpetua & constanti dat unicuique rei quod suum est . . . Sic in qualibet re tantundem est de jure, quantum de entitate: habet enim res quælibet jus seu titulum id habendi, quod habet ex dictamine rectissimo primæ Justitiæ. Jus vero sic describitur. Jus est potestas, seu facultas propinqua conveniens alicui secundum dictamen prima Justitiæ."

45. See Richard M. Golden, *The Godly Rebellion: Parisian Curés and the Religious Fronde, 1652–1662* (Chapel Hill: University of North Carolina Press, 1981).

46. Richer's otherwise not particularly satisfactory biographer has aptly described him as "un parlementaire égaré dans l'Eglise"; see Pierre Edouard Pujol, *Edmond Richer: Étude historique et critique sur la rénovation du gallicanisme au commencement du XVIIe siècle*, 2 vols. (Paris: T. Olmer, 1876), 1:176.

printed in Paris, in both French and Latin versions. It raised a storm of controversy—indeed, a council of the province of Sens condemned it. The Faculty of Theology expelled Richer from his post as its syndic, and he failed in his attempts to have the Parlement intervene on his behalf.[47] What is interesting here about Richer's doctrine is one particularly striking image that he used to describe the way in which God gives authority immediately to all ecclesiastical orders without the intervention of the pope: "as in France the inferior judges and magistrates, though they depend on the parlements, nevertheless derive their authority as immediately from the Most Christian king as do the parlements."[48] Obviously this retained and even strengthened the well-established episcopalism of the French secular clergy, but at the same time it suggested that the jurisdiction of bishops was not in any way fundamentally different from that of secular magistrates—an impression, it must be said, that the rest of the tract did almost nothing to dispel.[49] Gerson, by way of contrast, was careful to make it clear that the similarity between the two jurisdiction lay in the fact that, ultimately, divine justice authorized them both.

This image of the Church as royal legal system proved remarkably durable. It persisted through at least four rounds of debate, so that in 1618 a theologian named Theophraste Bouju was making the following argument: the fact that the good of hierarchical inferiors is undoubtedly the final cause of ecclesiastical jurisdiction does not mean that those inferiors have any title to that jurisdiction, "because even though a parlement is given sovereign ju-

---

47. On Richer's career and fall, see Pujol, *Edmond Richer;* Aimé-Georges Martimort, *Le gallicanisme de Bossuet* (Paris: Editions du Cerf, 1953), 53–56; and a pamphlet apparently released by Richer himself, *Recueil de plusieurs Actes remarquables pour l'Histoire de ce temps* (s.l., 1613).

48. [Edmond Richer], *De la puissance ecclesiastique et politique* (Paris: n.p., 1612), 10. This was not, in fact, a statement calculated to endear its author to the Parlement, since that body held exactly the opposite view: the *procureurs du roi* in inferior courts, for example, were styled and held to be simply substitutes for the *procureur general* of the Parlement. Perhaps this is why the courts failed to back him in the fight over the Syndicate, though Richer had a facility seldom equalled for alienating anyone and everyone.

49. Equating sacred and secular governance got Richer into trouble on other fronts as well. Since he denounced papal monarchy as tyranny and claimed that the proper government of the Church was aristocratic, opponents questioned his loyalty to the French monarchy. See, e.g., Jacobus Cosma Fabricius [, S.J.], *Notæ stigmaticæ ad Magistrum triginta paginiarum, qui libello uno Ecclesiasticam & politicam potestatem complexus est* (Frankfurt, Germany: Jacob Fischer, 1612), 31: "Tu vero lege quam absoluto unius imperio gubernari multo præstare, in Gallia audes scribere. Legis regiæ hostis, quam in principem omne imperium transtulit, quo tibi Aristocraticum placet solum. Verbera non times? Nos enim ad ea tempora revocas, quibus parricidam neffandissimum sanctorum numero adscribendum, publicè disputatisti."

risdiction for the love and in favor of all the persons residing in its resort
... nevertheless, the jurisdiction and sovereign power is only given formally
and immediately to ... the presidents and councilors." As enamored of—
and trapped within—political metaphors as his opponent, Bouju ended up
explicating the relation between pope and General Council as identical to
that of the king and the Estates General, which "can do nothing without
the king, if there is one, [but] could elect another if the race of our kings
should have failed."[50] Neither Gallicans nor ultramontanists, it seems, neither *bons français* nor *dévots*, felt any great desire any longer to follow Gerson
with particular fidelity. It is ironic that the jurists, in preferring to concentrate on order rather than jurisdiction as the characteristic of the Church,
remained in a way closer to the master than did his successors among the
theologians.

How did the Gallican jurists understand legitimate ecclesiastical jurisdiction? If they preferred not to describe even their own jurisdiction in terms
of direct divine institution and transcendental authorization, still less
would they accept such descriptions of ecclesiastical jurisdiction. The difficulties involved in that rejection, however, were even more considerable in
the case of ecclesiastical than of secular jurisdiction. Clearly, the relation of
the ecclesiastical polity to a divine and eternal justice was much clearer than
in the secular case, since the ecclesiastical polity had a definite foundational
moment or moments, and a legislator who had clear access to the mind of
God, being God himself (either the Father, as founder of the covenants
with the Jews, or Christ in his various charges to the apostles). Furthermore,
the records of that legislation were preserved in the authoritative texts of
Scripture and subject to the authoritative (if infinitely redefinable) interpretation of the Church. Thus, the problem of historical skepticism—and the
opportunity of historical authority—did not arise in anything like the way
they did for the secular polity. On the other hand, if the jurisdiction of the

50. Theophraste Bouju, *Deffence pour la Hierarchy de l'Eglise et de nostre S. pere le Pape* (Paris: Denys Langlois, 1620), 31–32, 196. According to the anti-Conciliarists, the only power a general council possessed without papal leadership was the election of a pope if there was no clear claimant to that office. Bouju's covert reference to the Leaguer Estates and the *arrêt* for the Salic Law is really quite neat: this passage draws on a move du Perron had made in his oration to the third estate, suggesting that Gallicanism rendered the Crown less, not more, stable (see below, Chapter 6). Bouju wrote this tract in reply to a counselor in the Grand Conseil named Simon Vigor, who had written in reply to André Duval, who had replied to Richer. Bouju follows Duval, the house theologian of the *parti dévot*, very closely.

secular courts was a contingent historical product, while that of the Church was the direct consequence of the revealed will of God, any attempt by the jurists to restrict or even define the latter would encounter severe problems.

The erudite Gallicans never tackled these issues head-on—there is no reason why they should have, since to do so would already have conceded a great deal to their opponents—but it is clear that they relied chiefly on two strategies to answer or deflect them. The first was to regard ecclesiastical jurisdiction as essentially *territorial*, and hence historically contingent, while only secondarily of direct divine institution. The second was, along the lines of a well-established Evangelicalism, to restrict the role of the Church as much as possible to what Gerson had called "the hierarchical acts," that is, the administration of the sacraments and the transmission of the divine Word, with all external organization and discipline becoming the province of the secular authority. Both of these strategies tended toward a radical depoliticization of the Church, to a degree, indeed, that ultimately proved untenable.

Early modern legal thinkers were acutely aware, as historians have been ever since, that one of the ways in which their society differed most greatly from that of the ancients was the phenomenon of multiple and juridically equal territorial states.[51] This circumstance had changed the definition of ultimate political authority: the maxim "a king is emperor in his own kingdom" was cited incessantly by Gallican jurists eager to demonstrate the temporal independence of the king of France.[52] In doing so, it had also increased the importance of the territorial circumscription of jurisdiction beyond even that which had prevailed in the later Roman Empire. Thus, as Dumoulin remarked in his commentary on the *Codex* of Justinian, a judge

---

51. One of the most striking instances of this comes from a minor quarrel over monetary policy. In 1611 the first president of the Cour des Monnaies objected to a proposal that France commemorate its victories on its coins in imitation of the Romans: "de comparer une mousche a un elephant cest simplesse et riser [?] tout ensemble. Aussy de comparer ce royaume foible petit et estroit a lempire Romain qui estoit fort, spacieux et de longue estendue voire que mettoit sa pied Rome sur les trois parties du monde cest trop impertinent. . . . Mais noz Roys qui sont chrestiens et qui ont affair avec dautres chrestiens grans et puissans princes avec lesquels apres les guerres il est besoing de se reconcillier et effacer touttes memoires dhostilite de part et dautre" (BN Dupuy 51, fol. 46v).

52. On the history of this maxim and its importance in the developing concept of territorial sovereignty, see Walter Ullmann, "The Development of the Medieval Idea of Sovereignty," *English Historical Review* 64 (1949): 1–33; and A. Bossuat, "La formule 'Le roi est empereur en son royaume': Son emploi au XVe siècle devant le parlement de Paris," *Revue d'histoire du droit français et étranger* 39 (1961): 371–81.

"may not exercise jurisdiction or proclaim the law in all places: for today there are distinct territories, and any court is delimited territorially," so that ordinary jurisdiction, at least, "is that which is given by the laws or the prince, *universally for certain territories*."[53] It occurred early on to the erudite Gallicans that the ecclesiastical jurisdiction, though it remained embedded in the universal sovereignty of the Catholic Church, was in practice subject to similar territorial delimitation into patriarchates, provinces, dioceses, and the like. Furthermore, the secular clergy, at least in France, had long defended as a Gallican liberty the proposition that these territorial jurisdictions held their authority originarily and by divine law.

In fact, at least in France, the physical divisions of ecclesiastical jurisdiction closely followed exactly that late-antique administrative geography to which the Roman law referred. "The Christian law having come into the world under the Roman Empire [and] while the dominion of that people was widely distributed in diverse regions and provinces" (as Servin said in one of his pleas), its hierarchy followed the divisions of the empire.[54] This fact does something to explain the fervor with which Gallican erudites studied the arcana of that subject.[55] Jacques Leschassier, for example, entered into a quarrel on the matter with the scholarly nemesis of the erudite Gallicans, the Jesuit Jacques Sirmond.[56] More to the point, most of Guy Coquille's numerous tracts on matters concerning the Gallican liberties begin with long accounts of the relation between diocesan boundaries and the urban organization of the late empire. This line of thought was developed to its logical conclusion in 1592 by a Protestant, probably the great erudite Denis Godefroy, who claimed that "we see that this institution [of the ecclesiastical hierarchy] was modeled on the temporal government of the world," and that "the ecclesiastical hierarchy was established, altered, and changed according to the pleasure and will of the emperors and not of the apostles."[57]

---

53. From a commentary on C.2.13, in Charles Dumoulin, *Omnia quæ extant opera*, 5 vols. (Paris: Charles Osmont, 1681), 3:617. Note the additions made to the *Digest*'s definition of ordinary jurisdiction at D.2.1.5, which lacks the final four words (my emphasis).

54. Louis Servin, *Plaidoyez*, vol. 2 (Paris: Pierre Hennequin, 1605), fol. 56r.

55. It is probably not coincidental, for example, that Pierre Pithou possessed one of the most important manuscripts of the key text for the study of imperial administrative geography, the *Itinerarium Antonini Augusti*; see Pauly-Wissowa, *Reallexicon der Altertumswissenschaft*, s.v. "Itinerarium."

56. Jacques Leschassier, "De vocabulis ad geographiam juris Romani pertinentibus observatio," in *Œuvres* (Paris: n.p., 1649), 457–81. Sirmond published the first complete collection of the Gallican councils, which had been Pithou's pet project.

57. Denis Godefroy (attr.), *Maintenue & defense des princes souverains et Eglises chrestiennes, Contre*

From this, one could conclude that the French king could, and should, install a primate (on the ominous models of the patriarch of Constantinople, or the archbishops of Canterbury and York) who would take over all papal jurisdiction in France—this was a course of action always hinted at, but never directly mentioned by French governments during crises in relations with the papacy.[58] This pattern of logical conclusions always ready to be drawn, but never quite able to be stated, is characteristic of Gallican jurisdictional thought.

Etienne Pasquier developed the notion of jurisdictional territoriality most consistently, within the limits of a reasonably orthodox Catholicism. For Pasquier, the foundational moment of the Church was the missionary mandate to the disciples, which instituted territorial division. The entire ecclesiastical hierarchy developed organically from this one imperative, in harmony with, but causally separated from, the institutions of Jesus' ministry: "thereafter in imitation of that holy *police*, the Christian religion transplanting itself, and necessity requiring various ministers . . . difference began little by little to be established therein." The first of these differences was between the episcopal and priestly offices, with the latter originally a territorial jurisdiction within the former; this condition was corrupted at a later date by "our bishops by their avarice." This was followed by the subordination of some episcopal sees to others, a process oddly assimilated to rhetorical exercise and civic virtue on a republican model. The apostles

had a very familiar custom, for having undertaken to win over all the world by their holy exhortations, they were accustomed to delegate the most capable and sufficient to the principal towns of each province. From which comes the ecclesiastical *police* whereby our Church being divided into patriarchs, archbishops, and bishops, you see the names of patriarchates and archbishoprics assigned to those cities where temporal power was settled.[59]

---

les attentats, usurpations, & excommunications des Papes de Rome (s.l., 1592), 268, 270. This tract was printed outside of France—probably at Heidelberg.

58. The only fully explicit call for such a move I have been able to locate is in a very obscure memoir from the reign of Henri III, "Que le Roy est souverain pontife en L'Eglise Gallicane," BN fr. 6396, fols. 98–135, written by a self-identified Protestant but theologically closest to old-fashioned Henrician Anglo-Catholicism. During the crisis of 1551, there had been rumors that the Cardinal de Lorraine would be made primate; in the 1590s, the name of Reginaud de Beaune was mentioned, and in the 1630s, Richelieu seems to have deliberately encouraged rumors that he was considering taking such a step.

59. Etienne Pasquier, *Les Recherches de la France*, ed. M.-M. Fragonard and F. Roudaut, 3 vols. (Paris: Honoré Champion, 1996), 1:514–15.

Coquille made much the same point when he said that "when the city of Rome commanded the entire world, the pope, being elected at Rome, was recognized as sovereign."[60] This was not meant to demonstrate the illegitimacy of Roman headship per se; as Servin remarked in the plea quoted above, à propos of the pretensions of Constantinople under the Byzantine Empire, "it was most reasonable that the old customs should be maintained for the reverence of antiquity."[61] What is particularly striking in this thought, though, is the degree to which the ecclesiastical constitution had come to resemble simple contigent custom, a second and secondary nature, rather than (as it was for Gerson) a direct or indirect emanation of divine Perfection.

This process of redefinition of the Church (situated uncomfortably between naturalization and denaturing) tended practically to result in a drastic curtailment of the jurisdictional reach of the hierarchy which, after all, had grown out of and easily sank back toward the purely political. Thus, in the anonymous tract *De la puissance royale et sacerdotale*, the decay of territoriality within the diocese exposed the Church's pretensions:

[P]romotion to orders has been separated and disjoined from the provision of benefices, which were formerly done together [whence] it has happened that what formerly was spiritual in the provision of titles and benefices, that is to say the promotion to ecclesiastical orders which may not be done by the laity has been separated from the collation of benefices . . . which is purely *de facto*.

This kind of deconstruction of the ecclesiastical body had the highly typical corollary that what remained supernatural, namely, the power of order, was locked up within the clergy. The conferral of Holy Orders is "spiritual, as is baptism, and other sacraments of the administration of which the laity are incapable."[62] In an error not untypical of the Gallican jurists, this was precisely backward: of all the sacraments, it was only Baptism that could (under certain circumstances) be administered by either the clergy or the laity.[63]

If one recalls that already in 1551 du Tillet had claimed that harmonious

---

60. Guy Coquille, *Œuvres*, vol. 1 (Paris: Guillaume de Luyne et al., 1665), 200.

61. Servin, *Plaidoyez*, 2: fol. 57r. Recall the discussion of Servin's very real reverence for ecclesiastical antiquity in Chapter 1, above.

62. *De la puissance*, 174–75.

63. On the administration of the sacrament of Baptism, see, e.g., Joannes Paulus Lancelotus, *Institutionum juris canonici*, in *Corpus juris canonici emendatum et notis illustratum* (Lyons, France: n.p., 1614), separately numbered: "Cura baptizandi ad solis sacerdotes spectat, sed ex causam neceßitatis quilibet potest baptizare" (col. 45). The sacrament of Matrimony, of course, could (in the Roman rite) be administered *only* by the laity, a point Louis Servin consistently failed to grasp in his writings on marriage law.

relations between Church and state began to break down with the decay of commensality between bishops and their clergy, and furthermore if one notes that the theorists of conciliarism had based some of their most important arguments on the idea that episcopal jurisdiction was derived from the diocesan chapter at election, a pattern begins to emerge.[64] The erudite Gallicans clearly preferred to think of territorial division in itself as the root of all ecclesiastical jurisdiction and, at the limit, of the visible Church itself. In this way the ecclesiastical *police* could be looked at as a historically contingent, but naturalized, political phenomenon essentially equivalent to the secular state. The question of what divine authority the visible Church carried could be deferred, though not resolved: without denying that in general terms that authority had been instituted by Christ, the Gallican jurists seem to have thought that its specific forms, having developed within the temporal sphere and according to its rules, should properly be judged by the same criteria as were the forms of state authority.

Thus, anything that threatened the derivation of ecclesiastical jurisdiction from the territorial unit as, for example, the decay of community between bishop and chapter, or, more seriously, an overweening and absolutist papacy, could only be signs of the corruption (in its full technical sense) of the Church. With this in mind, it becomes easier to understand the seemingly contradictory attitudes toward the integrity of diocesan jurisdiction shown by du Mesnil and du Vair at the beginning of this chapter. On the one hand, restructuring a diocese according to an illegitimate and innovative alteration of secular jurisdiction was exactly as dangerous as any other political innovation and could only be expected to result in disaster. On the other hand, the basis of ecclesiastical jurisdiction was no different from, and in an important way secondary to, its secular counterpart, so that where a fully legitimate secular boundary conflicted with an ecclesiastical territory, it was perfectly valid that the latter should cede to the former.

In a plea on behalf of the University of Paris in 1583 Simon Marion (later Servin's colleague as *avocat du roi* and maternal grandfather of the great

---

64. See Brian Tierney, *Foundations of the Conciliar Theory: The Contribution of the Medieval Canonists from Gratian to the Great Schism* (Cambridge, U.K.: Cambridge University Press, 1955), 243 and passim. The *ordinary* power of bishops was derived from their episcopal consecration at the hands of other bishops. The importance of episcopal election to conciliar ecclesiology (besides its legislation at Basel) doubtless does much to explain the erudite Gallicans' defense of that institution in the face of political reality, though they themselves may well not have understood the connection in detail.

Jansenist clan of the Arnaulds) alluded to the idea that the constitutional development of the Church was bound up with that of the Roman Empire. He did so, however, to make a somewhat different point than did the jurists we have just considered. "In fact," he said, "when the seat of temporal power ceased to be [in Rome] that of the Church commenced, by a rich exchange of material for spiritual arms, of bodies for souls, and of the earth for heaven."[65] In this case the necessary condition for the establishment of ecclesiastical jurisdiction seems to be not the presence, but the absence, of Roman power. One potential problem with an identification between secular and ecclesiastical territoriality was that if taken far enough the latter might threaten to take over the former by a kind of *translatio imperii* from the emperors to the popes. According to Roman law, after all, jurisdiction (at least usually) included *imperium*. Thus, to make their historicized account of ecclesiastical polity serve the political ends for which it was intended, the erudite Gallicans had to show not only that the jurisdiction of the Church was installed by the historical configuration of secular authority, but that it did not include the kind of coercive force that might allow it to displace that authority. As Marion suggested, they did this by a kind of *Aufhebung* whereby the power of the Church was identified as immaterial, spiritual, and not of this world.

The jurisprudential aspects of that process can conveniently be traced in the case that Julien Peleus, with whom we began this chapter, used to illustrate them. The case, of no particular political import and argued by an anonymous substitute for the *avocat général*, was one of those matters of honor that clogged early modern dockets. A royal judge, Jean Bonnefoy (the elder), who had some reputation as a neo-Latin poet and was in general a good example of the ideal humanist magistrate, had been assaulted by a cleric. His assailant claimed the privilege of being handed over for trial to the ecclesiastical courts. He eventually took the case on appeal to the Parlement of Paris. The substitute for the *avocat du roi* argued that the appellant was in no way entitled to the privilege he claimed, since insulting a royal judge was a direct attack on royal justice itself and a patent abuse of the ecclesiastical state. In making such an argument he was well within a long tradition of French jurisprudence, which had reserved all attacks on the regalian rights to the king's own courts.

65. Simon Marion, *Plaidoyez* (Paris: Pierre le Mur, 1620), 3 (plea of 14 March 1583). The issue was the validity of a self-proclaimed papal monopoly on printing breviaries. Like those of Peleus and Servin, this collection of Marion's pleas was led off by a case involving the extent of ecclesiastical jurisdiction.

To support his contention that the appellant's case was groundless, the substitute attempted to give an exact definition of the ecclesiastical jurisdiction, showing in particular that by its own nature and by divine law the Church was not exempt from the secular realm. This too was (in France anyway) a relatively uncontroversial position, constituting what is generally known as "jurisdictionalism." Even the Sorbonne supported it, condemning in 1612 the proposition of a Portuguese Franciscan that "persons and goods consecrated to God are by divine law exempt from secular jurisdiction."[66] In choosing where to draw the line, our author was no more original—the Church in itself judges only spiritual matters and inflicts only spiritual pains.

> The duty and power of priests and prelates consists in instructing and teaching the people, administering the sacraments, giving orders, [and] making rules and canons concerning ceremonies, so that all things may be done with order and without confusion. Moreover they may and should decide controversial points of religion to the exclusion of all others.
>
> . . .
>
> Now the Church does not in any way have by right the temporal sword . . . if she enjoys it this is only by the concession and privilege of princes, against whom, moreover, she cannot use it.[67]

Attentive students of ecclesiology would have recognized that this last claim paraphrased the doctrine of the great radical theorist Marsilius of Padua that "no minister of the Church . . . has or ever has had in this world coercive jurisdiction over anyone, cleric or lay, . . . unless the human legislator has conceded such jurisdiction to them, and it is also possible to remove it whenever it seems good to the legislator."[68] However, despite this provocative echo, the reasoning behind this doctrine was purely that of the erudite Gallicans themselves.

 66. *Propositiones exerptæ ex libello cui titulus est Compendium Quæstionum Regularium R. admodum P. Emanuelis Roderici Lusitanis &c.* (s.l., n.d.), 1. The *procès verbal* of the condemnation of these writings is to be found in BN Dupuy 670, fol. 111r. Although this document is dated 1 June 1612, and explicitly calls for the preparation of a list of condemned propositons, the printed list (of which the Dupuys preserved at least two copies) is taken from a 1620 edition of Rodriquez, suggesting that the Paris doctors were unconscionably slow at their work. Richer was fired from his syndicate in October 1612, which may well have suspended action on this case.

 67. Peleus, *Œuvres*, 4, 6. The *arrêt* in the case was issued on 27 July 1607.

 68. Marsilius of Padua, *Œuvres mineures: Defensor minor, De translatione Imperii*, ed. Colette Jeudy and Jeannine Quillet (Paris: Editions du C. N. R. S., 1979), 176–78 (*Defensor minor* 1:7). The "legislator," for Marsilius, was the Holy Roman Emperor.

First of all, the repeated use of the term "order" is important. According to Peleus, the significance of the case was that it established the secular origins of "ecclesiastical *temporal* jurisdiction," but clearly there was a tendency to identify what the Church did independently possess with the power of orders rather than with jurisdiction.[69] A parallel though distinct tendency within juristic Gallican thought identified the proper realm of the Church as the spiritual, as opposed to the physical. This was a perfectly valid distinction in canon law, though one that cut across the distinction between orders and jurisdiction.[70] Perhaps this tendency was influenced by the legal distinction between jurisdiction and mere *imperium*, but the strongest and most visible source was much more purely religious. Our author began his list of ecclesiastical duties with "instructing and teaching the people," only then moving on to the sacramental order on which Gerson, for instance, had founded the entire Church. This is recognizable as the doctrine of the early sixteenth-century Evangelical humanists in the tradition of Erasmus, which stressed above all the Scriptures and the instructional mission of the Church, though without rejecting either sacramentality or institutionalism.[71]

William Bouwsma has analyzed Gallicanism as a kind of international conspiracy among humanistically trained defenders of this kind of religious outlook.[72] This point of view involves considerable dangers—notably, its

69. Peleus, *Œuvres*, 3 (emphasis in original).

70. The distinction is actually somewhat more complex than that, at least for the canonists. See, e.g., Lancelottus, *Institutio*, col. 43: "Summa rerum Ecclesiasticarum divisio in duos articulos deducitur: nam aut spirituales sunt, aut temporales. Spirituales sunt, quæ spiriti deserviunt, atque animæ causa sunt institutæ, ut Sacramenta Ecclesiæ; alteria, & his similia. Temporales sunt, quæ non tam spiritus, quàm corporis gratia pro Ecclesiasticis ministeriis, sacrorumque ministrorum usu sunt comparatæ; ut sunt: prædia, domus & fructus decimales. . . . Rursus spiritualium quædam sunt incorporales, quædam verò corporales. Incorporales sunt, quæ neque tangi, neque sensu corpores percipi possunt: quales sunt, virtutes, & dona Dei, aut quæ in jure consistunt. Corporales sunt, quæ tangi & humanis sensibus percipi possunt. Harum autem quædam sunt Sacramenta." The erudite Gallicans seem to have used mainly the former distinction (privileging the latter would result in a distinctly Calvinist ecclesiology), but at times it seems to have been corrupted by the latter.

71. The literature on French Evangelicism is, like the movement itself, both immense and diffuse. Its influence was greatest in literature, and for that reason it is literary scholars who have provided the most illuminating treatments of it. See, e.g., Gérard Defaux, *Le curieux, le glorieux et la sagesse du monde dans la première moitié du XVIe siècle: L'exemple de Panurge (Ulysse, Demosthene, Empedocle)* (Lexington, Ky.: French Forum Publishers, 1982); and Augustin Renaudet, *Préréforme et humanisme à Paris pendant les premières guerres de religion (1494–1517)* (Paris: Honoré Champion, 1916).

72. William Bouwsma, "Gallicanism and the Nature of Christendom," in *Renaissance Stud-*

tendency to take at face value the Gallicans' ideas about their Romanist opponents—but Bouwsma is quite right to point out its centrality to any explanation of the way in which Gallicans spiritualized the Church. Unfortunately, it is easier to make such general statements than to point to any details, for few sources allow us to approach the strictly religious thought of the Gallican jurists—particularly those of the later school who, we have said, were deeply unwilling to criticize the orthodoxy of the Roman Church. Pierre Pithou, however, left a set of very curious prayers he apparently composed for himself, consisting of various biblical, patristic, and liturgical texts arranged under the headings "faith, hope, and charity."[73] The texts are notable for their conservatism ("what is earlier is more true") and their tendency toward the theology of *docta ignorantia* favored by the northern humanists. A collection of prayers for the king of France "from an old sacred codex" tacked on to the end either indicate an exceptional degree of personal spiritual involvement with the royal cult or, more likely, the results of scholarship undertaken for a distinct political purpose.[74] Pithou's typicality is questionable—he converted from Protestantism fairly late in life—but the overall impression left by this piece confirms the picture of a historicized humanist Evangelicism.

In fact, the one opinion about the way in which contemporary religious life should be changed that one can comfortably attribute to erudite Gallican opinion in general is that it should be more biblicized. Practically all surviving religious writing by erudite Gallicans, aside from Pithou's patristic excursus, is closely based on the Bible. J.-A. de Thou wrote a poetic commentary on Job, for example, while Servin translated part of the Song of Songs into Latin verse.[75] What is more, the Parlement of Paris at least had

---

ies in Honor of Hans Baron, ed. Anthony Molho and John A. Tedeschi (Florence: G. C. Sansoni, 1971), 811–30; which must be read in the context of Bouwsma's idea of Renaissance (i.e., Evangelical) religiosity, in his *Venice*, 27–33—as, the Church's "peculiar responsibilities, the preaching of the Gospel and the administration of the sacraments, were generally entrusted to the clergy under the spiritual leadership of the pope. But the essence of the church, on this, its highest level, was precisely its spirituality" (30). The erudite Gallicans, however, never developed a theory of the Church as *purely* spiritual.

73. Pierre Pithou, "Comes Theologus sive spicilegium ex sacra messe," in *Opera sacra, juridica, historica, miscellanea* (Paris: Sebastien Cramoisy, 1609).

74. Pithou, "Comes," 43, 69. On *docta ignorantia*, see, e.g., 42: "Melius & utilius est idiotam & parum scientiem existere, ac per charitatem proximum fieri Dei, quàm putare multum scire, & in Deum blasphemam inveniri." See also Defaux, *Le curieux*, passim. This was most likely redacted early in the reign of Henri IV when, as we shall see, enforcing prayers for the king became a significant political issue.

75. Jacques-Auguste de Thou, *Jobus, sive de constantia libri IIII: Poetica metaphrasi explicati* (Paris:

no compunctions about imposing, or attempting to impose, this view of religiosity on the Gallican church, and in particular on the Univerity of Paris Faculty of Theology. As early as 1535, the Parlement had stipulated that all candidates for theological degrees in France should read a certain amount of Scripture.[76] The reform of the university that followed the Wars of the League and was carried out by what amounted to a Gallican cabal, made an increased emphasis on the study of Scripture one of the centerpieces of the new program.[77] On the promulgation of that reform Servin, de Thou, and First President Achille de Harlay all delivered orations in which they undertook to teach the theologians their own business. Of the three, de Harlay put it most diplomatically:

[S]ince then all those religious controversies in which this age is excessively fertile may only by stopped by the sword of Scripture, apply yourselves most of all to that care so that the divine Spirit, sharpened by your genius, may shine forth.... You study the Scriptures rather than histories. Dividing and gathering the thoughts of Thucydides, Polybius, Livy, and Tacitus is hardly necessary for theologians: rather, [their concern is] the testimonies of sacred letters.[78]

The contrast here between Scripture and history helps to clarify the ideological load carried by the biblicism of the *parlementaire* Gallicans. Assigned the realm of the divine Word, ecclesiastics were simultaneously excluded from the realm of historical knowledge from whence the erudite jurists de-

---

Denis Duval, 1587); and Louis Servin, *Poetica paraphrasis Cantica canticorum Salomonis Regis* (Paris: Pierre Mettayer, 1612). It should be noted, though, that neither of these cases was exclusively religious in inspiration. De Thou, as his title implies, was concerned to expound upon the Christian-Stoic tendencies in his thought, while Servin was interested above all in flattering Henri IV, whom he identified with Solomon. Two aspects of Servin's piece are suggestive as to his religious outlook. First, his translation privileges a reading of the Song of Solomon as descriptive of the direct and personal relation of the Soul to God in the Word, bypassing any ecclesiological reading: "Sat per se *Deus* est locutus, olim Per sacros dedit osculum Prophetas: Sat est polliciti, *fides* sequatur: Jam tu Sponse veri, osculare sponsam" (sig. aii r–v). Second, before each paraphrase he gives the original text twice, "secundum Hebraica veritas & vulgato versio" (sig. Bi r), indicating a less than Tridentine respect for the Vulgate!

76. This is discussed by Louis Servin, *Plaidoyez* (Paris: Pierre Hennequin, 1604), 1:95. In fact, the affair was not confrontational; for a full treatment, see James K. Farge, *Le parti conservateur au XVIe siècle: Université et Parlement de Paris à l'époque de la Renaissance et de la Réforme* (Paris: Collège de France, 1992).

77. On the reform of the University of Paris, see Anne Magnaudet-Barthe, "Edmond Richer et la réforme de l'Université de Paris (1594–1610)," in *Positions des thèses soutenues par les élèves de la promotion de 1983 pour le diplôme d'archiviste paléographe* (Paris: Ecole des Chartes, 1983), 143–50.

78. BN fr. 4397, fol. 295v. Servin's and de Thou's orations on the occassion are in Louis Servin, *Actions notables et plaidoyez* (Paris: Alphonse Picard, 1619), 449–51.

The Problem of Jurisdiction 165

rived their own authority as political counselors. We have already mentioned the topos of clerical incompetence in the study of secular history and the role it played in robe historiographical theory. Here we see how that topos could be deployed in a concrete political and institutional context.

It is important to make clear, though, that the erudite scripturalism never replaced, but merely supplemented, the idea of a sacramental Church. It did not, in other words, evolve into a doctrine of *sola scriptura*. As Quentin Skinner has pointed out, Luther's belief that salvation was effected entirely by the direct operation of the divine Word in the heart of each believer, and the consequent doctrine of the priesthood of all believers, led him to repudiate "the idea that the Church possesses jurisdictional powers, and thus has the authority to direct and regulate Christian life."[79] If in practice the erudite Gallicans sometimes came close to adopting this essentially Erastian position, they never accepted the theology that underlay it. We shall see how difficult it was, as long as the legitimacy of order was maintained, to avoid a concurrent necessity for ecclesiastical jurisdiction. This ongoing tension is best seen in the practice of Gallican politics.

One may see how the legal, historical, and religious elements in the *parlementaire* Gallican view of ecclesiastical authority were integrated (or failed to be integrated) in another and less friendly speech to the Faculty of Theology, this time by the *procureur général* Jacques de la Guesle. It was delivered in 1596 in the course of the Florentin Jacob affair, which we shall examine in more detail in the following chapter. For the moment, it is enough to note that this particular oration formed part of the general project undertaken by the *parlementaire* Gallicans after the fall of Leaguer Paris to consolidate their own doctrine while systematically answering, if not silencing, all opposing voices. It was included in many later collections of Gallican documents, thus forming part of the erudite Gallican historical-ideological corpus, while at the same time finding a prominent part in the collection of de la Guesle's harangues, issued to guarantee his place in the pantheon of French eloquence.[80] His pretensions to originality were few—most pro-

---

79. Quentin Skinner, *The Foundations of Modern Political Thought*, 2 vols. (Cambridge, U.K.: Cambridge University Press, 1978), 2:12. On Luther's view of ecclesiastical jurisdiction, see 2:10–14. Calvinist ecclesiology, particularly under the influence of covenant theology, was very different; it could (and did) easily lead to a fairly theocratic ideology. There is no sign that any of the erudite Gallicans had any familiarity with covenant theology.

80. Jacques de la Guesle, *Les remonstrances de Messire Jacques de La Guesle, Procureur general du Roy. Dediees A la Royne Regent* (Paris: Pierre Chevalier, 1611). This volume has a particularly fine en-

grammatic statements about the Gallican liberties one finds in his orations are close paraphrases of Pasquier or Jacques Leschassier[81]—but he accurately reflected sentiment among the erudite magistrates and, in the case at hand, he made explicit much of the heart of their doctrine.

After starting off with a bracing dose of divine-right theory, de la Guesle moved on to a brief exegesis of one of the erudite Gallicans' favorite texts, the saying of Optatus Milevitanus that "the Church is in the Republic, not the Republic in the Church."[82] As he made clear, this was taken to express the temporal and logical priority of secular, territorial jurisdiction. (That particular tag works best if one keeps in mind an argument advanced by Bignon, among others; since temporal jurisdiction already existed at the time of Christ, who "did not come to abolish the law but to accomplish it, nor to take away the rights of nature," it should continue unabated in the Christian era. At the same time, one must not claim that conversion to Christianity caused monarchs to lose rights they had had before their conversion. Such a circumstance would not only be a manifest injustice, but it could never "induce infidel monarchs to join the Christian religion."[83]) As one would expect from our earlier analysis, de la Guesle proceeded to an argument for the purely spiritual nature of the papacy and the Church in general. The early popes, rather than infringing on princely jurisdiction,

> were in truth totally spiritual men, entirely given to what concerned the repose of spirits and the salvation of souls, and totally occupied in the administration of sacraments, by which that salvation is mediated, together with remonstrances and holy preaching which teach the way to that repose.[84]

Here we have the primacy of sacramental order and the stress on Word and preaching admirably combined.

---

graved title page, reproduced in Fumaroli, *L'age de l'éloquence*, plate 21. On de la Guesle's importance in the history of robe eloquence, see Fumaroli, passim.

81. See, e.g., BN Dupuy 392, fols. 46r–50r, where he draws from Leschassier to describe the nature of the Gallican liberties (the ancient constitution of the Church), and on Pasquier for the history of Franco-papal relations.

82. Optatus Milevitanus, "De schismate Donatistarum adversus Parmenium," in J. P. Migne, ed., *Patriologia Latina*, vol. 11 (Paris: Vrayet, 1845), cols. 883–1104, col. 999.

83. Bignon, *Grandeur*, 45, 46. This was the received interpretation of Optatus's text. In his edition of that author published in 1700, the ultra-Gallican scholar Louis Ellies Dupin (who had also succeeded Richer as the editor of Jean Gerson) glossed it as follows: "Imperium Romanum erat ante Ecclesiam constitutam, Ecclesia in ipso constituta est et ædificata, non autem imperium in Ecclesia" (*PL* 11, col. 1000n).

84. De la Guesle, *Remonstrances*, 416. De la Guesle refers a bit later to the Church holding the "clefs ministerialles de la parole & des Sacremens."

It might be objected that this stress on orders and spirituality left the Church not only without *imperium* or coercive jurisdiction (whatever that was), but without any jurisdiction at all. In a discussion that followed of Bernard of Clairvaux's views on papal authority, de la Guesle actually seemed to say as much. Bernard, said the orator,

> concludes that *domination is forbidden to the apostles or to apostolic men*. It even seems that after the example of the apostles he denies to their successors all jurisdiction, when he says that he had not read that they had ever sat in judgment, but rather that they had sat down to be judged.... Also, to show that ecclesiastical jurisdiction is not truly jurisdiction, there is the fact that formerly it was called audience, cognizance, and by any other name rather than by that of jurisdiction.[85]

The point is clear. The Church (and above all the pope) has no right to judge anyone, in the sense of applying a law to a particular case with force and authority. By this logic, the very idea of a visible and hierarchical Church might be called into question, since it would lack both independent internal regulation and the possibility of temporal effectiveness. Moreover, the secular sphere would at the same time be desanctified, becoming something to which the advent of Christianity made no difference and on which the Church had no grip. There is a palpable movement here toward the invisible and otherworldly Church of Lutheran ecclesiology, and toward the purely temporal republic of Machiavelli and Hobbes.

But this was not the direction the erudite Gallicans wished to take. If the logic of their historicism led them toward such a view, the historicism of their logic militated against it. The concept of the Church as the invisible assembly of the elect appears nowhere in erudite Gallican discourse, and as long as the Gallican jurists continued to address ecclesiology from the point of view of the history of institutions, there was really no way it could. At the same time the historical fact that France was a Christian, and Catholic, monarchy remained inescapable. It was more deeply embedded in Pasquier's narrative, for example, than any number of ritualistic declarations that the king might convert to Islam without damaging his legitimacy could erase. Perhaps the monarchy *should* have been able to have remained stable under such conditions, but the Gallicans saw no real way in which it *could* have. The experience of Henri IV's early days must have erased any illusions the Gallicans might have held on this score. This may account for the noticeable hes-

---

85. De la Guesle, *Remonstrances*, 424–25. He was right about when the term "jurisdiction" entered canon law, but it was characteristic of the French historical school of legal studies to deny any necessary connection between terms and legal institutions.

itancy in de la Guesle's rejection of ecclesiastical jurisdiction. Most of it was placed in indirect discourse, with the orator's own voice thrown in only as an aside.

What is more, the erudite Gallicans remained wedded to a much different vision of Christian society. This vision was clear, for example, in du Tillet's nostalgia for an originary unity of purpose and action between the state and the ecclesiastical establishment, and de la Guesle set it out explicitly. He hoped "always to keep a close union between the church and the state, so that those two bodies of which the City of God is composed should mutually succor each other, and that maintaining love and Christian charity between them they should form one body in Jesus Christ his son."[86] This was nothing other than the ancient idea of Christendom, as the Middle Ages had inherited it from Augustine. The *parlementaire* Gallicans had no particular inclination to look back to the foundation of this new society by Christ as the Kingdom of God, nor yet did they look forward to its millennial conclusion. They quietly abandoned most of the traditional language of Church reform based on the collective action of Christian rulers. They even rejected an ideal that for centuries had been almost indissolubly connected with the concept of Christendom, that of the crusade.[87] Still, the central, emotional notion that the Church and the temporal order should be one in their final cause and that civil life would thus be sanctified and religious life realized remained very much alive. To appreciate the constraints that this fact placed on Gallican discourse, one must examine an issue that pushed the antijurisdictional logic of the *parlementaire* position to its limits.

Before concluding this discussion of the shadowy world of jurisdictional theorizing, then, it is in order to visit its murkiest corner: the never-quite-formulated doctrine of the French king's inexcommunicability. This half-doctrine is one of the most extraordinary and revealing aspects of the erudite Gallican ideology, demonstrating in its very silences and inconsistencies much about the structure and limits of that mode of thought and discourse. In particular, this phenomenon nicely illustrates three tensions. Gallican ideology was constructed out of a miscellaneous collection of legal, theological, and humanist components, and confusion sometimes arose about how mutually compatible they might be. The *parlementaire* Gallicans also frequently found themselves in the difficult position of attributing

---

86. De la Guesle, *Remonstrances*, 426.
87. On the Gallican distaste for the crusade, see Bouchel, *Bibliotheque*, 1, s.v. "croisade."

more authority to the monarchy than the king himself felt it politic to claim. Finally, despite its pretensions to a monolithic unity of all right-thinking Frenchmen over all time, the institutional structure of erudite Gallicanism could not, and did not, systematically muffle dissent. The sovereign courts, both in their actions and in their records, labored mightily to produce an illusion of unanimity that in general was only broken in the realm of rumor, or in extreme cases like the Wars of the League. The other pillar of erudite Gallicanism, however—the armature of publication, collection, scholarship, and rhetoric that incarnated the Gallican ideology—was by its very nature a locus of contestation, and furthermore provided a host of textual interstices in which phantom debates with very real stakes could be carried out.

Disputes about the excommunication of French kings were older than the Capetian dynasty itself. The pro-Carolingian papacy had not hesitated, in the tenth century, to use the weapons of excommunication against the Robertian candidates for the West Frankish throne, and at one point some of the Robertians' episcopal supporters had counterattacked with the claim that only a national council could validly excommunicate a king.[88] The fact that national councils never really existed as an institution limited the resonance of this claim, but it remained as an option for anyone who wanted to contest papal excommunication without denying completely that kings could be excommunicated. The problem of the excommunication of kings first achieved genuine European prominence, though, in the aftermath of Pope Gregory VII's excommunication of Emperor Henry IV in 1076. In a pair of letters to Bishop Hermann of Metz, Gregory felt called upon to answer the claim that "it is not right to excommunicate a king," or, more strongly, that "King Henry, a man who contemns Christian law, a destroyer of the Church and the Empire and a creator and companion of heretics may not be excommunicated by the authority of the Holy and Apostolic See."[89] It is not particularly easy to reconstruct what precise arguments the imperialists had advanced for such propositions. Gregory largely restricted himself to providing historical counterexamples of dubious relevance, and posing the rhetorical question "who . . . would esteem himself to be excluded from that universal concession to be bound and loosed by the power of Peter, ex-

---

88. See Odette Pontal, *Les conciles de la France capétienne jusqu'en 1215* (Paris: Les Editions du Cerf, 1995).

89. *Das Register Gregors VII*, ed. Erich Caspar, M. G. H., Epistolae selectae, vol. 2 (Berlin: Weidemannsche Buchhandlung, 1920), 294 (25 August 1076), 547 (15 March 1081).

cept that most unfortunate man who, not wishing to bear the Lord's yoke, submits himself to the toils of the devil, and withdraws himself from the number of Christ's sheep?" One passage does suggest, however, that they relied on an elevated notion of the royal office's sacral dignity. "But they claim boldly," Gregory said of his opponents, "that the royal dignity is more excellent than the episcopal," a notion that he lost no time in refuting.[90] On this question, at least, the Gregorian Reform emerged triumphant, and while the notion of a sacral kingship maintained a popular afterlife in France as elsewhere in Europe, it largely vanished from serious political theory.[91] Thus, when Philip the Fair found himself excommunicated by Boniface VIII a century and a quarter later, his most effective defender, Jean de Paris, in his *Treatise on Royal and Papal Power*, began by admitting the formal inferiority of the royal to the episcopal dignity, relying instead on the intrinsic separation of the two powers to protect the realm from papal interference.[92]

If the two powers were essentially separate, though, each with its own particular sphere of activity over humanity, it would be hard to deny Gregory's jab that anyone putting himself beyond excommunication would be rejecting the status of a Christian. Even the most radical ecclesiological theorist of the Middle Ages, Marsilius of Padua, did not attempt a frontal assault on that view. While, in his *Defensor pacis*, he rejected with scorn the idea that any "bishop or priest or particular group of them," not excluding the pope, "has the authority to excommunicate any ruler, province, or other civil community," this was simply because the power to excommunicate, in his view, came from the civil community of the faithful and its leaders in the first place. Indeed, he held that rulers could perfectly well be excommunicated by general councils, where the community of the faithful legislated for themselves under the supervision of their supreme leader, the Holy Roman Emperor.[93] Since an emperor armed with such powers would have

90. *Das Register Gregors VII*, ed. Erich Caspar, 548, 295.

91. On the decay of sacral kingship in political thought, see Ernst Kantorowicz, *The King's Two Bodies: A Study in Medieval Political Theology* (Princeton, N.J.: Princeton University Press, 1957), passim; on its afterlife, see Marc Bloch, *Les rois thaumaturges: Étude sur le caractère surnaturel attribué à la puissance royale, particulièrement en France et en Angleterre* (Strasbourg, France: Librairie Istra, 1924).

92. See Jean de Paris, *On Royal and Papal Power*, ed. J. A. Watt (Toronto: Pontifical Institute for Medieval Studies, 1971).

93. Marsilius of Padua, *Defensor pacis*, trans. Alan Gewirth (Toronto: University of Toronto Press/Medieval Academy of America, 1980), 293. The main discussion of excommunication occurs in Bk. 2, chap. 6; that of the jurisdiction of general councils in Bk. 2, chap. 21. There is, of course, a difficulty (which Marsilius does not address) in imagining

posed infinitely more difficulties to the kings of France than any pope, it is not surprising that the theories of the rector of the University of Paris found little support in the kingdom he was soon constrained to flee.

The mainstream of French thought therefore remained true to the doctrines of Jean de Paris. Thus, the great conciliarist Jean Gerson distinguished two extreme and heretical positions, namely, (paraphrasing Marsilius) that "the pope and all the Church together may not punish anyone with a coactive punishment unless the Emperor grants them authority," and that "all princes are subject to the pope, of whom none of them may in any circumstances demand 'why do you act as you do,' but who on the contrary can change, depose, or transfer them."[94] In the latter case, though, it was not clear whether Gerson rejected only the "direct" power of papal deposition (which the papacy itself in general did not defend), or whether he was also attacking the "indirect" power, whereby a contumacious and excommunicated monarch would inevitably lose the obedience of her or his Catholic subjects and be deposed, but by the subjects rather than by the pope. This became a major bone of contention throughout Europe in the sixteenth century, and in its most basic form the Gallican doctrine regarding the excommunication of kings was merely a strong rejection of the indirect deposing power. Given the absolute separation of spiritual and temporal jurisdiction, it claimed, a purely spiritual penalty could have no temporal effects. Thus, a character in the *Satyre Menipée*, a *politique* polemic from before Henri IV's conversion, asked rhetorically, "[W]hat laws, what chapter, what gospel teaches us to dispossess men of their goods, and kings of their kingdoms over religious differences? Excommunication extends only over souls, not bodies and fortunes."[95]

A number of commentators, though, went much farther, suggesting that the kings of France were in fact entirely immune to excommunication. It seems as if this version of the doctrine sprang fully formed from the Zeus-

---

how an errant emperor might be excommunicated, but it is formally identical to the problem posed to papalists by a heretical pope, and they never suggested that popes were immune to excommunication. The most common solution was to say that a heretical pope was excommunicated *ipso facto*, something that an emergency council could declare as a matter of fact. Marsilius would probably have favored a more direct right of action by the people against an unsuitable ruler.

94. Jean Gerson, in an undated "Determinatio seu positio de jurisdictione spirituali et temporali," in his *Opera omnia*, col. 270.

95. *Satyre Menippée de la vertu du Catholicon d'Espagne et de la tenue des Estats de Paris*, ed. Charles Labitte (Paris: G. Charpentier, 1880), 219.

like head of the *avocat du roi* Séguier in 1591, in his plea against the papal bulls fulminated against Henri IV. He contended

> that the Church went more than eight hundred years without an excommunication [of a king], and during those eight hundred years it was directed by more than sixty popes, all good men . . . they never made use of this instrument, which has never produced good effects.

He concluded, after a rather conventional account of the medieval conflicts between the papacy and secular princes, that "the kings [of France] have this preeminence, that they cannot be excommunicated. There are eleven declarations of this in the Trésor des chartes."[96] Although Séguier cited no specific authority, it is clear from later writers that the reference to the eleven declarations in the Trésor des chartes was drawn from a passage in Bodin's *République* which, however, claimed that these privileges granted immunity to the realm from interdict, not to the king from excommunication.[97] It certainly was not a privilege Henri had ever claimed for himself, although admittedly his formal response to his excommunication dated to the period before his accession to the throne. Needless to say, it is also far removed from a simple denial that the excommunication of a monarch entails his or her deposition or even (taking the text literally) that the excommunication of French kings pertains to some ecclesiastical authority other than the pope.

It is fairly easy to trace a few of the doctrine's actual sources. The most obvious tributary was the much more traditional doctrine that royal *officers* could not be excommunicated in the course of their duties, both because this would be an invasion of the royal jurisdiction and, presumably, because it was the king who bore the moral responsibility for what was done in his name.[98] There was also a doctrine of canon law whereby a corporation could not be excommunicated, since it lacked a soul.[99] This would apply to the French Crown, which could also be seen as the true author of the official

---

96. *Receuil du plaidoie de Monsieur Seguier Conseiller du Roy en son Conseil d'Estat, & son Advocat en la Cour de Parlement. Contre la Bulle de Gregoire soy disant Pape 14. de ce nom. A Tours le Parlement y seant, en Aoust 1591* (Châlons-sur-Marne, France: n.p., 1595), 2, 6.

97. The passage in question is from Bk. 1, chap. 9; Jean Bodin *Six livres de la République*, 6 vols. (Paris: Fayard, 1986), 1:280–81. The context is a refutation of any papal claims to direct secular superiority over the kings of France. Bodin holds at any rate that these documents are abusive since they grant as privileges an independence that is held by right.

98. See Génestal, *Les origines*, 62. For a statement of this doctrine, see Bourdin's article 6 (Pithou no. 16).

99. For this bit of canon law, see Kantorowicz, *King's Two Bodies*, 305–6.

actions of its agents. The pope, under canon law, could not be excommunicated, for lack of a competent judge, by an extension of the principal *princeps legibus solutus*—though he could be deposed and subsequently excommunicated in the case of heresy or (according to the conciliarists) other high crimes and misdemeanors.[100] On a number of occasions in the Middle Ages the kings of France had received papal privileges exempting them from excommunication by anyone *other than* the Holy See but not, as several writers claimed, by Rome itself.[101]

In addition to the privileges in the Trésor, which they might have done better to ignore, the Gallican commentators cited one other significant text. This was an act whereby the Parlement of Paris had, in 1550, registered papal bulls allowing the Cardinal de Lorraine to found a university in Rheims and granting various privileges to him and to Henri II for this pious act. Among the restrictions that the court placed on the bulls before accepting them was,

first, in that the king is absolved by the said bulls ... from all sentences, excommunications, and censures that he may have incurred, one cannot and does not infer or conclude the king to have been, or now or in the future to be in any way or for any reason whatsoever subject to apostolic excommunications or censures, nor prejudice or derogate from the rights, privileges, and preeminences of the king and the kingdom.[102]

At first glance this seems to be a categorical statement that the king of France could not be excommunicated by the pope, but it is in fact more

---

100. Interestingly, this was a doctrine at least tepidly supported by Bodin, who ascribed it to Charlemagne; see his *Republique*, 6:30.

101. Privileges of this kind, which also protected against certain types of excommunication *latæ sententiæ*, were widely distributed in the Middle Ages; see Vodola, *Excommunication*, 139–40. An immunity to papal excommunication would arguably have been abusive and void since (a) the jurisdiction renounced would have been *jure divino* and thus inalienable; and (b) it would have amounted to pardoning crimes not yet committed. Pasquier, whose command of the archives left little to be desired, admitted (even while arguing for the existence of these privileges) that "nous n'en voyons la constitution expresse" (Pasquier, *Recherches*, 1:643–44).

102. *Conclusions de la tres-sacree Faculté de Theologie de Paris, sur la Censure des livres de M. Jean de Mansencal quand vivoit premier President au Parlement de Tholose* (s.l.: 1615), 13 (*arrêt* of 30 January 1549 [o.s.]). This particular pamphlet was part of a long and obscure exchange between Louis Richeome and Louis Servin over the Parlement's condemnation of Suarez for being soft on tyrannicide. The same *arrêt* is reproduced (without comment) in, e.g., Dupuy, *Preuves*, and *Copie d'une lettre d'un prelat deputé du clergé à l'assemblée des Estats, sur ce qui s'est passé touchant l'article contentieux employé pour le premier au cayer du tiers Estat* (s.l., 1615), 2, where it appears to serve as an example of the outrageous jurisdictional overreaching of the Parlement.

plausible to read it much more narrowly. Gallican jurists held that the prohibitions in the Pragmatic Sanction and the Concordat on papal judgments against French subjects either in the first instance or outside the realm included a prohibition on *latæ sententiæ* excommunication—that is, automatic excommunication without formal judicial procedures. Such arguments appeared, for example, during the affair of the queen of Navarre. Since any excommunication that had been incurred by the king without the pope's explicit knowledge would have been *latæ sententiæ*, the Parlement's caveat was most likely meant to flag and refute this implication. Since the Parlement was given to broad language and refused on principle to justify its actions, it is impossible to be more precise. Already we can see both the degree to which the historical record, supposedly a source of stable and stabilizing counsel, was open to divergent readings and the ambiguity that was to haunt the question of royal excommunicability.

The idea of the king's complete immunity to papal excommunication may actually have been dreamt up to deal with a specific legal problem, namely, the excommunication of Henri III. Since he had actually murdered a priest of the diocese of Rome (namely, the Cardinal de Guise), Henri could not reasonably claim either that his excommunication was unfounded or that it was outside the jurisdiction of the pope. From a practical point of view, Jacques Clément solved that problem before it could be properly addressed. Henri III was absolved *in articulo mortis*, a perfectly canonical procedure by even the most Romanist light, and the issues for his successor were rather different. The official line was that, though Henri IV had been excommunicated as a heretic, he had in fact never been properly instructed in the Catholic faith, and since one cannot deviate from a doctrine of which one is ignorant, this could not be valid. Furthermore, in the end, Henri IV converted and was absolved by both the Gallican clergy and the pope. If that course of action was to be effective in impressing those prelates, ex-Leaguers, and religious moderates whom it was intended to mollify and on whom Henri's government increasingly relied, Henri was almost forced to acknowledge that his original excommunication had had some legitimacy.[103]

If that account is correct, excommunicability was an orphaned Gallican doctrine, never used in the circumstances that had called it forth and disowned by the king when the possibility arose of reconciliation with the papacy. In this regard it was typical of the entire post-Concordat history of *parlementaire* Gallicanism. These circumstances kept the doctrine from affect-

---

103. See Wolfe, *Conversion*, 27 and passim; and Chapter 3, above.

The Problem of Jurisdiction 175

ing jurisprudence after 1595, but they did not kill it entirely. Two programmatic statements on inexcommunicability appeared around 1610. The first was a chapter added by Pasquier to the third book of the *Recherches* in the 1611 edition. Entitled "That Our Kings Are Free and Exempt from the Censures of the Court of Rome," it was inserted in the middle of his historical narrative and made a characteristically historical argument. As Pasquier admitted, inexcommunicability was a "proposition which will seem *prima facie* very bold."[104] He attributed it to the historic dependence of the papacy on French military and political support and implied that French kings might validly be excommunicated by a national (or, presumably, general) council.[105] In essence and insofar as the distinction was meaningful to the erudite jurists, his was a political rather than a legal argument, based on the elaborate account of the interdependence of monarchy and papacy developed through the third book of the *Recherches*. If the papacy and the French monarchy were necessary for each others' stability, it would have been self-defeating for one to call the other into question.

A more comprehensive and theoretical statement of this theory was contained in a long and obscure pamphlet published in 1612 under the name Anthoine Piard and entitled *Apologie royalle*.[106] Piard concerned himself with the entire range of issues pertaining to the independence of royal power as they were defined in the contemporary controversial literature, but the largest part of his treatise was devoted to the question of excommunication. Both the tone and the claims of the *Apologie* were far less moderate than Pasquier's, which may partially explain the obscurity of the pamphlet and of its authorship. Piard based his arguments on a very strong claim for the divine right of (French) kings: "the authority of our kings is ordained by the Divinity, the principal work of his hands, image of his sublime majesty and proportionate with his immense grandeur," and so on.[107] Piard's notion of

104. Pasquier, *Recherches*, 1:643. This is chap. 18 of the final editions, "Que nos Roys sont francs, & exempts des Censures de la Cour de Rome."
105. He cites the cases of Lothar and Philip I and II, excommunicated in this fashion (though at papal initiative) for bigamy. One of the historical arguments he offers for inexcommunicability is that many French monarchs richly deserving of excommunication have gone unpunished! On the significance of that argument, see Nancy Streuver, "Pasquier's *Recherches de la France:* The Exemplarity of His Medieval Sources," *History and Theory* 27 (1988): 51–59.
106. *Apologie royalle. Par M. Anthoine Piard S. du Monguenant, premier Advocat du Roi en la Vicompté de Neufchastel* (s.l., 1612).
107. Piard, *Apologie*, 2. This is a direct, unacknowleged quotation of the opening phrases of Jacques de la Guesle's speech to the Sorbonne discussed above; cf. de la Guesle, *Remonstrances*, 409.

the dignity of the royal office was so strong, in fact, that it determined his entire political theology.

He divided the issue of royal excommunication into three questions: (1) May the pope excommunicate the king of France at all? (2) If so, is it ever prudent for him to do so? And (3) would a valid excommunication deprive the king of his right to rule? Any Gallican doctrine would answer the third question in the negative,[108] while Pasquier and the author of the *De la puissance royale et sacerdotale* had done so for the second.[109] Piard's position on the first was confused—he frequently confounded the various questions he was treating—but he was evidently in the radical tradition of Séguier, and in fact gave the clearest exposition ever of that point of view:

> As to the first point, that is, whether it is licit for the sovereign pontiffs to excommunicate our kings, we say that insofar as they attribute to themselves a plenitude of power in the Church . . . by which they think it permitted to do what seems good to them without accounting for their actions to a greater power, in this manner it is licit and permissible to excommunicate them. . . . Thus, for our kings in their kingdom . . . everything is licit and permissible because they can command by an absolute power whatever they wish, and have their commands executed, but doing so is *to act not rationally but willfully, not by judgment but by appetite.* . . . But if we take as a licit action one that is accompanied by law and reason, we say that it has not been licit for the sovereign pontiffs to use violence against our kings or to excommunicate them, because there is no law, reason, or tradition on which they can rely.[110]

The triad of "law, reason, and tradition" clearly marks Piard's discourse as the one with which we are by now familiar, wherein individual action must be constrained by a natural or paranatural order to which erudite jurists have privileged access. At the same time it remained firmly within a territorial and absolute concept of jurisdiction.

Still, there was a degree of tension between Piard's advocacy of divine right and his condemnation of *plenitudo potestatis*.[111] One factor that con-

---

108. See, e.g., Bourdin's article 5 (Pithou no. 15).

109. The *De la puissance*, 23–27, argued against excommunicating monarchs on the grounds that it had never produced good effects (citing the disaster of Henry VIII)—the sort of prudential argument of which its author was fond.

110. Piard, *Apologie*, 42–43. On the legal basis of these anti-absolutist arguments, see Kenneth Pennington, *The Prince and the Law 1200–1600: Sovereignty and Rights in the Western Legal Tradition* (Berkeley and Los Angeles: University of California Press, 1993), passim.

111. Martimort, doubtless correctly, sees this tension as one of the fatal flaws of *parlementaire* Gallicanism in the seventeenth century; see his *Gallicanisme de Bossuet*, pt. 1.

tributed to this state of affairs was a tendency to collapse the classic distinction between the king's "two bodies."[112] Ralph Giesey and his students have shown persuasively that it was at precisely this period that the traditional notion of a mystical, immortal, and quasi-corporate Crown (to use the English term), incarnated in the system of justice and symbolized by such ceremonies as the royal funeral and coronation and the *lit de justice*, declined precipitously. It was replaced by a very close identification of royalty with the royal blood and the physical person of the monarch, and, at the limit, the doctrine of "l'état, c'est moi." As William Church put it, the legists "had shifted divine authorization from the authority of the king to his person."[113] The parlements were the traditional guardians of the older view of the Crown, and they certainly did not officially or consciously abandon it between 1588 and 1615. Still, the strong rhetoric of divine-right monarchy that dominated the Gallican response to the deposition controversy did not sit at all well with a vision of the king's two bodies, for it was the individual, reigning monarch rather than the monarchy in general who was the principal beneficiary of divine right.

The doctrine of inexcommunicability, especially in Piard's very strong version, tended to deny entirely the king's character as a Christian soul and hence a mortal individual. That a corporate body was not subject to the pains of excommunication was, after all, a well-established principle both of canon law and of Gallican thought.[114] It was from the inviolability of the

---

112. The literature on this subject is large. In addition to Kantorowicz, *The King's Two Bodies*, see Alain Boureau, *Le simple corps du roi: L'impossible sacralité des souverains français, XVe–XVIIIe siècle* (Paris: Editions de Paris, 1988); and Jacques Revel, "La royauté sacrée: Éléments pour un débat," in Alain Boureau and C. S. Ingerflom, eds., *La royauté sacrée dans le monde chrétien (Colloque de Royaumont, mars 1989)* (Paris: Editions de l'Ecole des Hautes Etudes en Sciences Sociales, 1992), 7–17, and literature cited therein.

113. William F. Church, *Constitutional Thought in Sixteenth-Century France: A Study in the History of Ideas* (Cambridge, Mass.: Harvard University Press, 1941), 316. See Ralph Giesey *The Royal Funeral Ceremony in Renaissance France* (Geneva: Droz, 1960); Sarah Hanley, *The Lit de justice of the Kings of France: Constitutional Ideology in Legend, Ritual, and Discourse* (Princeton, N.J.: Princeton University Press, 1983), passim; and Richard Jackson, *Vive le roi!: A History of the French Coronation from Charles V to Charles X* (Chapel Hill: University of North Carolina Press, 1984). Erik Middlefort has detected a similar shift of emphasis onto the physical person of the prince in the treatment of mentally unstable rulers in sixteenth-century Germany; see his *Mad Princes of Renaissance Germany* (Charlottesville: University of Virginia Press, 1995).

114. We have already mentioned the Gallican principle that an officer could not validly be excommunicated for official acts. This could imply royal inexcommunicability if it were granted that the king could take *no* action *apart from* the royal office—if, that is, his private self were entirely *aufgehebt*.

royal office that Piard argued for the immunity of the king to censure: "[W]ill it then be licit for the bishops of Rome to dispossess our kings of their throne, ... and envy [or, invade?] the grandeur of their majesty?"[115] Erudite Gallicans never abandoned the notion that the royal office participated in the sacerdotal, which meant for them that the king was a part of the Church considered not only as the assembly of the faithful but even as the body of the clergy. This idea of sacerdotality, never fully spelled out, can be seen even in Pasquier's moderate theory, which derived royal immunity from the indispensability of the French Crown to the papacy. When Piard asked,

> What do the sovereign pontiffs think they do when they wish to exterminate our kings, excommunicate them, and remove them from the body of the Church, [making it] less than a deformed monster which lacks some of its members? For the king of France [being] the first son of the Church, ... the right arm of the Holy Apostolic See, as the popes themselves confess, how will it be licit for them ... to strike him off from the body of the Church?[116]

he was very much in the tradition of Pasquier's exposition of the mutual dependence between France and the papacy. Clearly this political relationship was more than *merely* a historical coincidence. Rather, the French monarchy should be coequal with the papacy in the functioning of the ecclesiastical polity. One could hope for no more striking example of the naturalization of history, the equivocation between historical development and divine legislation, or the radical separation of the secular from the spiritual jurisdiction.[117]

There is something peculiar about the specific way in which this doctrine confounded the royal bodies, though. The partial or total immunity of the king to excommunication depended on the censure being, as it were, intercepted by his corporate being. This in turn implied a *subordination* of the indi-

---

115. Piard, *Apologie*, 44. One should perhaps read "envahir" for "envier."

116. Piard, *Apologie*, 46–47. This reverses arguments made by papalist theologians, and by Bodin in the secular sphere, that a polity with more than one locus of power would be monstrous.

117. Ecclesiological thinkers agreed that a pope who fell into heresy either was *ipso facto* deposed or could be deposed by a competent tribunal. This was because of the juridical necessity that the pope remain in the body of Christians of which he was the head, and since that body was defined sacramentally, this was necessarily a question concerning the individual person of the pontiff. The doctrine of French royal inexcommunicability might in some sense have been an attempt to avoid having to face the equivalent issue for the French kingdom, whose Catholicity and participation in Christendom were never denied.

vidual to the corporate personality. For one thing, if the metaphysical reality of the corporate king was not at least equal to that of the physical king, it is hard to see how the one could preserve the other from highly metaphysical spiritual penalties. For another, and more concretely, if the individual had absolute control of the office, then his actions in that office should really entail sufficient moral responsibility to incur excommunication in the event that they would ordinarily merit it. This was not an ordering that would necessarily appeal to the *individual* king. The inexcommunicability doctrine preserved the French Crown from external interference—which was, of course, exactly what the Gallican jurists wished to do—but at the same time it suggested that the will of the king was not the most important component of that Crown. This line of thought certainly meshed well with the idea that political action was or ought to be controlled by a historical custom which, like the "corporation sole" of all the successive kings of France, existed almost entirely in the past and which (for Montaigne at least) might effectively block the possibility of action in accord with private morality. It was much less compatible with the spirit of absolutism, involving as the latter did a personalization of the monarchy and a veritable cult of the royal will. A king might well prefer to run the risk of excommunication and damnation while exercising absolute power rather than be the mindless avatar of the historical monarchy. It seems likely that Louis XIII, for example, took exactly this attitude.

Such, at any rate, was the substance of the doctrine of inexcommunicability. It remains to describe in detail its ambiguous place in the textual corpus of erudite Gallicanism and the significance of that curious status. As we have seen, the details of the doctrine were generally not stated explicitly, but rather mixed in with a mass of parallel argumentation and left to the ingenuity of the reader. It was not infrequently refuted, sometimes as an ostentatious gesture of moderation, but, as in the case of the 1550 decree of the Parlement, even apparently straightforward statements of it turn out on closer examination to hover uncomfortably between two contradictory readings. One source even allows us to see such divergent readings under production in the mind of a contemporary reader. A curious pamphlet printed in 1613 by Edmond Richer or his friends as part of an elaborate dispute over his tenure as syndic of the University of Paris Faculty of Theology included an "Advis de M. George Froger, Docteur de Sorbonne, . . . Extraict des notes dudit Froger sur le Livre, *de la puissance Ecclesiastique & politique*," Richer's controversial work.[118] A passage at the beginning of that section reads as follows in the copy preserved at the Library of Congress:

> Mais combien que le Pape [ms.: '†'] puisse de droit special frapper les Roys de France du fouldre d'excommunication, (afin que je n'en entre en preuves plus amples, les privileges concedez par les Papes aux Roys tres-Chrestiens nous le monstrent, par lesquels ils ne doivent jamais craindre, ny aussi leurs femmes, & enfants, le foudre d'excommunication),

and thence goes on to discuss the indirect power of deposition. A manuscript note in the margin reads: "† selon le sens de lauteur et sa parenthese, il faut adjouster .ne."[119]

The exact words of the anonymous annotator are interesting. He or she distinguished between the "sense" and the "parenthesis" of the offending "author." The referent of the last word is unclear: are we to take it to be Dr. Froger, or the editor of the pamphlet as a whole? Since the editor was probably Richer himself, on whose (nominally anonymous) text Froger was commenting, this may be a distinction without a practical difference. That the annotator had in mind the pamphlet as a whole, however (with or without an awareness of the identity of its editor), is indicated by the fact that, while there are no further marginalia in the Froger section, an earlier passage where the editor had criticized for its weak language a papal bull condemning a supporter of tyrannicide had drawn a comment that it "is put here by a malicious or deceived person; given that . . . the Catholic Bishop has severely and promptly censured this evil book."[120] Evidently this reader saw

---

118. *Recueil de ce qui s'est fait en Sorbonne et ailleurs, contre un Livre de Becanus Jesuite* (s.l., 1613). This forms a set with *Recueil de plusieurs Actes remarquables pour l'Histoire de ce temps* (s.l., 1613) and other unpublished material. The handling of the Becanus affair came up during the Estates General of 1615; see below, Chapter 6. Cf. Richer *De la puissance*.

119. Due to the importance in this case of the exact wording, I have relegated my translation to the notes. *Recueil*, 27: "But insofar as the pope may [†] by a special right strike the Kings of France with the bolt of excommunication (so that I do not enter into more ample justifications, the privileges conceded by the popes to the most Christian Kings demonstrate this, by which they, nor their wives and children, need never fear the bolt of excommunication) . . ."; "† according to the sense of the author and his parenthesis, one must add 'not.'"

120. *Recueil*, 24: the marginalium reads, as far as it can be reconstructed, "Ce que dessoubs est mis par personne malicieux ou trompé; attendu que le mot de 'respectivement' est admis esgallement que [illeg.] que ce [illeg.] est [illeg.] faux francois et esprits n'entendant le langage et lobeissance et que l'Evesque Catholique a censuré severement et instament ce meschant livre comme le debvois et en bons termes." Gallicans objected strongly to the practice of styling the pope "universal bishop," which implied that he was the fount of all episcopal jurisdiction.

the entire outlook of those who considered the papacy complicit in attempts to destroy the legitimacy and jurisdiction of the French monarchy—the "sense" of the author—as one that would logically imply the doctrine of inexcommunicability. We might well ask ourselves why this should be so. At the same time, the parenthesis is itself ambiguous. The annotator read it as meaning that the pope had no power to excommunicate the king, but it might as naturally be taken to mean that, since the pope had granted freedom from excommunication to the royal family, he might by a "special right" take it away.

In essence the annotator claimed to have uncovered a subversive agenda hidden, purposely or inadvertently, behind the typography of that pamphlet and, more generally, behind the logic of erudite Gallicanism.[121] There is something emblematic about this claim and the way it was made, for the ambiguity of statements of the doctrine of inexcommunicability is often doubled by an ambiguity or liminality in their textual position. The clearest exposition of inexcommunicability, Piard's *Apologie*, was not only difficult to read, but probably difficult to find. Only two copies survive, though admittedly they were strategically placed. One was in the papers of the de Harlay family, while the other was in the library of the Jesuit Collège de Clermont![122] Piard himself is otherwise completely unknown, and the name might well be fictitious. Even across the Channel James I, defending the Oath of Allegiance he had prescribed for recusant Catholics, deflected responsibility for the doctrine: "[T]he truth is, that the Lower house of Parliament at the first framing of this Oath, made it to containe, that the pope had no power to excommunicate me; which I caused them to reform."[123] In

---

121. The idea that this argument was being carried out by means of deliberate typographical games is not as far-fetched as it might sound. The *recueil factice* in which the annotated copy of this pamphlet was preserved, and which may very well have been put together by the annotator himself—an example, by the way, of the manner in which polemical and historical documents were constructed into locations of public memory—includes a copy of a pamphlet by the Jesuit Richeome against Servin. In the first signature of this copy the word "Jesuites" has been consistently replaced with "Judaisants" or "Jesuates," presumably by a worker in the print shop. We have here a similar phenomenon of two voices speaking against each other in the same textual space.

122. Newberry Library C 7583.686 bears the *ex libris* "Collegii Parisiensis societatis Jesu." The other surviving copy is bound into BN fr. 15733, a manuscript belonging originally to the de Harlay collection.

123. James I & VI, *An Apologie for the Oath of Allegiance* (London: Robert Barker, 1609), 9. Pierre Dupuy buried his (typically ambiguous) discussion of the matter in an apology for his collection of Gallican treatises, which was not published for a further century (*Traitez* 1731, 1: [separately paginated section], 7).

a strange twist, James's own papers preserve an early draft of the climactic political expression of *parlementaire* Gallicanism, the "first article of the Third Estate" from the Estates General of 1614. This version of the article (which, its opponents alleged, was modeled on the English Oath of Allegiance) included the confident dogmatic statement "that the punishment of the faults and sins that the said lord king may commit, of whatever species or quality they may be, belongs to God alone."[124] In other words, the king of France had God alone not only as his secular but also as his spiritual superior. Again, however, this statement immediately became occult, dropped by its supporters from their actual proposal, physically transferred to a heretical foreign power, and even formally disowned. Thus, the Prince de Condé began a public statement in favor of the article by stating specifically that "since Your Majesty is a sheep like the least [of the Christian flock], you should not doubt that you are subject to that spiritual power [the papacy], both to bring you salvation and to cut you off and excommunicate you from the members of the Church if your faults and sins give occasion."[125]

The problem was that the border between the secular and the ecclesiastical jurisdiction, the line that the erudite Gallican project had above all to draw, ran through the person of the king. On the one hand, the idea that the pope had no power whatsoever, even in the forum of conscience, over the person of the French king was the logical limit of the *parlementaire* Gallican quest to delimit and demonstrate the absolute independence of the secular sphere. At this point, however, the Gallicans ran up against both their stress on the fallible humanity of the French kings (in Pasquier, for example) and their faith in the unity of the Catholic Church under the headship, however attenuated, of Rome. Even with its jurisdiction constrained as firmly as could be to dogma, sacrament, and moral teaching, the Church could not be kept out of the political realm, for the fact remained that a single physical body linked the immortal soul of the king and the immortal corporation of the Crown. Moreover, the inexcommunicability of the king would entail the dissolution of any idea that the secular and the ecclesiastical destinies of the

124. This document, sent to London by the British ambassador at Paris in November 1614 and preserved in the Public Record Office, has been published and analyzed by Eric W. Nelson, "Defining the Fundamental Laws of France: The Proposed First Article of the Third Estate at the French Estates General of 1614," *English Historical Review* 115 (2000): 1216–30, p. 27: "Recognoissans tous que la punition des fautes et pechez que ledit sieur Roy peut commettre de quelque espece ou qualite qu'ilz puissent estre, appartient a Dieu seul."

125. Henri de Bourbon, Prince de Condé, *Advis de Monseigneur le Prince au Roy. En son conseil tenu au Louvre, le jour des Roys: 6. Janvier 1615. Sur l'article du Tiers Estat Contradictions du Clergé, & Arrest du Parlement touchant la souveraineté du Roy* (s.l., 1615), 4. Note the repetition of the phrase "fautes et pechés."

Christian world went hand in hand, since the two powers would lose their claim to be the same kind of thing. In short, it would leave the erudite Gallicans in exactly the same bind in which de la Guesle found himself, between an unwillingness to abandon the vision of a harmonious Christendom and the inability to imagine either a deinstitutionalized Christianity or a de-Christianized state.

Thus, to avoid revealing a potential contradiction in Gallican theory, the doctrine of inexcommunicability had either to be abandoned entirely—an alternative against which the very logic of the system militated—weakened, stated ambiguously, or buried. A comparison to the psychological process of repression would not be inapt. Furthermore, just as the process of repression typically is supposed to occur in response to or in fear of a hostile external authority,[126] the tendency of the erudite Gallicans to repress the doctrine of inexcommunicability in its full form responded to the reality that neither the royal government nor, of course, the Church were willing in any way to countenance it. The former relied too heavily on the papacy in external and the prelates in internal affairs to take up such a theoretical challenge in the absence of compelling necessity, while the latter saw in the Gallican doctrine a basic threat to its role in secular society.

This complete subtraction of the royal person from the jurisdiction of the Church, not only in the exterior but even in the interior forum, was necessarily a threat not only to Rome but to the French clergy as well, for in important respects it left France in the position (so hypothetically dear to nonresistance theorists) of being ruled by a non-Christian. It is not surprising that Claude d'Angennes de Rambouillet, the bishop of Le Mans, who took a leading role in the diplomacy leading to Henri IV's papal absolution, in his unpublished tract on relations between the Crown and the Church, very clearly distinguished the two royal persons that were systematically elided by Séguier and his followers:

> When the pope commands the king to believe or to do something necessary for his salvation, he ought to obey . . . and if he does not, he may justly be excommunicated. . . . For in this world kings hold two ranks, one as children of God and of the Church, and the other as king. Insofar as he is regenerated by baptism and made a child of the Church, he is made equal to his brothers. . . . In this quality kings owe obedience to the popes, but when they hold the rank of a temporal king, they no longer owe that obedience.[127]

---

126. The classic statement of this theory is Sigmund Freud, *Civilization and Its Discontents*, trans. James Strachey (New York: W. W. Norton, 1961).

127. BN fr. 15733, fol. 18r, 24v.

Certainly Rambouillet's diplomatic activities on behalf of Henri's absolution would have been rather vain had he not held such beliefs, but at least as importantly to reject this vision of the monarchy would leave the Church with no jurisdiction at all over the soul of the king, and the king with no suprapolitical reason to heed his clergy.[128] It is not surprising that these sentiments would be echoed later by leaders of the clergy: in their broad outlines, indeed, they differed little from what Gerson had taught two hundred years earlier, that "the ecclesiastical power may be superior [to the secular] with respect to direction toward eternal life, as the temporal is ordered to the spiritual, but it does not follow that it has all power to the full."[129] Nor, of course, is it surprising that two such opposed visions of how secular and ecclesiastical jurisdiction functioned would come into conflict in the legal and political, as well as the ideological and theoretical, arenas.

128. Clearly ecclesiastics had, if anything, more pressing reasons than their *parlementaire* opponents not to desire a public and open debate over the limits of excommunication. The Cardinal du Perron refuted the idea of inexcommunicability, though—once again—not in print; see *Perroniana* (Cologne: n.p., 1694), 156–58, s.v. "excommunication." Oddly enough, the *Perroniana* was edited by none other than Pierre Dupuy, the last defender of royal inexcommunicability!

129. Gerson, *Opera*, col. 270.

CHAPTER 5

Gallicanism as a Political Ideology

BY THE END OF THE WARS OF RELIGION, the erudite Gallicans' jurisdictionalism was more explicit, more systematic, and more vigorous than it had ever been before. After 1588, it had been a vital instrument of a royal policy faced with the desperate and seemingly implacable hostility of the papacy and of much French Catholic opinion. As that hostility receded, though, the cooperation between the pope and the Most Christian King that had prevailed with few interruptions since the Concordat of Bologna was quickly restored, leaving Gallican jurisdictionalism once more politically isolated. Meanwhile, the structures of both church and state had suffered serious damage during thirty years of civil war and both required considerable rebuilding. This resulted in an increasing dynamism in each sphere individually, and in a struggle over how the burdens and rewards of reconstruction should be distributed. Finally, the textual, institutional, and discursive consolidation of erudite Gallicanism, together with a corresponding movement among the clergy, made it increasingly likely that local disputes would take on a national and ideological character. The result of all these factors was a noisy proliferation of disputes pitting prelates against the secular courts throughout France. It is hard to judge objectively how this situation compared with that of earlier years. Studying conflicts between bishops and cathedral chapters, which, as we shall see, almost inevitably involved the secular courts, Frederic Baumgartner has claimed that such cases became less common during the Wars of Religion as other concerns took precedence.[1] Certainly that trend was reversed with the arrival of peace, and it seems likely that this was the case for other forms of institutional conflict as well. Beyond such very incomplete views, we can only study contemporary perceptions and the modalities of debate. Contemporaries at least found the level and nature of conflict novel and threatening.

Conflict between the Gallican courts and the ultramontanist clergy proceeded on two parallel tracks, a structure imposed by the structure of the French state itself. On the one hand, an almost continual series of incidents clustered around the monarchy and the consultative institutions it sponsored—notably, the assemblies of the clergy, the Estates General, and assemblies of notables. These incidents involved conscious and explicit attempts by the various parties to influence government policy and the fundamental laws of the nation. This will be the subject of the next chapter. On the other hand, at this point neither the French state nor the French church was truly a centralized system. Thus, almost of necessity, the struggle over the Gallican liberties was also played out in a multitude of local conflicts all over the country: conflicts which, nevertheless, were profoundly influenced by and immediately took their own place within a national ideological matrix. An account of this phenomenon can only be anecdotal, given the fragmentary and episodic nature of the incidents themselves. Therefore, this chapter examines those local conflicts that seem to have had the most prominence in the minds of contemporaries. That is not to say that these stories have no unifying themes. First, of course, there was the national political struggle of which all these conflicts formed a part. Individual incidents took form and importance from that struggle, and in turn influenced the ideological development of the respective parties. Second, the language used by the Gallican side throughout these widely dispersed cases conformed closely to the discourse we have already analyzed. The central importance of custom, the unique role of the magistrates in providing historically and legally informed counsel to the king, the historical tradition from which this counsel was drawn, and the jurisdictional concerns that informed it were all consistently and unambiguously present. This was not merely the theory of a few intellectuals: it was a widely shared, though not uncontested, political ideology.

Finally, the cases we will examine in this chapter are tied together by their place in the Gallican tradition. It is above all for their prominence within

---

1. Frederic J. Baumgartner, *Change and Continuity in the French Episcopate: The Bishops and the Wars of Religion 1547–1610* (Durham, N.C.: Duke University Press, 1986), 102–4. In the cases Baumgartner cites, there is no readily visible jurisprudential trend.

Gallicanism as a Political Ideology 187

the documentary monuments of that tradition that these incidents have been selected, and in fact much of this account is drawn from those monuments. More importantly, the assimilation of Gallican ideology and erudite scholarship meant that such events were quickly and easily incorporated into the Gallican tradition as texts, as commonplaces, and as new sites of conflict; indeed, they were necessary for the continued viability of that tradition, which otherwise would have sunk (as it did at the very end of the old regime) into pure antiquarianism. A political movement that lived and died by precedent—where each case became part of a carefully guarded record and was liable to be fitted willy-nilly by the guardians of one or another institutional interest into an overarching narrative of legal or political change—was particularly likely to confer importance on otherwise minor clashes that might offer an opportunity for or a threat to its development. Some such clashes, even, were not lacking in a touch of romance.

Among the collection of young rakes who fought, gambled, and loved their way through Henri IV's court, François de Bassompierre was far from the least in ancestry and *ésprit*. What concerns us, though, are not his duels, his losses at the table, nor even his distinguished career as a soldier and diplomat. Rather, it is the long affair that he carried on with Charlotte Marie de Balsac d'Entragues. Their relationship began in 1605, shortly after Bassompierre returned to Paris from the then-fashionable pastime of fighting the Turks in Hungary, and continued with a brief interruption until the birth of their child in August 1610. The boy, named Louis after the new king, was Bassompierre's only son and heir (something that proved to be of purely formal interest when both father and mother died bankrupt), but a dispute arose as to the baby's legitimacy. The couple had drawn up a secret contract of marriage during d'Entragues's pregnancy; Bassompierre contended that this had been a fiction concocted for the benefit of d'Entragues's mother and was nullified by yet another secret understanding. About a year later, though, the younger d'Entragues brought suit against her lover in the episcopal court of Paris, denying that the marriage was fictitious and demanding that it be solemnized. Bassompierre later claimed that she did so at the instigation of his personal enemies, though this seems relatively unlikely. At any rate, the case dragged on for at least four years—not, actually, a particularly long time by the standards of the old regime—and produced what was even by those standards a pretty considerable legal mess before finally being decided in Bassompierre's favor.

There was never any real doubt that the decision would turn out that way, because Marie de Medicis, the queen mother, was willing to support him in any fashion that might prove necessary. Bassompierre's influence among the restive magnates was considerable, and his help was badly needed to keep as many as possible of them from revolt. By his own account, he played a key role in maintaining the loyalty of the ducs de Guise and d'Epernon. Moreover, Charlotte's sister Henriette had apparently received a similar promise in 1599 from her lover, Henri IV, suppressed only with difficulty, which was certainly not an incident of which the queen mother would wish to be reminded.[2] Thus, after losing in the ecclesiastical courts of Paris and of the metropolitan see of Sens, Bassompierre was granted an *appel comme d'abus* in the Parlement of Paris. Since d'Entragues's mother was related to the Hennequin clan, and thus to practically everyone in the Parisian robe, Bassompierre sought and was granted an evocation to the royal council, which sent the case to the Parlement of Rouen. Unsurprisingly, d'Entragues failed in a similar appeal against that venue, and in July 1615 the court decided for the appellant. The most notable feature of the *arrêt* is that the preliminary account of the history of the case, normally a brief paragraph, in this case filled ten folio pages in manuscript.[3]

In part this was because of another complication that had occurred in the mean time. In 1614, d'Entragues appealed the decision of the official of Sens to Rome. Since that decision had actually been in her favor, she must have done so with the intention of making a political and diplomatic issue of the matter. In conformity with the Concordat of Bologna, the pope appointed a French delegate, choosing Paul Hurault de l'Hospital, archbishop of Aix. Despite Bassompierre's assertions to the contrary, l'Hospital was a sane, well-respected man and indeed a logical choice to hear the case since, as a former *conseiller clerc* in the Parlement of Paris, he could be expected to know the relevant civil and canon law. Although l'Hospital upheld the decisions of the other two ecclesiastical courts, Bassompierre had no trouble getting the Parlement to quash his verdict.[4] First, Bassompierre's appeal to the royal courts should have suspended ecclesiastical proceedings, and, second, the Concordat specified that (except for nebulous *causæ majores*) an ap-

2. See Katherine B. Crawford, "The Politics of Promiscuity: Masculinity and Heroic Representation at the Court of Henry IV," *French Historical Studies* 26 (2003): 232. This was the kind of mess that made *préciosité* seem like a good idea at the time.

3. There is a copy of the final *arrêt* of the Parlement of Rouen in BN Dupuy 493, fols. 242–47. Copies of its other *arrêts* in the case may be found in BN 500 Colb. 153, fols. 238–39.

4. An official copy of l'Hospital's verdict is preserved in BN 500 Colb. 153, fols. 222–34 (marked "Pour le Curé de St. Germain L'auxerrois," the parish of the unhappy couple). It was also printed; a copy is bound into the same manuscipt.

peal to Rome would only lie after two appeals to ordinaries, and then only if the prior verdicts had not been uniform. Bassompierre even obtained an arrest warrant against l'Hospital and, although it was never served, the archbishop complained bitterly of his treatment to the representatives of the Assembly of the Clergy then in session.[5]

This not very edifying affair highlights the well-known vulnerability of old-regime justice to searches for sympathetic venues and the undue exercise of political influence. It had as a subtext the hostility between robe and sword nobilities dramatically played out at the Estates General of 1614. It took a substantial place not only in Bassompierre's own memoirs but also in two of the major erudite Gallican manuscript collections, those of Pierre Dupuy and Matthieu Molé, and therefore can be presumed to have lingered in the minds of the jurists. Most importantly for our purposes, though, it is emblematic of what had by then become an endemic conflict between the sovereign courts, on the one side, and an alliance between the French bishops and the papacy, on the other. The conflict fed and fed off of both the politicization of justice and conflict within the "society of orders"—both of which, in the public perception, were on the increase. Robe intellectuals had an increasing conviction that a republican and Ciceronian mode of political participation was in the process of disappearing, endangering their own political and ideological position in the state.[6] At the same time, the development of the fiscal state and the growth of a class of *grands serviteurs du roi* distinct from the traditional robe nobility slowly but steadily eroded the political standing of the courts. Sully's ascendancy over Bellièvre in the royal council around 1603 has been suggested as the point at which a fiscal and administrative view of the monarchy definitively replaced a traditionalist and juridical one.[7]

---

5. The outlines of this account are drawn from François de Bassompierre, *Journal de ma vie: Mémoires du maréchal de Bassompierre*, ed. M.-J. de Chantérac, 4 vols. (Paris: Veuve Jules Renouard, 1870), 1:293–99 and passim, 2:2–7. Louis de Bassompierre eventually became bishop of Saintes, presumably with his father's assistance (1:399–400 [Appendix 15]). L'Hospital's complaint to the clergy, which prompted an official protest, may be found in *Collection des procez-verbaux des Assemblées-Générales du Clergé de France*, 8 vols. (Paris: Guillaume Desprez, 1767), 2:284B. The arrest warrant against l'Hospital may have had more to do with the prelate's simultaneous interference in the Estates of Provence, which drew the ire of the government, than with Bassompierre's case; see BN Dupuy 91, fols. 184–85, and BN 500 Colb. 153, fols. 232–34.

6. See *inter alia* Marc Fumaroli, *L'Age de l'éloquence: Rhétorique et «res literaria» de la Renaissance au seuil de l'époque classique* (Geneva: Droz, 1980), 585–612.

7. This interpretation seems to have been originated by Roland Mousnier, "Sully et le Conseil d'état et des finances," *Revue historique* 192 (1941): 68–86; and has been furthered by

On the other hand, starting with the end of the Wars of Religion and continuing for some decades thereafter, the social and political position of the French prelates improved considerably. This was, after all, the *siècle des saints*, and the increased prestige and human resources of the Church could not but redound to its political benefit.[8] Moreover, as the Protestant threat waned, both the French church and the government turned their attention to other matters, notably to a major program of institutional rebuilding and reform. While the main long-term beneficiary of all these trends was the centralizing monarchy, they expressed themselves to a large extent in conflict between the first and third estates. This conflict turned around exactly those issues of the law and constitution, the availability of authority in the civic realm, and the nature and extent of legitimate jurisdiction and sacerdotal order that we have been examining. The quarrel involved the first complete operational deployment of a mature erudite Gallicanism, and it called forth a competing ideology from representatives of the high clergy. It is thus both a key moment in the development of Gallican thought and a perfect opportunity to see at the most concrete level of political engagement the effect of that thought on the structures and function of old-regime governance.

Paul Hurault de l'Hospital, who got himself into trouble over the Bassompierre marriage, would not seem to have been a likely candidate to become a lightning rod for conflict between the courts and the higher clergy. In the words of an annoyed Parlement of Provence, he had "had the honor of growing up in the sovereign courts."[9] He was a grandson of the great chancellor, and his brother Michel—also a *conseiller* in the Parlement of Paris—had served in the hyper-*politique* Chamber of Justice of Guyenne in the early 1580s, later becoming a propagandist for Henri IV. Paul himself

---

Bernard Barbiche, *Sully* (Paris: Albin Michel, 1978). A recent survey of the period cautiously endorses this view; see Mark Greengrass, *France in the Age of Henri IV: The Struggle for Stability*, 2nd ed. (London: Longman, 1994), 149–55.

8. A recent study has detected a considerable, albeit slow and unsteady, improvement in the quality of episcopal nominations from 1580 through the 1630s, with troughs during the Wars of the League and the beginning of Henri IV's reign and the minority of Louis XIII; see Joseph Bergin, "'Pour avoir un évêque à son souhait': Le recrutement de l'épiscopat au temps d'Henri IV et de Louis XIII," *Revue d'histoire de l'Eglise de France* 81 (1995): 413–31. In particular, the influence of magnates on episcopal appointments seems to have declined in this period, with the result that nominees would be more likely to put the interests of their estate (and of the monarchy) above those of one or another faction.

9. BN 500 Colb. 153, fol. 192r (*arrêt* of 5 May 1601).

had been sufficiently royalist to serve at Tours.[10] Nonetheless, he thoroughly earned the tribute accorded to him by the *Gallia christiana* of being "a very bitter defender of ecclesiastical rights and episcopal authority."[11] Trouble seems to have begun almost immediately after l'Hospital's appointment to his see in 1600. A fine old-fashioned precedence dispute in that year over seating in the church of St. Sauveur had pitted the bishop of Sisteron against the presidents of the Parlement in Aix, which issued a decision requesting the archbishop, as metropolitan, to keep his suffragans in line.[12] This was not calculated to make a friend of the new prelate, and indeed matters soon became much more serious. The following year, a priest of the diocese of Aix was convicted of rape and sodomy by an ecclesiastical court which, however, failed to turn him over to the secular arm for punishment. The Parlement rectified this oversight through an *appel comme d'abus* and sentenced the miscreant to be degraded from the priesthood and executed.

L'Hospital, however, refused to carry out his part in that sentence, presumably because he objected to the matter having been removed from the Church courts in the first place. The Parlement then proceeded with the execution, notwithstanding the fact that the criminal remained in orders, and l'Hospital responded by excommunicating all those involved in the execution, citing provisions of the papal bull *In cœna domini*.[13] As l'Hospital no doubt knew full well, this was waving a red flag in front of the *parlementaires*, both because it had long been held that officers of the Crown could not be excommunicated in pursuit of their duties and because there had been an enormous controversy over *In cœna domini* in 1580, the upshot of which was that the bull was not to be published or accepted as law in France.[14] The

---

10. On Michel, see Jotham Parsons, "The Political Vision of Antoine Loisel," *Sixteenth Century Journal* 26 (1996): 453–76, p. 456. It should be noted that Paul's tenure at Tours was marked by a bitter quarrel within the court that nearly involved him in a duel with one of his colleagues; see Maugis, *Histoire*, 2:151–54.

11. *Gallia christiana*, 1:336: "accerimus [*sic*] juris ecclesiatici & auctoritatis episcopalis assertor, in dissidiis quæ habuit cum senatu Aquensi pro jurisdictione."

12. BN Dupuy 677, fols. 60–61 (*arrêt* of 31 January 1600).

13. This bull, so called because it was read by the pope with great ceremony on each Holy Thursday, specified a large number of actions—mostly attacks on the property or the authority of the Church—that would incur *latæ sententiæ* excommunication. The Gallican jurists, who disliked *latæ sententiæ* excommunication at the best of times, found its extension under various recensions of the bull excessively broad.

14. On the excommunication of officers, see Pithou no. 16 (Bourdin article 6): this is what l'Hospital's *parlementaire* upbringing should have taught him. On the *Cœna domini* affair, see Martin, *Le gallicanisme*, 173–81; it is also worth consulting Montaigne's flippant discussion

parlement appealed to the royal council and l'Hospital to the papal representatives at Avignon, but neither of these parties seems to have been at all eager to become involved at this point. Next, the *avocat général* of Aix lodged an *appel comme d'abus* against the excommunications, characterizing them as "so great, so exorbitant, so enormous, so injurious, so scandalous, that one might say that since the establishment of the kingdom, among the greatest disorders that have prevailed, no prelate has been found to have attempted such a thing."[15] Simultaneously, in a very murky incident, l'Hospital held a man accused of involvement with the murder of an official of the church of St. Sauveur prisoner in his residence, thus seeming to arrogate ordinary criminal jurisdiction to himself. The parlement began proceedings to distrain the archbishop's temporal holdings, and within a few weeks l'Hospital capitulated, absolving the officers he had excommunicated.[16]

From this point on, he seems to have decided that nonresidence was the better part of valor, but in 1614 another jurisdictional storm blew up, this time over issues much less grave than rape and murder but nonetheless of great symbolic importance. On a visit back to his diocese, l'Hospital tried to carry the cross that was the symbol of his authority as a metropolitan into the council chamber of the parlement, and when the *procureur général* prevented him from doing so, he appealed to the royal *conseil privé* against that officer personally and against the parlement. The remonstrance that the Parlement of Provence directed to the king on this occasion gave an unusually complete statement of the court's position.[17] According to the court, the authority of the *procureur général*, which l'Hospital had attacked, was a

---

of the ceremony that accompanied the annual reading of the bull at Rome in his "Journal de voyage en Italie," in *Œuvres complètes*, ed. Albert Thibaudet and Maurice Rat (Paris: N.R.F./Gallimard, 1962), 1231. The publication that set off the fight in France was *Litteræ processus, S. D. N. D. Gregorii PP. XIII lectæ die Cænæ Domini, Anno M. D. LXXX* (Paris: Thomas Brummenius, 1580), of which there is a copy in BN Dupuy 493. Similar concerns had arisen in 1536, though without exciting the same kind of public quarrel; see BN Dupuy 423, fols. 107–8 (letter of the *parquet* of the Parlement of Paris to the chancellor, 27 March 1536, orig.).

15. BN 500 Colb. 153, fol. 192r. On l'Hospital's citation of *Cæna domini* and the involvement of royal and papal representatives, see the *procès-verbaux* of various interrogations in the case preserved in BN Dupuy 423, fols. 142–49.

16. There is a copy of the *procès-verbal* of his submission (23 May 1601) in BN 500 Colb. 153, fol. 194. The documents in BN Dupuy 423 include records of various abortive legal maneuvers on l'Hospital's part to fend off the parlement.

17. BN fr. 3888, fol. 157–66: "Remonstrances treshumbles de la Cour de Parlement de Provence au Roy, sur la Poursuite de l'Archevesque d'Aix au Conseil Privé, contre le Procureur general du Roy au dict Parlement, & autres Differens l'an 1614."

particularly important one: he was "the censor of all the orders, at whose glance the greatest magnates of your realm should tremble and examine their conscience." Moreover, it was absolutely necessary to maintain the authority of the parlement in order to assure the stability of the monarchy. The spokesman for the parlement advanced some fairly original arguments for this proposition. In the first place, the orator claimed that the French constitution left to the king in person the administration of "graces, favors, and benefits," while assigning retributive justice to his courts.

In doing so your majesty in the first place is discharged before God for things that you could not take up because of the demands of the government of the state. Moreover, you are discharged in your conscience, by having these things done by persons of understanding and experienced in the legislation, which you cannot be yourself.[18]

Moreover, the king must not encourage "the importunity of the magnates . . . who would doubtless induce you by their importunity to grant them things very prejudicial to the state."[19] Here, the orator attached his ideas about the role of the parlements to the criticism of noble pensions circulating during the run-up to the Estates General.

Two other issues raised in this speech give a more immediate idea of the roots of this kind of imbroglio. The first was a stern warning that "it is more necessary now than ever to take care, for a venomous ambition has taken hold of some spirits, and has so denatured them from the French humor, that they call what our ancestors believed blasphemy," referring to the *parlementaire* conception of the Gallican liberties.[20] This went to the heart of what separated the Gallican and ultramontanist parties: the former believed that a substantial, organized party was seeking to destroy the ecclesiological consensus on which the stability of the French monarchy had always depended, the latter that a similar party sought to foment schism under the color of patriotism. The other key passage was a throwaway comment on l'Hospital's original offense in attempting to bring his cross into the parlement: "[H]e cannot even carry it in the chapter of his church, because his jurisdiction there is not sole, but shared with his chapter; to the point where

---

18. BN fr. 3888, fols. 162r, 163v. The reference is obviously to the doctrine of the court as the embodiment of the law within the corporate body of the prince.

19. BN fr. 3888, fol. 164r. The Estates requested the restoration of episcopal elections, a strict curtailment of noble pensions, and an end to the venality of offices, all with a similar lack of realism or genuine conviction.

20. BN fr. 3888, fol. 164v.

this very year, when he tried to bring it into the chapter a complaint was made about it, and the chapter resolved that they would not tolerate this from him."[21] One would already have guessed from l'Hospital's imbroglio with the parlements of Paris and Rouen that jurisdictional issues were at the heart of many, if not most, conflicts between prelates and courts. Here we see that in fact concerns over the excesses of episcopal jurisdiction, conceived in highly technical terms, lurked behind even apparently unrelated disputes. Moreover, these concerns seem to have leaked out into relations between bishops and their clergy as well. This kind of conflict between bishop and chapter—sometimes closely homologous with similar disputes between the bishop and secular justice—was more often than not a factor in larger conflicts between prelates and the courts, with significant consequences for the legal and ideological development of those fights.

This level of tension over jurisdictional boundaries between the orders of the realm had not arisen overnight. During the Wars of Religion, some members of the sovereign courts began to develop a real fear that a party within the Gallican church sought nothing less than the destruction of the state. Initially, though, the direct objects of concern were not the (overwhelmingly monarchist) prelates of the realm but rather elements within the University of Paris and the Parisian lower clergy more generally. The earliest and probably the most important intimations of this were the Jesuit and Tanquerel affairs. The former we have already encountered in relation to the career of Estienne Pasquier, and the only thing to add now is that the theme of the Society of Jesus as a danger to the civil, as opposed to the ecclesiastical, order was relatively muted in the 1560s, coming to prominence only in the final stages of the religious wars.[22] The Tanquerel affair, on the other hand, involved the regulation of existing institutions within the French church. Sometime in the fall of 1561, a bachelor of theology named

---

21. BN fr. 3888, fols. 160v–161r. For more details on this and similar affairs, see Jean-Remy Palanque et al., *Le diocèse d'Aix-en-Provence* (Paris: Beauchesne, 1975), 99–101. The conflict described continued until Mazarin intervened on behalf of the bishop.

22. Eric Nelson is currently preparing a detailed study of the Jesuits and their enemies in France under Henri IV. In the meantime, the most recent account of their adventures is Claude Sutto's introduction to his edition of Estienne Pasquier, *Cathechisme des Jesuites* (Sherbrooke, Quebec, Canada: Les Editions de l'Université de Sherbrooke, 1982), 11–121. See also Fumaroli, *L'age de l'éloquence*, 233–46; and the old but thorough work of Henri Fouqueray, *Histoire de la Compagnie de Jésus en France des origines à la suppression*, 5 vols. (Paris: A. Picard, 1910–1925).

Jean Tanquerel defended a thesis supporting the temporal supremacy of the pope.[23] When the Parlement got wind of this, it took action to suppress Tanquerel's theses, with vigorous support from Catherine de Medicis's government. Tanquerel was induced to sign a retraction, and though he subsequently fled, his retraction was read to a full meeting of the Faculty of Theology called for the purpose, which was also harangued by the *procureur général* Gilles Bourdin. This was consistent with the government's action in the affair of the queen of Navarre some months later, and more generally with its attempt to keep a lid on religious quarrels and inflammatory preaching in hopes of restoring national unity. The *parlementaires* were generally willing partners in this policy, but they were not its driving force: many would have preferred sterner action.

The Parlement of Paris's policy toward the mendicant orders throws some light on the development of Gallican politics. Like the affair of the Jesuits, these affairs turned largely on rights in the University of Paris and the restrictions on the regular clergy in that institution—hence, to some extent, on control over the doctrine of the Gallican church. In 1536, the Parlement decided that the general of the Dominicans had no right to interfere in decisions about which members of that order would sit for the doctorate of theology, basing their decision on the papal privileges of the Parisian Jacobins.[24] In 1552, the same court agreed to register a papal bull doubling the number of Franciscans who could sit for the same degree.[25] While the Parlement continued in the second half of the century to uphold the privileges

---

23. The offending thesis was "Ecclesia, cujus solus Papa Christi Vicarius Monarcha spiritualem & secularem habens potestatem omnes fideles subjectos continens principes suis præceptis rebelles regno & dignitatibus privare potest: nec suam hæræsim occultam alteri revelare tenetur." The Parlement summarized it as "Quod Papa Christi Vicarius Monarcha, spiritualem & secularem habens potestatem, principes suis præceptis rebelles, regno & dignitatibus privare potest," clearly interpreting the inherently ambiguous thesis as defending the direct, rather than the indirect, power of the pope to depose princes; see Laurent Bouchel, *Decretorum Ecclesiæ Gallicanæ . . . Libri VIII* (Paris: Bartholomeus Maceus, 1609), 732. Bouchel reproduces (as 5:4:6, pp. 729–33) the *procès-verbal* (12 December 1561) of the execution of an *arrêt* of 2 December 1561. Tanquerel himself was interrogated on 13 November 1561.

24. *Arrêt* of 14 December 1536. There are copies in BN 500 Colb. 153, fols. 120–22, and in César Egasse du Boulay, *Historia universitatis parisiensis*, 6 vols. (Paris: Petrus de Bresche & François Noël, 1665–1673), 6:296–99. Du Boulay also notes a similar case in the same year involving the Carmelites.

25. BN 500 Colb. 153, fols. 152–57 (*arrêt* of 22 August 1552), with the pleas of the parties. The apparent motive of the papal bull was to train more preachers to counter the Huguenots. The characterization of the pope as "dispensateur et ordinaire des ordinaires" (fol. 152v), which would have been anathema to the court in a later period, went unre-

of the local mendicants, it did so with increasingly nationalist and anti-Roman overtones. In a case heard in 1574, very similar to that of 1536 and again involving the Jacobins, the substitute for the *procureur général* complained bitterly of the disrespect the (usually foreign) generals of that order showed for French law and custom.[26] These issues reached a kind of climax with the affair of the Cordeliers, a terribly complex internecine struggle in which the authority of both pope and Parlement were freely invoked by opposing factions within the Franciscan convent. At one point, the court condemned the papal nuncio for having excommunicated a group of Franciscans; the proceeding was important in setting a precedent both for increasingly bitter conflicts over the power of excommunication and for increasingly frequent diplomatic conflicts with Rome. Over all, the Parlement showed a growing eagerness to defend French monastic houses against the authority of the pope and of foreign generals. The swiftly developing tradition of *parlementaire* Gallicanism, forwarded by a traditionalist faction within the mendicant orders, was the most important factor behind this development.[27]

Not surprisingly, the consolidation of Gallican ideology after Henri IV's victory was accompanied by newly concerted and vigorous juridical action against all traces of clerical subversion. This action was carried out, however, on models already in place from the Wars of Religion. The Tanquerel and Jesuit affairs above all remained foremost in the *parlementaire* imagination. In 1595 an incident very similar to the former occurred, the protagonist this time being one Florentin Jacob, whose name suggested the Italian corruption he was accused of introducing.[28] Still, though the Parlement acted on

---

marked. Over the course of the sixteenth century, the constitution of the Cordeliers was altered to give more authority to friars with university degrees, thus presumably increasing their desireability within the order.

26. BN 500 Colb. 153, fols. 164–70 (*arrêt* of 3 June 1574), with the pleas of the parties. On an earlier stage of the affair, see fol. 175 (*arrêt* of 29 March 1582).

27. *Arrest de la Cour de Parlement, contre le Nonce du Pape, pour avoir excommunié les Cordeliers de Paris, & iceux absous à la baguette* (s.l., n.d.): *arrêt* of 29 March 1582. On the Cordelier affair and its diplomatic complications, see Martin, *Le gallicanisme*, 188–96; and, above all, Megan Armstrong, "Spiritual Reform, Mendicant Autonomy, and State Formation: French Franciscan Disputes before the Parlement of Paris, 1500–1600," *French Historical Studies* 25 (2002): 505–30. Armstrong detects an increasing willingness among the Franciscans in the second half of the sixteenth century to appeal to the secular courts, in reaction to centralizing, Observant-inspired reform movements.

28. His propositions were clearer than Tanquerel's: "Huic porro sedi successor, in qua sedet etiam numc Clemens huius nominis octavus, omnium Pontificum maximus & supremus. Qui cum in terris vices Dei gerat, ab eodem esse spiritualia & temporalia non est ambigendum, spiritualem enim & temporalem in omnes habet potestatem. Eique universi Cardi-

the precedent of 1561, there were notable differences in the way it proceeded this time. First, learning from experience, it kept Jacob under lock and key until he had publicly recanted. There is no sign that the *parlementaires* sought or received approval for their actions from Henri IV or his ministers. Nor were they content, as they had been thirty-four years before, simply to elicit a retraction. Rather, they took it upon themselves to judge the theological value of the offending propositions, condemning them as "false, schismatic, contrary to the word of God, to the holy *decreta*, the canonical constitutions and the laws of the realm, tending toward rebellion and the disturbance of the public peace."[29] At the time, the Faculty of Theology was sufficiently cowed that it accepted without objection what amounted, after all, to a judicial determination of doctrine. Finally, where in 1561 the Faculty of Theology had only been forced to listen to a brief and relatively collegial speech, in 1595 they were subjected to a full-dress oration by Jacques de la Guesle on the temporal incompetence of the clergy.

At the same time, in the wake of Jean Chastel's attempted assassination of Henri IV, the Parlement of Paris revived the case against the Jesuits and excluded them entirely from its jurisdiction.[30] For some reason, they directed very little energy and animus against the order most sympathetic to the radical Leaguers, the Capuchins.[31] This order was, for example, the principal target in a series of attempts by the Parlement in Tours and the presidial court of Besançon in the first five or six years of Henri IV's reign to enforce public prayers for the monarch.[32] As late as 1603, missals were being printed in France without the prayers for the health of the king, and in 1606 the Parlement of Toulouse thought it necessary to take action to prevent this from

---

nales, Episcopi, & omnes omnis generis homines parere & obedire, & veluti membra capiti adhærere perpetuo tenentur," and "Domus Ecclesiastica cum duplicis gladii habeat potestatem, Temporalis usum ad bonorum defensionem & malorum exterminium Regibus & magistratibus concedit." This, of course, took place while Henri still lay under papal excommunication: the court could not fail to take a serious view of the case. See Bouchel, *Decreta*, 734 (the *procès-verbal* is reproduced as 5:4:8, pp. 734–56).

29. Bouchel, *Decreta*, 734 (*arrêt* of 19 July 1595).

30. On this subject I follow the information that Eric Nelson has kindly shared.

31. Of anti-Capuchin literature I have been able to discover only the draft of an unpublished pamphlet: "Regles et Statuts de lordre antimoral des Capucins nouvelement establis en Guyenne," BN fr. 15463, fols. 527–30. This does, however, have the distinction of being perhaps the most virulent polemic I have ever read.

32. BN Dupuy 493, fols. 123–34, memoirs and *procès-verbaux*, labeled "Des Prieres publiques pour les Roys." I assume the episode from Besançon dates to the 1595–1598 French occupation of the Franche-Comté.

occurring again.³³ It was not until 1605, after repeated warnings from the Parlement of Paris, that the chapter of St. Martin of Tours conformed to a custom that granted Henri IV collation of the first benefice to open after his accession.³⁴ Even if it did not amount to a crisis, the survival of monarchomach sentiment within the clergy was not a product of the Gallican jurists' imagination. Less rational was the conviction that any supporters of an Italian-style Tridentine reformation must be enemies of the Crown. The premier, though far from the only, representatives of this supposedly dangerous tendency were the Jesuits, against whose reintroduction into the realm the Parlement waged a long and ultimately futile campaign.

Jesuits had at least had demonstrable ties to the League: some other religious organizations seem to have suffered guilt by association. In 1602 Henri himself urged the Parlement of Burgundy to crack down on confraternities of the rosary, which had supposedly been vehicles of Leaguer sentiment.³⁵ On his own initiative, Servin had a confraternity of "blue penitents" from Bourges dissolved in 1601, not merely for continuing the piety of the League but for an excessively literal and materialistic spirituality: "they would understand [the Psalms] well if they took the words *in flagella* for the visitations of God's scourges and for spiritual afflictions, instead of taking the meaning literally and corporally."³⁶

The distressing phenomenon of public displays that combined a show of Leaguer sympathies with a spiritual ideal of the immanence and physicality of divine action was not confined to simple monks and laypersons. The most famous such case was the Marthe Brossier affair of 1599. The public and continuous exorcisms of this supposedly possessed young woman, who had been brought from Remorantin to Paris for the purpose, were supported (unsurprisingly) by the Capuchins; by André Duval, who led the ultramontanist faction in the Faculty of Theology; and by the la Rochefoucauld brothers: Alexandre, the prior of St. Martin de Randan, and François, bish-

---

33. BN Dupuy 493, fols. 138–39, 222–23; the former is an anonymous memoir, the latter a letter of Nicholas de Verdun (first president at Thoulouse) to Henri IV, 21 June 1606 (orig.).

34. Laurent Bouchel, *Receuil d'arrests notables et decisifs, de plusieurs questions qui sont presentées en la Cour de Parlement, & Cour des Aydes de Paris* (Paris: Guillaume Loyson, 1630), 58–59 (*arrêts* of 20 July 1591 and 18 June 1605).

35. BN Dupuy 670, fols. 101–2: two undated letters of Henri IV to the *procureur general* of the Parlement of Burgundy, labeled in another hand "1602" (copies).

36. Louis Servin, *Plaidoyez*, 4 vols. (Paris: Jean de Heuqueville, 1603–1614), 1:227. From his plea for an *arrêt* of 7 June 1601 (pp. 217–34). The case originated as a dispute over a property sale, appealed by the *penitents* themselves, who ought to have known better.

op of Clermont and soon-to-be cardinal.³⁷ Both had been diehards of the League during the wars and could reasonably be suspected of attempting to revive its spirit, an impression strengthened by the fact that Brossier apparently took to prophesying doom for the Huguenots. Brossier's clerical supporters, on the other hand, felt that the courts were attempting to regulate divine action, "complaining that ecclesiastical liberty was destroyed by the actions of the magistrates."³⁸ The matter was not closed until royal diplomacy (with the cooperation of the Jesuit Jacques Sirmond) had foiled an appeal to Rome, and the sequestration of his temporal holdings and Henri's extreme displeasure had brought about the submission of the Bishop of Clermont. The younger la Rochefoucauld brother retreated to Rome, where he remained until his death in 1602.

This is far from an exhaustive account of legal conflict between Gallican and anti-Gallican forces in the four years that followed the consolidation of Henri IV's power, but it serves to show that by the beginning of the new century issues, parties, and modes of combat had been established and were well on their way to becoming conventional. On one side were the parlements, especially their *gens du roi*, and on the other side a somewhat diffuse grouping of the newer religious orders, pious lay Catholics of former Leaguer tendencies, papal diplomats, a party in the Faculty of Theology, and, most importantly, a significant number of French bishops. In the early years of the seventeenth century, one issue above all others brought out the divisions between these parties: the European controversy over tyrannicide. The French part of this quarrel combined with the increasing national visibility of ecclesiastical infighting to radically harden *parlementaire* fears about the stability of the monarchy.³⁹ That political assassination was a major prob-

---

37. See Joseph Bergin, *Cardinal de la Rochefoucauld: Leadership and Reform in the French Church* (New Haven, Conn.: Yale University Press, 1987), 31–34. There is a convenient pamphlet edition of de Thou's account of the Brossier affair from his *Historia: Histoire de Marthe Brossier pretendue possedee tiree du latin de Messire Jacques Auguste de Thou* (Rouen, France: Jacques Herault, 1652). The most enlightening treatment is the classic study by Robert Mandrou, *Magistrats et sorciers en France au XVIIe siècle: Une analyse de psychologie historique*, 2nd ed. (Paris: Editions du Seuil, 1980), 163–85. See also Jonathan Pearl, *The Crime of Crimes: Demonology and Politics in France, 1560–1620* (Waterloo, Ontario, Canada: Wilfrid Laurier University Press, 1999), 48–56, stressing the partisan nature of the incident.

38. De Thou, *Histoire de Marthe Brossier*, 9–10.

39. The best introductions to the controversy are Roland Mousnier, *L'assassinat d'Henri IV: Le problème du tyrannicide et l'affermissement de la monarchie absolue* (Paris: N.R.F./Gallimard, 1964); and John Neville Figgis, *The Divine Right of Kings*, 2nd ed. (New York: Harper & Row, 1965

lem in late-Renaissance Europe William the Silent, Henri III, Henri IV, two generations of the Ducs de Guise, and many other figures, less fatally, could testify. At a very early stage, the question of whether political assassination could ever be justified became inextricably entangled with the question of the so-called indirect power of the pope to depose rulers in order to safeguard the faith, a doctrine that had been invoked most memorably against Elizabeth I (and, by extension, James I) and against Henri IV himself.[40] Just as the tyrannicide doctrine had been a target of the Parlement in the Barrière and Chastel cases and the subsequent offensive against the Jesuits, the court had set itself against the doctrine of the indirect power in the Tanquerel and Florentin Jacob affairs. Through the first two decades of the new century, the Parlement posed very self-consciously as the bulwark of the realm against both pernicious ideologies.

The bulk of this effort consisted of a systematic attempt to censor any publication of the suspect doctrines within its jurisdiction. There is no need here to describe this process in detail as its more interesting episodes have already been ably treated.[41] The ceremony quickly became repetitive and even routine: a new (or not so new) publication would be brought to the attention of the *parquet*, which would profess itself shocked and obtain a decree from the Parlement banning its sale or possession, ordering all existing copies destroyed, and perhaps fining or imprisoning the printer if he or she could be found. The Faculty of Theology or some group of bishops might issue its own condemnation, either in cooperation or in competition with the Parlement. This was about as effective as most early modern law enforcement ever was—that is, not particularly so. If the author was promi-

---

[1896]). Valuable insights may also be found in J. H. M. Salmon, "Gallicanism and Anglicanism in the age of the Counter-Reformation," in *Renaissance and Revolt: Essays in the Intellectual and Social History of Early Modern France* (Cambridge, U.K.: Cambridge University Press, 1987), 155–90; and Albert Soman, "Book Censorship in France, 1598–1607" (Ph.D. dissertation, Harvard University, 1968). There is now a comprehensive treatment of Western thought on tyranny and tyrannicide from ancient to modern times; see Mario Turchetti, *Tyrannie et tyrannicide de l'antiquité à nos jours* (Paris: Presses Universitaires de France, 2001).

40. For a brief and cogent summary of this controversy and the literature thereon, see the recent article of Francis Oakley, "Complexities of Context: Gerson, Bellarmine, Sarpi, Richer, and the Venetian Interdict of 1606–1607," *Catholic Historical Review* 82 (1996): 368–96, and "Bronze-Age Conciliarism: Edmond Richer's Encounters with Cajetan and Bellarmine," *History of Political Thought* 20 (1999): 65–86.

41. On the early period, see Soman, "Book Censorship"; and in general, Perrens, *L'église et l'état*, 1:306–38, 2:195–283. Eric Nelson discusses some of these incidents in his forthcoming book on the Jesuits.

Gallicanism as a Political Ideology 201

nent, like Bellarmine or Suarez, Rome would object to these actions as an insult and an enterprise of jurisdiction. Generally, the government would force the court to rescind its action wholly or in part.[42] The level of change or development in this structure over the years seems to have been minimal during the first quarter of the seventeenth century.

There was, however, a very substantial international dimension to these related quarrels, which strongly influenced their direction. Besides France and the papacy, Britain and Venice were directly involved. The former sustained a controversy over the oath of allegiance required of recusants, which was defended by James I himself, by Lancelot Andrews, and by many others; their principal French opponent was the Cardinal du Perron. Venice entered the lists on the occasion of the Interdict crisis of 1607, in the person principally of Paolo Sarpi, though the pamphlet war was in fact opened by the publication of one of Edmond Richer's works. As Alain Tallon has shown, French Catholics had powerful traditions of negative identification with the Anglican church and (despite Lemaire de Belges) of positive identification with the Venetians.[43] Both of these affairs thus touched on matters deeply felt in France. The international situation rendered the incidents even more delicate, for Henri IV's diplomatic strategy required friendly relations with Britain, Venice, and the papacy simultaneously, in order not to present an opening to potential Hapsburg aggression. While the controversy over the English Oath of Allegiance was in general civil enough not to disturb this policy, the government frequently felt compelled to intervene in other facets of the quarrel, imposing a particularly stringent censorship during the Venetian crisis.[44] Still, it is very difficult to muzzle an ideological dispute,

---

42. On the Suarez episode, see Pierre Blet, "L'Article du Tiers aux etats généraux de 1614," *Revue d'histoire moderne et contemporaine* 2 (1955): 81–106, pp. 83–89. A notable exception to this pattern was the case of Becano in late 1610, where the Faculty of Theology and eventually even the pope joined in the chorus of condemnation. A shadowy incident at the Estates General in 1615 seems to have been an attempt by the clergy to use this example to demonstrate the Church's ability to police itself, something Richer had earlier questioned; see the Richerist *Recueil de ce qui s'est fait en Sorbonne et ailleurs, contre un Livre de Becanus Jesuite* (s.l., 1613); BN fr. 15733, fols. 429–434 (conclusions of the Faculty of Theology and of the Congregation of the Index); and *Procez-verbaux*, 2:182B–184B. Filesac, Richer's successor as syndic of the Faculty of Theology, was the key figure in both 1610 and 1615.

43. Alain Tallon, *Conscience nationale et sentiment religieux en France au XVIe siècle: Essai sur la vision gallicane du monde* (Paris: Presses Universitaires de France, 2002), 185–211.

44. Even this was only moderately successful: both Servin and Leschassier managed to publish Latin pamphlets on behalf of the Venetians, while Bruslart de Sillery offered tacit protection to pro-papalists. See Soman, "Book Censorship," chap. 14; [Louis Servin], *Pro lib-*

since almost anything can be an occasion for its reemergence. This one broke out in any number of directions.

The affair of the Dominicans in 1611 was particularly interesting.[45] In its outlines, this was a replay of the Tanquerel and Florentin Jacob cases, but this time with a much more distinguished supporting cast and a slightly different theological issue at stake. The Dominicans held their Chapter General in Paris on 20 May of that year, and among the celebrations marking the occasion were theological disputations. The Parlement got wind of some papalist theses that a German friar was scheduled to dispute on 27 May, among them that "in no case is the council superior to the pope"—no mention was to be made of papal temporal supremacy, let alone of the question of the absolute temporal monarchy of the pope that had been the crux of earlier cases. Nevertheless, the court ordered the deletion of all propositions "tending to destroy the liberty of the universal Church and overthrow the administration of France," and on the appointed day a *président à mortier*, the *prévôt des marchands* of Paris, several other councilors, and Richer, the self-appointed theological champion of conciliarism, showed up to make sure that this order was obeyed. On the other hand, a variety of ecclesiastical dignitaries including two Jesuits, the papal nuncio, and Cardinal du Perron attended as well, with the obvious intention of seeing to it that the clergy's interests came to no harm. The stage was thus set for a battle royal.

Richer began it by musing aloud that "if the late King Henri the Great had lived, they would not have dared to insert the said propositions into their theses. It seemed as if one wished to tempt the patience of the French during the minority of the king."[46] The prior of the Jacobins, Nicolas Coeffeteau, made a conciliatory speech apologizing for the introduction of the

---

ertate status et reipublicæ venetorum Gallofranci ad Philenetum Epistola (Paris: n.p., 1606); and Jacques Leschassier, "Consultatio Parisii cujusdam, de controversia inter Sanctitatem Pauli Quinti et Serenissima Republica Venetam," in *Les œuvres de M. Jacques Leschassier* (s.l., 1649), 401–55.

45. This account is drawn from a *procès-verbal* of the disputation, "Recit veritable de ce qui s'est passé à Paris, en la dispute publique du chapitre General des Religieux de l'Ordre de S. Dominique, le Vendredy 27 May, 1611." What is almost certainly the original of this document is preserved in BN Dupuy 37, under that title. It was also printed separately. The most accessible version is in Laurent Bouchel, *La bibliothèque ou thresor du droict francois*, 2 vols. (Paris: Eustache Foucault et al., 1615), 1:716–18, s.v. "concile." The author of the *procès-verbal* is unknown. Other accounts of the affair may be found in Armand-Jean du Plessis de Richelieu, *Mémoires* (Paris: Renouard, 1907), 1:158–60; Richer, *Histoire*, 16–30; and Perrens, *L'Eglise et l'état*, 2:34–58.

46. Bouchel, *Bibliothèque*, 1:117.

disputed points. Coeffeteau, however, was a protégé of du Perron's, and had recently intervened in the tyrannicide controversy, contending among other things that "if [kings] depart from their duty and instead of defending the faith seek to ruin it, it is up to the pope to rein them in and to apply his just censures, in order to prevent the evil that would threaten religion."[47] Perhaps suspecting that the Dominicans were engaged in a conspiracy to spread such sentiments (for he was a pathologically suspicious man), Richer refused to accept this apology, demanding that the suspect theses be refuted publicly. No doubt he had arranged for this in advance, and a bachelor in the Sorbonne named Claude Bertin proceeded to argue the conciliarist position, basing himself on the canons of the Council of Constance. This in turn enraged the clerical party. The nuncio and du Perron both contended that the proposition at hand was problematical rather than dogmatic, that it was to have been defended as such, that Richer and his supporters were violating the decree of the Parlement in bringing the matter up at all, and that having been publicly attacked the proposition should now be publicly defended. The *parlementaires* in the audience were opposed to this idea and booed it loudly, but the president of the disputation, Cosme Morelles, did in fact offer an anti-conciliarist argument drawn in its essentials from the hundred-year-old works of the then-general of the Dominicans, Cajetan.[48]

Of course, neither side was convinced by the other, and the meeting broke up amid general dissatisfaction. A few days later a similar thesis was again proposed; this time the court shut down the disputations altogether, and they were only restored through the intervention of the royal government in the persons of Villeroy and Bruslart de Sillery, and with the assurance that questions about the powers of the pope would be dropped. Thereafter, all went smoothly. The author of the surviving account of this incident sided strongly with Richer and the *parlementaires* and faithfully expressed their views both on the extent of the secular jurisdiction and on its importance for the state given the political conjuncture:

47. Nicolas Coeffeteau, *Responce a l'advertissment, adressé par le Serenissime Roy de la grande Bretagne, Jacques I. à tous les Princes & Potentats de la Chrestienté* (Paris: François Huby, 1610 [1609]), fol. 14 r–v. Coeffeteau, renowned for his eloquence, had been appointed as *predicateur ordinaire du roi* by Henri IV (an appointment that made him a subordinate of the *Grand aumônier*, du Perron), and later became bishop of Marseille. Himself a doctor of the Sorbonne, he was a longtime opponent of Richer's. On his life, see Charles Urbain, *Nicolas Coeffeteau dominicain, évêque de Marseille, un des fondateurs de la prose française (1574–1623)* (Paris: Thorin & fils, 1893), esp. 39–83.

48. Thomas de Vio Cajetan, *De comparatione auctoritatis Papæ et Concilii cum apologia eiusdem tractatus*, ed. Vincent Pollet (Rome: Institutum Angelicum, 1936).

The wisest believe that henceforth the council will keep closer guard, particularly during the minority of the king, that no new doctrine attributing an absolute power to the pope is introduced, seeing that it would only serve to make those of the so-called reformed religion more stubborn in their opinions, and to dishearten and discourage the Catholics who shiver to see such plots, which are almost plans to cause disturbances in religion and in the state.[49]

In the end, however, a very large segment of robe opinion remained unsatisfied with the efforts of both the Council and the theologians to arrest what seemed an ever-broadening complex of threatening innovations. At the same time, a largely separate set of conflicts over the details of episcopal authority served to embitter relations between the leaders of the clergy and the courts even further, in ways that would poison the entire French political landscape.

The case of Paul Hurault de l'Hospital with which this chapter began was far from being unique; in fact, it was typical of the relationships between a large number of prelates and the sovereign courts in the first years of the seventeenth century. Some such cases involved the very old question of the extent of episcopal jurisdiction over the regular clergy within a given diocese. But a larger and more important group concerned a similar issue that, while even older, had less obvious connections with the great issues of papal jurisdiction and fundamental ecclesiology: the relation between bishops and the chapters of their cathedrals and collegiate churches. The royal courts had long been accustomed to embroilment in such affairs—Loisel in his "Dialogue des avocats" mentioned in passing a case from the mid-sixteenth century in which the Parlement of Paris had sustained the right of a canon of Chartres to have a liturgically highly inappropriate "Te Deum" sung at his funeral.[50] Such disputes resumed with renewed vigor after 1595. In part, this was certainly due to the influence of the Tridentine reform movement with its emphasis on diocesan life and episcopal activism, partic-

---

49. Bouchel, *Bibliothèque*, 1:718. This kind of case was not confined to the Faculty of Theology. In 1607 the Parlement moved to supress a thesis of Georges Critton, one of the royal professors of law, that was felt to promote papalism; see Perrens, *L'Eglise et l'état*, 1:298. The theses were printed as *Selectæ juris utriusquæ sententiæ, partim consonæ, partim dissonæ* (s.l., 17 December 1607), dedicated to du Perron. It is interesting that the major defenders of papal prerogative within the University of Paris, Critton and André Duval, were appointed directly by Henri IV.

50. Antoine Loisel, "Pasquier, ou le Dialogue des avocats," in André Dupin, *Profession d'avocat: Receuil des pièces concernant l'exercise de cette profession*, 2 vols. (Paris: Alex Gobelet and B. Warré, 1832), 1:147–258, pp. 207–8.

Gallicanism as a Political Ideology 205

ularly as exemplified by Carlo Borromeo whose vision, one commentator has remarked, "became a historical fact only outside of Italy in a Gallican context."[51] In part, it sprang from inevitable disputes over how the burden of reconstruction would be spread after the devastation of the religious wars.[52] Finally, it is clear that the growing importance Gallican jurisprudence assigned to jurisdictional issues was itself a factor in the increasing volume and prominence of litigation over such matters.

An important piece of background to these quarrels is that, by and large, *parlementaires* and canons were of the same social background, and indeed were often the same people, since *conselliers clercs* (who held seats in the parlements reserved, at least in theory, for clerics) were often canons as well.[53] Thus, it was only natural that they should have an affinity with *parlementaire* political positions.[54] For a time, the lower clergy supported the *parlementaires* against their ecclesiastical superiors in the struggle over the publication of

51. John M. Headley, ed., *San Carlo Borromeo: Catholic Reform and Ecclesiastical Politics in the Second Half of the Sixteenth Century* (Washington, D.C.: Folger Library Books, 1988), 23. On the Borromean model in France, see also Marc Venard, "The Influence of Carlo Borromeo on the Church of France," in the same volume, 208–27. For a defense of the originality and importance of a broadly conceived Tridentine current of reform in the Catholic Church, see the review article by William Hudon, "Religion and Society in Early Modern Italy: Old Questions, New Insights," *American Historical Review* 101 (1996): 783–804; and, more polemically, Eric Cochrane, "Counter Reformation or Tridentine Reformation?: Italy in the Age of Carlo Borromeo," in *San Carlo Borromeo*, 31–46.

52. One suspects that disputes over this issue could be found in most of the harder-hit dioceses of France in the early part of Henri IV's reign. Consider, e.g., the case of the bishop of Castres, condemned by the Parlement of Toulouse to "deux mil escus d'amende envers le Roy applicable a la reparation du palais [whether the bishop's palace or the *palais de justice* is unclear]" (*arrêt* of 9 September 1599: BN 500 Colb. 153, fol. 188), after he had excommunicated some members of the Chambre de l'Edit in his city who had tried to force him to reconstruct a church. The young Richelieu first tested his political mettle in Luçon in a dispute with his chapter over how reconstruction expenses should be apportioned; see Gabriel Hanotaux, *Histoire du Cardinal Richelieu*, 2nd ed.(Paris: Librairie Plon, 1934), 1:93–94. According to Bergin, "'Pour avoir un évêque,'" 421–22, dioceses were also exceptionally heavily burdened with pensions in the early years of Henri IV's reign.

53. A quick indication of the interpenetration of the two worlds may be given by the fact that the two capitular deputies from the ecclesiastical province of Sens (which at the time included Paris) who signed a document on behalf of the Assembly of the Clergy in 1604 were an Odart Hennequin (from Troyes—the same name as one of Mmle. d'Entrague's recused relatives), and "Jean du Villier Chancelliart, Chanoine de l'Eglise de Paris conseiller du Roy en sa cour de Parlement de Paris" (BN fr. 2760, fols. 301v–302r).

54. Nevertheless, it does not seem that the social background of a *bishop* made much difference to the harmony of his relationship with his canons. Horror stories run the gamut from a *robin* like Hurault de l'Hospital, through an hereditary humanist like François Miron, to a sword noble like the Cardinal de Sourdis.

the Tridentine canons.⁵⁵ Moreover, this sociological relation was accompanied by a very similar ideological self-conception. The canons of Bordeaux, for example, complained to the pope in 1602 that their bishop did not give them the respect he ought, seeing that among their number were "senators in the parlement, public professors of theology, and preachers of the divine word, in addition to experts on canon and civil law, and teachers of the Hebrew, Aramaic, Syriac, Arabic, Greek, and Latin languages."⁵⁶ This little constellation of attributes—senators, orators, jurisprudents, philologists—is strikingly reminiscent of the self-conception the Gallican jurists had fashioned for themselves as a means of authorizing their own political discourse. It is significant too that the canons' identity as magistrates took precedence over their identity as theologians!

Beyond this, there was a significant homology between the ways in which the constitutional roles of the sovereign courts and of the diocesan chapters were conceptualized. Those canons of Bordeaux, who took such pride in being secular *senatores*, described their relation to their bishop as being "in a way the natural senate of the pastor."⁵⁷ This suggested a kind of aristocratic constitutionalism completely foreign to the legislation of the Tridentine fathers, but that had been considerably developed by conciliarist thinkers, including Edmond Richer.⁵⁸ By the mid-1570s, the upper and lower clergy had

55. See Martin, *Le gallicanisme*, e.g., p. 239.
56. BN Dupuy 594, fol. 199v (Canons of St. André of Bordeaux to Clement VIII, second half of 1602, copy).
57. BN Dupuy 594, fol. 201r.
58. Edmond Richer, in *De la puissance ecclesiastique et politique* (Paris: n.p., 1612), 13, defines the Church as "une police Monarchique, instituee pour une fin supernaturelle & spirituelle, conduite d'un gouvernement Aristocratique par le souverain Pasteur des ames nostre Seigneur" (also quoted on the title page). The monarchic element involves not so much the pope as Christ, true Head of the Church. Richer, like most of his conciliarist predecessors, remained vague on the question of who exactly constituted the Church's constitutional aristocracy. The most developed form of aristocratism in canon law had the College of Cardinals (which served as the chapter of the Roman, and, by extension, the Universal Church) fill that position—this had been Hostiensis's view, for example; see Brian Tierney, *Foundations of the Conciliarist Theory* (Cambridge, U.K.: Cambridge University Press, 1955), 249–53—while the Council of Basel, which contained few prelates, had tended toward an almost democratic view—see Antony Black, *Monarchy and Community: Political Ideas in the Later Conciliar Controversy, 1430–1450* (Cambridge, U.K.: Cambridge University Press, 1970), passim. The lack of a direct connection between episcopalism and conciliarist aristocratism may well have served as a barrier to the development in France of an Anglican-style view of the Church as being constitutionally an assemblage of bishops and dioceses. The English, of course, lacked the French history of a commitment to conciliarism and were thus more inclined to ecclesiastical insularity.

reached an understanding whereby the latter would accept the principles of Trent in return for a guarantee that the status quo between bishops and their chapters would be retained, but as individual quarrels multiplied some form of what would later be called "Richerism" retained value as a reserve position. More importantly, to the Gallican legists, the chapters were an important link in the organic unity of clergy and laity, and a link as well to an earlier and less corrupt era of Church governance. This appeared, for example, in du Tillet's vision of the Carolingian church. According to du Tillet, episcopal jurisdiction originally flowed from and remained united to the geographical circumscription of the diocese and the society (that is, the laity) within that circumscription; the ecclesiastical constitution kept personal ambition sufficiently in check to preserve that unity, not least by uniting the entire clergy:

> There was then no division between the tables of the bishops and their chapters. For the canons had no personal property, and lived regularly and in common. The said bishops did not dispose of the goods of the church without the council of their chapter, regular colleges were not exempt from the said bishops, . . . nor was there plurality of benefices: each minister resided in his administration.

When papal interference disturbed this dispensation,

> good government and the means [of its preservation] began to be destroyed. The said popes divided the goods of the bishops and their chapters, regular canons were secularized, each had his own root and source of avarice, which soon drove out the community and charity of the ecclesiastical state.[59]

This not only degraded the Church itself, but led it into conflict with the secular power. As the guardians of a disinterested and republican virtue in the French state, the magistrates could not shirk their duty to attempt its reintroduction into the Church.

We have seen how these ideals made their way from du Tillet, through Pasquier and his contemporaries, to Servin and his generation. There was a countervailing impulse in the courts—going back to the quarrels of the mendicants and the seculars—to defend episcopal authority as the regular and constitutional jurisdiction, particularly because exemptions were often based on papal grants. In practice, suspicion over exemption tended to fall much harder on collegiate churches and religious houses than on cathedral chapters.[60] Rather than determining jurisprudence (though they did often

---

59. Jean du Tillet, "Traitte des droict & usages du Royaume de France, envers l'eglise & le sainct siege apostolique," BN fr. 473, fol. 2v, fol. 4v.

60. See Servin's pleas in cases involving François de la Guesle, archbishop of Tours, and

so), however, these theoretical considerations were important above all in vastly increasing the political importance of otherwise routine legal battles by elevating them into tests of principle. Three examples are worth discussing at length on account of their bitterness and *éclat*. A case from Senlis led to serious arguments over the nature of jurisdiction by and surrounding the lawyer Jacques Leschassier. A series of cases, particularly the affair of the breviary of Angers, pitted Charles Miron of Angers against his lower clergy and against Louis Servin. Finally, there were the endlessly prolonged quarrels of the Cardinal de Sourdis in Bordeaux, mainly but not exclusively before the parlement of that city.

The most obdurate of the Leaguer prelates—even more so than the de la Rochefoucauld brothers—had been Guillaume Roze, bishop of Senlis. Consistent with Henri IV's post-civil-war strategy, though, he was left in peaceful possession of his diocese after the collapse of his cause, and was even allowed to pass it on after his death in 1602 to his nephew, Antoine Roze. The new bishop showed signs of sharing his uncle's general outlook; among other things, he received his episcopal confirmation at the hands of the pope himself.[61] Moreover, a major legal dispute with his chapter in 1606–1608 suggested that the new bishop lacked the full confidence of the government. While he received a good deal of support from the clergy, the royal council seemed unusually reluctant to back him up, even against a lawyer who cannot have been in its good graces, with the result that in the end he was forced to abandon the legal fray, and eventually the diocese of Senlis itself, in defeat. In the meantime his opponent, Jacques Leschassier, took advantage of the public forum the case had provided to advance some unusually radical ideas about the nature of ecclesiastical jurisdiction, its relation to the power of orders, and the structures of diocesan governance. The main significance of the affair is the clarity with which it demonstrated the fundamental issues at stake between prelates and the courts.

Leschassier presents something of an enigma. Firmly planted within the circles of *parlementaire* jurisprudence—he was a client of the prominent judge Guy du Faur de Pibrac and served for a while as a substitute for the *procureur du roi*—he also maintained an unusually close connection with Italian affairs, most notably as a correspondent of the Venetian propagandist

---

the bishop of Toul (*arrêt* of 16 May 1611), in Louis Servin, *Actions notables, et plaidoyez* (Paris: Claude Morlot, 1631), 406–15.

61. See *Gallia christiana*, 10: cols. 1445–46.

and historian Paolo Sarpi. Whether as the effect or, more likely, as the cause of these connections, he held not entirely typical views concerning the nature of law in general and of canon law in particular.[62] Whether he developed these ideas before or after taking on the case of the canons of Senlis one cannot say, since he published his one full-length treatise in 1606, while the case was already underway. This, together with other material that he wrote during the course of the controversy and in its wake, demonstrated a strong and quite literalistic concern for ancient law, together with a vision of the organic unity between upper and lower clergy more pronounced even than du Tillet's.

The case, which was before the Grand Conseil—the body normally charged with ecclesiastical affairs, but lacking the Parlement's prestige, stature, and, as we have seen, inclination toward Gallican enthusiasm—involved a dispute over when the chapter could issue letters permitting candidates for orders to receive their ordination at the hands of someone other than the bishop of the diocese. That they could do so when the see was vacant was not in dispute: given the frequency of long vacancies in the period, and the constant need for new clergy, it could hardly have been otherwise. The contention was over whether this right continued while there was a sitting bishop, particularly during periods of nonresidence—which were, of course, equally frequent, but during which the bishop would provide a vicar to perform his ordinary duties. One obvious tack for Roze to have taken would have been to claim that the granting of these letters was part of the episcopal *jurisdictio* which, with the rest of the jurisdiction, devolved to the chapter when the see was vacant, and was resumed by the bishop when it was filled. For some reason, though, perhaps because of the generally unfriendly attitude of the sovereign courts toward episcopal *jurisdictio*, he seems not to have made this argument.

Instead, as far as one can reconstruct the matter from Leschassier's pleas (those of Roze's lawyers seem not to have survived), he argued that these letters were either part of or at least intimately and inextricably linked to his power of *ordo*, whereby the sacramental orders were actually conferred. Leschassier replied in his plea and in a memoir entitled "That, by the Ancient and Canonical Liberty of the Church, the Senate Composed of the

---

62. For what little is known about Leschassier's life and works, see Paolo Sarpi, *Lettere ai gallicani*, ed. Boris Ulianich (Wiesbaden, Germany: Franz Steiner Verlag, 1961), lxxii–lxxxiii. Their actual correspondance consists largely of citations of French case law to back up the Venetian position in the Interdict crisis and of reflections on the history of canon law in general.

Bishop and the Priests Together Ordained Priests and Other Clerks." He held, in effect, that the episcopal office was itself largely a corruption. "Today, bishops divide their authority into two parts, of which one consists of those things *which are of orders*, and the other of those *which are of jurisdiction*. Both powers belonged originally to the entire ecclesiastical college," that is, the primitive community including bishop, chapter, and even laity, of which du Tillet had been so enamored.[63] Leschassier believed that the old order was preferable to the modern forms, and that the chapter should and did retain much if not all of the "ecclesiastical college's" authority to control and confer ordination. Lest there should be any doubt about the basis for and implications of this argument, Leschassier wrote (and, in one case, published) two brief tracts on the legal foundations of the Gallican liberties, among which the rights of his clients in Senlis were to be numbered. One, *On the Ancient and Canonical Liberty of the Gallican Church*, addressed to the Parlement, stressed the obligation of that body to preserve the constitution of the Church, a protection due

> to the honor of the Church in general, due to the liberty of the order of justice ... but ... due even more to the assurance, so necessary in these times, of the crowns of kings. For just as there is nothing so friendly to their security as the purity of the first apostolic and canon law, so is there nothing so contrary to it as the corruption and depravity thereof.[64]

It thus tied the issues of the Senlis affair to the general problem of the security of the state.

The other tract, *Against Those Who Say That the Judges of the Realm Should Say and Specify Which and How Many Are the Liberties of the Gallican Church*, developed further a legal philosophy already outlined in justification for the former memoir. According to Leschassier, law in general could not be codified in the way his opponents demanded, because of the nature of its historical development. The continual flux of events, which could never be fully foreseen by the laws, meant that new law was continually taking shape—a process, moreover, that at different times would be the responsibility of different bodies within the polity. This was as much true of the Church as of secular

---

63. "Que par l'ancienne et canonique liberté de l'Eglise, le Senat composé de l'Evesque et des Prestres ensemblement, ordonnoient les Prestres, & autres Clercs," in Leschassier, *Œuvres*, 396. There is a copy of this memoir in BN Dupuy 37, which may be contemporary with the trial itself.

64. "De la liberté ancienne et canonique de l'Eglise Gallicane," in Leschassier, *Œuvres*, 290–91. This was published as a pamphlet by Claude Morel in 1606.

states, where the apostles, the ecumenical councils, the emperors and French kings, national councils, the sovereign courts, and "unwritten custom" had all made their contribution. This is recognizable as the *parlementaire* doctrine of naturalized custom we have already described, where the constitutions of state and church are homologous, not to be violated on pain of chaos and collapse. They are necessarily the product not of some rational and visible legislation, such as could be demonstrated and delimited, but of the continued play of fortune and prudence through a long history. Leschassier did show a greater tendency than many of his colleagues to fetishize laws sufficiently old to be truly originary. He specified that the Roman law was built on a foundation of what "nature and the law of nations had first dictated," while "among the political laws of the Church, the divine or apostolic are the eternal and perpetual laws, the others temporal and provisional, made for human and temporal causes," a belief that encouraged him in the search for early canonistic sources.[65]

What was troubling to contemporary prelates was the clear attack against their authority that Leschassier's entire range of arguments involved. The tendency to style the diocesan chapter a "senate," and to expand its powers at the expense of the bishop's, was of ongoing concern to the leaders of the French church. At the same time, both Leschassier's specific arguments about diocesan governance and his entire legal philosophy deeply threatened the claims of the ecclesiastical hierarchy to a legislative, jurisdictional, or even sacramental role completely independent of the laity or of the lower clergy. The Assembly of the Clergy responded by issuing a censure of Leschassier's plea and his writings, extracting from them eight objectionable propositions of which the first was "that the two powers *of orders* and *of jurisdiction* belonged in the primitive Church, not only to the bishops, but in common to the entire ecclesiastical college."[66] Leschassier appealed to the Conseil Privé against the action of the Assembly on the grounds, first, that it had no doctrinal jurisdiction at all, and second, that pleas in the royal

---

65. "Contre ceux qui disent que les Juges de ce Royaume doivent dire & compter, quelles, & combien sont les libertez de l'Eglise Gallicane, & de quelle authorité elles sont procedees," in Leschassier, *Œuvres*, 295; "De la liberté," 290. As can be clearly seen in his correspondance with Sarpi, Leschassier was a believer in "les pretendües Regles et Canons des Apostres," which even the unscholarly Jacques de la Guesle admitted "ne se voyent point" (from a memoir of de la Guesle's in BN Dupuy 392, fol. 53v; there is also a copy in BN Dupuy 37 alongside the works of Leschassier).

66. Leschassier, *Œuvres*, 337. The censure is dated 18 January 1607. On the episode of the censure and its suppression, see Soman, "Book Censorship," 140–42.

courts were only subject to the censure of the courts themselves or of the king. He prevailed, in a relatively rare clear victory for the *parlementaire* Gallicans over the ultramontanists in the forum of royal policy. It is probably significant that the institution that gained the most was the Grand Conseil, much more moderate in its religious politics than the parlements and generally much more tractable to the royal will.

One of the memoirs Leschassier wrote in the course of his suit against the Assembly of the Clergy made it clear how much what was, after all, a local and highly technical affair had become caught up in the great issues of ecclesiological and political theory and in the constitution of the erudite Gallican tradition. There, he traced "four principal abuses" to which the Church was prone "in France, as it appears from history and from books made by our ancestors on the rights of the Crown," with historical examples. These were (1) the deposition of kings, (2) leveling accusations of heresy against defenders of the Gallican liberties, "which abuse is being renewed today," (3) interdicts against royal towns, and finally (4),

> so frequent today, when bishops excommunicate or prohibit the absolution of the companies of parlements, of *procureurs généraux*, of judges, of *avocats*, for performing their duties. . . . These abuses will never be committed with good counsel, nor by the counsel of chapters, since it is easier for an individual to become corrupted than an entire company.[67]

To Leschassier, his case was just part of a pattern: a pattern of ecclesiastical abuses through history, preserved in the historical record to which the erudite Gallicans had privileged access (largely because they had created it themselves); a pattern in contemporary politics that duplicated the historical pattern but was all the more threatening because of the dangers to which the Crown was exposed; a pattern of political theory, where the shunting aside of learned counsel, organized (both for the chapters and for the parlements) in "companies," led to imprudent action and the decay of public order. To the bishops, it was also part of a pattern: a pattern of attacks on their jurisdictional and sacramental rights. This was not a situation that left a great deal of room to avoid conflict.

The cause célèbre that both generated the most noise of any in the conflict between Gallicans and ultramontanists and brought out most clearly the jurisdictional and philosophical issues at stake was the affair of the bre-

---

67. Leschassier, *Œuvres*, 329–30.

viary of Angers. This was the greatest, though by no means the last, of the disputes that enveloped the tenure of Charles Miron as bishop of that diocese. Miron had been installed as a loyalist of Henri III, being the son of his personal physician, and he immediately transferred this loyalty to Henri of Navarre. The first years of his episcopate were devoted to the political struggle of the Wars of the League, but thereafter he made a pretty good figure of the Tridentine prelate, if not so energetic as some. He introduced the Capuchins, centralized and rationalized the administration of the diocese, and attempted to regulate popular religiosity.[68] This did not increase his popularity with the champions of the religious status quo, including the Gallican jurists.

The name of Miron's legal disputes was legion. Already in 1601 he had come before the Parlement of Paris in a dispute over the attempted reform of a convent of Cordeliers into Recollects. He had backed the reformers, blocking a visitation of the house by the unreformed congregation, who appealed from that action *comme d'abus*.[69] Servin characteristically opposed the reformers, finding their piety altogether Italianate and innovating. He also objected to the support they had received from Rome, "for they can obey the laws of the Catholic, Apostolic, and Roman Church without wandering out of the kingodom ... they, being subjects of the king and wishing to live in the kingdom, should have recourse to this court of France to be governed by its sentence."[70] They were perhaps guilty of being too like the Jesuits— Servin cited against them the decree of the Fourth Lateran Council against the foundation of new orders, one of the cornerstones of anti-Jesuit theory. More immediately, though, they had made the mistake of basing their original case on a ruling by Cajetan, the papal legate to the Leaguer government and one of its most tireless supporters, which the court was certainly not prepared to recognize as legitimate. The Parlement upheld the appeal, although on this occasion it did no more than send the case back to the ecclesiastical courts for retrial, refusing to involve itself in the details of the dispute.

68. On his career, see François Lebrun et al., *La diocèse d'Angers* (Paris: Beauchesne, 1981), 114–17. He was, incidentally, related to the *prévôt des marchands* of Paris François Miron, who also presided over the third estate at the Estates of 1614–1615 and was thus a considerable figure in legal Gallicanism. This is yet another case of institutional loyalty trumping family ties on issues of Gallicanism!

69. Servin, *Plaidoyez*, 1:969–1014 (*arrêt* of 30 June 1601). As in the more famous case, Bouchel was counsel for Miron, and Montholon for the Recollects.

70. Servin, *Plaidoyez*, 1:989.

The breviary case, which came to trial two years later, arose as a direct consequence of Miron's embrace of the French bishops' broad attempt to introduce Tridentine discipline into the individual dioceses. In this case, the events in question went back to 1599. At that time Miron had tried to abolish the local breviary in the collegiate church of Sainte Trinité (not the cathedral) and substitute for it the Roman version as revised by the Tridentine fathers. The chapter of that church, or at least its "plus grande et plus saine partie," appealed the acts instituting this change (which included the burning of some copies of the old breviary) as abusive, and were received by the Parlement of Paris. The case turned not only on this particular action, but also on the way in which Miron had antagonized a considerable portion of his clergy, including the chapter of the cathedral—it seems likely that the canons of Ste. Trinité pursued their case at the instigation of the cathedral canons.[71]

When the case reached the Parlement of Paris, Louis Servin professed to regard it as the most significant he had ever pled. It appeared a few months later at the head of his first collection of pleas (which were otherwise in no sort of order), and maintained that position in a later edition where they were divided into groups dealing with ecclesiastical, royal, and private affairs.[72] Even by his standards it was long, and even by his standards it raised an unholy row, which came to involve the Faculty of Theology, papal diplomacy, and the Assembly of the Clergy. He began his oration with the doubtless hyperbolic claim that "since the establishment of the Christian religion and the Crown of France in the state of the Gauls no more important case than the one before us now has been brought up either in the council of the [presumably Carolingian] emperors or in this Parlement."[73] Servin did not restrict himself to a consideration of the procedural issues at hand. Rather, he developed a systematic attack on Miron's methods of epis-

71. The canons of Ste. Trinité had obtained a ruling from the cathedral chapter contradicting Miron's decision on the breviary, and several cathedral canons were murkily involved in the court proceedings.

72. "Plaidoyé et arrest de la Cour de Parlement... Sur l'appel comme d'abus du changement du Breviaire d'Anjou ordonné par l'Evesque d'Angers en l'Eglise de la Trinité audict Angers" (*arrêt* of 27 February 1603), in Servin, *Plaidoyez*, 1:1–130; cf. Servin, *Actions notables, et plaidoyez* (Paris: Claude Morlot, 1631).

73. Servin, *Plaidoyez*, 1:15. The identification of the political and religious constitutions of the realm, the prominence of the Carolingian constitution, and the implicit valorization of the Parlement's role in maintaining the ecclesiastical and political stability of the kingdom all included in this brief exordium alerted the audience immediately to Servin's ideological position.

copal governance and, more importantly, on the entire idea of liturgical innovation. In the first third of the plea he argued that the establishment of forms of service "are never undertaken except in Assemblies of the Clergy convoked with the permission of kings" and confirmed by them, though "the care of reforming prayers and breviaries is left to the bishops."[74] Considering that such reforms also had to be carried out in consultation with the diocesan chapter, it is clear that Servin was willing to leave very little jurisdictional authority to the prelates; they needed permission from the secular authorities and approval from their hierarchical subordinates, keeping only the hard technical work of reform. This was not likely to prove popular with the French bishops, but in the event it aroused less controversy than the remaining part of the plea.

There, Servin played upon two well-established themes of *parlementaire* Gallicanism: the necessity for pride in the national religious tradition (with the adoption of the Roman breviary "even the most excellent and memorable things belonging not only to our glory, but also to our salvation, will be taken away"), and the naturalization of custom, which provided a philosophical justification for respecting tradition.[75] To bishops attracted by a Borromean reform the former tack was likely to seem subversive, while the latter of course conflicted with the ecclesiological assumptions of the clergy—a situation aggravated by a long digression that seemed to tend toward an idea of Scripture as, besides custom, the only valid norm of religious organization. Most fatefully, Servin enlisted in his cause a resolution of the chapter of Notre Dame de Paris and a "rescript" (his term) of the Faculty of Theology, both issued in 1583, condemning the idea of introducing the Roman breviary. The latter did so with a singular vehemence, taxing Rome with pride and avarice. At the time, at any rate, all of these arguments had their desired effect.[76] The Parlement received the appeal and after Miron's lawyer (the Gallican scholar Laurent Bouchel) refused to proceed further a default judgment was entered for the appellants.

By invoking the authority of the Faculty of Theology, however, Servin had inadvertently or purposefully expanded the scope of an already highly

74. Servin, *Plaidoyez*, 1:26, 38.
75. Servin, *Plaidoyez*, 1:94. Compare Pithou's remarks in his introduction to Salvian of Marseille.
76. The document in question is in Servin, *Plaidoyez*, 1:99–105. Like Servin's plea, the theological document is concerned to valorize diversity of custom, but it does so with the tools of Thomistic theology, arguing that "Deus Optimus Maximus semper gavisus & usus est varietate, ut patet in ipsa creatione, in qua diversitate delectatus est" (99).

charged conflict. The Faculty of Theology was deeply divided, and in this instance the ultramontanist faction was not prepared to see its authority invoked against the Tridentine reforms. Indeed, Servin's highly ideological plea and its almost immediate publication had left his opponents with little choice but to respond, while there were suspicions, and not ridiculous ones, that Richer had supplied Servin with the decree of the Faculty of Theology that he had cited. As early as December 1603, the matter was brought up in the Sorbonne, though both the dean of the Faculty of Theology and the royal council seem to have issued orders that it be dropped. Nevertheless, in February 1604 an assembly of the Faculty of Theology, which consisted almost entirely of doctors of the College of the Sorbonne, condemned Servin's plea as heretical and schismatic, and the decree that he had cited as spurious.[77] The opposing party, including the dean of the Faculty of Theology, disavowed this action. Either at their instigation or of its own accord, the Parlement took up the issue and summoned some of the theologians to explain their actions. The ultramontanists claimed that Chancellor Bellièvre had approved their action. Given the chancellor's Leaguer past and his strong Tridentine sympathies—during the Venetian Interdict affair, for example, he allowed several pro-papal tracts to be produced, in spite of his government's strong and explicit policy of neutrality—their claim had some credibility.

The fact that, despite the insult to its jurisdiction, the Parlement took no action at this point suggests even more strongly that the defenders of the Roman breviary were receiving high-level support.[78] Over the following year, Servin's opponents among the theologians, supported by the papal legate and the Assembly of the Clergy, and with the close involvement of the curia, lobbied strenuously to have the king suppress both the decision of the Parlement and Servin's printed plea. The Parlement, in turn, lobbied just as hard to prevent such an outcome. In the end, though, nothing much happened at all and the matter was allowed to drop, doubtless much to Henri

77. See BN fr. 15733, fols. 420–26: "Recit veritable de ce qui s'est passé en lassemblee de Sorbonne le xvi febvrier 1604," with some other documents. The leader of the ultramontanist forces, one Pierrerive, claimed to have recieved letters from Rome indicating that the Faculty of Theology's inaction was eroding its credibility there. The level of dissimulation and outright lying in this affair was so great, however, that such statements must be taken with great caution.

78. See *Arrests de la cour de Parlement des 17. & 18. Febvrier 1604 sur l'assemblée de Sorbone touchant le Plaidoyé du Breviaire d'Anjou. Extraict des registres de Parlement* (s.l., n.d.), and a *procès-verbal* of the Parlement's interrogation of the Sorbonnists in BN Dupuy 594, fols. 223 and 225. The *Arrests* was most likely a publication of the Richerist faction in the Sorbonne, which was given to such gestures, rather than of the Parlement.

IV's relief.⁷⁹ While the entire controversy generated far more heat than light, it demonstrated the volatility of the political climate that the growth of juridical Gallican ideology had created, where minor and local ecclesiastical disputes could quite easily become major national and even international incidents. The threats to the fabric of the nation that the erudite Gallicans perceived were so grave, the rhetoric and the jurisdictional claims with which they combated them were so extreme, and the cleavages both within and between the institutions involved in legal and theological disputes were so deep that strong polarization was inevitable.

Nor did the affair of 1603–1604 mark the end of Miron's conflicts with the Gallicans and with his lower clergy. In 1612, the Parlement rejected his attempt to give the ecclesiastical offices of promoter and penitencer to one man simultaneously, accepting Servin's argument that this unacceptably confounded the spheres of orders and jurisdiction.⁸⁰ In 1616, Miron felt himself to be in so untenable a position with his clergy that he resigned his benefice, though he returned in 1621 when his successor died prematurely.⁸¹ Two years later he was condemned by the Parlement of Paris after excommunicating his archdeacon for having lodged an *appel comme d'abus*, and after having "preached publicly that appeals *comme d'abus*, and those who promoted them, were more damaging to the Church than heretics."⁸² The Parlement, as sometimes happened, had a good deal of trouble finding someone to absolve the offending archdeacon in conformity with its order. It turned eventually to the grand vicar of Lyons, a M. Ruellé, who happened also to be a councilor in the Parlement itself. The chapter continued to make an issue of this case even after Miron had capitulated, and in 1627 he left his see again, this time to become archbishop of Lyons.⁸³ He died less than a year later. His successor as primate of the Gauls was Alphonse de Richelieu, brother of the cardinal.

79. For a full account of this phase of the incident, see Soman, "Book Censorship," 64–72.
80. Servin, *Plaidoyez*, vol. 4, pt. 6. Oger, the offending individual, was himself continually at loggerheads with the Parlement.
81. See *Gallia Christiana*, 4:584–85.
82. In Laurent Bouchel, *La somme beneficiale, reduite à l'usage et pratique de France* (Paris: Rolet Boutonne, 1628), 87–101, s.v. "Apellations comme d'abus" (*arrêt* of 30 June 1623), p. 101.
83. See *Arrest de la cour de Parlement, par lequel Commission est decernée à Monsieur Ruellé Grand Vicaire de Monseigneur l'Archevesque & Primat de Lyon pour absoudre* ad cautelam *M. Pierre Garande Archidiacre d'Angers des prettendües sentences de Suspension & Excommunication contre luy rendües par M. l'Evesque d'Angers, avec l'absolution donnee par ledict Sieur Ruellé en consequence dudict Arrest* (s.l., n.d.), with an open letter from the chapter of 16 February 1624.

François Cardinal de Sourdis, archbishop of Bordeaux, was vastly more troublesome to the government as a whole than were Leschassier, Servin, and the entire Roze and Miron clans together. He was almost continually embroiled with his chapter, with the local parlement, and often with the king from late February 1602 until his death. We have already encountered one of these incidents in the complaints his chapter sent to the pope and the self-conception they revealed. Sourdis was of a sword-noble family, a relative of Henri IV's mistress Gabrielle d'Estrées, to whom he owed his swift preferment.[84] Though he came to the church somewhat tardily, only being ordained in 1600 after he had already received both cardinalate and archbishopric, he made a fairly good model of the Tridentine prelate, introducing many religious orders including Jesuits, Capuchins, and Carmelites, and undertaking a full set of reforms on a quite strict Borromean model.[85] He was a local magnate of considerable importance and, given his high social and ecclesiastical status and his considerable energy, an influential voice in the French clergy.

His career demonstrates the scope of jurisdictional conflict between clergy and magistrates in several ways. It shows how quickly a local issue far from the metropolis could call into play national and international powers: the king, the pope, and in one case even a rebellious prince of the blood. Moreover, the fact that so intense a conflict arose in Bordeaux at all says something important about how the erudite Gallican ideology functioned, for the Parlement of Bordeaux was—comparatively speaking—a bastion of ultramontanism. For example, the only published statement I have found in which a member of a sovereign court (other than the Leaguer bodies) explicitly attacked the tenets of legal Gallicanism was produced by an *avocat* and later councilor at Bordeaux, precisely in support of Sourdis's reforms.[86]

---

84. Henri IV's other *maîtresse en titre* in the 1600s was Henriette de Balsac d'Entragues. That both came from families with evident ultramontanist sympathies is not really sufficient to show a pattern, but it does suggest something about the environment at Henri's court.

85. *Gallia Christiana*, 2:851–54. On his impressive reform program, see Bernard Peyrous, "La réforme institutionelle de l'archidiocèse de Bordeaux au temps du Cardinal François de Sourdis (1599–1628)," *Revue d'histoire écclésiastique* 76 (1981): 5–47. Of some value for divining de Sourdis's religious attitude is a monitory he issued in 1609, admonishing the family of two sisters not to interfere with their vocation as nuns, the whole incident being couched in stereotypical terms revealing a wide, and rather uncritical, familiarity with hagiographic literature (BN fr. 15518, fol. 58).

86. The tract in question was by one de la Chaize, "Des appellations comme d'abus, & de la residence que doibvent les Archidiacres pres de leur Evesque & de leur Eglise Cathe-

Bordeaux was also the only parlement that prosecuted witchcraft at all agressively; as Jonathan Pearl has shown, this was a very accurate measure of conservative Catholic political affiliation.[87] The fact that even there a series of bitterly contested disputes erupted along lines essentially indistinguishable from those of the broader debate over the Gallican liberties shows both the structural importance of that debate and the degree to which the erudite Gallican ideology had been adopted by the parlements as a group.

There are no clear indications as to precisely when the bad blood between the cardinal and his enemies first arose or precisely why, though an early onset connected with the new prelate's attempts at reform seems likely. The proximate cause of the first imbroglio, however, was a dispute over the arrangement of altars in the cathedral.[88] Sourdis thought that two altars in the nave interfered with and were profaned by the crowds that came to hear preachers, while the canons considered them important for their antiquity and because they traditionally carried an indulgence for the newly baptized.[89] The line was thus once again roughly drawn between an innovating bishop and a practically and ideologically conservative chapter. Rather than taking the matter to the courts, Sourdis simply sent in workmen during a chapter meeting (which presumably kept the canons out of the cathedral), who proceeded to demolish the disputed altars. Naturally, this led to a nasty confrontation with the chapter, which immediately took its case to the Parlement of Bordeaux. Both the parlement and the chapter sent parties to at-

---

drale," in *Plaidoyers et Actions Grans et Eloquents de plusieurs fameux Advocats du Parlement de Bourdeaus* (Bordeaux, France: Gilbert Vernoy, 1616), 1–36. The historian Florimond de Raemond, whose perspective was distinctly Tridentine, was also a Bordeaux *parlementaire*. As we shall see in the following chapter, the voting record of the Guyenne delegates to the Estates General of 1614–1615 was consistently the most ultramontanist of any province.

87. See Pearl, *Crime of Crimes*, 127–49 and passim. Pearl implies, however, that even at Bordeaux witchhunting fervor was a minority position.

88. The most comprehensive source for this incident is a "Discours de ce qui se passa a Bordeaux entre le Parlement & le Cardinal de Sourdis & des ecclesiastiques 18 Mars 1602," BN Dupuy 594, fols. 177–80, which is not particularly sympathetic to the cardinal, and a dossier of *arrêts* and correspondance that follows (through fol. 222). There is another copy of the chapter's letter to Rome in BN fr. 15730, fols. 1056–63. See also Phillipe Loupès, *Chapitres et chanoines de Guyenne aux XVIIe et XVIIIe siècles* (Paris: Editions de l'E. H. E. S. S., 1985), 361.

89. This, at least, is what the respective parties told the pope: it is hard to know how much credence to give them. Note that no. 40 of Bourdin's list of liberties specifies that the pope "Ne peut . . . dispenser des coustumes et statuz des eglises cathedrales ou collegiales du Royaulme qui concernent la decoration et entretement du service divin," a prohibition that Pithou clarifies as being due to the royal rights as the fictive founder of major churches (no. 64). There is no clear reason, though, why this should apply to the bishop as well.

tempt to rebuild the altars; when the cardinal and his retinue encountered the latter, "M. le Cardinal hit them hard several times with the stick from the very cross which is carried in front of him, and also with his fists."[90] The cross in question was the symbol of the archbishop's jurisdiction—whether or not the incident actually occurred as stated, the symbolic import is evident. The councilors of the parlement received a spiritual rather than a corporal rebuke in the form of excommunication, from which of course they appealed *comme d'abus*.

In court and in letters to Henri IV and Pope Clement VIII, the chapter based its case on the claim that they, and the altars in question, were exempt from episcopal jurisdiction by papal edict. Both the parlement and the cardinal, on the other hand, freely brought up broader jurisprudential issues. A court ruling of 17 March 1602, for example, forbade Sourdis to cite the bull *In cœna domini* in his case.[91] Sourdis sought and obtained a papal brief requesting the chapter to comply with his demands, though it was not as "harshly written" as Clement had promised Sourdis it would be.[92] One thing for which the curia did strongly reproach the chapter, and for which the chapter sought to defend itself, was having recourse to the secular courts. The canons assured the Cardinal d'Ossat (official guardian of French interests in the curia) that they did so only after "being unable to obtain satisfaction elsewhere according to the privileges granted by the Holy See to the king and his officers to hear all cases of the *possessoire* of all ecclesiastical property," and they rather unconvincingly assured Rome that they would not have taken such steps had Sourdis acted through the procedures of canon law rather than by fait accomplie.[93]

Henri was thoroughly annoyed at Sourdis for his precipitous action, for initiating a vexing diplomatic imbroglio, and because "it was not reasonable for the said cardinal, having requested justice from us, to appeal to his Holiness," demonstrating that the royal administration viewed the case not as one of legal and political principal but rather in terms of a lack of personal loyalty and administrative tact.[94] Nevertheless, Henri saw fit to extract Sourdis

90. BN Dupuy 594, fol. 177r.
91. BN Dupuy 594, fol. 192.
92. BN fr. 6379, fol. 9r (Clement VIII to Sourdis, July 1602, orig.): the letters to the chapter are described as "acriter scriptas," but in the actually brief (BN Dupuy 594, fols. 193–97) phrases such as "quam opinabamur rem evenire audimus" (fol. 195r) recur frequently.
93. BN Dupuy 594, fol. 215r (Chapter of St. André de Bordeaux to the Cardinal d'Ossat, 11 December 1602, copy). The chapter's reassurances to the pope are on fol. 205v.
94. BN Dupuy 594, fol. 210r (Henri IV to the Chapter of St. André, 11 December 1602, copy).

from the troubles he had brought on himself who, with "several of his people would have been in a bad way if I had not interposed my authority . . . and omitted nothing that could be done on his behalf without too much injustice."[95] Clearly the king felt that good relations with Rome and the maintenance of Sourdis's personal dignity were more important than a strong defense of the principals of Gallicanism and the parlements' authority.

Thus it is not surprising that Sourdis proved a recidivist. Matters next came to a head in 1606, when he launched a frontal attack against appeals by his subordinates to the secular arm, excommunicating the entire Parlement of Bordeaux (and opposing counsel) when it upheld an *appel comme d'abus* from his official by one Philip Preniur, a Bordelais priest. Of course this resulted in another round of sentences against him, freezing his temporal property and fining him fifty thousand *livres*.[96] Sourdis again appealed to Henri (though not to Rome as well—he was learning some lessons), on the grounds that the court was interfering with his charitable enterprises while, "as for the church, besides the fact that they are perverting the order that Jesus Christ established for it, they are attacking its principal columns, which are the cardinals, who cannot be touched without causing the collapse of the entire structure."[97] Henri by this time was showing some sympathy for such arguments in defense of the ecclesiastical jurisdiction. At any rate, the matter was once again smoothed over.[98]

In 1615, perhaps emboldened by the fact that, during the regency of

95. BN Dupuy 594, fol. 212r–v (Henri IV to Phillipe de Béthune, French ambassador to Rome, 11 December 1602, copy). Béthune was the younger brother of Sully, and very much a member of the inner circle of Henri IV's government.

96. BN Dupuy 770, pp. 527–529 (*arrêt* of 30 December 1606). This copy is wrongly dated 30 March—for the correct date, see a copy in BN 500 Colb. 153, fols. 196–98. The error doubtless arose by contamination from the affair of March 1602. An interesting section of the *arrêt* declares: "inhib{itions} audit Torel curé de Puipaulin et tous autres de prescher en quarrefours marchés & places publicques contre l'ancienne forme & coutume, ny faire aucunes assemblees nouvelles et extraordinaires hors les eglises et lieux et jours non accoustumes au despit [?] des Magistrats et sans permission du Roy ou de ladite Cour soubs pretexte de predication a peine d'estre punis comme infracteur des edicts du Roy." Such preaching had often inflamed passions during the Wars of Religion.

97. BN Dupuy 493, fol. 231v (Sourdis to Henri IV, early 1607, orig.).

98. In 1609, Henri IV wrote to Sourdis saying that "communiquer par vostre chappitre que je veoy avec deplaisir n'estre pas bien d'accord avec vous j'en ay icy deux depputez qui se plaignent destre de vous trop rigoreusement traittez tant de faict que de parolles. Jay renvoye la requeste quils mont voulu presenter a mon conseil ou je masseure quil ne se fera rien a vostre prejudice" (BN fr. 6379, fol. 30r: Henri IV to Sourdis, 22 October 1609, orig.). Sourdis retained Henri's support, though the king showed some impatience with these never-ending conflicts.

Marie de Medicis he (like Bassompierre) provided vital support to the government against the rebellious magnates, and thus could not be alienated, Sourdis pushed his luck again.[99] During a royal visit to Bordeaux, his henchmen forcibly freed an imprisoned Protestant who had been condemned for murder by the parlement, killing a guard in the process. This was "an action that demonstrated either the lack of esteem in which the royal authority was then held, or the inconsiderate boldness of he who undertook it with impunity," according to the Cardinal de Richelieu, "but the affair went no farther since, because of his piety, his majesty took the side of the Church."[100] On the other hand, a pamphleteer writing on behalf of the Prince de Condé, who was then in a state half-way between opposition to and rebellion against the regime, took the occasion to pose as a defender of the Gallican liberties. He advised the cardinal

above all [to] remember that Jesus Christ never interfered with the tribute of Caesar, and that the French . . . desire no change of superiors, for fear that by admonitions, and then by excommunications, and then by the naming of enemies of the Roman Church, one might put fire to the sacred couches of our repose.[101]

In sponsoring these remarks, Condé was continuing a pose of defender of the Gallican liberties that he had adopted a few months earlier during the tenure of the Estates General.[102] Sourdis had become a "wedge issue" in the major political divisions of the realm.

One last act in this serial tragicomedy is worthy of attention because it demonstrates the degree of sophistication that Sourdis eventually achieved in carrying out this kind of quarrel. In 1625 or 1626, Sourdis excommunicated a lay couple for cohabitation outside the bonds of matrimony. The man appealed this act to the Parlement of Bordeaux, on the grounds that bishops had no jurisdiction over the laity on such matters. The case was transferred

99. This appears clearly from the extensive correspondance preserved in BN fr. 6379.

100. Richelieu, *Mémoires*, 411–12, 413. In the following chapter we will have occassion to analyze the beliefs that led Richelieu to adopt the attitude displayed here. Sourdis and his associates sought and received papal absolution for their actions; see BN fr. 6379, fols. 291–93.

101. *Advis salutaire donné au sieur illustrissime Cardinal de Sourdis pour sagement vivre à l'advenir* (s.l., 1615), 14. Condé and his party were at the time trying to make common cause with the Parlement of Paris in its support of the Article of the Third Estate and its demands for more accountable government.

102. See *Advis de Monseigneur le Prince au Roy. En son conseil tenu au Louvre, le jour des Roys: 6. Janvier 1615. Sur l'article du Tiers Estat Contradictions du Clergé, & Arrest du Parlement touchant la souveraineté du Roy* (s.l., 1615), one of Condé's quasi-official publications.

to the Parlement of Toulouse, which ruled against Sourdis.[103] The case was an important one because it advanced a truly radical theory of the extent of secular jurisdiction over marriage, removing not merely the transfer of property and the definition of families but even the matter of public morals from the cognizance of ecclesiastical courts. If the Church did not have jurisdiction over the laity in this kind of case, it is hard to conceive what jurisdiction it would have had at all. Sourdis thus sought support from the king and from the agents of the General Assembly of the Clergy to have the ruling suppressed.[104] It was not enough to have this done "by the simple cassation of the sentence," though. Circumstances called for "something more thorough, having it ordered torn from the registers of the court in order to bury its memory," a remedy generally only used when the king felt his authority directly threatened by the decree of a court.[105] In arguing his case, Sourdis employed two parallel strategies. On the one hand, he mounted a strong defense of the ecclesiastical jurisdiction with its scriptural foundations and its religious necessity. "How can this sentence sustain itself against the word of the Gospel?" he asked: "the Gospel says, Tell it unto the Church; the parlement says, Tell it to us." Louis XIII would ignore this at his peril. "Let your majesty weigh well that God changes powers and empires, moving them from nation to nation for the sins of the peoples and the disobedience that is shown to him in the persons of the prelates of his church."[106] At the same time, though, Sourdis did not hesitate to turn the weapons of the Gallicans against them. He cited the Pragmatic Sanction in his defense. An "Addition aux susdictes raisons," written in a different hand, drew a series of arguments from Bouchel's *Decreta ecclesiæ Gallicanæ* while defending the Council of Trent: this despite the fact that Bouchel in his index "is silent about these decrees of the Gallican church in order not to displease the parlement to which he dedicated his book."[107]

Here we have, in addition to a degree of moderation and political acumen that the brawling prelate had not always possessed, a carefully devel-

---

103. BN Dupuy 670, fols. 133–34 (*arrêt* of 5 September 1626).

104. BN 500 Colb. 153, fols. 262–75: "Brieve narration de la procedure de Monseigneur le S.r Card. de Sourdis Arch. de Bord. primat d'Aquit. contre le S.r de Saugeau et Jamine Chalonbic excommuniez pour concubinage avec l'arrest du Parlement de Tholoze au contre. Ensemble les raisons de M. le Card. sur la nullité dudit Arrest."

105. BN 500 Colb. 153, fol. 276r (Sourdis to the Assembly of the Clergy, 6 November 1626, auto.).

106. BN 500 Colb. 153, fol. 269r; 270r. The reference in the former quote is to Mt 18:15–18, one of the foundational texts of Christian ecclesiology.

107. BN 500 Colb. 153, fol. 271v.

oped counterdiscourse directed against the *parlementaire* Gallicans, based both on an unabashed appeal to scriptural authority and claims to know the secret designs of God, and on a thorough familiarity with the practices and documents of the erudite Gallicans themselves. Given the skill and power with which the Gallican jurists attacked many of the higher clergy's interests, and the coherence of the ideology that underlay those attacks, it is far from surprising that the prelates developed their own ideological tools in response. They also developed a textual corpus that parallelled that of the erudite Gallicans. They built the archives of the Assemblies of the Clergy into a formidable instrument, with a regular and carefully supervised program of publication. They even commissioned, from Pierre de Marca, a synthetic statement of their ecclesiological theories. They did all this in the same atmosphere of late humanism in which the erudite Gallicans operated—as we have seen, more than one anti-Gallican cleric was of robe background—which led them toward an interest in many of the same theoretical issues that concerned their opponents, and toward a similar set of rhetorical and historical commonplaces. However, they chose to defend rather than to attack the transcendental ideal of political organization and thus undertook a comprehensive philosophical as well as political conflict with the Gallican jurists.

This was not in any strict sense inevitable: the Anglican bishops, faced by critics who saw in Scripture a divinely legislated form of church governance, developed a mode of argument from tradition and custom that had much in common with that of the erudite Gallicans.[108] The French prelates, however, were not called on to deviate from the main international currents of their own Church. Indeed, in the seventeenth century they took over from Italy the lead in the development of the Catholic Reformation. Nor were they alienated from the medieval tradition of transcendental politics. While they may have made occasional and tactical use of skeptical arguments as weapons against Protestants,[109] the Church had a sufficient prescriptive

---

108. Technically, only the congregationalist Independants claimed to find positive divine legislation as to church governance; Presbyterians and episcopalist Puritans generally argued only that certain high-Anglican practices were *forbidden* by Scripture. On the development of Anglican ecclesiology, see Paul Avis, *Anglicanism and the Christian Church: Theological Resources in Historical Perspective* (Minneapolis: Fortress Press, 1989), 23–153.

109. This is the thesis of Richard Popkin, *The History of Scepticism from Erasmus to Spinoza* (Berkeley and Los Angeles: Univeristy of California Press, 1979), 66–86. However, Susan Rosa, in "Seventeenth-Century Catholic Polemic and the Rise of Cultural Rationalism: An Example from the Empire," *Journal of the History of Ideas* 57 (1996): 87–107, has argued convincingly that strict rationalism formed the true basis of Catholic apologetics in the seventeenth century.

claim on the possession of ultimate truth to make the abandonment of such a notion and a resort to history generally unappealing. Most importantly, the adoption of a transcendental model of both church and state by the clergy in its official discourse proved to be highly effective politically because of its consonance with many of the ideas that governed the monarchy: for while the erudite jurists might claim that the firm foundations of the French royal house lay in the customary constitution of the realm, the king himself was much more inclined to discern them in the will of God.

Although it was generally presented as being directed first and foremost against the pope and the curia, matters were of course very far from being so simple in practice. In the first place, since erudite Gallicanism was from its origins a reaction against currents of reform within the Catholic Church generally emanating from Italy and which may be subsumed under the generic label "Tridentine," it tended to bring about conflict between the courts and the Church wherever the Tridentine reform was at work within the latter. As erudite Gallicanism and Tridentinism became more and more influential within the third and first estates, respectively, after the accession of Henri IV, a situation developed of nearly pandemic conflict between the prelates of the French church, on the one hand, and the parlements and their sympathizers, on the other. This conflict was all the more bitter because, as we saw in the previous chapter, Gallican thought tended to minimized the potential political role of the clergy as a body, not merely of the papacy.

Furthermore, it is evident that this structural conflict did not consist simply of an attack by the courts on a passive and disorganized clergy. Rather, it was met and not infrequently preempted by a vigorous and determined counterattack and a clearly visible sense of solidarity. How far this solidarity went requires some further examination, though, as does the broader form taken by the counterattack. As it turns out, there can be no doubt that the clerical response was highly self-conscious and broadly conceived. There is a tendency in the literature on early modern French political thought, or at least on that segment of it that eschewed revolutionary and monarchomach extremism, to stress the activity and contributions of the robe above those of all other groups. Thus, for example, J. H. M. Salmon has claimed that "the institutional development of early modern France owes almost everything to the robe. The men of the law did not merely build the state: in a sense they were the state"—this even though the sovereign courts per se played rather a small role in directing the French state during the seventeenth century.[110] While the juristic contribution should by no means be denigrated, it would be most surprising if the political enemies of the *parlementaires* had not developed a competing political theory, or set of theories, as well. It will be worth our while to attempt to locate this countertheory and to make a preliminary estimate of its form and influence.

Having traced the doctrine of the erudite Gallicans from the empyrean heights of metaphysical speculation to the depths of actual litigation, then, we must proceed into the even less exalted arena of political conflict before we can again breath the pure air of theory. We have seen that the institutional structure of the robe was an essential component both in the theoretical development and the practical expression of erudite Gallicanism, and it seems reasonable to suppose that the same would hold true within the clergy. Clearly, both the dioceses and the Paris Faculty of Theology played important roles in the conflict between the prelates and the magistrates, but it is equally clear that neither was suited to form the basis of a coordinated response on the part of the former, since the diocese was an inherently local organization, and the Faculty of Theology was itself one of the principal battlegrounds in the Gallicans' struggle for hegemony.[111] On the other hand, the traditional tripartite division of society institutionalized in the three estates made it inevitable that the clergy should be at least intermittently organized on a national level. In fact, precisely during the period under discussion, this organization was becoming much denser and more effective.

110. J. H. M. Salmon, "Protestant Jurists and Theologians in Early Modern France: The Family of Cappel," in Roman Schnur, ed., *Die Rolle der Juristen bei der Entstehung des modernen Staates* (Berlin: Dunker and Humblot, 1986), 357–79, p. 357. To give another example, Nancy Roelker claimed in her synthesis of current scholarship on the matter that "[t]he great majority of those who wrote on the subject [of the French constitution], whether on the more conservative (consitutional) side, or tending toward absolutism, were members of the parlementaire class" (*One King, One Faith*, 60) While this is true as far as it goes, it carries with it the tendency to equate the composition of treatises with the formation of the *res publica*.

111. The Faculty of Theology retained this character at least through the fight over Molinism in which Blaise Pascal famously intervened. There is a revealing discussion of divisions in the Faculty of Theology in Soman, "Book Censorship," chap. 14. One might also cite a remark attributed by Richer's supporters to Chancellor Bellièvre in early 1613. See *Recueil de ce qui s'est fait . . . contre un Livre de Becanus*, 20–21: "Que c'estoit un tres-grand malheur, que la sacree Faculté de Theologie de laquelle tout le Royaume de France doit dependre, ès choses qui concernent la Religion, fust aujourd'huy divisee en divers parties & factions: Que donc la Faculté devoit de tout son soing veiller à la recerche [*sic*] d'une paix & concorde salutaire."

CHAPTER 6

Assemblies of the Clergy and Absolute Monarchy

B ETWEEN THE MID-SIXTEENTH and the eighteenth centuries the machinery of the old regime gained only two entirely new institutions. Both were religious in character, and both arose as a direct result of the religious wars. The first, and less durable, was the *religion prétendue réformée*, the Protestant church itself, recognized in the pacification edict of 1561 and dissolved by Louis XIV. The other had its origins as a fundraising expedient for the wars against the Huguenots, but survived the revocation of the Edict of Nantes without breaking stride. This was the Assembly of the Clergy, which began to take form at the Colloquy of Poissy in 1561, and more solidly after the Estates General of 1576. It represented the first estate before the king in fiscal matters and administered the funding of the *rentes* on the Hôtel de Ville of Paris, which quickly became one of the monarchy's principal financial instruments and one of the major resources of French *rentiers*.[1] While it was not new for the clergy to play a collective role in the kingdom's affairs, or in the defense and interpretation of the Gallican liberties, such in-

---

1. On the early history of the assemblies, see Louis Serbat, *Les Assemblées du Clergé de France: Origines, organisation, dévelopement 1561–1615* (Paris: Honoré Champion, 1906); and M. Perronet, "Naissance d'une insitution (dans la seconde moitié du XVIe siècle): Les Assemblées du Clergé," in André Stegmann, ed., *Pouvoir et institutions en Europe au XVIème siècle* (Paris: J. Vrin, 1987), 249–61.

tervention had previously been episodic and at the pleasure of the king.² As the assemblies entrenched themselves, they permanently changed the dynamic not only of disputes over Gallicanism, but of French political life as a whole. The sovereign courts lost their near-monopoly on the systematic interpretation of and institutional memory concerning the relations of church and state. To a lesser extent, the assemblies even represented a new option in French political culture, alongside the aristocracy of the sword nobles and the robe's "justice state." For all these reasons, the development and political stance of the assemblies, their bitter conflicts with the parlements and the third estate, and the overall political vision they put forward are of the first interest. Examining these phenomena illuminates the final stages in the development of Gallican ideology, and suggests how that was related to the broader development of the old regime itself.

The institutional conflict between the Gallican jurists and the first estate developed slowly. It appeared at the beginning of the religious wars, with the dispute over the introduction of the Tridentine canons.³ Through the 1570s, though occasionally bitter, their fight remained largely confined to this single issue. The hostility of the jurists was directed primarily at Roman ambition rather than against the native clergy, while the Huguenot peril preoccupied both parties. The institutional development of the assemblies of the clergy sharply broadened this dispute. Their real corporate existence dated from the Assembly of Melun in 1579–1580, their first regularly scheduled meeting, and, significantly, the one at which they formally organized an archive for themselves.⁴ From the first, these meetings took cognizance of "ecclesiastical jurisdiction and privileges, and the usurpations of [the ecclesiastical courts'] duties to the prejudice of the clergy."⁵ They also made it clear to both the king and the robe exactly how they understood and intended to protect their own political and jurisdictional position. The first major

---

2. See Jotham Parsons, "The French Assemblies of the Clergy from Philip the Fair to Louis XIII," *Parliaments, Estates and Representation* 23 (2003): 1–16. In this essay I expand on some of the issues treated in this chapter.

3. On the different attitudes of courts and clergy to Trent, see Victor Martin, *Le gallicanisme et la réforme catholique: Essai historique sur l'introduction en France des décrets du concile de Trente (1563–1615)* (Paris: Picard, 1919), 127–210.

4. AN *G⁸ 2846, "Inventaire des papiers communs du clerge de france au thresor et archif dicelluy." Previously, papers had been scattered around the boardinghouses of Paris. For more details on the clergy's archives, see Françoise Hildesheimer, "De la conservation à l'impression: Les archives du clergé de France," *Histoire et archives* 8 (2000): 59–99.

5. *Procès-verbaux*, 1:136B.

statement on the subject came shortly after the deputies of the clergy had opened negotiations on a new royal subsidy. The Archbishop of Lyons, in a long and eloquent harangue to the royal negotiator Pomponne de Bellièvre, explained the clergy's commitment to "the conservation of the privileges and immunities of the Church, held dearer than our own lives."

While his immediate concern was to preserve the principle of clerical tax exemption, he made it clear that both the issue and his own claims were much broader. He strongly implied that only those polities that had assigned priests a determining role in government had thrived, and he referred obliquely to the Gallican jurists' attacks on ecclesiastical jurisdiction, whereby "our ecclesiastical privileges . . . are today more than they have ever been, placed in doubt."[6] He also indicated the powerful weapon that the clergy could now wield in defense of its position: the king needed money, and the clergy would not provide it unless their position was respected. This placed them in conflict with the robe in a very immediate and nonideological way, for without the clerics' subsidy the *rentes* on the Hôtel de Ville that played such a large role in their portfolios would not be paid. At one point in the negotiations the Parlement, at the instigation of the Paris Bureau de Ville, tried to place the entire Assembly under house arrest in order to force concessions—an ill-advised fit of pique that the king promptly countermanded but that can only have promoted ill feeling between the first and third estates.[7]

By 1583 the permanent committee of agents set up to represent the clergy between their meetings produced a wide-ranging set of grievances over the intrusion of the secular on the ecclesiastical jurisdiction, though it received a lukewarm response from the king.[8] The Assembly of 1584 took up the matter of parlements imposing vicars on bishops to carry out absolution *ad cautelam* "against the liberty of the Church, the conscience of the lords prelates, and enterprise against the ecclesiastical jurisdiction."[9] With the accession of Henri IV, matters took a further and decisive turn for the worse.

6. AN *G^8 599 fols. 107r, 122r (session of 24 July 1579, *de relevé*).

7. This happened in mid-December. See AN *G^8 599 fols. 344–49; and Paul Guérin, ed., *Histoire générale de Paris: Registres des délibérations du bureau de la ville de Paris*, vol. 8 (Paris: Imprimerie nationale, 1896), 212–13.

8. *Articles accordez au Clergé de France, sur les remonstrances faicts au Roy par les Agens generaux d'iceluy, à sainct Germain en Laye le douzieme du mois de Novembre, 1583* (Paris: n.p., 1584); see Serbat, *Les Assemblées*, 301. There are fifty-seven articles, all of which deal with issues of jurisdiction. The complaints were provoked by certain actions of a *grand jours* of Troyes.

9. AN *G^8 608, fol. 58v (session of 16 June 1584, *du matin*). This incident involved the bishop of le Mans.

Conditions were indeed ripe for such a conflict. The League had stripped the sovereign courts of those of their members more inclined to caution and to ultramontanism, while Henri's desperate need for Catholic support (and for money) left the bishops in a very strong position and little inclined to compromise. One of the new king's first acts had been to promise to protect the Church and receive instruction in Catholicism. At intervals before his conversion he received endorsements of this position from assemblies of bishops; without these declarations of support it is doubtful whether he could have remained in power for very long.[10]

Nevertheless, not all of Henri's supporters were happy with the position the bishops had taken. An anonymous "Advis sur l'assemblée du Clergé à Chartres," from September 1591, complained bitterly of both the tone and the jurisdictional claims of that body.[11] The author was obviously close to the *parquet* of the royalist parlement sitting at Tours, and he was particularly concerned about injuries the prelates had supposedly done to that court. His defense of the parlement's authority was of a thoroughly familiar type, but it expressed much more explicitly than anything we have heretofore examined whom the *parlementaires* saw as the principal enemies of their constitutional position, and what they claimed the stakes were in the struggle.

> The court of the Parlement of Paris has from all time had such force in this realm, that the authority of the prince seems to reside in it. Even the three estates of the realm are always bound by its rulings. By means of this authority it has also maintained the state against the usurpations and enterprises both of its subjects and of its neighbors, and in particular against the violence of the popes . . . , so much so that this state almost alone has for so many centuries escaped all attacks and enterprises.[12]

---

10. See Michael Wolfe, *The Conversion of Henri IV: Politics, Power, and Religious Belief in Early Modern France* (Cambridge, Mass.: Harvard University Press, 1993), 72–80.

11. BN Dupuy 422, fols. 134–37. A copy of the declaration of that assembly (which was merely a meeting of prelates, not a real Assembly of the Clergy) may be found in BN fr. 5045, fol. 306. This text does not, however, correspond to the discussion in Dupuy 422. The author of the memoir may have been working from a draft version or from mere rumor. The one claim substantiated by the record is the proposed embassy by the bishops to Rome: they recommended sending the bishops of Angers and le Mans, and in fact the latter was included in the Duc de Nevers's mission a few years later. The only clue to the origin of the document under consideration is Henri's reply to the bishops' request that he approve this embassy; he asked to wait to hear from, among others, "les Présidents de Tours & de Caen, qui ont des remonstrances à me faire, & prie de ne résoudre ce qu'ils ont à me dire ou faire entendre sans les avoir ouis" (*Procès-verbaux*, 1, pièces justificatives: 148B).

12. BN Dupuy 422, fol. 135 r–v. The echo of Pasquier is extremely strong.

The author suggested that Henri should refer the declaration of the prelates to the *parquet* of the Parlement (as would have been done with, say, a papal bull or the *cahiers* of an Estates General), which would of course have returned a negative opinion. In the absence of such oversight, "each of the three estates will be a law unto itself, where the Parlement had given the law to all, and held all three bound by its rulings."[13] This tract seems to conflate assemblies of royalist prelates with the potentially republican meeting of the Estates General then being canvassed by the League—an elision that speaks volumes about the state of relations between the two pillars of Henri IV's support!

This memoir's author worried that when the prelates asked Henri to keep his promise to receive instruction in the Catholic faith, and to convert to that faith, they concealed the threat of a *tiers parti* and would turn against him if this were not done. This threat was intimately linked to defiance of the parlement's authority: "which is to say that if his majesty does not give them satisfaction on this point, there would no longer be a parlement to say that one is obliged to obey one's prince, despite any putative heresy."[14] The historic role of the parlement as the seat of stabilizing counsel was now identified with its specific support of doctrines of nonresistance. Under the circumstances, this was an easily comprehensible interpretation of that by now classic topos. However, this stabilizing role could only be fulfilled if the parlement's jurisdiction was respected, and indeed expanded as much as possible. Thus, our author found it particularly threatening that the clergy might be attempting to intrude on some of those areas of state affairs over which the Parlement claimed jurisdiction. The prelates supposedly wished both to undertake their own mediation among the parties in conflict and to exclude the Parlement from jurisdiction over beneficial and other ecclesiastical disputes arising from the suspension of relations with Rome. From our author's point of view, these plans all amounted to much the same thing: a self-serving attempt to shoulder aside a body necessary for the support of the monarchy,

which would be to remove the authority attributed to the court from all time to judge alone and to the exclusion of all others any differences between the pope and the king, the power he claims, and the privileges of the realm. That is, it would not only abolish what was ordained for the preservation of the authority

---

13. BN Dupuy 422, fol. 136v. The importance of this line of argument will become apparent when we examine the events surrounding the Estates General of 1614.

14. BN Dupuy 422, fol. 134v.

of the king by its ruling [on ecclesiastical administration during the break with Rome], but everything it could do and ordain on the same subject in the future.[15]

This was indeed a period fertile in extreme claims for the king's secular jurisdiction. We have already seen that it was around this time that the doctrine of royal inexcommunicability first emerged. Another anonymous memoir, this one on the powers of the papal legate to the League, went about as far as it is possible to go: "our kings are sovereign not in temporal matters alone, but they maintain that they have the same power in spiritual affairs"—a statement that a later reader found striking enough to underline and mark in the margin. The two swords were completely collapsed here, although it seems that the scope of the argument was meant to be restricted to strictly legal matters (the main issue at hand), since the next sentence reads "and there is no one who would dare to undertake any judicial act except under [royal] authority."[16] Having once staked out such an advanced ideological position, the courts proved very unwilling to retreat. It is not hard to interpret the particularly intransigent Gallicanism of Henri IV's Parlement—which Edouard Maugis, for instance, has noted—as the logical extension of the polemics undertaken during the wars of the League.[17] The continuing instability of the monarchy, both apparent and real, provided ample reinforcement to the magistrates as they played the role of guarantors of stability at least through the minority of Louis XIII. Thus, there was no particular reason for the reflexive hostility toward the jurisdictional pretensions of the clergy documented in 1591 to dissipate.

In the mean time, the leaders of the French church appear to have been infused around the turn of the century with a new self-confidence and institutional assertiveness. This is most clearly seen in the persistent demands of the assemblies of the clergy from 1597 on for royal action to restrain the *appel comme d'abus* and other intrusions of the secular courts on what they con-

15. BN Dupuy 422, fol. 134r.
16. BN Dupuy 670, fols. 93–94 (two speeches of 29 November 1590), 93r. It is not at all clear either who gave them, or whom they were given to. The first is signed "L. D. O. V. M. D. A," the second more briefly "L. D. O.": the latter seems to have been a plea, perhaps in the Grand Conseil. It is clear from the second speech that the extension of jurisdiction is meant to encompass primarily beneficial matters: "nos Roys sont seigneurs souverains de tous les biens temporelles des ecclesiastiques, tout ainsi que de leurs autres subjectz; mais encore qu'à eux originellement & naturellement apartient la collation & distribution de tout les benefices de leur Royaume" (fol. 94v).
17. See Edouard Maugis, *Histoire du Parlement de Paris de l'avenement des rois Valois à la mort d'Henri IV*, 3 vols. (Paris: A. Picard, 1913–1916), 2:277–304.

sidered to be their proper jurisdiction. No such campaign had been undertaken prior to the reign of Henri IV; certainly, the gathering momentum of religious revival contributed to the bishops' boldness. The more immediate root of this policy, though, was the disorder that the break with Rome had left in the French church and the courts' attempts to regulate this state of affairs on their own. The interruption of contact with the papacy had left a power vacuum in the French ecclesiastical order, or perhaps just greatly accentuated one of very long standing, and this was a vacuum that the papacy, the prelates, and the magistrates all hoped to fill.[18] They were all well equipped to make their respective bids for authority: the papacy under the firm and intelligent leadership of Clement VIII, the prelates supported by a new crop of vigorous reformers able to apply their policies consistently in the new atmosphere of stability, and the magistrates with a Gallican ideology now fully developed and tested under fire.

The edicts forbidding recourse to Rome had provided that people named to ecclesiastical benefices receive their investiture *in spiritualibus* from their ordinary superiors. For many posts (the major benefices covered by the Concordat, in general) this was a canonically dubious procedure, at least from the point of view of those more tolerant of papal jurisdiction than were the Gallican legists. Worse yet, in a number of cases the appropriate superior had been a Leaguer, a vacant see, or someone otherwise unable or unwilling to provide investiture. In such cases other prelates chosen at hazard had provided the investiture on a commission from the courts.[19] In oth-

---

18. The depth of commitment to reform on the part of both Henri III and the League is clear, but it is equally clear that in practice these two valences tended to cancel each other out. See, e.g., Frances Yates, *The French Academies of the Sixteenth Century* (London: Warburg Institute, 1947); A. Lynn Martin, *Henry III and the Jesuit Politicians* (Geneva: Droz, 1973); and Philip Benedict, *Rouen during the Wars of Religion* (Cambridge, U.K.: Cambridge University Press, 1981), 190–208. That the clergy, at least, was fully aware of this vacuum and had some sort of plan for filling it is made clear by a speech which the promoter of the Assembly of the Clergy of 1595–1596 gave at the close of the meeting. See *Procez-verbaux* 1: 626A: "ci-devant le Clergé de ce Royaume étoit appuyé & assisté de quelques-uns de Messeigneurs les Cardinaux Princes, d'un bon nombre d'autres Cardinaux, Archevêques & Evêques ordinaires au Conseil du Roi au préjudice du Clergé; mais qu'à présent il étoit tellement affoibli & diminué, qu'il n'y avoit en l'Ordre Ecclésiastique de ce Royaume, aucun Prince, fort peu de Messeigneurs les Cardinaux, & encore ceux qui y sont, ne sont ordinaires près la personne du Roi ou au Conseil, & de Messeigneurs les Archevêques & Evêques, n'en y a que bien peu qui soient ordinaires audit Conseil, de sorte qu'on pourroit justement dire que *Obscuratum est aurum, mutatus est color optimus* tant le Clergé a changé depuis peu d'années."

19. What was apparently actually the most common procedure, a provisional investiture

er cases of vacancy, the courts had bypassed the (generally pro-League) cathedral chapters and appointed *œconomes in spirtualibus* to carry out the spiritual functions of the bishops. One of the first actions of the Assembly of the Clergy of 1595 was to call for a declaration that all such doubtful investitures were null and void, thus erasing a precedent that had allowed the secular arm to rule on the cure of souls. According to the minutes, "other complaints that the Assembly might make were common and ordinary ... but ... this one, besides being entirely new and without precedent in this kingdom, was of very great weight and importance."[20]

This initiative gave rise to a brief but significant exchange of pamphlets. The Parlement counterattacked with a collection of documents on the conduct of French ecclesiastical affairs during previous breaks with Rome. Such pamphlets had been issued before, notably one that formed a pendant to Pithou's *Libertez*.[21] In this case, though, there was a brief preface explaining what the reader was to make of the documents, "even though it is not reasonable to inquire and ask after the reasoning on which the rulings of the sovereign courts are based, either in private or in public matters."[22] The pamphlet went on to defend in the strongest terms the rights of the par-

---

by the Grand conseil, seems never to have become a matter of controversy. I have not been able to track down the details of this procedure, which must have been less objectionable to the prelates, who also doubtless wished to preserve their generally good relationship with that body.

20. *Procès-verbaux*, 1:573A.

21. *Ordre et reglement sur les provisions des benefices en l'Eglise Gallicane pendant les empeschemens d'aller à Rome* (Paris: Denys Duval, 1596). A note in the BN catalogue attributes this work to Jacques de la Guesle, which certainly seems reasonable enough, though I do not know what its authority is. Cf. Pierre Pithou, *Ecclesiæ Gallicanæ in schismate status. ex acte publicis* (Paris: s.l., 1594).

22. *Ordre*, 1. Cf. Bk. 1, chap. 2, of Pasquier's *Recherches de la France*. The nonjustification of the actions of the Parlement was one of the attributes of its sovereign status, along with judging at equity rather than at law and, for the *parquet*, pleading in the name of the *procureur du roi*. An early (c. 1337) *stylus* of the Chambre des Enquêtes explains the matter. See Paul Guilhermoz, *Enquêtes et procès: Etude sur la procédure et le fonctionnement du Parlement au XIVe siècle. Suivie du Style de la Chambre des Enquêtes, du Style des commissaires du Parlement et de plusieurs autres textes et documents* (Paris: Alphonse Picard, 1892), 221–22: "Nec debent cuilibet apparere secreta curie supreme, que non habet nisi Deum superiorem, que curia quandoque contra juris rigorem, vel eciam contra jus aliquociens, ordinat ex causa, justa apud Deum suum superiorem, que forte forte non reputaretur justa sive procedere de jure, quod jus non ligat Regem, tanquam superiorem et solutum legibus et juribus, et contingit aliquociens propter causas quas non licet cuique dicere nec exprimere, et hoc frequenter fit, prout qualitas negociorum, excessuum, malefactorum, scandalorum, periculorum ... qualitates personarum et insidiose frequenter et obscure deliquencium ... et plures alie cause innumerabiles requirunt, que cause ex bono judicio dominorum expertorum in talibus perpenduntur." In short, the prin-

Assemblies of the Clergy   235

lements, in troubled times, to intervene in ecclesiastical affairs for the general good.

It was a matter of the king's dignity and of the duty of the sovereign judges of his courts, to whom belongs the direction of public affairs that might bring benefit to the state, or even the ecclesiastical administration, and peace to the subjects of the kingdom . . . to induce prelates, pastors, superiors, or other ecclesiastical persons of dignity, by his majesty's authority, to see to these things as conveniently as possible.[23]

Another memoir on the same subject, unpublished but almost certainly known to the clergy, made the implications of such claims clearer. This writer began with the assertion that "the Church being in the republic and not the republic in the Church, as the good Optatus said, and kings and princes being heads and sovereign moderators of the republic, it follows that their moderation and government extend to all parts of the whole." From this classic position he quickly developed in two directions very typical of the new Gallicanism, and threatening to the clergy. First, based on Roman and Carolingian precedents, the author claimed "that kings and princes have superintendance over the discipline of the Church even in what is purely ecclesiastical, and spiritually," and hence certainly over the matter in question.[24] Second,

just as pieces of wood newly joined and glued together come apart at the slightest jolt, but when the solder is made firm by time, it is all a blade can do to take them apart, so at the beginning of a reconciliation it takes less than nothing to break it. Let us then be on guard lest we alter this one, so useful to France and to all Christendom, by importunate disputes, allowing time to do its work.[25]

In other words, not only was long custom the only true guarantor of political stability, and not only were the courts the only competent judges of what that custom was, but they should even be given the authority to nur-

---

ciple that the Parlement's actions participated in the "mystery of state" formed part and parcel of its claims to authority. From this perspective, the presentation of historical documents was a particularly appealing mode of public argument, since they tended rather to reduplicate and hence authorize than to rationally justify the courts' actions.

23. *Ordre*, 2. On the principle of belt and suspenders, this pamphlet also justified the parlements' actions by "une probable necessité."

24. From a memoir with the later and incorrect title "Memoires des choses que Messieurs du clergé desiroient du Roy 1576," in BN fr. 6396, fols. 87–90, fol. 87r, fol. 88r. There is no doubt, from internal evidence, that this memoir dates from 1595–1596, and that it was produced by officers of either the Parlement or, less likely, the Grand Conseil.

25. BN fr. 6396, fol. 90r.

ture recent innovations of their choosing to the point where they would become customary and stable!

If these arguments went unopposed, the bishops would surely lose a part of their vital constitutional position. The inevitable clerical riposte presented a sophisticated argument backed up by extensive historical and canonistic erudition.[26] The core of the clerical writer's argument was very simple: "to provide laws and ordinances on the ecclesiastical administration, [Christ] gave authority to his apostles and to the bishops, their successors, when he said to them, 'Whatever you bind on Earth. . . .'" Since this disposition was *jure divino*, even the plea of necessity did not excuse its violation: "in matters of faith, such as the power and authority of the Church, one may not allege necessity."[27] Nor was it acceptable to contend that the courts' acts were *res judicata* and thus should stand even if inequitable, since the courts were without jurisdiction in the first place and their acts were a nullity. "Not everyone can give dispensations, but only those to whom the authority belongs by law," while "the Gallican church cannot be represented except by a national council."[28] The entire argument rested on the claim that ecclesiastical jurisdiction was both put in place and defined in its details by a single, visible act of divine legislation. Indeed, the author of the *Response* went into great detail on the theory of ecclesiastical jurisdiction. He pointed out that the laity might exercise offices of spiritual jurisdiction "such as collecting tithes . . . conferring benefices . . . electing prelates . . . hearing and judging ecclesiastical cases . . . [and] preaching the word of God," but only when they had been delegated to do so by the ecclesiastical authorities. This contrasts with the doctrine expounded most clearly in the *De la puissance* whereby any functions exercised by both clergy and laity could only have been delegated from the latter to the former. Moreover, even if "a layperson has permission to perform these spiritual acts, he can only have it from the pope."[29]

The reader then received a carefully nuanced account of the relation be-

26. *Response au traite intitulé, Ordre & reglement sur les provisions des benefices en l'Eglise Gallicane, pendant l'empeschement d'aller à Rome. A Messieurs les Prelatz & autres Ecclesiastiques tenans l'assemblee generale du Clergé de France à Paris* (s.l., 1596). The level of erudition in this treatise is very high, demonstrating an encyclopedic knowledge of the canon law and a fair grasp of Protestant ecclesiology.

27. *Response*, 11, 60. This follows from either a Thomist or an Ockhamist view of natural law: "necessity" is nothing but the operation of the divine will through natural causes, and it is impossible that that will should come into conflict with itself. Therefore, any perceived necessity to violate divine law must be illusory.

28. *Response*, 4, 7.

29. *Response*, 32, 33. Panormitan, incidentally, was the most conciliarist of the great canonists.

tween the papacy and ecclesiastical jurisdiction, carefully pitched between traditional Gallican and ultramontanist modes. The author of the *parlementaire* pamphlet had argued that it was perfectly legitimate for bishops other than hierarchical superiors to perform episcopal confirmations, citing in his defense a passage from St. Cyprian that characterized all bishops as holding their dioceses as one, *in solidum*.[30] The author of the *Response* countered that

> all bishops hold that universal bishopric entire and united when their churches are not separated from that head, that root, that fountain [the Church of Rome]. . . . To take a similar case, even though the bishopric of Rome is a portion of the Universal Church, or that universal bishopric, as is the bishopric of Paris, nevertheless that of Rome maintains and governs that of Paris, and not the other way around.

Still, this did not negate the divine institution of the episcopacy considered *individualiter*, or imply that the pope held universal as well as supreme jurisdiction: "St. Cyprian does not mean to say that the pope is the only bishop in the whole Church, or that the others are only vicars or commissioners of the pope, but that they are true titularies and true bishops."[31]

One sees very clearly here the foundations of the ultramontanist tendency that marked the French higher clergy for most of the seventeenth century. Placing ecclesiastical jurisdiction outside of human law and its unifying source outside of the kingdom enabled the prelates to reject any interference with their affairs by the secular authorities, while leaving the dignity and independence of the episcopacy untouched and available for deployment against any papal interference.[32] Since the legal Gallicans also stressed a deep and inviolable distinction between clergy and laity, such arguments were potentially very effective. Furthermore, any who might contest this account of ecclesiastical jurisdiction could be equated with Luther, "who pretends that [Christians] are all priests by baptism, and thus have the power to perform any spiritual act."[33] This pamphlet had a substantial fortune. It ei-

---

30. The passage, which had been included in the *Decretum* (D. 2 c. 7, 1, 7), was a favorite of writers on ecclesiology.

31. *Response*, 34–36. Cf. Yves Congar, "Aspects ecclésiologiques de la querelle entre mendiants et séculiers dans la seconde moitié du XIIIe siècle et le début du XIVe," *Archives d'histoire doctrinale et littéraire du moyen âge* 28 (1961): 34–151, p. 79.

32. Rambouillet, the bishop of Le Mans whose ecclesiological writings we discussed in Chapter 3, in fact deployed arguments about the divine institution and indispensibility of certain beneficial matters against the papal legate, who wished to regularize some of the expedients of the religious wars; see Martin, "La reprise," 251–52.

33. *Response*, 31–32. The author (pp. 17–19) carefully distinguished between Luther's and Calvin's positions on church governance.

ther represented or determined the general thinking of the Assembly of the Clergy of 1596, for its substance was included in their official remonstrances.[34] The king proved unwilling to face the political and practical consequences of annulling so much of what his courts had done over the previous decade, but the clergy were at least able to extract from him an edict to the effect that the objectionable actions were "against that which has been heretofore observed" and would not be allowed to form a precedent.[35] Even this did little good, though, despite very considerable episcopal solidarity. Decisions of the Parlement of Paris from 1612 and 1613, for example, confirmed Edmond Richer and Pierre de Bailly purely and simply in prebends, despite the fact that the bishops of Paris, Sens, Autun, Noyon, Chartres, Lyons, and Beauvais had all refused, *seriatim*, to install them![36]

As we have said, two external factors contributed to this combination of political solidarity and activism with at least a moderate ultramontanism—namely, papal policy and the character of the upper ranks of the episcopate. While conflict between the papacy and the French bishops was by no means unknown, the sort of direct control over local affairs that the curia attempted to impose, for example, on Venice was simply out of the question in France. Thus, when Rome supported ecclesiastical jurisdiction against the intrusions of the French monarchy, this meant in practice supporting the power of the Gallican church and of its local leaders. And in fact the defense of ecclesiastical jurisdiction was a central focus of papal diplomacy. The crisis of the Venetian interdict revealed this, as did the entire tenor of the administration of the Papal States.[37] In France, papal representatives routinely intervened against the courts, a situation that the disputes surrounding the Council of Trent rendered chronic.

---

34. *Recueil des actes, titres et memoires concernant les affaires du Clergé de France* (Paris: Pierre Simon, 1740), cols. 220–24; cf. article 11 of that year's *cahier*, ibid., cols. 1147–51. In the course of the Assembly the promoter, Desaigues, gave a speech advancing very similar arguments; see *Procès-verbaux* 1, pièces justificatives: 152A–156A.

35. *Les remonstrances, edicts, contracts, et autres choses concernans le Clergé de France*, 3 separately foliated secs. (Paris: Jean Richer, 1621), 3: fol. 120r.

36. BN 500 Colb. 153, fols. 210–12 (*arrêts* of 27 July 1612, 5 December 1612, and 15 January 1613).

37. On the interdict, see Bouwsma, *Venice*. On the influence of jurisdictional theory on the papacy's domestic policies, see Paolo Prodi, *The Papal Prince, One Body and Two Souls: The Papal Monarchy in Early Modern Europe*, trans. Susan Haskins (Cambridge, U.K.: Cambridge University Press, 1987), passim.

Clement VIII's instructions to his diplomats reveal that this was a conscious and deliberate policy, and was tracked carefully by the chancery. The text regarding the defense of jurisdiction was preserved from mission to mission, but always with additions in the sense of a greater specificity. The most complete version summarizes the principles of papal diplomacy on the issues of concern to us so completely that it deserves quotation *in extenso:*

> Ecclesiastical jurisdiction is under attack in that kingdom, wherefore your excellence [Matteo Barberini] should recommend it to the king, that he might not permit it to be oppressed by the lay courts and the temporal jurisdiction. Remind him of what Our Lord Jesus Christ said: "Render unto Caesar the things that are Caesar's, and unto God the things that are God's": moreover, that if the bishops and ecclesiastics do not have their hands free to exercise their [spiritual] arms and jurisdiction, they will not be feared and it will be almost impossible for them to reform the clergy and their churches, from which would arise the peace of the people and hence the quiet of the kingdom. Represent also to his majesty the blame that princes who occupy the things of the Church and its jurisdiction receive, and your excellence will remind his majesty that the bounty of the kings his predecessors privileged the ecclesiastical jurisdiction in that kingdom above all other kings. . . .
>
> Some things came up on this matter under the Cardinal del Bufalo, in which God permitted him, through his skill and resolution, to overcome the difficulties of the Parlement and of the others who oppose such things, so that the jurisdiction was somewhat raised up and advanced in its reputation above its enemies. Your excellence should continue to maintain it in that state and to move it forward, but skillfully and avoiding acrimony, and rather through negotiation than by threats, since in this court and in particular with this king this is much more effective . . . than force or fear.[38]

Rome's strategy was to quietly arrange an alliance of the bishops and the king against the parlements, and this policy met with a fair degree of success.

In a kind of back-handed acknowledgment of the effectiveness of the papal diplomats, the Parlement undertook a concerted effort to detach

---

38. *Die Hauptinstruktionen Clemens' VIII. für die Nuntien und Legaten an den Europäischen Fürstenhöfen 1592–1605*, ed. Klaus Jaitner (Tübingen, Germany: Max Niemeyer Verlag, 1984), 734–35 (98: IV, 3). See also pp. 460 (54: III, 8); 584 (73: III, 3); and 672–73 (88: IV, 3). I elide an account of Phillip IV and Pierre Bertrand's thwarting of Pierre de Cugnières's plans for the curtailment of ecclesiastical jurisdiction which first appeared in del Bufalo's instructions (1601). A similar account of this incident appears in the *Response*, pp. 68–69: "la memoire duquel [Cugnières] a esté par le passé, & sera à jamais opprobre à la posterité pour un si mal'hureux [*sic*] dessein."

them from the Gallican hierarchy. Over the first few decades of the seventeenth century, the court consistently asserted that, first, legates should be considered as representatives of the pope purely in his capacity as a secular prince, and, second, that since legates and nuncios were the representatives of a foreign prince it was an act of lèse majesté for any French subject to meet with them without the king's prior consent.[39] They based the former position on the tenet that the pope had no jurisdiction in the first instance within France, and the latter on an understandable though unenforceable interpretation of the law of treason. As it turned out, the entire enterprise came to grief on the complete unwillingness of the monarchy to countenance these doctrines, but attempts to enforce them could be a fairly effective form of harassment. A striking example of this occurred in the aftermath of the Faculty of Theology's abortive attempt to condemn Richer's *De ecclesiastica et politica potestate* in January 1612. At least according to those members of the Faculty of Theology questioned by the Parlement, the nuncio had been the animating force behind that enterprise, which greatly annoyed the court. The theologian who had cooperated most closely with the nuncio was "warned that it was the act of a bad Frenchman to communicate with foreigners without the permission of the king and to aid in seducing and suborning his subjects against all the law of nations," and sentenced to be "castigated by the *gens du roi*." The Parlement also sent one of its presidents to the king to ask that a closer watch be kept on the nuncio and his staff.[40]

A variety of internal factors also predisposed the leadership of the French clergy toward ultramontanist views and toward an assertive view of their own jurisdictional competence. Episcopal pluralism by this time had been largely eliminated and nonresidence at least brought under some kind

---

39. For an overview of this quarrel, see Pierre Blet, "Le nonce en France au XVIIe siècle: Ambassadeur et délégué apostolique," *Revue d'histoire diplomatique* 88 (1974): 223–58.

40. BN fr. 15734, fols. 17–20 (*procès-verbal* of a meeting between the Parlement and representatives of the Faculty of Theology, 1 February 1612), fols. 19r, 20r. The court's annoyance extended to Richer, who seems to have been generally unpopular. He was dressed down in private by Achille de Harlay "de la faulte davoire imprudemmment & sans sujet compose ledit traicté et icelluy faict imprimer avec les decretz de la faculté sans [?] authorité," that is, for violating the principle that institutional authority and counsel must go together. This incident had a precedent the previous year when, in the course of the diplomatic quarrel over the condemnation of Belarmine, the *gens du roi* "avoient priée ledict sieur Chancelier nommer ceux qui avoient esté vers le Nunce [pour lui révéler quelques détails des délibérations du Parlement sur l'Affaire] et qu'ils prendroient leur conclusions contre eux comme criminels de lese Majesté, d'avoir conferé sans permission avec un ambassadeur estranger"; see BN fr. 4397, fol. 309v.

of control. Even politically ambitious prelates like du Perron or Richelieu—then just beginning his career as bishop of Luçon—considered it a good idea to devote considerable energies to their pastoral obligations. With the conversion of Henri IV, moreover, the prospect of the general conversion of the Huguenot elite opened up, and the prelates, led by the "great converter" du Perron, were not slow to exploit their new opportunity or the prestige it could bring. This situation led to increased conflict with the courts and intensified the annoyance powerful prelates felt at such conflict. The specific model of diocesan reform that Carlo Borromeo had developed in Milan was significant for the politics of the clergy. Two of Henri IV's cardinals were explicitly disciples of the Milanese saint: Sourdis, as we have seen, and la Rochefoucauld who, while developing his own organizational ideas, maintained an intense devotion to his Italian cousin.[41] Borromeo's model involved a considerable extension of the bishop's power within the diocese, resulting inevitably in a wave of conflict, litigation, and resentment. Being Italian, the model was also by its nature ultramontanizing, involving, for example, the introduction of the Roman breviary—the case of Angers showed how much trouble this could cause. If successful, of course, such reforms would also make the Church more coherent institutionally and presumably more attractive to converts, thus reinforcing the other factors we have noted.

The logic of anti-Protestant apologetics also reinforced the ideal of an authoritative hierarchy. The key arguments used in such apologies or cited by recent converts turned on the historical continuity of Catholic institutions and the need for a stable institutional authority to establish and interpret Scripture. One typical account cites as the most important factor in a prominent conversion

the abuse found among the Protestants, where the artisan . . . and even simple women indifferently interpret the sacred letters, each one according to the maxim of reform and liberty, and *by the interior persuasion of the individual spirit* which enlightens and guides them infallibly (as they say), although hardly consistently.[42]

41. On la Rochefoucauld, see Gabriel de la Rochefoucauld, *Un homme d'Eglise et d'Etat au commencement du XVIIe siècle: Le Cardinal François de la Rochefoucauld* (Paris: Plon, 1926); and Joseph Bergin, *Cardinal de La Rochefoucauld: Leadership and Reform in the French Church* (New Haven, Conn.: Yale University Press, 1987). According to the former of these works (pp. 106–7), la Rochefoucauld was instrumental in having those canons of the Council of Basel produced after its break with the pope excised from official editions.

42. *Conversion de Pierre Marcha en l'église de Saint-Ouen à Rouen*, in Societé des Bibliophiles Normands, *Miscellanées historiques et littéraires*, 4th série, 20 (Rouen, France: Imprimerie Léon

This was opposed to Catholicism's dignified unity, personified in this case by François de Harlay, archbishop of Rouen. The invisibility and interiority of ultimate authority within the Protestant churches was seen as a particularly important source of instability and weakness; thus, the visibility and visible signs of authority in the Catholic hierarchy took on an added strategic importance.[43] This structure paralleled, though with important differences, the distrust of particularity and the search for non–*a priori* modes of authorization that characterized Gallican thought.

In the seventeenth century too, more than ever before, the French cardinals provided the leadership of the Gallican church. The three cardinals raised to that dignity by Henri IV's patronage were particularly important both because their position was undisputed—the Cardinal d'Ossat was permanently resident in Rome, and the Cardinal de Joyeuse, though fabulously wealthy,[44] was neither young nor energetic—and because each in his way was emblematic of the chronic conflict between the prelates and the Gallican magistrates. Sourdis, though he made only episodic forays beyond his province of Guyenne, was exceptionally energetic in his local reforms and disputes. Du Perron, besides his role in the tyrannicide controversy, launched magisterial attacks from on high on what he took to be definitive statements of Gallican doctrine: Richer's *De potestate* and, as we shall see, the article of the third estate in 1614. La Rochefoucauld was a diehard Leaguer, though, apart from the Marthe Brossier affair and an episode in 1626, he generally refrained from direct political involvement after his reconciliation with Henri IV. He symbolized, however, the ongoing power of the Leaguer spirit within the French church, and thus epitomized most completely its rejection of the Gallican line.

In 1597, while still in his diocese of Clermont licking his wounds after the defeat of his party, la Rochefoucauld wrote a small book on ecclesiastical authority which, as he ingenuously noted, was largely derived from the works of Bellarmine. Far from repenting of it after being received into the

---

Gy, 1905), 9 (emphasis in original). Marcha was a Protestant minister whose conversion was made the occasion of a *coup de théâtre* during the Assembly of Notables of 1617.

43. A very clear statement of this line of thought may be found in Thomas Pelletier, *La conversion du Sr Pelletier à la Foy Catholique. En laquelle il represente au naif les vrayes & infaillibles marques de l'Eglise* (Paris: Jean Junnon, 1609).

44. In 1615, la Rochfoucauld and du Perron were assessed for the *décime* at l. 4,000 apiece, Sourdis at l. 7,000, and Joyeuse at l. 20,000! See Pierre Blet, *Le clergé de France et la monarchie: Études sur les Assemblées Générales du Clergé de 1615 à 1666*, 2 vols. (Rome: Librairie éditrice de l'Université Grégorienne, 1959), 2:398.

Assemblies of the Clergy 243

royal confidence, though, he prepared a new edition, which was provided with a fine engraved, allegorical title page and a dedication to Henri himself.[45] It was presented as a guide for diocesan priests in controversy with Protestants though, as Joseph Bergin has noted, it clearly had Gallicans in view as at least a secondary target. What strikes the reader, though, is not so much the body of the text as the tone of the new dedicatory epistle added for the second edition. There, the author preached a political sermon to the ruler whose legitimacy he had only recently and with the greatest reluctance accepted, and he evidently did so without provoking any objection from Henri, who was notoriously disinclined to be told his own business.[46] Clearly, the cardinal enjoyed considerable support from his king.

The theme of the dedication was the actions necessary to preserve the state. La Rochefoucauld's ideas about the foundations of political prudence, however, differed radically from those advanced by the *parlementaire* Gallicans. From the beginning he radically denied the possibility of contingency:

Nature can teach us, sire, and it is confirmed by experience and placed beyond debated by the rules of our religion, that nothing occurs in this world haphazardly or by chance: that fortune and destiny having contributed nothing to the building of this great work, they cannot pretend to guide it, nor yet attribute to themselves its conservation.

It is not merely that all things are the work of divine providence, which any Christian would admit; the operations of that Providence are openly accessible in natural law. Divine Wisdom,

having deigned to communicate with men by providing them with reason, has drawn from it justice, equity, prudence, laws and administration, which are need-

---

45. François (Cardinal) de la Rochefoucauld, *De l'auctorité de l'Eglise en ce qui concerne la foy, et la religion*, "Seconde Edition reveue et augmente de plusieurs Chapitres" (Paris: Ambroise et Hierome Drouart, 1604). The title page repeats the sense of the dedication to the king. There are three registers, the middle one being the title surrounded by pillars. Above, the Pantocrator gives the crossed keys to Ecclesia (with triple tiara), and the scepter to Henri (with crown), both figures kneeling. Below, "Regale" and "Sacerdotium" stand before the pillars, the former as Plenty or Prudence, the latter as Moses with censer and tablets. On this book see Bergin, *Cardinal de la Rochefoucauld*, 29–31.

46. The most famous expression of this impatience is the speech Henri gave to the Parlement of Paris ordering it to register the Edict of Nantes, of which easily twenty manuscript copies are preserved in the BN alone. It is printed in Roland Mousnier, *L'assasinat d'Henri IV: Le problème du tyrannicide et l'affermissement de la monarchie absolue* (Paris: N.R.F./Gallimard, 1964), 334–37.

ed to govern the world . . . an eternal and immutable law: an infallible rule, and a complete model for human action. On this law, the order of conduct in the world takes its seat and foundation."[47]

This suggests that the prelates put much greater reliance on the power of pure reason in human affairs than we have seen in erudite Gallican thought. Indeed, the author of the *Response au traicté* lamented at one point that "it is a vice of these times, . . . that the world regulates its actions more by human standards . . . than by reason or the law, which is an infallible rule."[48]

For the Gallican jurists, the only possible guide to political action and the only guarantor of civil stability was custom, to which (at least within the political sphere) both reason and revelation were ultimately subordinate, and which was only accessible to a certain class and by a certain method. For the prelates, reason and revelation stood autonomously as a single, transcendent model for political action. The former might, at least in principle, be immanent to all, but the latter was the privileged domain of what is now called the *magisterium*. Two considerations tended to complicate this model, however. The first was not broached by la Rochefoucauld, but it was nonetheless important: the arguments advanced against the transparency of reason, which we touched on above, still stood—and as the pamphleteer suggested, reason seemed at any rate not to be operative among the bulk of humanity. Second, it was important to clarify the boundary between those aspects of public affairs governed by reason or natural law and those governed by what might be called *revealed* reason. The latter would be the exclusive preserve of the clergy, who had an interest in making it as broad as possible.

For la Rochefoucauld, who was preoccupied with soteriological issues, the very sublimity of natural existence revealed the need for eternal life, and hence for salvation, revelation, and ecclesiastical authority. "And from this relation of Earth to Heaven, and of time to eternity results the concord, harmony, and connection of the two sovereign powers God established for the government of men." This is recognizable as the doctrine of the medieval curialists, that the final cause of secular government is the saving work of the Church, but la Rochefoucauld contented himself with deriving from it the corollary that the form of relation between the two powers was

47. La Rochefoucauld, *De l'auctorité*, sigs. aiiir, aiv r–v.
48. *Response*, 55. This outlook is characteristic of the seventeenth-century Catholic anti-Machiavellians studied by Robert Birely in *The Counter-Reformation Prince: Anti-Machiavellianism or Catholic Statecraft in Early Modern Europe* (Chapel Hill: University of North Carolina Press, 1990).

determined by revelation, a "marriage consummated by the new law of the Gospel."⁴⁹ From this in turn it followed that the ecclesiastical hierarchy alone could determine the proper bounds of its own competence.

This reading would seem to run the danger of soliciting the text, were it not for the existence at that time of a very well-developed tradition of episcopal addresses to the king, to which this dedication conformed. The roots of this genre lay at least as deep in the constitution of the French monarchy as did those of robe eloquence. In a celebrated passage Claude de Seyssel had described it as one of the basic checks on the power of the monarchy:

> Now if the king lives according to the law and the Christian religion he cannot do anything tyrannical. And if he should, it is permissible for any prelate ... to remonstrate with him and criticize him and for a simple preacher to take it up with him and to argue publicly and to his face. And yet the king would not even dare to mistreat or abuse him for it ... which does not happen in any other kingdom.⁵⁰

Such constitutionalist language fell out of favor as the sixteenth century progressed, but the reality it described continued undisturbed. Indeed, the reality came to approach the rhetoric rather more closely than before due to the institution of the assemblies itself. In a practice borrowed from the Estates General from which they had emerged, at the close of an Assembly one of its members was deputized to deliver a harangue to the king presenting the *cahier*. The speech was essentially ceremonial, but, unlike the sermons Seyssel had in mind, it had behind it the implicit threat of the most effective known weapon against royal tyranny: fiscal obstructionism.

From the beginning these harangues were occasions for presenting a consistent theory of the correct relationship between the monarch and his prelates—the closest equivalent for the magistrates were the speeches given at the opening of a *lit de justice*.⁵¹ The first such oration, in 1579, touched already on a number of themes that we have seen in la Rochefoucauld, and were to recur again and again. The cardinal's very strong providentialism, for example, was present and explicitly linked with the problem of political durability. To this ontologically grounded causal connection between religious policy and the continued existence of the state was added an empirically grounded one, namely, that correct religious observance by the popu-

49. La Rochefoucauld, *De l'auctorité*, sig. aix v, sig. ax v.
50. Claude de Seyssel, *La monarchie de France*, ed. Jacques Poujol (Paris: Librairie d'Argences, 1961), 116. This is from Bk. 1, chap. 9: "De la religion qui est le premier frein des rois."
51. For an analysis of how those orations functioned, see Sarah Hanley, *The Lit de justice of the Kings of France: Constitutional Ideology in Legend, Ritual, and Discourse* (Princeton, N.J.: Princeton University Press, 1983), passim.

lace at large guaranteed civil stability, and was in turn guaranteed by a correct ecclesiastical order.

Also, the experience of past centuries up to today has demonstrated that among Christians ... censures and excommunication are more useful for intimidating and containing hard and felonious hearts in good faith and civil society than are the grandeur, valor, power, laws and ordinances of kings and magistrates.[52]

This stabilizing power competed directly with that of the courts. The clergy also added a private consideration to these public ones, namely, the king's concern for his own soul—an appeal to the personal royal body uniquely available to the clergy, who alone held jurisdiction over it. The oration ended with a quote from Louis the Fat: "Royal authority is nothing but a procuratorship and public charge, for which you must give a most exact and rigorous accounting after death."[53] Such statements contrasted sharply with the *parlementaire* flirtation with royal inexcommunicability.

The harangue delivered in 1596, after the conflicts with the Parlement we have already noted, was given by none other than Claude d'Angennes de Rambouillet, bishop of le Mans. He had been a leader of the assemblies since their institution, and as a loyalist of the first hour he was likely to find favor with the king.[54] He was not, however, a master of this particular genre and his speech added little to what had been said in 1579. Again one finds the themes of the king's personal responsibility for the government of the French church, the desirability for the sake of civil peace of a strong religion, and the providential sanction of good ecclesiastical management: "the alteration of races in this monarchy has only come about when the church has been ill governed in this way and its goods given over to the laity."[55] Two years later it was the turn of François de la Guesle, brother of the *procureur général*. He was also somewhat more explicit about the authority with which and for which he spoke. The assembled clerics were "servants, ministers, and

---

52. *Recueil des actes*, col. 5. Note the similarity to the papal diplomatic instructions quoted above, where the nuncio is requested to remind the king that ecclesiastical reform will lead to "la pace dei popoli et in conseguenza al quiete del Regno."

53. *Recueil des actes*, col. 14. The other possible source of such private authority was through education; the authority of a royal tutor or (female) parent was, as we shall see, cited in distinguishing the king's two bodies.

54. Not only Rambouillet but also Renaud de Beaune, Henri's other pillar of support within the episcopacy, had been a leader of the Assembly in the 1580s, which may help account for Navarre's partiality toward the order. See Serbat, *Les Assemblées*, e.g., 293, 299, 304–5, and 312.

55. *Recueil des actes*, col. 218.

ambassadors of the eternal God of peace and of justice, dispensers of his sacred mysteries, by whose mouths his holy will is announced."[56] The magistrates might claim to be "priests of justice," as they were styled in Justinian's *Institutes*, but that could only ever be a derivative claim, while the clergy were free to claim a more exalted and immediate contact with true Peace and Justice and to provide a more effective transcendental ideal for political conduct.

One might also suspect, though it would be hard to prove, that such claims of oracular authority were more in sympathy with an emerging discourse of absolutism than the less universalizing language of the erudite Gallicans. While the idea of absolute monarchy, and in particular of its exemplification in seventeenth-century France, has been vigorously attacked and in many ways has fallen out of fashion, it still retains its utility in the study of political culture.[57] Few scholars would deny that the style of the French monarchy changed significantly under the Bourbons, becoming more personalized, more extravagant in its claims to exclusive authority, and more magnificently self-centered in its display. Perhaps the most typical symptom of this new ideology was a cult of strong, decisive, unilateral action, the so-called *coup d'état*, that would have turned Donald Rumsfeld slightly green.[58] Combined with the secular trend toward a more powerful central government, this was enough to alter the political landscape radically. Perhaps, as some scholars have suggested, it would be more accurate to call the result a "baroque" or a "confessional" rather than an "absolute" monarchy.[59] The former terms would have the advantage of stressing the link between the new style and post-Tridentine Catholicism.[60] For the sake of convenience

---

56. *Recueil des actes*, cols. 251–52.

57. Nicholas Henshall, in *The Myth of Absolutism: Change and Continuity in Early Modern European Monarchy* (London: Longman, 1992), summarizes all of the possible arguments against "absolutism."

58. The best introduction to this cult is the text and introductory essay of Gabriel Naudé, *Considerations politiques sur les coups d'état*, ed. Louis Marin (Paris: Editions de Paris, 1989).

59. A recent German controversy, which will delight conoisseurs of academic invective, hashes all of these issues out quite thoroughly. See Peter Baumgart, "Absolutismus ein Mythos? Aufgeklärter Absolutismus ein Widerspruch? Reflexionen zu einem kontroversen Thema gegenwärtiger Frühneuzeitforschung," *Zeitschrift für historische Forschung* 27 (2000): 573–89; and Heinz Duchhardt, "Die Absolutsimusdebatte: eine Antipolemik," *Historische Zeitschrift* 275 (2002): 323–31, and "Absolutismus: Abschied von einem Epochenbegriff?," *Historische Zeitschrift* 258 (1994).

60. Eric Nelson, *The Monarchy and the Jesuits: Political Authority and Catholic Renewal in France*,

and tradition, however, I will continue to use the term "absolutism" to refer to this new style of monarchy.

The next clerical harangue in 1605 included another, far more obvious adaptation to that absolutism. This was the first such speech not to include a call for that Gallican classic, the restoration of episcopal elections. A closer examination of the record shows that in this matter the assemblies of the clergy had been moving away both from Gallican ideas of the autonomy of canon law and from classical republican notions of civic virtue for some time. In 1579 their *cahier* included a long and impassioned plea for elections, but the Assembly of the Clergy of 1595 had already debated "whether it would be good, in case the king does not wish to restore free elections to the clergy, to consider more convenient remedies so that they may be provided with good and sufficient prelates?"[61] Evidently the clergy decided in the affirmative, for in their *cahier* they greatly reduced the call for elections both in length and in emphasis, and followed it by an article proposing as an alternative a new procedure for the examination of candidates for the episcopacy. They followed the same form in 1605, while dropping the call for elections entirely.[62] The orator (this time, Jerôme de Villars, archbishop of Vienne) merely requested

> that your majesty, as he has done in the happy nomination of the prelates who are [now] in the churches of your realm, should henceforth choose such capable persons for nomination to prelacies that you may be discharged in your conscience, which is strictly bound and obliged in the matter.[63]

As Bergin has pointed out, these proposals "contained in embryonic form the idea of a *conseil de conscience*," such as was eventually put in place under Louis XIV.[64] This is not the last case we shall see in which the policies of

---

1590–1615 (Aldershot, U.K.: Ashgate, forthcoming), delves much more deeply than I do into these connections.

61. *Procès-verbaux*, 570B.

62. In 1595 the restoration of elections was requested in article 4, while article 5 (*Recueil des actes*, cols. 1144–45) began "Et où il plairoit à votredit Majesté l'accorder[,] pour le present attendant qu'il plaise à Dieu vous en faire la grace, afin qu'il y soit bien & heureusement pourvu ausdites Prelatures à la decharge de votre conscience," continuing to request a system whereby the life and morals of episcopal candidates would be vetted by a commission consisting of the metropolitan bishop and three canons from the vacant bishopric. The same pattern was followed in 1605 (*Recueil des actes*, cols. 1165–66).

63. *Recueil des actes*, col. 271.

64. Joseph Bergin, *The Making of the French Episcopate, 1589–1661* (New Haven, Conn.: Yale University Press, 1996), 436. Bergin seems unaware that these ideas had been put forward prior to the Estates General of 1615, though, as we shall see, that assembly marked another

high absolutism were first adumbrated in the assemblies of the clergy under Henri IV.

In fact, the clergy came to accept not only the possibility but the desirability of legislation by the monarch—whether the pope or the king did not need to be specified—and the supremacy of the royal will (under God, of course) in determining public virtue. They accompanied this with a still more definite turn toward the rhetoric of absolutism. In domestic and foreign affairs, Henri was portrayed as all-powerful, his will taking effect with neither delay nor mediation: "all foreign provinces, of which the single, double, and triple crowns are not held firm and assured on the heads of their possessors, but the simple laying down of your arms," paralleled the French people conquered by their king's love; "love does not wander or delay, but delights in speeding to its desire."[65] If it was in fact at just this moment that such absolutism became dominant in the French monarchy, the prelates must be given credit for a truly extraordinary political sense in accommodating themselves to it so promptly.

An accommodation, however, should not be confused with a capitulation. Even the most absolute prince had limitations, among them his own conscience and the need to take counsel. Moreover, he remained a mortal with a soul subject to the Church. There was no reason, in fact, why an absolute monarch should not be absolutely responsive to the needs of the Church. They were after all identical to his own ultimate needs and those of his state, and the ecclesiastical hierarchy was uniquely qualified to express them. Indeed, it could not but express those needs, and with a perfect transparency:

What crime for a prelate, speaking for the entire church of France, for a subject to conceal from his king what touches the salvation of his soul? . . . If, by keeping silent on this truth, some ill were to occur, would we not be guilty and criminals of divine and human treason, and unworthy to live and to see the light of the world, and to breath the air that gives us life? . . . Your majesty, sire, is to this state what the head is to the human body. . . . Your subjects represent the exterior sens-

---

important step away from support for episcopal elections. Villars by the way, like Paul Hurault de l'Hospital, had been a *conseiller clerc* in the Parlement of Paris; see Bergin, *The Making of the French Episcopate*, p. 715.

65. *Les remonstrances*, 1: 118v, 117r, marginal note (later editions lack the marginal notes doubtless introduced for a contemporary printing). On the immediacy between the royal will and its effect as a characteristic absolutist topos, see Louis Marin, *Le portrait du Roi* (Paris: Les Éditions de Minuit, 1981), 236–50. Given Henri's personal life, though, it is hard to read the references to his amorous motivation other than ironically.

es.... And among your subjects, the eyes are represented by the most noble part, by the first rank, which the ecclesiastics possess as the highest part of your state. They conjure your majesty by his royal bounty to find it good that this truth should be represented by my mouth.... Those who are dedicated to holy things should carry [truths] ever on the tips of their tongues.[66]

The transparent access to a necessary and state-preserving truth that the magistrates justified through a complex and subtle ontology and epistemology, their jurisdictional rivals could claim as a direct consequence of their position with respect to God and to the body politic. Their claims of a right to offer authoritative counsel extended to both the public and the private royal body, both of which were subject to the same divine legislation. Nor did the bishops need to distinguish between a "public" and a "private" reason with different scopes and capabilities. It was enough that the reason be duly illuminated by faith and the Holy Spirit for it to undertake all things.[67] It might be objected that the prelates, like the king, were moved by human as well as divine impulses and might be as untrustworthy as any other counselors, but this cavil could be countered in its own terms. Ecclesiastics "are disinterested, having no children to succeed them in whatever designs they might have."[68] The structure of the Church was as effective a machine as the Venetian constitution for detaching will from interest.

The Assembly of the Clergy of 1605 was also notable for the vigor with which it pressed its attack on the Gallican courts. Already in 1596 the Assembly had investigated reports of unorthodox statements about marriage made by Servin, though concluding that these were unfounded.[69] The otherwise uneventful small Assembly of 1600 had taken up and included in its *cahier* a precedence dispute between the Parlement of Provence and the Bish-

---

66. *Recueil des actes*, cols. 271–72. Recall that *parlementaires* too had used the topos of the "eyes of the body politic" to justify a position of preeminent public authority, attached there as here to a transcendental idea of political organization.

67. See, e.g., *Recueil des actes*, col. 279: "Mais en ceste consideration, nous avons à nous plaindre, que la prudence humaine prenant le timon, & s'en faisant ordinairement trop à croire dans la conduite des grandes affaires, nous fait souvent un mauvais parti, lorsqu'entrant seulement en son conseil particulier, & n'y apellant que sa raison & que ses prevoïances humaines, elle ne jette point les yeux sur ces grandes causes qui agissent hors d'elle," etc. (harangue of 1608). What "conseil particulier" lacks here is not integrity, but merely *information*, which the hierarchy alone can supply.

68. *Perroniana*, 115, s.v. "Ecclesiastiques."

69. *Procès-verbaux*, 1:609B. Servin was supposed to have said: "que le mariage étoit bon & parfait sans la Bénédiction Sacerdotale, nonobstant l'ordonnance du Concile de Trente; ... qu'auparavant & sans ledit Concile, le Royaume ne laissoit d'être Catholique."

op of Sisteron.⁷⁰ In 1605, though, the clergy jumped with both feet into the individual disputes between bishops and parlements that were rampant by that time, a practice kept up at subsequent meetings. The quarrel between the Archbishop of Aix and the court of that city over the demission of clerics received a long hearing and inclusion in the *cahier*. This pales in comparison, though, to the stress the clergy laid on the Breviary of Angers affair. Not only was Miron's cause given a full hearing and taken up in the *cahier*, but "that ruling being the most important thing, and the most prejudicial to the Church that had yet been, and could in the future be proposed in the Assembly," a separate delegation was sent to the king, led by the Cardinal de Joyeuse himself, to demand that Servin henceforth be barred from pleading in cases involving the Church!⁷¹ There was also some shadowy dispute over certain actions of a Grand Jours in the Auvergne: no trace of it is to be found in the *procès verbaux*, but some jurist drew up a reply to *possible* objections on the part of the Assembly, giving vent at the same time to no little spleen:

It is difficult to discern from what motives the Assembly of the Clergy has engaged itself to demand their revocation from the king . . . but one may easily presume that, a stay in Paris not being disagreeable to those who compose the Assembly, they have been quite content to consume their time in long deliberations and thus to delay their return to their dioceses, which they consider an exile.⁷²

Tensions, and resentments, were running exceptionally high.

What is more, for the first time the Assembly requested that the *appel comme d'abus*, the cornerstone of the entire Gallican edifice, be restrained. Representatives of the clergy and the Parlement of Paris even had a conference on the matter—with how little effect can easily be imagined.⁷³ To all

---

70. *Procès-verbaux*, 1:675B. The dispute was part of the saga of Paul Hurault de l'Hospital discussed in the previous chapter.

71. *Procès-verbaux*, 1:758B–760B, 753B–756A, 755A. It seems clear that l'Hospital personally played a considerable role in pioneering the involvment of the assembly in specific jurisdictional disputes.

72. BN fr. 15463, fols. 108–14: "Memoires envoyez de Clermont en Auvergne sur larrest des grands Jours du xxx octobre 1605," fol. 113r–v. The author, no doubt a Parisian himself, must have felt very keenly the attractions of the capital from which he was detained!

73. *Procès-verbaux*, 1:722B. An undated set of eleven "Articles proposez par le Clergé de France assemblé a Paris par la Permission du Roy sur la conference accordée par sa Majesté a ladicte Assemblée avec Messieurs du Parlement de Paris," BN fr. 2760, fols. 299–300, may well be from this meeting. If so, the proposals of the clergy would have revolutionized legal affairs. They asked among other things that the *appel comme d'abus* be limited to questions of

this the royal response, though still rather vague, was far more sympathetic than any the clergy had received on jurisdictional issues before. This may have been due to Villar's skillful flattery; more likely, it was a sign of Henri's (and Villeroy's) displeasure at continual *parlementaire* interference with royal diplomacy. Whatever was the case, the prelates can only have felt encouraged in their new stance, though for the time being they did little to push it further.

In a rather extraordinary display of consistency, the orator at the Assembly of 1610 (François de Pericard, bishop of Avranches) took the prelates' faith in the power of Providence so far as to ascribe Henri IV's death to divine displeasure—a punishment, he said, for the sin of pride. This was a striking illustration of the freedom the prelates felt to speak to the private life of the monarch. To the child-king, Pericard preached obedience to his parents: not only his mother, but God, "whom you have as a father, just as you have the Church for your mother."[74] What this meant in practice was clear: above all, he should restrain the secular courts.

What shame and dishonor is it to this kingdom, which once merited the title of most Christian, . . . which was the refuge and protection of those who were persecuted elsewhere for the defense of the Church, and of its rights—take, for example, that great archbishop of Canterbury, St. Thomas—that today one sees here ecclesiastics held in such opprobrium and disrespect, and the authority of the Church so thrown down?[75]

Concretely, the clergy proposed a return to the old system whereby one of the two *avocat général* positions in each parlement had been clerical; this was a thinly disguised attack on Servin.[76] Unsurprisingly, no progress was made, and tempers grew worse.

For the next five years, as Marie de Medicis struggled to hold the kingdom together, the clergy did not meet, but in the mean time the enmity between it and the magistrates only grew. We have already discussed the rea-

---

jurisdiction, that the competence of the secular courts be limited to the cassation of ecclesiastical verdicts, and that the practice of seizing the temporal of recalcitrant beneficiaries be ended, although this was the principal means of coercion available to the secular courts.

74. *Recueil des actes*, col. 289.

75. *Recueil des actes*, col. 302. The tract *De la puissance royalle* gives a precisely contradictory interpretation of the lessons to be drawn from Thomas à Beckett's career.

76. *Procès-verbaux*, 2:33A–B. On the old system, see Bernard de la Roche Flavin, *Treze livres des parlemens de France* (Bordeaux, France: Simon Millanges, 1617), 92. According to him, this practice prevailed only in Paris. One aspect of the clergy's unhappiness with the sovereign courts was a pervasive concern over the decay of the institution of the *conseiller-clerc*.

sons for this: the multitude of lawsuits, concerns over tyrannicide, and so on. *Parlementaire* efforts to stamp out dangerous writings, in particular, were redoubled, leading to increased friction with Rome. Villeroy, who was responsible for relations with the papacy, began to take a deeply pessimistic view of the whole affair. While urging on Isaac Casaubon (who was writing on behalf of James I) the danger of the entire dispute, "so that I would rather seek to smother such an enormous and unnatural crime than to keep up the memory of this dispute,"[77] he wrote a meditative letter to one of his agents at the papal court that drew a very alarming picture. Like the former Leaguer he was, he sympathized more with the papalists than with their opponents, but he found even his allies extreme in their views and heedless of consequences, "so much so that those writers do exactly the opposite of what they claim."

"Perhaps," he continued,

there was a time when such writers could be useful ... but we see that the season for this is past in Europe, where the number of those who hope to diminish the power of the popes increases in a variety of ways rather than diminishing: which it seems that they cannot or will not understand in Rome.

At this time, in particular, the success of Christian von Anhalt's maneuvers in the Rhineland and the weakness of Catholicism in the Austrian territories made the prospect of a Protestant hegemony in the Holy Roman Empire seem a real possibility.[78] This and the ever-present Turkish threat made Villeroy gloomy about the future of Christendom itself,

which is becoming weaker and disintegrating before our eyes ... I think that they do not have so little foresight in Rome that they cannot perceive this, and nevertheless, seeing that they do not understand the consequences and the events as the size and proximity of the peril merits, it seems that God has judged them and we other Catholics in his wrath.[79]

77. BN fr. 15733, fol. 243 (Villeroy to Casaubon, 1 December 1611, copy). Casaubon, it should be remembered, was personally very close to de Thou (and, incidentally, to Paolo Sarpi).

78. For a good account of the international situation in the first part of the seventeenth century, see Geoffrey Parker, ed., *The Thirty Years' War* (London: Routledge, 1984), 2–38. Under the influence of Sully and Richelieu, historians often forget the degree to which French policymakers found it necessary to negotiate between the Scylla of the Hapsburg Empire and the Charybdis of international Calvinism, each of which had its own potentially rebellious partisans within the kingdom, and neither of which could be allowed to become dominant.

79. BN fr. 15733, fols. 245–46 (Villeroy to a French representative at Rome [?], undated but probably contemporary with the previous letter, copy), 254r. The letter ends: "Monsieur

These were, perhaps, the night thoughts of an aging man, or perhaps a persona adopted for the benefit of the curia. However, a deep apocalyptic strain had moved Catholics during the Wars of Religion, and under Marie de Medici's regency it retained sufficient vigor that fears about the collapse of Catholicism could be very real.[80] A set of prophecies from this period, familiar in their outline but now far removed from any Gallican program, predicted just such an eventuality, to be followed by the defeat of the Turks at the hands of the French king and a general renewal of Christendom.[81] Perhaps more significantly, a brief tract attributed to Cardinal du Perron dating from the period of the Venetian Interdict crisis used the same language. The pope's mismanagement of the affair led the author to believe that

> it was not certain whether God, to punish the vices of Christendom, would one day permit the Catholic religion to be oppressed in Italy, or possibly even banished from Europe as it had been from Africa and Asia, and in the end to be transferred to the Indies and into the other hemisphere.[82]

It is difficult to tell how much significance one should assign to this line of thought, but it does throw some light on the bitterness with which Gallican designs were opposed.[83]

Such millenarian fears shared with the rest of the anti-Gallicans' political thought the metaphysical presuppositions of the direct activity of supernatural forces in history and the availability of (reasonably) precise knowledge concerning those forces to those who knew where to look. At a practical level, they both also reinforced a deep distrust of activist Gallicanism and a fear that, unchecked, it could tear down the divinely instituted order of the kingdom and, more importantly, of the Catholic Church. A particularly

---

me trouvant icy avec quelque loisir, j'ay bien voulu descharger en vostre sien ces mesmes cogitations et pensées sur les affaires qui se presentent desquelles vous userez ainsy que vous jugerez pour le mieux" (246r).

80. On Catholic chiliasm in the religious wars, see Denis Crouzet, *Les guerriers de Dieu: La violence au temps des troubles de religion (vers 1525–vers 1610)*, 2 vols. (Paris: Champ Vallon, 1990).

81. BN fr. 2760, fols. 376–89: "Extraict des Propheties et revelations des Ss. Peres." This version seems to have been recycled in the minority of Louis XIV.

82. "Raisons, representees au Pape, par le Cardinal du Perron sur l'affaire d'entre sa Steté. & les Veneciens en l'an 1607," BN fr. 4770, fols. 178v–180r, fol. 178v.

83. Another example of this type of thinking may be found in a brief pamphlet entitled *Prophetie faite par M. Abel Ongeur* (Paris: P. Buray, 1614), 4, which expresses the fear that in the year of its publication "Chacun sera lors en danger, De voir le bien en mal changer. L'Aigle son vol abbaissera; L'Isle de l'Ange haussera Le coq mangera ses poußins, L'Autriche perdera ses dessins," though all would be redeemed by the *fleur de lys*.

frightening development from the point of view of the clergy was a project, seriously advanced after Henri's assassination, to restrict the secrecy of the confessional. In addition to unambiguously violating conciliar decrees, this would have imposed secular oversight on the innermost recesses of ecclesiastical jurisdiction—on the forum of conscience in its sacramental expression.

This idea resembled that of royal inexcommunicability not only in its radical approach to the sacraments, but also in that no official proposal to this effect ever appeared. It did, however, develop a certain prominence in the pamphlet literature. The issue seems first to have been brought up by James I of England in the preface to his *Apologie for the Oath of Allegiance*. There the royal pamphleteer claimed that the view

that no treason nor devilish plot, though it should tend to the ruine or extermination of a whole Kingdom, must be revealed, if it bee told under Confession; no not the matter so far indirectly disclosed, as may give occasion for preventing the danger thereof, . . . is such a new and dangerous head of doctrine, as no king nor State can live in securitie where that Position is maintained.[84]

While the alternative he proposed to this "conceit of some three or foure new *Jesuited* Doctors"—that, without revealing the name of the penitent, the plot be found out to the authorities—had perhaps an even better claim to be called Jesuitical, it did attempt to preserve in principle the secrecy of the confessional. We have already mentioned that the Jacobin Coeffeteau published a reply to James's *Apologie*. In his reply, whether deliberately or not, he construed James's position to be that confession was "pernicious to states if it is not permissible to violate its seal and declare its secrets for the good of republics."[85]

At any rate, Gallican jurists soon took up the same ideas. The clearest statement in favor of compromising the secrecy of confession was included in a pamphlet written as a "confession of faith in matters of state" by a fairly obscure lawyer and *litterateur* named Pierre de Nancel. Composed in deadly, protoclassical Alexandrine couplets and glorying in the title *De la Souveraineté des Roys: Poeme epique, divisé en trois livres*, it was a compendium of

---

84. James I and VI, *An Apologie for the Oath of Allegiance . . . Together with a Premonition of his Majesties, to all most Mightie Monarches, Kings, free Princes and States of Christendom* (London: Robert Barker, 1609), pt. 1 (the "Premonition"), 125.

85. Nicolas Coeffeteau, *Responce à l'advertissement, adressé par le Serenissime Roy de la Grande Bretagne, Jacques I. à tous les Princes et Potentats de la Chrestienté* (Paris: François Huby, 1610 [1609]), fol. 157r–v.

Gallican-royalist commonplaces.[86] The discussion of confession came at the end of the first "book," explicitly as a cure for the evils brought about by the doctrine of tyrannicide. The sacramental aspects of confession, Nancel acknowledged, were divinely instituted and unalterable,

> But the duty of silence imposed, for its part
> Is a positive law, and goes not to the heart.
> There may be dispensation: God has not ordained
> That silence in these things be strictly maintained.[87]

Since those who assassinate kings are motivated not by hope for worldly gain but rather by the vision of an eternal reward, Nancel argued, they will not carry out their heinous designs if they cannot first safely have them cleared in the confessional. He rather undercut his own thesis by holding at the same time that assassins were merely the pawns of the subtle doctrine of tyrannicide, an ecclesiastical creation whose sponsors would presumably be unlikely to betray their simple followers, but this is of little moment. In practice, Nancel wanted the death penalty for confessing an urge to kill the king, and (despite the ingenious suggestion that would-be assassins could confess their sins in a foreign country) the chances of anyone gaining support from the Church for imposing such a punishment for partaking of the sacraments were unmeasurably small.[88]

This relatively minor controversy shows how deep the polarization between the clergy and the Gallican jurists ran. Combined with the doctrine of royal inexcommunicability, it threatened to remove not only the person of the king but everything that might (literally) touch it from the realm of sacramental order. Nor was it a simple response to a specific case of "tyrannicide": indeed, the dispute over the seal of the confessional straddled the assassination of Henri IV. There were fundamentally incompatible understandings of both the Church and the French monarchy at play here, and the leaders of clergy in particular were well aware of this. It is only in this context that the escalating conflict over tyrannicide and its condemnation

---

86. Pierre de Nancel, *De la Souveraineté des Roys: Poeme epique, divisé en trois livres* (s.l., 1610), 7. Sacramental confession is discussed on pp. 29–40.

87. *De la souveraineté*, 31: "Mais le seau du segret, le devoir du silence, Est du droit positif, & n'est pas de l'essence, On peut en dispenser, Dieu n'a pas commandé Que le silence y fust ettroittement gardé." The entire poem reads like dime-store Corneille.

88. Nancel was not alone in his beliefs. In one of his earlier pleas, for example, Servin opined "que le secret de Confession en cas de crime de Leze-Majesté non seulement se peut, mais encore se doit reveler"; see *Plaidoyez*, vol. 1 (Paris: Jean de Heuqueville, 1603), 126. This is one of the points on which he was attacked by Louis Richeome, *Advis et notes donnees sur quelques plaidoyez de Maistre Louys Servin* (Caen, France: Georges de la Mariniere, 1615), 303.

that culminated with the Estates General of 1614 makes sense. With minimal exceptions (perhaps a few Capuchins and even fewer Jesuits), there is no evidence that the French clergy had any real commitment to Suarez's doctrines on assassination.[89] On the substance of whether any subject could raise his or her hand against the king of France, there was no dispute. To understand the clergy's actions when the third estate tried to legislate this principle in 1614–1615, we must understand the climate within which they acted and the associations which Gallican rhetoric would conjure up.

The political situation in 1614 was not truly dire—certainly not compared to that which had prevailed during the previous meeting of the Estates General in 1588 (or 1593, if one counts the Leaguer Estates)—but with a government in transition, princes in intermittent rebellion, and finances deteriorating, the circumstances were not propitious for mature and effective deliberation. Still, even by the dubious standards of the institution, the Estates General of 1614 were a debacle, resulting in an enormous amount of infighting and no action to speak of.[90] Almost all of their energy was taken up by two grand quarrels: the first between the commons and the nobility and the second between the commons and the clergy. In fact, both incidents did little more than rehash tensions that were already well established in French society and that the issues before the Estates General were calculated to bring out. Those substantive issues that arose were for the most part centered around the question of office holding, which was the chief bone of contention for the French elites.

A few aspects of the complex problem of office holding in the old regime are worth bearing in mind.[91] The first is the parallel between offices in the church and the state. Before the imposition of the *paulette* (a tax that guaranteed the heritability of royal offices), the transfer of both had been

---

89. On the Jesuits, see Claude Sutto, "Le Roi et le Parlement dans la pensée et l'action des Jésuites français (1590–1625)," in Stegmann, ed., *Pouvoir et institutions*, 263–74; and Nelson, *Monarchy and the Jesuits*, passim. A study of the French Capuchins is badly needed.

90. As J. Michael Hayden has pointed out, the government actually *wanted* a debacle, but in the event they got more than they could reasonably have hoped for; see *France and the Estates General of 1614* (Cambridge, U.K.: Cambridge University Press, 1974).

91. The classic treatment is Roland Mousnier, *La venalité des offices sous Henri IV et Louis XIII*, 2nd ed. (Paris: Presses Universitaires de France, 1971); for a recent discussion of the issue, see William Doyle, *Venality: The Sale of Offices in Eighteenth-Century France* (Oxford, U.K.: Clarendon Press, 1996). On some of the theoretical issues surrounding the question, see Jotham Parsons, "The Roman Censors in the Renaissance Political Imagination," *History of Political Thought* 22 (2001): 565–86.

governed by essentially the same law. Both the courts and the prelates increasingly depended on a visible display of character, expressed through ceremonial and an elaborate code of conduct, to buttress their authority.[92] Moreover, in the lay and ecclesiastical realms alike, the distribution of offices was at the heart of a perceived decline from ideals of republican virtue.[93] As the *paulette* consolidated the regime of venality for royal offices and as the Church recognized the impossibility of ever restoring elections to the major benefices, it became necessary to find a new way of explaining how virtue might be rewarded, and how the king might receive virtuous counsel—though the Estates General made no progress at all on these tasks, as each estate restricted itself to criticism of the regimes under which its colleagues operated. The crisis at hand rendered the destructive power of these critiques very great.

In this context it is clear why each estate's claim to be the guarantor of stability for the monarchy were so vital. The clergy was in a basically stronger position, since its claim, based on divine legislation and the order of nature, was not necessarily dependent on any particular virtue on the part of the prelates themselves. Against the support of the Holy Spirit and the natural disinterestedness of the celibate, the magistrates could only advance their expertise as judges and erudite historians and as the avatars of ancient custom. Much more than their rivals in the first estate, the jurists tended strongly, and perhaps even increasingly, to bolster this with nostalgic depictions of a past marked by civic virtue, to which it might or might not be possible to return. Their peculiar bitterness in 1614–1615 was as much as anything a reaction to relative political impotence. The commons did in fact devote a truly extraordinary amount of time and effort to scoring points off

---

92. On both these issues, see Colin Kaiser, "Les cours souveraines au XVIe siècle: Morale et Contre-Réforme," *Annales: Economies, sociétés, civilisations* 37 (1982): 15–31. For background on the culture of social appearance, see Jacques Revel, "Les usages de la civilité," in Phillipe Ariès and Georges Duby, eds., *Histoire de la vie privée*, vol. 5 (Paris: Seuil, 1986), 169–209. This phenomenon also deeply involved the nobility—*Il corteggiano* was one of its founding texts—on which see Norbert Elias, *The Court Society*, trans. Edmund Jephcott (Oxford, U.K.: Basil Blackwell, 1983).

93. The clergy, though, had never had the same enthusiasm as the magistrates for the language of republicanism. In the first estate's most complete early statement on behalf of episcopal election, namely, the article in the *cahier* of 1579 calling for its restoration, the potential to restore republican virtue was only one of three arguments advanced in favor of elections: the other two were the sacred antiquity of elections, and the evil of simony. This is not to say, however, that when it appeared, republican language lacked clarity: "Votre Majesté remediera à ce mal, quand aïant remis les élections, chacun estimera ne pouvoir venir à aucun degré ou avancement, si ce n'est par le merite de son sçavoir, vertu, & en suivant la vocation ecclesiastique" (*Recueil des actes*, col. 1092).

the other estates; in one incident with eerie echoes of 1788, they succeeded after much squabbling in sending a double-sized deputation to a conference with the king.[94] The major vehicle for their self-assertion, however, was the famous first article of their *cahier*, a thorough expression of the synthesis of Gallican and divine-right theory.

One important problem is the degree to which the third estate in 1614 was an instrument of the hard-core Gallican tendency among the jurists. With the exception of the delegation from Guyenne, the answer seems to have been that it was very much so, with the delegations from Picardy, and to a lesser extent from Orleans and Champagne, showing a tendency even to be *plus gallican que les Gallicans*.[95] The first article itself was obviously the result of a carefully drawn-up strategy, since it appeared in similar wording in the *cahiers* of Paris, Normandy, Champagne, Lyons, and Orleans, as well as being introduced (with no result) in the first and second estates—in the former, by the heavily robe lower clergy of Paris.[96] The article's original redactors were all highly placed Parisian lawyers; they included Antoine Arnauld himself, the *avocat du roi* of the Cour des Aides, and a *conseiller* in the Parlement.[97] Within the Estates General, Robert Miron pushed the article forcefully enough to produce some feeling that he was hijacking the assembly.[98] Considering as well the parallel effort in the Parlement, led by Servin and Molé, on behalf of the same text, one is led to the conclusion that this was a genuine and conscious full-court press on the part of the Gallicans, designed as a show of political strength.

The text of the first estate's article ran, in part,

That, to arrest the course of the pernicious doctrine that was introduced several years ago by seditious spirits against kings and sovereign powers established by God and which troubles and subverts them: the king shall be asked to declare in

94. Pierre Clapisson, "Recueil journalier de ce qui s'est negotié & arresté en la chambre du tiers estat de France en l'assemblée generale des Estats tenus a Paris es annees 1614 & 1615," BN Dupuy 520, fols. 56–58.

95. This is based on voting patterns during the affair of the first article. See also Hayden, *France and the Estates General*, 145n35.

96. *Harangues, Propositions, Opinions, Resolutions, & arrestez de la Chambre du Tiers Estat. Avec le procez verbal, de tout ce qui s'est passé de jour en jour en ladicte Chambre, & l'Ordre tenu en icelle* (Paris: Pierre Mettayer, 1616), 20–32.

97. *Harangues*, 3–4. Among the *quarteniers* for Paris were Antoine Loisel and Jacques Leschassier (though this does not suggest that they held leadership positions). One of Loisel's sons was also a deputy for the *baillage* of Senlis; see Hayden, *France and the Estates General*, 267.

98. BN Dupuy 520, fols. 94v–95r. Later, Miron was accused of caving in to royal pressure to excise the article from the cahier; see Hayden, *France and the Estates General*, 145.

the assembly of his Estates as a fundamental law of the kingdom . . . : that since he is known to be sovereign in his state, holding his crown from God alone, that there is no power on earth whatever, spiritual or temporal, which has any authority over his kingdom, to take away the sacred nature of our kings, to dispense or absolve their subjects of the fidelity and obedience which they owe them for any cause or pretext whatsoever. That all subjects, of whatever quality or condition they might be, shall hold this law to be holy and true as conforming to *the word of God*, without distinction, equivocation, or limitation. . . . That the contrary opinion, that it is lawful to kill and depose our kings, to rise up and rebel against them, to shake off the yoke of obedience, for whatever reason, is *impious*, detestable, against truth, and against the state of France, which is responsible only to God. . . . All subjects of his majesty who hold to this, of whatever quality and condition they might be, shall be . . . guilty of treason in the first degree. And if any book is found that contains a proposition directly or indirectly contrary to this law written by a foreigner, cleric or not, the clerics of the same orders established in France will be obliged to respond to it, impugning and contradicting it incessantly.[99]

Considering the disastrous results with which the previous meeting of the Estates General had taken up the task of defining a fundamental law—admittedly, of exactly the opposite tenor—the distaste that the government quickly developed for this article is understandable. However, the government did not take, and had no need to take, the lead in opposition to this innovation, since the first estate was more than happy to do so.

From the clergy's point of view, the article had two offensive features. First, it would have attributed to the Estates general the authority to interpret what was and what was not conformable to the Word of God, a power the Counter-Reformation had marked out as the very foundation of the Catholic Church's superiority. Second, if it went into effect, the article would have given the secular courts the task of judging the doctrinal content of ecclesiastical publications for their conformity to the interpretation of the divine Word that the Estates General had established. This is why, in the printed edition of their *procès-verbaux*, the clergy italicized the text of the article in the manner reproduced above. One may add the fact that, as the leaders of the clergy probably knew, the original text of the article, and thus presumably the intentions of its promoters, were even more radical. Besides the including doctrine of royal inexcommunicability, a surviving early draft

---

99. The translation is from Hayden, *France and the Estates General*, 131–32. The French text may be found in *Procès-verbaux*, 2: pièces justificatives, 21A–B, from whence I take the emphasis, and in Mousnier, *L'assassinat*, 348–49.

Assemblies of the Clergy 261

would have given royal officers unlimited control over the proposed oath of adherence to the article, and would also have required that oath of any foreign visitor who did not have diplomatic immunity.[100] In a word, the proposed article epitomized the jurisdictional claims of the Gallican jurists, and the prelates felt that no effort should be spared in blocking its progress. In the ensuing battle, the clergy attacked the Gallicans with every weapon at their disposal.

The details of this battle were tragicomic. When it got wind of the article, the first estate (represented by Hurault de l'Hospital of Aix) requested that the third estate send it official notice of any articles involving matters of faith. The commons resolved "to say to the gentlemen of the clergy, that the third estate had nothing in its *cahier* concerning the doctrine of the Church. . . . That as to the *police* of the Church, it did touch on it to some extent."[101] This was done by a *capitoul* of Toulouse in a harangue whose baroque involution was only exceeded by its ineptitude, so far departing from decorum at one point as to compare the third estate to the eagle of Jupiter and the Church (or its doctrine, or the clergy: clarity was not the orator's strong suit) to the god's catamite, which cannot have pleased the reverend gentlemen.[102] After some grumbling the third estate did decide to send the first estate a copy of the article, without further comment. They rebuffed the clergy's suggestion that a simple republication of the Canons of Constance be substituted for the disputed text.[103] Than, having secured the support of the nobility (already at loggerheads with the third estate over an earlier incident), the clergy sent the Cardinal du Perron to explain their opposition to the commons.

Du Perron was in some respects the model of a humanist statesman. He

---

100. See Eric Nelson, "Defining the Fundamental Laws of France: The Proposed First Article of the Third Estate at the French Estates General of 1614," *English Historical Review* 115 (2000): 1216–30.

101. *Harangues*, 34–35.

102. *Harangues*, 35–50.

103. According to the *Harangues*, 118 (not, on this question, a reliable source), Aix suggested a compromise text that would bring the condemned doctrine into close, but not perfect, agreement with Constance, forbidding "toute sorte d'attentats contre les sacrees personnes des Roy, ou leur Estat, souz quelque couleur, pretexte, ou occassion que ce soit, et en quelque estat que se trouvent les consciences de leurs Princes." The text of the proposed republication of Constance was printed with a Gallican reply: *Article de l'Eglise apporté au tiers estat par Mongeur* [sic] *L'Evesque de Masçon, le matin 5. jour de Janvier 1615* (s.l., n.d.), which makes the point that since the tyrranicide theorists, against whom the entire enterprise was directed, already accepted the Canon of Constance, its republication would be of little use.

had begun his public career with a celebrated oration (on the death of Ronsard), and at this point he closed it with another. It was difficult to follow him, because of the great crowd ("thirty or forty" ecclesiastics accompanied him) and because, at his advanced age, "his tongue was not quick enough to follow his imagination," and he frequently corrected his choice of words, "taking up a better word, more suitable than the first."[104] One result of this is that a number of different versions of the speech survive: the one he himself published is the most authoritative, though it seems to have been fairly heavily edited.[105] As one might expect, he deployed the claims of his order to a leading place in the councils of the realm more carefully than ever before. Their interests were aligned with France's,

for the other orders come to the charges and to the honors and dignities of this kingdom, some ... at the price of their blood and peril of their lives: and others, besides what is due to their merit, by the contribution of a part of their means and their goods. But as for us, we arrive at them by the sole and pure grace and bounty of our kings.

This certainly squeezed the maximum advantage out of the clergy's abandonment of traditional Gallicanism and its insistence on the election of prelates! Beyond this, according to du Perron, the hierarchy had unique access to firm and eternal truth, which alone could provide the state with a permanent foundation. It also needed exercise control over innovation,

for fear of weakening the authority of that which is certain and infallible, by the admixture of that which is contested and contentious. For experience has taught us only too well that for those evils that proceed from a perverse and corrupted imagination of religion, mere human laws ... cannot serve as a sufficient remedy.... But it is necessary for them to be effective that they proceed from a certain, absolute, and infallible ecclesiastical authority.[106]

This argument carried the burden of the harangue. The cardinal pointed out his own immediate adherence to Henri IV, and he insinuated that, by re-

104. BN Dupuy 520, fols. 89v–90r.
105. "Harangue faitte de la part de la Chambre Ecclesiastique en celle du tiers Estat, sur l'Article du Serment," in *Les diverses œuvres de l'illustrissime Cardinal du Perron* (Paris: Anthoine Estienne, 1621), 594–644. Note that the term "article du Serment" for the disputed article attaches it to James I's anti-papal oath of allegiance, against which du Perron had already written. Characteristic of the immediate interest which this speech generated is an *Advis à un des grands de ce Royaume, sur la harangue faicte au Tiers Estat le 2. Janvier 1615. Par Monseigneur le Cardinal du Perron, touchant la puissance du Sainct Pere, sur les Princes Souveraines* (s.l., 1615), which provides a brief though generally accurate summary of the session and the cardinal's speech.
106. Du Perron, *Œuvres*, 597, 598.

moving ecclesiastical judgment from the political realm, the proposed article would in fact open the door to the *popular* deposition of the king. If tyrannicide was illicit when a prince has been determined to be engaging in the destruction of religion, but (as William Barclay, for example, had argued) was to be allowed if a prince was destroying the nation, what would prevent any self-appointed judge from deciding that the latter was the case? "The judgment that the people may feign of the one is much more perilous to princes than that which the Universal Church may make of the other." In effect, du Perron asked, what guarantees the king of France his throne if not the inerrant pronouncements of the Church on the absolutely stable dictates of God?[107]

This speech provoked a small pamphlet war, drawing a response from no less a figure than King James I.[108] The Parlement immediately issued a text equivalent to the article as an *arrêt*,[109] which only embittered the clergy the more, prompting discussion of the Parlement's ongoing attacks on ecclesiastical jurisdiction, "of which several examples were brought up."[110] The prelates sent the king a list six demands directed against the Parlement, one of which was "that M. Servin should be forbidden from speaking in cases concerned with the Church."[111] A fortnight later, the government returned a

107. Du Perron, *Œuvres*, 644. Du Perron, and the clergy after him, also raised the specter of a schism within the Catholic Church as a result of the proposed article: "Et non seulement cet article nous jette en un schisme inevitable, mais mesme nous precipite en une heresie evidente, nous obligeant necessairement de confesser que l'Eglise Catholique est perie depuis plusieurs siecles, en la terre" (p. 635; see also Hayden, *France and the Estates General*, 144). This fear, though doubtless played up for the benefit of the public, echoes the apocalyptic fears for the fate of the Church discussed above.

108. For details on this, see Hayden, *France and the Estates General*, 144n. To the items cited there one might add François de Kermadec, *Relation veritable envoyee au Serenissime Roy de la Grand' Bretagne* (Nantes, France: n.p., 1615), which as one would guess is the reply of a Breton noble; "Response à trois passages de Maistre Jean Gerson alleguez par le Cardinal du Perron en sa Harangue," BN 500 Colb. 154, fols. 79–84; and "Lettre escripte de Rome touchant la Harangue de Monseigneur l'Illustrissime Cardinal du Perron," BN fr. 15730, fols. 532–37. The last of these is so confusing that it is hard to tell on which side of the issue it comes down.

109. *Arrest de la Cour de Parlement du 2 Janvier 1615. Touchant la Souveraineté du Roy au temporel, & contre la pernicieuse Doctrine d'attenter aux personnes sacrées des Roys. En suite duquel sont les Arrests donnés sur le mesme subject* (Paris: F. Morel & P. Mettayer, 1615).

110. *Procès-verbaux*, 2:186B: a discussion "sur divers procédés desdits Sieurs du Parlement, en plusieurs affaires qui regardent la doctrine de la Foi, Religion & dépendance ... desquels néantmoins ladite Cour, sous prétexte de police, ou autre semblable considération recherchée, en prend la connoissance, qui est une notoire entreprise sur la Jurisdiction Ecclesiastique & spirituelle, dont quelques exemples ont été représentés."

111. *Copie d'une lettre d'un prelat deputé du clergé à l'assemblée des Estats, sur ce qui s'est passé touchant*

vague but friendly reply promising to consider the first estate's advice on the disposition of the offending article and announcing at the same time that the Parlement's edict had been quashed and its printer imprisoned.

In the end, the king had the third estate deliver the article to him separately from the *cahier* with the promise—which no one believed and which was in fact never fulfilled—that he would reply to it in due course. After much dispute, the commons acquiesced to this arrangement; since the only thing the government wanted from the Estates General was for it to go away, they had no real choice but to obey. The pope was sufficiently pleased with this outcome to send an official letter to the clergy praising them for their actions, a move perhaps more generous than politic.[112] One prelate was relieved enough to announce that "by the grace of God we see that we have most of what we are asking for: that the article be suppressed, that it should not give occasion for a schism, and we have some hope of settling accounts with the Court of Parlement."[113] Over the next few months the Estates General gradually wound down to the general dissatisfaction of all concerned. The only other significant step taken by the clergy was their last, and the one that posterity has found most worthy of note: the selection to give the closing remonstrance to the king of the little-known bishop of Luçon, Armand-Jean du Plessis de Richelieu.

Richelieu's so-called *Mémoires*—actually a history of Louis XIII's reign produced by the corporate authority of the cardinal's staff, but certainly reflecting his opinions and political rationale—took a very dim view of the Estates General:[114]

---

l'article contentieuse employé pour le premier au cayer du tiers Estat (s.l., 1615), 3–4. The full list of demands was as follows: "1. Que sa M. eust à casser l'arrest du Parlement du 2. Janvier, 2. Qu'elle eust à interdire ledict Parlement de la cognoissance des affaires d'Estat. 4. Qu'il luy pleust accorder l'evocation des causes des deputez à son Conseil la demandans dans les presens Estats; & six mois apres. 5. Qu'il fust defendu à Monsieur Servin de se lever ès causes qui regardent l'Eglise. Le 6. estoit, Qu'il pleust à sa Majesté nous donner communication de l'Estat de ses finances par le menu." Clearly, the clergy saw the Parlement as a more promising target than the third estate, and were quite happy to exploit the monarchy's own frustration with the Parlement's pretensions. See also Hayden, *France and the Estates General*, 145.

112. The text is in *Procès-verbaux*, 2: pièces justificatives, 23A–24A. The French cardinals seem to have received papal letters individually as well; there is one addressed to Sourdis in BN fr. 6379.

113. *Copie d'une lettre*, 8.

114. Corporate authorship and authority were a basic characteristic of Richelieu's modus operandi, as has been extensively demonstrated by Orest Ranum, in *Richelieu and the Councillors*

Assemblies of the Clergy   265

They concluded fruitlessly, the entire assembly having had no other effect than to burden the provinces with the taxes needed to maintain their deputies and to show to all that it does not suffice to understand ones ills if one lacks the will to remedy them.[115]

The connection between this assessment and Richelieu's own policies is evident: from the failure of representation to absolutism, from theoretical pieties to stern and decisive action. It is, of course, also just what the author of the passage wishes the audience to see. Nevertheless, it is possible to discern a genuine connection between the Estates General and the career of the cardinal-minister. It is in the institutional voice of the clergy that this link is to be found.

One building block of Richelieu's ministry so obvious that it is liable to be overlooked is the simple fact that a great churchman should be the chief counselor of the king. The clergy in fact disputed with the magistrates the preeminent right to give counsel to the monarch, and Richelieu in 1615 was at pains to emphasize this tradition: "It is certain that in past centuries in all the nations of the world . . . persons consecrated to the ministry of religion have, under sovereign princes . . . held the first ranks, not only in what concerns the spiritual, but in what regards the civil and political government as well."[116] His encomium on the prelate as perfect counselor, though drawn almost verbatim from earlier ecclesiastical harangues, could have served as a preemptive political testament.

Now, so that your majesty may know the justice of our complaints . . . consider, if you please, what reason there may be to distance the ecclesiastics from the honor of your councils and the cognizance of your affairs, since their profession is most serviceable to render them suitable for such employment, in that it obliges them particularly to acquire capacity, to be full of probity, to govern themselves with prudence, which are the only necessary conditions for serving a state with

---

of Louis XIII (Oxford, U.K.: Clarendon Press, 1963); and Christian Jouhaud, in *La main de Richelieu; ou, Le pouvoir cardinal* (Paris: Gallimard, 1991). This fact may very well be connected to the cardinal's early experience of clerical politics that were forced both by the institutional arrangements of the the first estate and, more importantly, by the principles of Christian ecclesiology to take such a form.

115. Armand-Jean du Plessis, Cardinal de Richelieu, *Mémoires*, vol. 1 (Paris: Renouard, 1907), 367–68. The harangue continues in this vein for three pages. On Richelieu's actions in and reactions to the Estates, see also Françoise Hildesheimer, *Richelieu: Une certaine idée de l'état* (S.l.: Publisud, 1985), 9–18.

116. Richelieu, *Mémoires*, 345. He echoes the concern we saw in 1596 that prelates are no longer prominent in the royal councils.

dignity; and that in fact they are, as they ought by reason to be, freer of all other personal interests which often interfere with public affairs, seeing that, remaining celibate as they do, nothing survives them after this life except their souls, which, since they cannot store up treasures on earth, obliges them to think of nothing here below when serving their king and their fatherland, but to acquire forever in heaven above a glorious and entirely perfect recompense.[117]

While all these arguments had been advanced before, Richelieu was the first to set them out so systematically and at such great length. This innovation bespeaks not only his personal ambition but also its intersection with the need the prelates felt as a body to press for authority within the state—a need occasioned more than anything else by pressure from the Gallicans in the courts and the third estate.[118]

Richelieu, obviously, did not fail to touch on that issue, with the usual double appeal to the king. "All sovereigns . . . are strictly obliged," to protect the ecclesiastical jurisdiction, "both by conscience, which is obvious, and by reason of state, for it is most certain that a prince could not better teach his subjects to scorn his power than by tolerating enterprises against that of the great God from whom he holds his own."[119] It may well have been in the (rhetorically) all-or-nothing struggle for the preservation of a divinely instituted ecclesiastical jurisdiction that the minister developed his zero-tolerance policy against the infringement of the royal prerogative. A parallel lesson from the same school was the one that Richelieu claimed to have drawn from the Estates General themselves, namely, the vanity of good intentions unaccompanied by action. The assemblies of the clergy complained incessantly that what protections the kings had granted them for their jurisdiction remained worthless because they were unenforced. This is another theme the Bishop of Luçon took up and amplified to a new and general importance.

That theme in fact occupied the entire final section of the speech, and it received several interesting developments. If the king's responses to his Estates General "are followed by execution not merely for a day, but forever," then "everything will be carried out with just weight and measure: we will see the reign of reason powerfully established; justice will recover the integrity that is its due," and the decay of the state will be averted.[120] In con-

117. Richelieu, *Mémoires*, 348.

118. The clergy had instructed its agents since 1586 to support actual clerics for positions of *conseiller clercs* in the parlements; see AN *G^8 609, 1036, and 1290–91. They kept an ongoing dossier from 1614 on their attempts to enforce this; see AN G^8 151.

119. Richelieu, *Mémoires*, 354.

120. Richelieu, *Mémoires*, 358.

trast to the ideology of the Gallican jurists, which sought the preservation of the state through the maintenance of its ancient form while dismissing the possibility of restoration through individual reasoning or action, Richelieu claimed that the king already had access to a reason of state that required only decisive and consistent action to impose itself on the body politic and render that body eternal.[121] Later theorists of absolutism would develop various ideas about what that reason was and how it might be accessible to the prince and his ministers, but in this moment it was quite clear what the prototype for such an infallible guide to statesmanship was: the inerrant canons of the ecclesiastical hierarchy, particularly the Council of Trent. It is this that Richelieu proposed as the "rule" for Louis's overdue ordering of his state.[122] The means, moreover, were consonant with the end, for once given access to this divinely mandated pattern for the state, the king also had a quasi-divine power to implement it: "in most good things it is for kings as it is for God, to whom to will is to do."[123] The divinization of the monarch was already a staple of political literature in France;[124] what its appearance in the discourse of the prelates did was to attach to it—vaguely and modestly at first—a distinct program of action. Du Perron's argument that grounding the monarchy in the doctrine of the Church gave it a power unavailable elsewhere appeared rather specious at the time, but there was more truth in it than he knew.

One final example will serve to illustrate this. The clergy was busy in these years: in addition to the Estates General of 1614, there were assemblies in 1615 (which unilaterally adopted the canons of Trent) and in 1617. The remonstrance for the last of these was given by Phillipe Cospeau, bishop of Aire, a protegé of the Angennes de Rambouillet family who was in his later career both a model of the spiritual director and an intimate of the Grey Eminence, Père Joseph.[125] Significantly, he was also a founding member of

---

121. On the central role of reason and rationality, conceived in the most transcendental terms, in Richelieu's political thought, see Françoise Hildesheimer, "Le *Testament politique* de Richelieu ou le règne terrestre de la raison," *Annuaire-bulletin de la Société de l'histoire de France* (1994): 17–34.

122. See Richelieu, *Mémoires*, 363.

123. Richelieu, *Mémoires*, 359.

124. William F. Church, *Constitutional Thought in Sixteenth-Century France: A Study in the History of Ideas* (Cambridge, Mass.: Harvard University Press, 1941), 316–17 and passim.

125. "Remonstrance du Clergé de france faict au Roy le dixhuict Juillet . . . l'an 1617," BN fr 2760, fols. 309–15. This speech was never included in the printed collections of the assemblies. It was printed separately, as *Remonstrance du Clergé de France: Faicte au Roy le 18. Juillet* (Paris: Jean Richer, 1617), but I have not been able to examine a copy of this edition. The manuscript I have used was most likely a copy of the printed version.

the *conseil de conscience* set up after Louis XIII's death to assure a competent and generally ultramontanist episcopacy.[126] The speech was distinctly more classical in style than its predecessors, though importing as well a Jesuitical taste for *ekphrasis*. One of the clergy's requests that year was what was to become a pet project of Richelieu's, the elimination of dueling. Interestingly, the mode in which Cospeau presented it was practically indistinguishable from the way the cardinal-minister later presented it to his king:

> Those unhappy men who ... destroy each other on the dueling field sin each one but once, are responsible each only for his own crime, but your majesty, who is obliged to stop them all ... failing in this duty sins alone for all, and makes himself guilty for all. ... It is not the law then, sire, that the Church requests but its execution, not threats but punishment, not an ordinance that does nothing for the sick, but a salutary bloodletting that stops and stanches at once this hemorrhage that is fatal to your state.[127]

The political theology of this passage is interesting: the king's person takes on the role of the body of Christ, assuming the sins of his people. Louis Marin has demonstrated that this line of thought was central to the absolutist theory put forward in the latter part of the century, and to its Jansenist critique.[128] It is not coincidental that so much of the political discourse of high absolutism should be outlined so early in precisely this space. Nor is it coincidental that Cospeau developed his line of political theology to protest the violation of ecclesiastical jurisdiction. He proposed to the king the image of Christ, crucified by the unjust decree of the Jews and Romans, absolving the bandits who flank him of their crimes, while in France Christ's Church, under the Most Christian King, was prevented from exercising the power of the keys by the secular courts. The erudite Gallicans, after all, supported their theories by eliding the personal body of the monarch that po-

---

126. The most notable member of the *conseil*, besides Mazarin and Anne of Austria, was St. Vincent de Paul. Cospeau was a native of the Spanish Netherlands and had studied at Louvian under Justus Lipsius before moving to Paris. On his career and the *conseil de conscience*, see Bergin, *French Episcopate*, 600–601 and 505ff. Cospeau was the subject of a contemporary biography, or rather hagiography: René le Mée, *Le prelat accomply, representé en la personne de l'illustrissime seigneur Phillipe Cospeau, Evesque et Comte de Lizeux. Dedié a Nosseigneurs les Prelats de l'Assemblée generale du Clergé de France* (Saumur: Jean Lesnier, 1647); and now of a modern biography: Emile Jacques, *Phillippe Cospeau: Un ami-ennemi de Richelieu, 1571–1646* (Paris: Beauchesne, 1989).

127. BN fr 2760, fol. 311r–v.

128. See Marin, *Le portrait*, 263–90, and "The Body-of-Power and Incarnation at Port Royal and in Pascal; or, Of the Figurability of the Political Absolute," in *Fragments for a History of the Human Body*, pt. 3 (New York: Zone, 1989), 421–47.

Assemblies of the Clergy 269

tentially mediated between the spiritual and the secular, and equally by minimizing any mediating physicality of the Church and its jurisdiction. The official spokesmen of the clergy took exactly the opposite tack, and by 1617 they were doing so more openly and more convincingly than their opponents.

Finally, lest one should doubt that Cospeau's discourse directly addressed the quarrel with the Gallican jurists, note that the author of the scurrilous and extremely polemical *Discours sur les meurs et humeur de M. Servin* took it up explicitly:

Now, as we have seen that the remonstrance of the clergy recently pronounced by the holy bishop of Aire moved the spirit of the king, and that his majesty has begun to deal with dueling by a holy edict, which he is having observed with severity ... we must hope that, by the advice that will be given him, he will see to the consequences of so pernicious a man [being] in his Parlement ... [and] will purge this great and august senate, court of peers of France and the triumphant seat of justice, of this putrefied blood that will insensibly infect this venerable body if no steps are taken.[129]

The Assembly simultaneously applied its oratorical production to the lowest level of political invective and (like the Gallicans) justified it by reference to what remained, after all was said and done, the supreme political value: the preservation of the state, its personnel, and its institutions.

By 1617, then, the clergy had developed in some detail key parts of Richelieu's program during his ministry: on the one hand, the strict duty that the king's public role imposed on his private soul, and, on the other hand, the necessity for swift and decisive action to put an end to intolerable evils and to preserve the state itself. Both elements were to be combined with a vigorous defense of the interests of the Church in France and indeed with a near-complete identification of French and Catholic interests. This tends to confirm the deep religiosity of Richelieu's political outlook and, by extension, that of the French monarchy in its period of maximum power, as it has been analyzed by William Farr Church.[130] Church's conclusion that Richelieu's political thought was developed to a very large extent as an ad hoc response

---

129. "Discours sur les meurs et humeur de Monsieur Servin Advocat General au Parlement de Paris," in *Archives curieuses de l'histoire de France depuis Louis XI jusqu'à Louis XVIII*, 27 vols. (Paris: Beauvais, 1834–1840), ser. 2, vol. 3, 208–9.

130. William F. Church, *Richelieu and Reason of State* (Princeton, N.J.: Princeton University Press, 1972).

270 CHAPTER 6

to his critics seems, on the other hand, to require some emendation.[131] Certainly, the way he explained many of his policies and seemingly arbitrary acts to himself and his king in the *Testament politique* came straight from the clerical rhetoric of his youth. Take, for example, the question of dueling that had preoccupied the Bishop of Aire, out of which Richelieu built a treatise in miniature on the reason of state:

> Since the best laws in the world are useless if they are not made to be observed without fail, and because those who fall into this kind of fault [dueling] use so many tricks to prevent its proof that it is usually impossible to convict them, I do not fear to say to your majesty that it is not enough to punish open duels by the rigor of the edicts but, where there is notoriety without proof, you should have the guilty parties taken and held prisoner at their own expense.[132]

This issue was a prime location for discussing certain aspects of the nature and morality of monarchical government, and the same discourse made its way into the extraordinary anti-dueling ordinances of Richelieu's ministry.[133]

A few pages later, Richelieu laid out the general principle behind his position; it was one that the assemblies had voiced repeatedly in their attempts to obtain fulfillment of promised restrictions on the secular courts:

> In many cases one cannot leave one fault unpunished without committing a new one.... The theologians, like the politicians, all agree that in certain circumstances where private persons would be wrong not to pardon, those who are charged with public government would be inexcusable if, instead of imposing severe punishment, they were indulgent.[134]

This principle, which lay at the heart of Richelieu's notion of the reasonable and justifiable raison d'état, rested in its turn on the king's special moral position. Richelieu took it sufficiently seriously to close his *Testament* with it:

> In order to finish this work happily I have only to represent to your majesty that kings, being obliged to do many more things as sovereigns than as private per-

---

131. This critique applies only to Richelieu's domestic policy. The very important case of his Protestant alliances, which called forth so much of the theoretical work of his ministry, is beyond our scope here.

132. Armand-Jean du Plessis Cardinal de Richelieu, *Testament politique*, ed. Louis André (Paris: Robert Lafont, 1947), 227–28.

133. See M. Isambert and A. Jourdan, eds., *Recueil général des anciennes lois françaises, depuis l'an 420 jusqu'à la Révolution de 1789*, 29 vols. (Paris: Belin-Leprieur, 1826–1833), 15:351–58 and 16:175–83.

134. Richelieu, *Testament*, 339.

sons, cannot shirk their duty even a little without committing more sins of omission than a private person could ever commit sins of commission. . . . One of the greatest kings of our neighbors, knowing this truth, cried on his deathbed that he feared not so much Philip's sins as the king's.[135]

Richelieu's politics were regulated by a very strictly Christian morality. One key factor of this morality was that it operated through the mediation of the king's person and his soul, subject to divine judgment and the jurisdiction of the Church. True, the cardinal-minister was not willing to accept interference from the "ordinary jurisdiction" of the royal confessor—when the *dévôt* Père Caussin raised moral objections to Richelieu's policies he was forced out, though his replacement was the erudite nemesis of the erudite Gallicans, Jacques Sirmond[136]—but the *Testament* testifies that Richelieu himself functioned above all as a spiritual advisor to his king. It was this function that enabled all purely political action, for

God being the principle of all things, the sovereign master of kings and he who alone makes them reign happily, if your majesty's devotion were not known to all I would begin this chapter . . . by showing you that, if you do not follow the will of your Creator and submit yourself to his laws, you should not hope to make your own observed and to see your subjects obey your orders.[137]

For Richelieu, as for the clergy in general, the knowledge that would make the body politic function was a knowledge of the divine will and, first and foremost, the province of the Church.

Even in many of the functional details of his political philosophy, Richelieu remained faithful to the views that his *corps* had put forth at the beginning of the century. His ideal of the disinterested statesman remained what it had always been: "The statesman should be faithful to God, to the state, and to himself. This will happen when, besides the qualities we have mentioned, he loves the public and is disinterested in his counsels."[138] What is more, he remained committed to maintaining the dignity and independence of the clergy within the realm, whatever his financial quarrels with them might have been. The *Testament* includes a detailed exposition of the

---

135. Richelieu, *Testament*, 451–54.
136. Sirmond's great achievement was to complete an edition of the early Gallic national councils, which had been the pet project of a number of Gallicans including Pierre Pithou: *Concilia antiqua galliæ*, 3 vols. (Paris: Sebastien Cramoisy, 1629). Robert Bireley is currently at work on a study of seventeenth-century Jesuit confessors that will analyze the Caussin affair in detail.
137. Richelieu, *Testament*, 264.
138. Richelieu, *Testament*, 292.

clergy's long-standing position on the *appel comme d'abus*, as well as the following general statement, which should be taken seriously and at face value:

> This great kingdom cannot flourish if your majesty does not maintain the *corps* of which it is composed in their order, the Church holding first place, the nobility second, and the officers who march at the head of the people the third. I say this boldly because it is as important as it is just to stop the enterprises of certain officers who . . . are so presumptuous as to wish to take the first place where they can only take the third.[139]

Among the infinity of pressing dangers menacing France, Richelieu did not fail to emphasize the jurisdictional pretensions of the Gallican magistrates. These included not only enterprises on the Church, but also spurious claims to offer the kingdom and their king better informed and more disinterested counsel than could the great prelates.

Richelieu's political outlook, then, as he himself presented it to his king and to the world, was in large measure built from elements forged by the assemblies of the clergy in their political disputes with the Gallican jurists. From this perspective we can better appreciate both the correctness and the significance of Pierre Blet's contention that the cardinal's regime was characterized by an adherence to "the wishes of the clergy."[140] This obviously excluded matters of the royal revenues and other issues where external constraints forced the government's hand, but it included Richelieu's basic conception of the kingdom, which was very much that of the clergy. One can see this concretely in a comprehensive project for national reform that Richelieu's circle probably drew up in 1625. It begins with the institution of a *conseil de conscience* and moves on to the publication of the Tridentine decrees. After specifying "that spiritual authority and ecclesiastical jurisdiction should be respected in all their rights," it "exhorts" (rather than commanding) the French bishops to exercise that jurisdiction vigorously, without "prejudicing in anything the rights of . . . the pope, superior judge of the Church."[141] If the prelates could have written a royal ordinance themselves, this might almost have been it.

---

139. Richelieu, *Testament*, 256. The *appel comme d'abus* is discussed at 1:2:2 (pp. 157–68).

140. Blet, *Clergé de France*, 2:416: "à Louis XIV réalisant une partie des vœux des Parlements, on peut opposer Richelieu réalisant les vœux du Clergé."

141. "Règlement pour toutes les affaires du Royaume," in M. Avenel, ed., *Lettres, instructions diplomatiques, et papiers d'état du Cardinal de Richelieu*, vol. 2 (Paris: Imprimerie Impériale, 1856), 168–83, p. 172 (Avenel's paraphrase). This document, drawn up in the form of a royal edict, moves directly from ecclesiastical affairs to dueling!

In this light, one must question the contribution of the jurists and of Gallicanism to the construction of the classical French monarchy. J. H. M. Salmon's conclusion that the influence of Jean Bodin, supposedly the greatest of the juridical contributors to absolutism, becomes nearly invisible in the seventeenth century, is not after all so surprising, since key aspects of his transcendentalist doctrine were picked up and promoted by the clergy and, eventually, by the cardinal-ministers without Bodin's troubling legal and philosophical baggage. The Gallican jurists' chief immediate influence was to push the clerics into developing and strengthening their own political doctrine. It is not particularly surprising that this should have occurred, for the traditionalist doctrine of the erudite Gallicans was not really suited to the strong and centralized monarchy that emerged from the religious wars. It gave the government no position from which it could operate outside the web of institutional self-interest in which historical contingency had wrapped France. Kings from Henri IV on were much more inclined to accept constraint by a timeless ideal, defined in religious terms by religious specialists, which could justify practically any action in its pursuit, than a home-grown historical account that would confine them for their own preservation within a customary framework and would leave them unable to develop new resources. The Gallicanism of the erudite jurists was much better adapted to be an oppositional ideology, patrolling the limits of the absolute monarchy and the Counter-Reformation Church. It had already begun to perform this role in the wake of the Council of Trent, and it started to dominate when the defeat of the League opened up the possibility of a renewed cooperation between king and church. The magistrates' inability to redefine the nature of the monarchy in the face of the prelates was confirmed in 1615, and from then on Gallicanism—a creation of the centralizing monarchy—became a force arrayed against it. It continued to be one well into the eighteenth century, up to and even beyond the Revolution.[142]

142. Dale van Kley discusses this question in *The Religious Origins of the French Revolution: From Calvin to the Civil Constitution, 1560–1791* (New Haven, Conn.: Yale University Press, 1996), but more work certainly remains to be done on the issue.

Conclusion

IN MANY WAYS, the Estates General of 1615 and the Assembly of the Clergy of 1617 marked the high point both of erudite Gallicanism and of the clerical reaction to it. Having failed in their attempt to impose their own vision of a stable monarchy controlling ecclesiastical jurisdiction, and faced with the ever more complete collapse of juristic influence within the corridors of royal power, the erudite Gallicans in fact had nowhere much to go. Their anti-Jesuit polemics continued almost unabated, but those polemics were increasingly cultural rather than political in scope. Jesuit rhetoric, Jesuit aesthetics, and, above all, Jesuit penitential practice were the favored targets of religiously minded French patriots, who could not expect to get much of anywhere by accusing Louis XIII or Louis XIV's confessors of treason and of undermining the kingdom's fundamental laws. The abject failure of the *parlementaire* Fronde a generation later confirmed all this in a most dramatic fashion.[1] Gradually, erudite Gallicans retreated from independent political action, looked to their own individual good, and often turned into royalist partisans (like Molé or Dupuy), or into Jansenists (like the Arnauds).[2] It was in the latter capacity that they would reenter the

---

1. See Orest Ranum, *The Fronde: A French Revolution* (New York: W. W. Norton, 1993).

2. In this sense, on the political rather than the economic level, and making allowance for the diversity of options, there may be some truth in the much-criticized thesis of Lucien Goldmann, *Le Dieu caché: Étude sur la vision tragique dans les* Pensées *de Pascal et dans le théâtre de* Racine (Paris: Gallimard, 1959). At the same time, there may be some connection between the erudite Gallicans' tendency to "privatize" sacramental order and the Jansenist subordination of sacramental efficacy to interior conversion. The best overview of the development of

theater of national politics in the eighteenth century, with an ideology once more transformed and renewed for a new era.

This is not to say, though, that the development of erudite Gallicanism and its opponents after 1617 was simple or linear. This can be seen as early as 1625, when the Assembly of the Clergy rehashed the issues of 1614–1615 in an even messier fashion than before. Much of what happened there was old hat. After bitter complaints about the enterprises of the Parlement of Rennes, for example, the prelates obtained their most definitive royal declaration to date against the harassment of bishops by the secular courts.[3] However, as the Assembly of the Clergy progressed, some cracks began to appear in the prelates' formerly united anti-Gallican front. This was above all the work of one man, Léonore d'Estampes, bishop of Chartres. In reaction to some jurisdictional excesses by a papal subdelegate, he drew up a statement on bishops' rights of visitation over regular clergy sufficiently radical in its episcopalism that the nuncio was able to get the Assembly to bury it.[4] D'Estampes could and did draw on the "regulations made by that great bishop, St. Charles Borromeo" and on the Tridentine reconciliation of episcopal authority and the papal role as "bishop of bishops and patriarchs."[5] Indeed, a document he drew up on the episcopal office was disowned by the Assembly of the Clergy, after it had already been printed at considerable expense, precisely for its use of that last phrase.

French Jansenism is now William Doyle, *Jansenism: Catholic Resistance to Authority from the Reformation to the French Revolution* (New York: St. Martin's Press, 2000).

3. On the dispute with the Parlement of Rennes (which was seconded by Molé and the Parlement of Paris), see Pierre Blet, *Le clergé de France et la monarchie: Étude sur les Assemblées Générales du Clergé de 1615 à 1666*, 2 vols. (Rome: Librairie éditrice de l'Université Grégorienne, 1959), 1:276–83. The edict granted to the clergy is in M. Isambert and A Jourdan, eds., *Recueil général des anciennes lois françaises, depuis l'an 420 jusqu'à la revolution de 1789*, 29 vols. (Paris: Belin-Leprieur, 1826–1833), 16:152–53. Isambert points out that, not surprisingly, no court registered this edict.

4. On this incident, see Michael K. Becker, "Episcopal Unrest: Gallicanism in the 1625 Assembly of the Clergy," *Church History* 43 (1974): 65–77; and Blet, *Le clergé*, 1:296–334.

5. "Supplement ou critique de l'assemblée du clergé de france tenüe en l'année 1625 par Mr. de chartres," AN *G^8 644, 92, 84. The *procès-verbal* of the Assembly does not give the justifications for suppressing this document, but according to a marginal note in this archival copy, "une des causes de la suppression de cet avis, est l'infaillibilité du pape. v. l'art. 137" (p. 3). What that article says about papal infallibility, however, is completely uncontroversial, applying it only to faith, not doctrine; the title of "evêque des evêques" that it gives the pope, however, is one the French clergy had disdained since the thirteenth century, as implying that episcopal jurisdiction was not *jure divino*. This must have been the excuse for suppressing d'Estampe's treatise.

This censure, however, was nothing more than an excuse to attack d'Estampes for a rather different element of his thought. At the end of 1625, d'Estampes drew up a "Judgment" against some pamphlets critical of France's Protestant alliance in the Valtelline War (which was, of course, a pet project of Richelieu's).[6] He published this under the name of the Assembly of the Clergy and, though he denied it, he seems to have done so without submitting it for their approval.[7] The Parlement immediately leapt to the defense of this judgment, linking it to its own condemnations of tyrannicide against the Jesuits and in the Estates General. The more conservative party in the clergy, led by the still-vigorous Cardinal de la Rochefoucauld, happily rejoined the old battle, which raged again for some months. Richelieu seems to have done his considerable best to avoid the ensuing rumpus, bowing out of a commission to investigate d'Estampes's actions with a plea of pressing royal business, and mobilizing the royal council against the Parlement only slowly and mildly. Nevertheless, he had no hesitation in defending his institution rather than his policies, and in private and in diplomatic channels he came down very hard on d'Estampes.

This imbroglio was old-fashioned enough to demonstrate that the politics of erudite Gallicanism were still very much a live issue. At the same time, there were enough suggestions of novelty to give some clue as to where those politics were headed. Thus, when the Cardinal de la Rochefoucauld or a writer in his service took up the attack on d'Estampes at length, he recited all of the commonplaces going back from the Estates General controversy, through the Oath of Allegiance and tyrannicide questions, to the Council of Trent and before. However, he concluded his treatise with a rather less familiar charge. The Gallicans, he claimed, were trying to separate church and state completely, and la Rochefoucauld joined Cicero in "criticizing the libertine doctrine of certain philosophers, who separate religion from the rules they give for human life, who 'to make men free have made them sacrilegious.'"[8] If this was true, it was not at all in the way that la Rochefoucauld meant it. What loomed here somewhat incongruously was a specter that

---

6. *Cardinalium, archiepiscoporum, episcoporum, caeterorumque qui ex universis regni provinciis ecclesiasticis comitiis interfuerunt, de anonymis quibusdam et famosis libellis sententia* (Paris: A. Stephanus, 1625).

7. On this affair, see, beside the manuscript cited above, Blet, *Le clergé*, 1:335–69; and Joseph Bergin, *Cardinal de la Rochefoucauld: Leadership and Reform in the French Church* (New Haven, Conn.: Yale University Press, 1987), 69–77. The secretary of the Assembly testified that he had been absent from the session in whose minutes the "Jugement" appeared, and had relied on d'Estampes's word when inserting it; see AN *G⁸ 644, 237 (extract from the *procès-verbal* of 29 November 1625).

8. François (Cardinal) de la Rochefoucauld, *Raisons pour le desaveu fait par les evesques de ce*

would haunt the clergy for the next three hundred years: the libertine, the *philosophe*, the secularist. Indeed, by the middle of the next century, this figure would replace the erudite Gallicans not only in the nightmares of cardinals, but in French ecclesiastical politics.

First, though, there was a long detour, which deserves to be reexamined in far more detail than we can give it here. Perhaps the most surprising thing about d'Estampes's activities in 1625–1626 is that they were undertaken by a bishop. His supporters were very much the usual suspects of erudite Gallicanism. Besides the Parlement (doubtless inspired by Servin), he was defended in a pamphlet issued by Edmond Richer, whom he probably knew from a stint teaching at the Sorbonne, and perhaps by Pierre Dupuy as well.[9] This was the first sign in a very long time that any kind of Gallicanism, let alone the new erudite Gallicanism, might have some purchase among the French bishops. Over the next sixty years, some of the clergy embraced the emerging tenets of Jansenism, and then sought refuge in sixteenth-century-style Gallicanism when they faced papal condemnation. Others, caught up in Louis XIV's politics of French cultural and military hegemony, found those old ideas appealing for new reasons; both groups had a very substantial number of counterparts among the robe magistrates. The result was a last alliance of royalist, clerical, and juridical Gallicans culminating in the Gallican articles that the clergy issued at royal insistence in 1682.[10] This document would have pleased Louis XII, Servin, or Richer in almost equal measure, but it was destined to remain an anomaly in the his-

---

roiaume d'un livret publié avec ce titre, Jugement des cardinaux, archevesques, evesques & autres . . . sur quelques libelles diffamatoires sans les noms des auteurs. Contre les scismatiques de ce tems (Paris: n.p., 1626), 339. This work has sometimes been attributed to la Rochefoucauld's secretary, Jean Phélypeaux, S.J.

9. [Edmond Richer], *Considerations sur un Livre, intitulé, Raisons pour le desadveu faict par les Evesques de ce Royaume, &c. mis en lumiere soubs le nom de Me François Cardinal de la Rochefoucault. Contre les vrais Schismatiques de ce temps. Par Timothee François Catholique* (s.l., 1628). The attribution to Richer is per AN *G⁸ 644, 106. There is a manuscript apology for d'Estampes's actions in the Dupuy collection; see BN Dupuy 376, "Escrits faicts sur le suict de la censure publiee par Monsr. l'evesque de chartres soubs le nom du clerge de France, MDCXXVI." While it is in d'Estampes's voice, Pierre Dupuy had some involvement in it; according to a marginal note (fol. 2r), he was "auteur de cet escrit," but another just below it reads "Cest mal a propos qu'on attribue ce livre à M. Dupuy comme autheur d'icelluy mais cest M l'Evesque de chartres. M. Dupuy la recuilly et . . . copié mais non autrement." On d'Estampes's brief career in the Sorbonne, around 1612, see Joseph Bergin, *The Making of the French Episcopacy, 1589–1641* (New Haven, Conn.: Yale University Press, 1996), 621–22. (On the other hand, according to Bergin, d'Estampes studied under the very ultramontanist Cospeau. Go figure.)

10. The definitive account of this episode remains Aimé-Georges Martimort, *Le gallicanisme de Bossuet* (Paris: Editions du Cerf, 1953).

tory of the old regime. By the beginning of the next century, the parties concerned had returned to their old positions and were once more at each others' throats.

Thus, skipping another few generations and examining the records of the Assembly of the Clergy of 1765, one has, at least at first glance, a feeling of déjà-vu.[11] Two years earlier, the Parlement of Paris had finally succeeded in expelling the Society of Jesus from the realm, using in combination arguments that dated back to Estienne Pasquier and Charles Dumoulin, and reasoning about the nature of the state and political society that owed a great deal to that most eloquent enemy of the Jesuits, Voltaire.[12] The magistrates had also recently renewed their attacks on the bull *Unigenitus*. In these actions the clergy saw a threat to their jurisdiction not matched, perhaps, since 1615. A standing committee on jurisdictional issues, the Bureau de Jurisdiction, which was now part of the Assembly's machinery, gave an alarming report on the subject, and in response the Assembly promulgated a set of acts including the condemnation of a number of books, a defense of *Unigenitus*, and an "Exposition on the Rights of the Spiritual Power."[13]

This document defended "the power that [the Church] received from Jesus Christ to preach and to instruct; to determine the objects of faith, of discipline and of morals; to dispense the sacraments," as well as to confirm or dispense vows (which had become an issue when the Parlement of Paris had dissolved the vows of the Jesuits along with the order itself).[14] The set of issues was almost exactly the same as those that had figured in the jurisdictional conflicts of the early seventeenth century, and the arguments marshaled against them had a long pedigree as well. In some respects the clerical understanding of and response to the *parlementaire* position had even grown clearer. The "Exposition" explicitly stated the spiritual subjection of kings to the Church, and the clergy took care to refute an argument that had been implicitly invoked but never (to my knowledge) explicitly discussed prior to

---

11. On this Assembly and its long-term significance, see Dale van Kley, "Church, State and the Ideological Origins of the French Revolution: The Debate over the General Assembly of the Gallican Clergy in 1765," *Journal of Modern History* 51 (1979): 629–66; and Jeffrey Merrick, *The Desacralization of the French Monarchy in the Eighteenth Century* (Baton Rouge: Louisiana State University Press, 1990), 105–16.

12. See Dale van Kley, *The Jansenists and the Expulsion of the Jesuits from France* (New Haven, Conn.: Yale University Press, 1975).

13. "Exposition sur les droits de la Puissance spirituelle," in *Procès verbaux*, 8.2: pièces justificatives, cols. 419–31. There was also an act aimed at promoting provincial councils.

14. *Procès-verbaux*, 8.2, col. 1364. This is from the report of the Bureau de Jurisdiction.

1615, but that had metastasized in the course of the Jansenist controversy. "One must not," they said, "distinguish between the interior and exterior administration [of the sacraments]; it is not the public nature of an object that determines which power it falls under and not all public actions are civil and temporal."[15] The clergy were addressing head-on the idea that the secular jurisdiction extended over the entire public sphere and even all visible things. Not unpredictably, the parlements reacted violently to this clerical initiative, condemning the "Exposition" and accusing the prelates of claiming an illegitimate "external and coercive jurisdiction."[16] As was customary, it was left to the king to resolve, or rather to end, the dispute. In an uncharacteristic act of decisiveness, Louis XV actually did so.

It is at this point that one begins to realize that, despite a surface familiarity, the world of 1765 was very different from that of 1615. First of all, the terms on which Louis XV closed the debate were highly unfavorable to the clergy: he issued a decree of his own on the matters in dispute that to all intents and purposes took the side of the jurists. Given his acquiescence three years earlier in the expulsion of the Jesuits, and indeed his entire policy since the death of Cardinal Fleury, this cannot have been unexpected, and the clergy was forced to withdraw, grumbling, from the fray. Between them, the expulsion of the Jesuits and the humiliation of 1765 seem to have destroyed ultramontanist clericalism as a political force in France—it was indeed ill-equipped to survive without royal support in an increasingly secular society. At any rate, from this time on such disputes between clergy and courts ceased to arise, and it may be that the capitulation of the first estate to the third estate in 1789, so different from what had transpired at the previous meeting of the Estates General, was already prepared twenty-three years earlier. Deprived of its enemy, *parlementaire* Gallicanism was hardly less prompt in expiring.

Behind this conjuncture of political fortunes, however, lay a much more profound shift in the French intellectual climate. To understand the significance of this shift, it will be helpful to recapitulate the itinerary that this study has traversed. Erudite Gallicanism, as we have seen, was a largely autonomous creation of a set of intellectual forces that may broadly be labeled "humanist," acting in the particular institutional structure of the

---

15. *Procès-verbaux*, 8.2: p. j., 429. On the history of the doctrine attacked here, see van Kley, "Church, State and Ideology," 642–45.

16. Parlement of Aix, *arrêt* of 30 October 1765, quoted in Merrick, *Desacralization*, 110.

sixteenth-century French state. It continued and was built on an earlier doctrine, the royalist Gallicanism that dated in some ways back to the beginning of the monarchy and that had been brought to a climax during the period of the Great Schism and the Italian wars. As successive kings lost interest in this ideology, and as the medieval ideals of a reformed Church and a just kingdom that had given life to it receded, it almost vanished from the public life of the realm. What revived it was neither the need of the authorities for support in secular politics, nor the challenge of Protestantism—though these factors played contributing roles—but rather the interest of a generation of humanistically trained jurists in finding a new way to understand the foundations of the state and their own role in it.

Basic to the revival of Gallicanism—so basic, indeed, that we have hardly discussed it—was the deep respect of the Renaissance for detailed, textual knowledge of the past. As political events and skeptical speculation made the search for a reliable guide to political organization in the present seem increasingly hopeless, it was natural that adepts of philology should turn to the historical record for guidance. Ideas about the power and importance of custom drawn from largely Italian political theory provided a way of systematizing this trend and, crucially, of extending it to religious as well as to purely secular practice. By the end of the sixteenth century law and history, and the professional skills they entailed, had become almost completely identified, and both were portrayed as vital to the conduct and preservation of the state. Only the jurists, on their own account, had the technique, the control of sources, and the disinterestedness to discern the customary structure of the kingdom, to defend it, and, where necessary, to rebuild it in the present. While this system was only drawn out in all its detail by the generation of the 1570s and 1580s, many elements had obviously been operative since the birth of the French historical school in the 1550s.

It was inevitable that the erudite jurists would turn their system to religious questions not only because religious thought and practice were undergoing revolutions unheard of for a millennium, or because these revolutions seriously threatened to tear France apart—though all this was true—but, above all, because France had always been nearly as much a religious as a political entity and because the main models of its nature were religious. In fact, the revolutions of the sixteenth century gave rise to new religious philosophies of politics, most notably a Tridentine Catholic one that yoked together reason, revelation, and an almost theocratic centralized authority in both church and state. In this respect the thought of the erudite Gallicans represented an important step in the secularization of European politics, but only a partial one. While moving away from a religious criterion of the political, the jurists retained an overriding concern with religious affairs and a deep belief that in France, at least, neither religion nor politics, inextricably linked by custom, could ever stand or fall alone.

Thus, when they came to treat the constitution of the Gallican church and its relation to the monarchy, the erudite Gallican jurists gave the subject their all. It was one of the very first to which the legal historians turned their attention, and it took a preeminent place in the textual collections that lay at the heart of erudite legal culture. A combination of the hazard of archival practice, the distribution of humanist education, and institutional position vis-à-vis the king and the public had conspired to concentrate erudite Gallicanism in the lower reaches of the Parlement of Paris—at the bar, the *greffe*, and above all the *parquet*. Over the course of the seventeenth century, as the offices of the *parquet* became venal and associated rather with the class of *grands serviteurs du roi* than with the Parisian lawyers, the center of Gallicanism drifted away from the parlements per se (Molé had, in a sense, formally delegated it to Pierre Dupuy), but it remained in Paris, particularly within the now formally organized *ordre des avocats*. At the very end of the old regime the dean of that order, the rabidly Jansenist and preternaturally prolific ideologue Louis-Adrien le Paige, was still maintaining the now venerable Gallican tradition after the model of Estienne Pasquier.[17]

One of the major consequences of the relative secularization of political theory by the erudite Gallicans was that they saw increasingly little role for even the French church in the public life of the nation. If, as they were predisposed to believe, custom was inherently territorial and history inherently national, then there was little room in the republic for a hierarchical, international, and spiritual institution. For the reasons we have mentioned, the jurists were never able to conceive of a purely secular society, but a tendency to remove the religious from public life and private life, even the king's, from the state was an enduring part of their thought. Even in its more moderate forms this tendency led the *parlementaires* to be deeply suspicious of any assertion of ecclesiastical jurisdiction, which might herald not only a return of Leaguer ideas but a fundamental subversion of the political order of which the *parlementaires* considered themselves the guardians. Thus, like the old ideology of royal Gallicanism, the ancient jurisdictional struggle of the

---

17. On the role of le Paige and the *ordre des avocats* in eighteenth-century French politics, see David Bell, *Lawyers and Citizens: The Making of a Political Elite in Old Regime France* (Oxford, U.K.: Oxford University Press, 1994).

secular against the religious courts was revived in a new guise, raised by the new Gallican ideology and the armature of sociability and erudition that it had built to the level of a coordinated national struggle.

At the same time the clergy was less inclined than ever to be pushed aside. The spirit of the Counter-Reformation, which the French church increasingly embraced (as it could hardly have avoided doing, given the power and prestige of the Tridentine movement), was scarcely one of quietism. The closing of religious divisions, a gradual improvement in the level of the episcopacy, and the first breaths of the *siècle des saints* gave them new prestige, while the demonstrated willingness of Catholic zealots to pull the country down around their ears if not accommodated gave them political leverage. This was increased by the institutional innovation of the General Assembly of the Clergy, which the parlements were to outlive by only one year. The result was that the clergy swiftly deployed a set of counterarguments against the erudite Gallicans, equally steeped in humanist ideals of erudition, eloquence, and disinterested counsel, but eschewing Gallican skepticism, historicism, and corporatism in favor of an emphasis on reason, divine revelation, and the personalization of the state. From that position the prelates offered an alliance with the absolute monarchy that Henri IV and Louis XIII, while being careful to maintain the balance of forces within the kingdom, were generally inclined to accept. Louis, indeed, accepted it in the person of the clergy's erstwhile spokesman, Richelieu.

What one seeks in vain in the clergy's 1765 "Exposition" are the vital signs of this alliance. There is no claim for the Church of a special role in guiding the state or the king. Even the claim that the Church was necessary for the preservation of the temporal order was restricted to the muted statement that "the world is well governed when the two powers are in accord; if they become disunited the wisest institutions are menaced with swift destruction."[18] Van Kley has detected in the apologists of the "Exposition" early signs of a despotic and reactionary monarchism of the Metternich or de Maistre variety, but this was unlikely to appeal even to Louis XV, let alone to the would-be "citizen king" Louis XVI.[19] More importantly, if this move did take place it was on the part of individuals rather than of the

---

18. *Procès-verbaux*, 8.2: p. j., col. 429.

19. There was an attempt on the occasion of Louis XVI's coronation to revive a religiously based and episcopally sanctioned model of the monarchy, which alienated fiscal reformers without producing a serious alliance between the new king and his clergy. See

clergy or of the prelates as a body. The reason for this is not difficult to discern. If there is one thing that the history of the Gallican liberties teaches us, it is the degree to which the political culture of old-regime France was driven by ideas and ideology. Both erudite Gallicanism and its clerical opposite number were above all the product of humanist culture. In important respects that culture lasted far into the seventeenth century and even into the eighteenth. By the 1760s, though, it had all but vanished. Veneration of antiquity and philological skill were on the wane, and both skeptical views of human political capacity and respect for the diktats of authority were, especially in France, passé.

However we choose to define the Enlightenment, this was its age, and it worked powerfully to dissolve the parties that had grown up around the issue of the Gallican liberties. At least since the final struggle against the Jesuits, the *parlementaire* Gallicans had begun speaking in the terms of Enlightened patriotism, of reason, natural law, social contract, and the rest. Such an outlook was of course incompatible with the idea that human society is governed by arbitrary custom and that the exposition of this custom is the province of erudite specialists in privileged social institutions. Yet the *parlementaires* (despite their success in thwarting Maupeou's attempt to abolish them in the 1770s) had little luck in coming up with convincing new justifications for their own political centrality, descending into the ignominious role of a stumbling block in the path of progress to be disposed of immediately when the revolution came. The clergy faced a similar dilemma and met it with a similar lack of success. One of the most revealing parts of the "Exposition" is one that never made it into the final version. The Bureau de Jurisdiction proposed in its report that the clergy offer the following defense of their contested powers: "that the free exercise of these rights is the very interest of the faithful; that we claim them only to guide them more surely in the path of salvation."[20] Perhaps this was merely a restatement of the doctrine that the final cause of ecclesiastical jurisdiction was the sanctification of the faithful, but in the context of the mid-eighteenth century it sounds more like an argument that the Church was instituted for a common welfare, conceived of not as a divine and hierarchical order but as the concatenation of the well-being of its individual members; this was what the American Continental Congress a decade later called an "inalienable right"

Richard Jackson, *Vive le roi!: A History of the French Coronation from Charles V to Charles X* (Chapel Hill: University of North Carolina Press, 1984), 215–17.

20. *Procès-verbaux*, 8.2, col. 1358.

to "the pursuit of happiness."[21] How France would then differ from a republic like that proposed by Rousseau is unclear: Who, after all, would be a better judge of the interest of the faithful than the laity as a whole? Perhaps it was because they saw this slippery slope that the redactors of the Assembly's *Actes* chose not to use that argument. If so, this exercise in self-censorship has an interesting parallel in the explicit decrees of the Assembly. Among the books they tried to suppress was Rousseau's *Social Contract*, with its famous advocacy of an exclusive civil religion. Needless to say, that attempt failed.

21. Anthony Pagden has justly remarked that it was characteristic of eighteenth-century political theory to take as its criterion of political success "what was widely known as 'public happiness,' what we today would call welfare. This was an inwardly directed and grounded claim that the interests of the state had primarily to be an expression of the well-being of those *individuals* of whom it was composed"; see *Lords of All the World: Ideologies of Empire in Spain, Britain and France c. 1500–c. 1800* (New Haven, Conn.: Yale University Press, 1995), 157. "Public happiness" showed a strong tendency to be measured in purely economic terms.

Bibliography

PRIMARY SOURCES

Manuscripts

Archives Nationales, France

Fonds de l'Agence générale du clergé:
G^8 151: Des conseillers clercs
*G^8 593^B: Procès-verbal de l'assemblée de Paris, 1567
*G^8 599: Procès-verbal de l'assemblée de Melun, 1579
*G^8 608: Procès-verbal de l'assemblée de Paris, 1584
*G^8 609: Procès-verbal de l'assemblée de Paris, 1585–1586
*G^8 644: Supplement ou critique de l'assemblée du clergé de France tenüe en l'année 1625, par Mr. de Chartres.
*G^8 2846: Inventaire des papiers communs du clerge de france

Bibliothèque Nationale de France

Collection Dupuy: 37, 117, 313, 376, 392, 422, 423, 477, 493, 520, 594, 670, 677, 770, 811.
Collection des Cinq Cents de Colbert: 153, 154.
Collection Duchesne: 47, 57.
Manuscrits français: 473, 2760, 3888, 4397, 4770, 5045, 6371, 6396, 4893, 10900, 15463, 15518, 15730, 15733, 15734.
Nouvelles acquisitions françaises: 5064.
Manuscrits latins: 1549^A, 1559, 9960.

Bibliothèque de l'Arsénal

Manuscrits 2562, 4114.

Bibliothèque Mazarine

Manuscrits 1368, 1369.

285

Case F 39.326 1579fr.

Newberry Library, Chicago

Pamphlets

Official Publications

Arrest de la Cour de Parlement contre les enfans, qui se marient sans le consentement de leurs peres & meres. Paris: Federic Morel & Pierre Mettayer, 1615.

Arrest de la Cour de Parlement, contre le Nonce du Pape, pour avoir excommunié les Cordeliers de Paris, & iceux absous à la baguette. S.l., n.d.

Arrest de la Cour de Parlement contre toutes provisions de Benefices decernees par les Cardinaux Cajetan & de Plaisance eux disans Legats de nostre St. Pere le Pape mesmes à ceus de leur faction. Paris: Jamet Mettayer & Pierre L'Huiller, 1594.

Arrest de la Cour de Parlement donné en l'audience de la Grand Chambre le 12. Juillet 1601. suivant l'ordonnance du Roy Henri III. . . . Sur la nullité alleguée contre un mariage clandestin pretendu promis par un mineur ayant pere & mere. En cest Arrest est inseré le plaidoyé de Mre. Loys Servin Advocat du Roy. Et au bas diceluy y a un aultre Arrest donné le XI. Decmbre 1576. sur pareille question . . . auquel Arrest est inseré le plaidoyé de Mre. Barnabé Brisson lors Advocat du Roy. Paris: Jean Heuqueville, 1601.

Arrest de la Cour de Parlement du 2 Janvier 1615. Touchant la Souveraineté du Roy au temporel, & contre la pernicieuse Doctrine d'attenter aux personnes sacrées des Roys. En suite duquel sont les Arrests donnés sur le mesme subject. Paris: F. Morel & P. Mettayer, 1615.

Arrest de la Cour de Parlement seant à Chaalons, sur certains libelles injurieux & scandaleux, intitulez, bulles monitoriales & imprimez à Rheims. Leu, & publié à Chaalons, en Parlement, l'audience tenant, le Lundy 10 jour de Juin, 1591: Et suyvant iceluy ledits libelles publiquement rompuz & lacerez. Châlons-sur-Marne: Claude Guyot, 1591.

Arrest de la Cour de Parlement sur le libvre faict par Gaspar Schoppius intitulé Ecclesiasticus . . . prononcé & executé le 24 de Novembre mil six cents douze. Paris: Pierre Mettayer, 1612.

Arrest de la cour de Parlement des 17. & 18. Febvrier 1604 sur l'assemblée de Sorbone touchant le Plaidoyé du Breviaire d'Anjou. Extraict des registres du Parlement. S.l., n.d.

Arrest de la cour de Parlement donné le 26 et executé le 27 Juin 1614. Contre le libvre imprimé a Cologne l'an present intitulé Francisci Suarez . . . Defensio fidei Catholicæ . . . contenant plusieurs maximes & propositions contraires aux puissances Souveraines des Roys ordonnez & establis de Dieu seureté de leurs persons, repos & tranquillité de leurs Estats. Paris: F. Morel & P. Mettayer, 1614.

Arrest de la cour de Parlement, par lequel Commission est decernée à Monsieur Ruellé Grand Vicaire de Monseigneur l'Archevesque & Primat de Lyon pour absoudre ad cautelam M. Pierre Garande Archidiacre d'Angers des prettendües sentences de Suspension & Excommunication contre luy rendües par M. l'Evesque d'Angers, avec l'absolution donnee par ledict Sieur Ruellé en consequence dudict Arrest. S.l., n.d.

Arrests de la cour de Parlement des 17. & 18. Febvrier 1604 sur l'assemblée de Sorbone touchant le Plaidoyé du Breviaire d'Anjou. Extraict des registres de Parlement. S.l., n.d.

Articles accordez au Clergé de France, sur les remonstrances faicts au Roy par les Agens generaux d'iceluy, à sainct Germain en Laye le douzieme du mois de Novembre, 1583. Paris: n.p., 1584.

Censure par les Evesques de la Province de Sens, d'un Livre intitulé, De Ecclesiastica & Politica potestate. Avec la Reservation des droicts du Roy, & de la Couronne de France, droicts, immunitez, & libertez de l'Eglise Gallicane. Publiee aux Prosnes des Messes Parochiales, le 18 Mars 1612. par l'ordonnance de Monsieur l'Evesque de Paris. Et quelques Procedures contre ladicte Censure. S.l., 1612.

Declaration de l'Assemblee generale du Clergé de France . . . sur l'attentat commis par Maistre Estienne Louytre, contre Monsieur l'Evesque de Laon. Paris: Antoine Estienne, 1625.

Facultez octroyees par nostre Sainct Pere le Pape Clement VIII. au Reverendissime Cardinal de Florence, Legat du S. Siege Apostolique au Tres-Chrestien Roy de France & de Navarre Henry IIII. & au Royaume de France: avec les lettres Patentes dudit Seigneur Roy. Paris: Jamet Mettayer & Pierre L'Huillier, 1596.

Harangues, Propositions, Opinions, Resolutions, & arrestez de la Chambre du Tiers Estat. Avec le procez verbal, de tout ce qui s'est passé de jour en jour en ladicte Chambre, & l'Ordre tenu en icelle. Paris: Pierrb [sic] Mettayer, n.d. [ms. note in BN Impr. 8° Le17-39: "1616"; first published as *Procez verbal, de tout ce qui s'est passé en la Chambre du Tiers Estat. Touchant le premier article de leur Cahyer presenté au Roy.* S.l., 1615.]

Litteræ processus, S. D. N. D. Gregorii PP. XIII lectæ die Cænæ Domini, Anno M. D. LXXX. Paris: Thomas Brummenius, 1580.

Anonymous Publications

Advis salutaire donné au sieur illustrissime Cardinal de Sourdis pour sagement vivre à l'advenir. S.l., 1615.

Ample discours des actes memorables de Poissy. Contenant le commancement de l'assemblee, l'entrée & issue du Colloque des Prelatz de France, & Ministres de l'Evangile: l'ordre y gardé: Ensemble la Harangue du Roy Charles IX. S.l., 1561.

Article de l'Eglise apporté au tiers estat par Mongeur [sic] *L'Evesque de Masçon, le matin 5. jour de Janvier 1615.* S.l., n.d.

Conclusions de la tres-sacree Faculté de Theologie de Paris, sur la Censure des livres de Mre. Jean du Mansencal quand vivoit premier President au Parlement de Tholose du 15. Decembre 1552. S.l., 1615.

Conversion de Pierre Marcha en l'église de Saint-Ouen à Rouen, in Societé des Bibliophiles Normands, *Miscellanées historiques et littéraires,* 4e série, vol. 20. Rouen, France: Imprimerie Léon Gy, 1905. [Originally published as "F. C.," *Ample et fidelle narré de l'heureuse conversion de Pierre Marcha, Sieur de Pras, Ministre de la Religion pretenduë reformée, ès pays de Languedoc. Faites en l'Eglise de S. Ouën, le jour de Noël dernier, en la presence de sa Majesté tres-chrestien, de Messieurs les Princes, de toute la Cour, & des Grands de son Royaume. Dedié au Roy.* Paris: Joseph Cottereau, 1618.]

Copie d'une lettre d'un prelat deputé du clergé à l'assemblée des Estats, sur ce qui s'est passé touchant l'article contentieux employé pour le premier au cayer du tiers Estat. S.l., 1615.

Defence du Traicté du Delict Commun et Cas privilegié, en la distinction des deux puissances, Ecclesiastique & Seculiere. A Monsieur Milletot, Sr. de Villy, Conseiller au Parlement de Bourgogne. Dijon, France: Claude Guyot, 1611.

Discours sur les meurs et humeur de Monsieur Servin Advocat General au Parlement de Paris. S.l., 1617.

Epistola tempore Philippi Pulchri Regis Christianissmi scripta, contra Bonifacii VIII usurpationes. S.l., n.d.

In Parricidas Regum, et Jesuites parricidorum impulsores, Et in Pædotribas plagiarios. Paris: Jamet Mettayer & Pierre L'Huiller, 1595.
Pieces du memorable proces esmeu l'an M. DC. VI. entre le Pape Paul V. et les seigneurs de Venise. Touchant l'excommunication du Pape publiee contre iceux Vénitiens Recueillies & fidelement traduits de Latin & d'Italien en François, sur les exemplaires imprimez à Rome & à Venise. S. Vincent: Paul Marceau, 1607.
Prophetie faite par M. Abel Ongeur, doyen de la grande Eglise de Theroneme, l'an 1477. Trouvez dans les papiers de Jean Anthoine de Baif, l'an 89. Paris: P. Buray, 1614.
Propositiones exerptæ ex libello cui titulus est, Compendium Quæstionum Regularium R. admodum P. Emanuelis Roderici Lusitani, S. T. Lectoris prov. S. Jacobi Reg. observ. ordin. Mino. diffinitoris ad commodiorem usum per Aphorismos ordine alphabetico digestum, opera ac studio quorundam fratrum Minorum Recollectorum. S.l., n.d.
Prosopopee de l'assassin du Roy. S.l., n.d.
Prosopopee de la Pyramide du Palais. S.l., n.d.
Quelques Propositions Recueillies de l'Epitome des Annales Ecclesiastics du reverendiss. Cardinal Baronius, faite par M. Henry Sponde, Prestre Romain, imprimee à Paris, chez le Nonce, l'an 1613. Et Arrests des Parlements de Paris, Thoulouse, et Rouen; et Edicts des Roys d'Espagne, qui condamnent semblables propositions, & ceux qui les publient. S.l., 1612 [*sic*].
Recueil de ce qui s'est fait en Sorbonne et ailleurs, contre un Livre de Becanus Jesuite. S.l., 1613.
Remonstrance à Messieurs de la Cour de Parlement sur le parricide commis en la personne du Roy Henry le Grand. S.l., 1610.
Response au Traite intitulé, Ordre & reglement sur les provisions des benefices en l'Eglise Gallicane, pendant les empeschemens d'aller à Rome. A Messieurs les Prelatz & autres Ecclesiastiques tenans l'assemblee generale du Clergé de France à Paris. S.l., 1596.
Le Tombeau de Monsieur Servin. Paris: Jean Bessin, 1626.
Le Tumbeau de messire Gilles Bourdin, Chevalier, Seigneur d'Assay, Conseiller au privé conseil du Roy, & Procureur general de sa Majesté au Parlement de Paris. En plusieurs langues. Recuilli de plusieurs scavans personnages de la France. Paris: Robert Estienne, 1570.

Publications with Known or Probable Authors

[Arnauld, Antoine]. *Antiespagnol autrement les Phillipiques d'un Demosthenes François touchant les menees & ruses de Phillipe Roy d'Espagne pour envahir la Couronne de France. Ensemble l'Infidelité, Rebellion & Fureur des Ligueurs Parisiens & Jesuites en faveur de l'Espagnol.* S.l., 1592.

[———]. *La Fleur de Lys. Qui est un discours d'un François retenu dans Paris, sur les impietez & desguisements contenus au Manifeste d'Espagne, publié au mois de Janvier dernier 93.* S.l., 1593.

Bodin, Jean. *Lettre de monsieur Bodin.* Paris: Guillaume Chaudiere, 1590.

Bouchet, Jean. *La déploration de l'église militante.* Edited by Jennifer Britnell. Geneva: Droz, 1991.

[Charron, Pierre]. *Discours Chrestien, qui'il n'est permis ny loisible a un subject, pour quelque cause & raison que ce soit, de se liguer, bander & rebeller contre son Roy.* Paris: Martin Durand, 1594.

Condé, Henri II de Bourbon, Prince de. *Advis de Monseigneur le Prince au Roy. En son conseil tenu au Louvre, le jour des Roys: 6. Janvier 1615. Sur l'article du Tiers Estat Contradictions du Clergé, & Arrest du Parlement touchant la souveraineté du Roy. Ensemble l'Extraict des Registres du Conseil d'Estat.* S.l., 1615.

———. *Lettre de Monseigneur le Prince à la Royne.* S.l., 1614.

———. *Lettre de Monseigneur le Prince de Condé envoyee à la Royne. Sur le refus qui luy a esté faict par Messieurs de Poictiers.* S.l., 1614.

Dumoulin, Charles. *Caroli Molinæ jurisconsulti, et in supremo Parisiensi Senatu antiqui advocati consultatio, an Jesuistæ* [sic] *sint recipiendi in regno Franciæ, & admittendi in Universitate Parisiensi.* S.l., 1594.

[Espesse, Jacques la Faye d']. *Advertissement sur la reception & publication du Concile de Trent.* S.l., 1583.

Fabricius, Jacobus Cosma. *Nota stigmaticæ, ad Magistrum trigina paginarum, qui libello uno Ecclesiasticam & politicam potestatem complexus est.* Frankfurt-am-Main, Germany: Jacob Fischer, 1612.

[Genebrard, Gilbert]. *Excommunication Des Ecclesiastiques, principalement des Evesques, Abbez et Docteurs, qui ont assisté au divin service, sciemment & volontairement avec Henry de Vallois, apres le massacre du Cardinal de Guyse. Traduit de Latin d'un Docteur par I. M.* Paris: Gilles Gourbin, 1589.

[Guesle, Jacques de la]. *Ordre et Reglement sur les Provisions des benefices en l'Eglise Gallicane pendant les empeschemens d'aller à Rome.* Paris: Denys Duval, 1596.

Guise, Charles, (Cardinal) de, dit "de Lorraine." *L'oraison de Monseigneur le illustrissime et reverendissime Cardinal de Lorraine, faicte en l'Assemblée de Poyssi, le Roy y estant present, le XVI. jour de Septembre, M. D. LXI.* Paris: Guillaume Morel, [1561].

James I & VI, King of England and Scotland. *Declaration du serenissime Roy Jacques I. Roy de la Grand' Bretaigne France et Irlande, Defenseur de la Foy. Pour le droit de Rois & independance de leurs Couronnes, Contre La Harangue De L'Illustrissime Cardinal du Perron prononcée en la chambre du tiers Estat le XV de Janvier 1615.* London: John Bill, 1615.

———. *An Apologie for the Oath of Allegiance. First set foorth without a name: and now acknowledged by the Authour, the Right High and Mightie Prince, James, by the Grace of God, King of Great Britain, France and Ireland; Defender of the Faith, &c. Together with a Premonition of his Majesties, to all most Mightie Monarchs, Kings, free Princes and States of Christendome.* London: Robert Barker, 1609.

[Jay, Nicolas le]. *Le Tocsin au Roy, à la Royne Regente mere du Roy, aux Princes du Sang, à tous les Parlemens, Magistrats, Officiers & bons & loyaux Subjects de la Couronne de France, contre le Livre de la Puissance Temporelle du Pape, mis n'agueres en lumiere par le Cardinal Bellarmin Jesuite. Par la Statue de Memnon. Avec Permission du bon Genie de la France.* Paris: "à l'enseigne de la Quaddrature du Cercle, en la rue du Tonneau des Danaides," 1610.

Kermadec, François de. *Relation veritable envoyee au Serenissime Roy de Grand' Bretagne, De plusieurs divers jugemens faits en France. Sur le sujet de la Declaration de S. M. Pour le droit des Rois & l'independance de leurs Couronnes.* "Sur le coppie imprimée à Nantes," 1615.

Loisel, Antoine. "Pasquier, ou le Dialogue des avocats." In André Dupin, ed., *Profession d'avocat: Receuil des pièces concernant l'exercise de cette profession.* 2 vols. Paris: Alex Gobelet and B. Warré, 1832. 1:147–258.

Mesnil, Baptiste du. *Plaidoié de feu M. l'advocat du Mesnil, en la cause de l'Université de Paris & des Jesuites.* Paris: Abel L'Angelier, 1594.

Nancel, Pierre de. *De la Souveraineté des Roys. Poeme Epique, Divisé en trois Livres. A la Reine, Mere* du Roy, Regente en France. Querimonia, super acerbo Henrici Magni funere. Elegiaco carmine expressa. S.l., 1610.

[Pasquier, Estienne]. *Le catechisme des Jesuites*. Edited by Claude Sutto. Sherbrooke, Quebec, Canada: Les Editions de l'Université de Sherbrooke, 1982.

―――. *Le plaidoyé de M. Pasquier pour l'Université de Paris deffenderesse, contre les Jesuites demandeurs en requeste*. Paris: Abel L'Angelier, 1594.

Pelletier, Thomas. *La conversion du Sr Pelletier à la Foy Catholique. En laquelle il represente au naif les vrayes & infaillibles marques de l'Eglise contre les erreurs & fausses opinions des Calvinistes*. Paris: Jean Junnon, 1609.

[Pithou, Pierre, et al.]. *Satyre Menipée de la vertu du Catholicon d'Espagne et de la tenue des Estats de Paris*. Edited by Charles Labitte. Paris: G. Charpentier, 1880.

[Richer, Edmond]. *De la puissance ecclesiastique et politique. L'Eglise est une police Monarchique, intstituee à une fin supernaturelle: Conduite d'un gouvernement Aristocratique, par le souverain Pasteur des ames nostre Seigneur Jesus-Christ*. Paris: n.p., 1612.

[―――]. *Recueil de plusieurs Actes remarquables pour l'Histoire de ce temps*. S.l., 1613.

[―――]. *Quædam acta ecclesiæ gallicanæ, pro libertatibus Ecclesiæ et Juris communis defensione*. Paris: n.p., 1608.

Seguier, Antoine. *Receuil du plaidoie de Monsieur Seguier Conseiller du Roy en son Conseil d'Estat, & son Advocat en la Cour de Parlement. Contre la Bulle de Gregoire soy disant Pape 14. de ce nom. A Tours le Parlement y seant, en Aoust 1591*. Châlons-sur-Marne, France: n.p., 1595.

[Servin, Louis]. *Comunefactio et postulationes Regiorum Cognitorum, necnon arrestum Curiæ Parlementi Parisiensis die 26 Novembr. 1610 latum Adversus librum inscriptum* Tractatus de Potestate Summi Pontificis in rebus Temporalibus adversus Guilielmum Barcleium autore Roberto S. R. E. Cardinali Bellarmino, *excursum Romæ anno 1610*. S.l., 1611.

―――. *Poetica paraphrasis Cantica canticorum Salomonis Regis*. Paris: Pierre Mettayer, 1612.

[―――]. *Pro libertate status et reipublicæ venetorum Gallofranci ad Philenetum Epistola*. Paris: n.p., 1606.

―――. *Recueil de ce qui fut dict par monsieur Servin Advocat General du Roy en la Cour de Parlement lors de la lecture des lettres patentes du Roy le cinquième Janvier mil cinqs cents quatre vingts dix, contenant declaration de sa Majesté à la venuë d'un des Cardinauls de la Cour de Rome envoyé par le Pape au Royaume de France*. S.l., n.d.

Thou, Jacques Auguste de. *Epistre de monsieur le president de Thou, au Roy*. Paris: Pierre Chevalier, 1614.

[Turgot, Georges]. *Le cayer general des remonstrances que l'Université de Paris a dressé, pour presenter au Roy nostre souverain Seigneur, en l'Assemblee Generale des trois Ordres de son Royaume, etc*. S.l., 1615.

Versoris, Pierre (alias le Torneur). *Plaidoyé de feu Maister Pierre Versoris advocat en Parlement, pour les prebstres & escoliers du College de Clermont fondé en l'Université de Paris demandeurs, contre ladicte Université deffenderesse*. S.l., 1594.

Printed Document Collections

Collection des procès-verbaux des Assemblées-Générales du Clergé de France, Depuis l'année 1560, jusqu'à présent, rédigés par ordre de matieres, Et réduits à ce qu'ils ont d'essentiel; Ouvrage Composé sous la direction de M. l'Evesque de Mâcon. Autorisé par les Assemblées de 1762 & 1765, & imprimé par ordre du Clergé. 8 vols. Paris: Guillaume Desprez, 1767.

Corpus juris canonici emendatum et notis illustratum: Gregorii XIII. Pont. Max. jussu editum. Lyons, France: n.p., 1614.

Corpus iuris canonici editio Lipsiensis secunda. 2 vols. Ed. Aemilius Friedberg. Leipzig, Germany: B. Tauchnitz, 1879; facs. rpt. Graz, Austria: Akademische Druck- und Verlagsanstalt, 1955.

Documents relatifs aux Etats Généraux et assemblées réunis sous Phillipe le Bel. Ed. Georges Picot. Collection des documents inédits sur l'histoire de France. Paris: Imprimerie Nationale, 1901.

Harangues et actions publiques des plus rares esprites de nostre temps. Faictes tant aux ouvertures des Cours souveraines de ce Royaume qu'en plusieurs tres signalées occasions. Reveuës & augmentées d'un grand nombre non encores imprimées. Paris: Jean de Heuqueville, 1609.

Ordonnances des rois de France de la troisième race, recueillies par ordre chronologique. Vol. 9. Paris: Imprimerie royale, 1755.

Plaidoyers et Actions Grans et Eloquents de plusieurs fameux Advocats du Parlement de Bourdeaus. Et Arrests sur ce intervenus. Bordeaux, France: Gilbert Vernoy, 1616.

Pragmatica sanctio cum glossis egregii, eminentisque scientiæ viri, Domini Cosmæ Guimier Parisini, in supremo Parisiensi senatu Inquestarum Præsidis. Quibus accesserunt ad cuiuslibet Decreti Parraphos summaria, suisque in locis Concordatorum concordia, & illorum dissonantia: Necnon glossæ, ac additiones, . . . Opera aut labore D. Philippi Propi Biturici. "Secunda editio quoad additiones." Paris: Apud Galeotum à Prato, 1555.

Recueil des actes, titres et memoires concernant les affaires du Clergé de France, Augmenté d'un grand nombre de Pieces & d'Observations sur la Discipline présente de l'Eglise, Et mis en nouvel Ordre suivant la Déliberation de l'Assemblée générale du Clergé du 29 Août 1705, etc. Paris: Pierre Simon, 1740.

Les remonstrances, edicts, contracts, et autres choes [sic] concernans le Clergé de France. . . . Illustree d'une Conference sous chacun article desdis Edicts. Et Augmentee de nouveau des Edict [sic], Lettres Patentes, & Arrests du Conseil d'Estat & du Grand-Conseil octroyez & donnez au faveur des Ecclesiastiques, ez annees 1616. 1620. & 1621. "Derniere edition." Paris: Jean Richer, 1621.

Les Remonstrances faictes au Roy Loys Unzieme, sur les privileges de l'Eglise Gallicane, & les plainctifs & doleances du peuple. Plus l'institution & ordonnance des Chevaliers de l'ordre des Treschrestiens Roys de France. Avec la forme et ordre de l'assemblée des trois estatz en la ville de Tours, soubz le regne de Charles huictieme, & ce qui y fut remonstré decidé & ordonné. Paris: Jean Dallier, 1561.

Traitez des droits et libertez de l'Eglise gallicane. 2 vols. Paris: n.p., 1731.

Traictez des droicts et libertez de l'Eglise gallicane. Paris: Pierre Chevalier, 1609. [also, 2nd exp. ed. Paris: Pierre Chevalier, 1612.]

Other Published Works

Anonymous. De la puissance Royalle & Sacerdotale. Opuscule politique. S.l., 1579.

Anonymous. Les Triomphes du Roy. A Monseigneur d'Espernon Duc, Pair & Colonel de France. Paris: Gilles Robinot, 1609.

Aristotle. On Rhetoric: A Theory of Civic Discourse. Translated by George A. Kennedy. Oxford, U.K.: Oxford University Press, 1991.

———. *The Politics.* Translated by Benjamin Jowett. Cambridge, U.K.: Cambridge University Press, 1988.
Arnauld d'Andilly, Antoine. *Mémoires.* In M. Petitot, ed., *Collection des mémoires relatifs à l'histoire de France,* vol. 33. 2nd ed. Paris: Foucault, 1824.
Bassompierre, François de. *Journal de ma vie: Mémoires du Maréchal de Bassompierre.* Edited by M.-J. de Chantérac. Sources de l'histoire de France 153. Paris: Veuve Jules Renouard, 1870.
Bellay, Jean (Cardinal) du. "Lettre du Cardinal du Bellay à M. de Mannes." *Revue de la renaissance* 4 (1903): 174–77.
Bellay, Joachim du. *La deffence et illustration de la langue francoyse.* Edited by Henri Chamard. Paris: Librarie Marcel Didier, 1961.
———. *Les regrets et autres œuvres poëtiques suivis des antiquitez de Rome, plus un songe ou vision sur le mesme subject.* Edited by J. Jolliffe and M. A. Screech. Geneva: Droz, 1966.
———. *Œuvres poétiques.* 6 vols. Edited by Henri Chamard. Paris: Klincksieck, 1991.
[Bignon, Jerôme]. *La grandeur de nos Roys, et de leur souveraine puissance. au Roy.* Paris: n.p., 1615.
Bodin, Jean. *Method for the Easy Comprehension of History.* Translated by Beatrice Reynolds. New York: Columbia University Press, 1945.
———. *Six livres de la République.* 6 vols. Paris: Fayard, 1986.
Boëtie, Etienne de la. *Œuvres complètes: Edition nouvelle augmentée.* 2 vols. Edited by Louis Desgraves and Paul Bonnefon. S.l.: William Blake and Co., 1991.
Bouchel, Laurent, ed. *La bibliothèque ou thresor du droict francois œuvre auquel non seulement tout ce qui est de de matieres civiles, criminelles, et beneficiales, Ordonnances & Coustumes de la France est sommairement rapporté: mais aussi les questions plus difficiles & remarquables d'icelles y sont expliquees & resoluës par les Expositions, Traittez & Decisions des plus celebres Jurisconsultes, Practiciens François, & Arrests des Cours Souverains Et encore illustré en plusieurs endroits par la conference & rapport des Loix & coustumes des nations etrangeres.* 2 vols. Paris: Eustache Foucault et al., 1615.
———. *Decretorum Ecclesiæ Gallicanæ, ex Conciliis eiusdem œcumenicis, statutis Synodalibus, Patriarchis, Provincialibus ac Diœcesanis, Senatusconsultis, Episcoporum Galliæ scriptis, aliisque cum veterum, tum recentiorum pietatis eximiæ virorum monimentis collectorum, Libri VIII.* Paris: Bartholomeus Maceus, 1609.
———. *La somme beneficiale, reduite à l'usage et pratique de France. Recueillie par M. Laurens Bouchel Advocat en la Cour de Parlement.* Paris: Rolet Boutonne, 1628.
———. *Receuil d'arrests notables et decisifs, de plusieurs questions qui sont presentées en la Cour de Parlement, & Cour des Aydes de Paris; Jugées és Audiences, & sur procés par escrit. Extraicts des memoires de Mes. Laur. Bouchel, & Jacques Joly, Advocats en Parlement.* Paris: Guillaume Loyson, 1630.
Bouju, Theophraste. *Deffence pour la Hierarchy de l'Eglise et de nostre S. pere le Pape, contre les faussetez, et calomniez de Maistre Simon Vigor Conseiller du Roy en son grand' Conseil, & autres.* Paris: Denys Langlois, 1620.
Boulay, César Egasse du. *Historia Univeristatis Parisiensis.* Vol. 6. Paris: Petrus de Bresche and François Noël, 1673.
Budé, Guillaume. *Forensia.* Paris: Robert Estienne, 1544.

---. *De Linstitution du Prince. Livre contenant plusieur Histoires, Enseignements, & saiges Dicts des Anciens tant Grecs que Latins. Faict & composé par Maistre Guillaume Budé, lors Secretaire & maistre de la Librairie, & depuis Maistre des Requestes, et Conseiller du Roy. Revue, enrichy d'Arguments, divisé par Chapitres, & augmenté de Scholies & Annotations, Par hault & puissant Seigneur, Missire Jean de Luxembourg, Abbé d'Iury*. L'Arrivour, France: Nicole Paris, 1547; facs. rpt. Farnborough, N.J.: Gregg Press, 1966.

Cajetan, Thomas de Vio (Cardinal). *De comparatione auctoritatis Papæ et Concilii, cum Apologia eiusdem tractatus*. Edited by Vincent Pollet. Scripta Theologica 1. Rome: Apud Institutum «Angelicum», 1936.

Camus, Jean-Pierre. *Homélies des Etats-généraux (1614–1615)*. Edited by Jean Descrains. Geneva: Droz, 1970.

Charondas le Caron, Louis. *Memorables observations du droit françois rapporté au civil et canonic: illustrees des arrests des Cours souveraines de France & auctoritez des plus celebres Aucteurs; Auquel livre sont representees plusieurs antiquitez Romaines & Françoises, non encore bien observees*. 3rd ed. Paris: Veufve Claude de Monstr'œil, 1614.

Clement VIII (Pope). *Die Hauptinstruktionen Clemens' VIII. für die Nuntien und Legaten an den Europäischen Fürstenhöfen 1592–1605*. 2 vols. paginated continuously. Edited by Klaus Jaitner. Instructiones Pontificum Romanorum. Tübingen, Germany: Max Niemeyer Verlag, 1984.

Coeffeteau, Nicolas. *Responce a l'advertissement, adressé par le Serenissime Roy de la grande Bretagne, Jacques I. à tous les Princes & Potentats de la Chrestienté*. Paris: François Huby, 1610.

Contarini, Gasparo. *De magistratibus et republica venetorum libri quinque*. Venice, Italy: Baldus Sabinus, 1551.

Coquille, Guy. *Les œuvres de Maistre Guy Coquille Sieur de Romenay, Contenans plusieurs traictez touchant les Libertez de l'Eglise Gallicane, l'Histoire de France & le Droict François. Entre lesquels plusieurs n'ont point encore esté imprimez, & les autres ont esté exactement corrigez*. 2 vols. Paris: Guillaume de Luyne et al., 1665.

Dumoulin, Charles. *Abus des petites dates, reservations, preventions, annates, et autres usurpations & Exactions de la Cour de Rome, Contre les Edictz & ordonnances des Roys de France*. Lyons, France: "pour ledit du Moulin," 1564.

---. *Commentarius ad edictum Henrici secundi contra parvas datas & abusus curiæ Romanæ, & in antiqua edicta & Senatusconsulta Franciæ contra Annatarum & id genus abusus, multas novas decisiones juris & praxis continens*. Lyons, France: Antoine Vincent, 1552.

---. *Omnia quæ extant opera*. 5 vols. Paris: Charles Osmont, 1681.

---. *Traicte de l'origine, progres et excellence du royaume & monarchie des françois, & coronne de France, oeuvre monstrant que toutes monarchies, empires, royaumes & seigneuries sont periz & ruinez par l'idolatrie*. Paris: "en la rue des Porees, à l'enseigne S. Julien," 1561.

Dupuy, Pierre, and Jacques Dupuy, eds. *Perroniana et Thuana ou, Pensées Judicieuses, bons mots, rencontres agreables & observations curieuses du Cardinal du Perron, et de Mr le President de Thou, Conseiller d'Estat*. Cologne [probably factitious], Germany: n.p., 1694.

Durand, Claude. *Advis d'un Docteur de Paris, Sur un livre intitulé,* De la puissance Ecclesiastique et Politique. Paris: n.p., 1612.

Fauchet, Claude. *Les Œuvres de M. Claude Fauchet. Reveues et corrigees en ceste derniere edition*. 2

vols. Paris: David le Clerc and Jean de Heuqueville, 1610; facs. rpt. Geneva: Slatkine Reprints, 1969.

Gerson, Jean. *Opera omnia . . . tomus secundus, Ea complectens quæ ad Ecclesiasticam politeian, & disciplinam pertinent*. Edited by Louis Ellies Dupin. Antwerp, Belgium: Sumptibus Societatis, 1706; facs. rpt. Hildesheim, Germany: Georg Olms Verlag, 1987.

Godefroy, Denis (attr.). *Maintenue & defense des princes souverains et Eglises chrestiennes, Contre les attentats, usurpations, & excommunications des Papes de Rome*. S. l., 1592.

Guesle, Jacques de la. *Les remonstrances de Messire Jacques de La Guesle, Procureur general du Roy. Dediees A la Royne Regent*. Paris: Pierre Chevalier, 1611.

Henri IV, King of France. *Lettres de Henri IV concernant les relations du Saint-Siège et de la France 1595–1609*. Edited by Bernard Barbiche. Studi e testi 250. Vatican City: Biblioteca Apostolica Vaticana, 1968.

[Hotman, Antoine]. *Traicté des libertez de l'eglise Gallicane. Laquelle composition monstre la pure & sincere intelligence de ces libertez*. Paris: Gilles Robinot, 1608.

Hotman, François. *Antitribonian ou discours d'un grand et renommé Jurisconsulte de nostre temps, sur l'estude des loix, Fait par l'advis de feu Monsieur de l'Hospital Chancelier de France en l'an 1567. Et Imprimé nouvellement*. Paris: Jeremie Perier, 1603; facs. rpt. Saint-Etienne, France: Publications de l'Université de Saint-Etienne, 1980.

———. *Francogallia*. Edited by Ralph E. Giesey. Translated by J. H. M. Salmon. Cambridge, U.K.: Cambridge University Press, 1972.

Isambert, M. François André, and A. Jourdan, eds. *Recueil général des anciennes lois françaises, depuis l'an 420 jusqu'à la revolution de 1789*. 29 vols. Paris: Belin-Leprieur, 1826–1833; facs rpt. Ridgewood, N.J.: Gregg Press, 1964–1966.

Jean de Paris (*alias* Jean Quidort). *On Royal and Papal Power*. Edited by J. A. Watt. Toronto: Pontifical Institute for Medieval Studies, 1971.

———. *On Royal and Papal Power*. Edited by Arthur P. Monahan. New York: Columbia University Press, 1974.

Joinville, Jean de. *La vie de saint Louis*. Edited by J. Monfrin. Paris: Classiques Garnier, 1995.

La Roche Flavin, Bernard de. *Treze livres des parlemens de France. Esquels est amplement traicté de leur origine et institution, et des presidens, conseillers, gens du Roy, greffiers, secretaires, Huissers & autres officiers; & de leur charge, devoir, & jurisdiction: ensemble de leurs rangs, seances, gages, privileges, reglements, & Mercurialles . . . Œuvre tres-utile non seulement a tous officiers des Parlemens: mais à tous autres Magistrats de France*. Bordeaux, France: Simon Millanges, 1617.

Lemaire de Belges, Jean. *Œuvres*. 4 vols. Edited by Jean Stecher. Louvain, Belgium: Lefever frères et sœur, 1885.

Le Maistre, Gilles. *Les Œuvres de feu Mesire Gilles Le Maistre, Chevalier et Premier President en la Cour de Parlement de Paris. Divisé en cinq livres, 1. Des Criées & Saisies réels. 2. Des Amortissemens & Franc-fiefs. 3. Des Regales. 4. Des Fiefs, Hommages & Vassaux. 5. Des Appelations comme d'abus. Reveuë, corrigée, augmenté de plusieurs decisions, & Arrests intervenus jusqu'à present par Maistre Claude Bernard, Advocat en Parlement*. Paris: Michel Bobin, 1653.

Leroy, Louis. *Des differens et troubles advenans entres les hommes par la diversité des opinions en la Religion*. Paris: Federic Morel, 1562.

---. *De la vicissitude ou varieté des choses en l'univers, et concurrence des armes et des lettres par premieres et plus illustres nations du monde, depuis le temps où a commencé la civilité, et memoire humaine jusques à present.* Paris: Fayard, 1988.

---. *Des troubles et differens advenans entres les hommes par la diversité des opinions des Religions. ensemble du commencement, progrez, & excellence de la Religion Chrestienne.* Paris: Federic Morel, 1568.

Leschassier, Jacques. *Les œuvres de M. Jacques Leschassier Parisien, Advocat en Parlement, Contenans plusieurs excellens Traittez; tant du Droit Public des Romains, que du celuy des François. Ensemble quelques memoires servans à l'antiquité de l'Eglise & à l'illustration de l'Histoire de France.* Paris: n.p., 1649.

Loisel, Antoine. *La Guyenne de M. Ant. L'Oisel, qui sont huict remonstrances faictes en la Chambre de Justice de Guyenne sur le subject des Edicts de Pacification. Plus une autre Remonstrance sur le Reduction de la ville & Restablissement du Parlement de Paris. Avec l'extrait d'un Plaidoyé de l'Université.* Paris: Abel L'Angelier, 1605.

Louet, Georges, and Julian Brodeau, eds. *Recueil d'aucuns notables arrests donnes en la Cour de Parlement De Paris. Pris des Memoires de feu monsieur Me Georges Louet, Conseiller du Roy en icelle. Cinquiesme edition. Reveuë, corrigée & augmentée de plusieurs Arrests, & autres notables Decisions, Par Julian Brodeau, Advocat en Parlement.* Paris: La veufve Abel L'Angelier, 1616.

Lucian (of Samosata). "The Way to Write History." In H. W. Fowler and F. G. Fowler, trans., *The Works of Lucian of Samosata*, 2:109–35. Oxford, U.K.: Clarendon Press, 1905.

Machiavelli, Niccolò. *The Prince.* Translated by Peter Bondanella and Mark Musa. Oxford, U.K.: Oxford University Press, 1984.

Mansi, Joannes Dominicus, et al., eds. *Sacrorum conciliorum nova et amplissima collectio.* Vol. 32. Paris and Leipzig, Germany: Hubert Welter, 1902.

Marion, Simon. *Plaidoyez et advis sur plusieurs grands et importans affaires, de Messire Simon Marion, Conseiller du Roy en son Conseil d'Estat, & son Advocat General au Parlement de Paris. Ensemble l'invintaire pour Monsieur le Connestable de Montmorency, en la cause de Chasteaubriant, fait par ledit sieur Marion. Le tout non encore cy devant imprimé.* Paris: Joseph Bucherin, 1625.

Marsilius of Padua. *Defensor pacis.* Translated by Alan Gewirth. Toronto: University of Toronto Press/Medieval Academy of America, 1980.

---. *Œuvres mineures: Defensor minor, De translatione Imperii.* Edited by Colette Jeudy and Jeannine Quillet. Paris: Editions du C.N.R.S., 1979.

Masselin, Jehan. *Journal des états généraux de France tenus à Tours en 1484 sous le règne de Charles VIII.* Edited by A. Bernier. Collection des documents inédits sur l'histoire de France. Paris: Imprimerie Royale, 1835.

Matthew Paris. *Matthæi parisiensis, monachi Sancti Albini, chronica majora*, Vol. 6: *Additamenta.* Edited by Henry Richards Luard. London: Longman, 1882.

Molé, Mathieu. *Mémoires de Mathieu Molé, procureur général, premier président au Parlement de Paris et garde des sceaux de France.* 4 vols. Edited by Aimé Champollion-Figeac. Sources de l'histoire de France 78. Paris: Jules Renouard, 1855–1857.

Montaigne, Michel de. *Les essais.* Edited by Pierre Villey. Paris: Quadrige/Presses Universitaires de France, 1992.

———. *Œuvres complètes.* Edited by Albert Thibaudet and Maurice Rat. Paris: N.R.F./Gallimard, 1962.

Optatus Milevitanus. "De schismate Donatistarum adversus Parmenium." In J. P. Migne, ed., *Patriologiæ cursus completus, series Latina,* vol. 11., cols. 883–1104. Paris: Vrayet, 1845.

Pasquier, Estienne. *Pourparlers.* Edited by Béatrice Sayhi-Périgot. Textes de la Renaissance 7. Paris: Honoré Champion, 1995.

———. *Les Recherches de la France.* 3 vols. Edited by Marie-Madeleine Fragonard and François Roudaut. Textes de la Renaissance 11. Paris: Honoré Champion, 1996.

Peleus, Julien. *Les œuvres de Me. Julien Peleus advocat en Parlement Contenant plusieurs Questions Illustres, tant en matieres Beneficials, Civiles & Criminelles, que des Coustumes de France, Droict Escrit, & consitutions de l'Eglise Gallicane. Ensemble les arrests notables sur ce intervenus. Avec les Plaidoyes des Anciens & fameux Advocats.* Paris: Pierre Billaine, 1638.

Perron, Jacques Davy (Cardinal) du. *Les diverses œuvres de l'illustrissime Cardinal du Perron, Archevesque de Sens, Primat des Gaules & de Germanie, & grand Ausmonier de France. Contenant plusieurs Œuvres, Conferences, Discours, Harangues, Lettres d'Estat & autres, Traductions, Poësies, & Traittez tant d'Eloquence, Philosophie que Theologie non encor veus ny publiez. Ensemble tous ses Ecrits mis au jour de son vivant, & maintenant r'imprimez sur ses Exemplaires laissez reveus, corrigez & augmentez de sa main.* Paris: Antoine Estienne, 1621.

Piard, Anthoine. *Apologie royalle.* S.l., 1612.

Pierre Godin, Guillaume de. *The Theory of Papal Monarchy in the Fourteenth Century: Guillaume de Pierre Godin, Tractatus de causa immediata ecclesiastice potestatis.* Edited by William D. McCready. Toronto: Pontifical Institute of Medieval Studies, 1982.

Pithou, Pierre. *Petri Pithoei opera, sacra, juridica, historica, miscellanea.* Paris: Sebastien Cramoisy, 1609.

Popilinière, Lancelot du Voisin de la. *L'histoire des histoires, avec l'idée de l'histoire accomplie.* 2 vols. Paris: Fayard, 1989.

Rabelais, François. *Le Quart livre.* Edited by Gérard Defaux. Paris: Le Livre de Poche, 1994.

Richelieu, Armand Jean du Plessis (Cardinal) de. *Lettres, instructions diplomatiques, et papiers d'état du Cardinal de Richelieu.* Vol. 2. Edited by M. Avenel. Collection des documents inédits sur l'histoire de France 128. Paris: Imprimerie Impériale, 1856.

———. *Mémoires.* Vol. 1. Sources de l'histoire de France 335. Paris: Renouard, 1907.

———. *Testament politique.* Edited by Louis Andre. Paris: R. Laffont, 1947.

Richeome, Louis. *Advis et notes donnees sur quelques plaidoyez, de Maistre Louys Servin Advocat du Roy, cy devant publiez en France, au prejudice de la Religion Catholique, de l'honneur du Roy, Tres Chrestien, & de la paix de son Royaume. A nos tres-honnorez Seigneurs les Gens tenans la Cour de Parlement de Paris.* Caen, France: Georges de la Mariniere, 1615.

[Richer, Edmond]. *Apologia pro Joanne Gersonio Pro suprema Ecclesiæ & Concilii generalis Auctoritate; atque independentia Regiæ Potestatis ab alio quam à Deo: Adversus Scholæ Parisiensis, & ejusdem Doctoris Christianissimi obtrectatores.* Louvain, Belgium: Paulus Moriaeus, 1676.

———. *Histoire du syndicat d'Edmond Richer Par Edmond Richer lui-même.* "Avignon: Alexandre Girard, 1753."

[———]. *Considerations sur un Livre, intitulé, Raisons pour le desadveu faict par les Evesques de ce*

Royaume, &c. mis en lumiere soubs le nom de Me François Cardinal de la Rochefoucault. Contre les vrais Schismatiques de ce temps. Par Timothee François Catholique. S.l., 1628.

Rochefoucauld, François (Cardinal) de la. *De l'auctorité de l'Eglise en ce qui concerne la foy, et la religion . . . Seconde Edition reveue et augmente de plusieurs Chapitres*. Paris: Ambroise et Hierome Drouart, 1604 [1597].

———. *Raisons pour le desaveu fait par les evesques de ce roiaume d'un livret publié avec ce titre, Jugement des cardinaux, archevesques, evesques & autres qui se sont trouvés en l'Assemblée generale du clergé du roiaume, sur quelques libelles diffamatoires sans les noms des auteurs. Contre les scismatiques de ce tems*. Paris: n.p., 1626.

Sarpi, Paolo. *Lettere ai gallicani*. Edited by Boris Ulianich. Wiesbaden, Germany: Franz Steiner Verlag, 1961.

Schard, Simon, ed. *De jurisdictione, et praeeminentia imperiali, ac potestati ecclesiasticam*. Basel, Switzerland: n.p., 1566.

Servin, Louis. *Plaidoyez de M.re Loys Servin conseiller du Roy en son Conseil d'Estat, & son Advocat general en sa Cour de Parlement. A la fin desquels sont les Arrests intervenus sur icelles*. Paris: Jean de Heuqueville, 1603.

———. *Second volume des plaidoyez de Mre. Loys Servin*. Paris: Jean de Heuqueville, 1605.

———. *Troisieme volume des plaidoyez de Mre. Loys Servin*. Paris: Jean de Heuqueville, 1608.

———. *Quatrieme volume des plaidoyez de Mre. Loys Servin*. Paris: Jean de Heuqueville, 1613.

———. *Actions notables, et plaidoyez de messire Louys Servin conseiller du roy en son Conseil d'Estat, & son advocat general en sa Cour de parlement de Paris. A la fin desquels sont les arrests intervenus sur iceux. Derniere edition, revuë, corrigee et augmentee de plusieurs plaidoyers dudit autheur: et mis en meilleur ordre qu'auparavant . . . Ensemble les plaidoyers de m. A. Robert, Arnault, & autres*. Paris: Claude Morlot, 1631 [1619].

Seyssel, Claude de. *La monarchie de France et deux autres fragments politiques*. Edited by Jacques Poujol. Paris: Librairie d'Argences, 1961.

[Telesphorus of Costenza et al.]. *Expositio magni prophete Joachimi in libris beati Cirilii de magnis tribulationibus & statu sancte matris ecclesie: ab his nostris temporibus usque in finem seculi: una cum compilatione ex diversis prophetes novi ac veteris testamenti Theolosphori de Lusentia*, etc. Venice, Italy: Lazaro de Soardis, 1516.

[———]. *Livre merveillieux, contenant en bref le fleur et substance de plusieurs traictez, tant des Propheties & revelations, qu'anciennes Croniques, faisant mention de tous les faicts de l'eglise universelle, comme des Scismes discords & tribulations qui doivent advenir en l'Eglise de Rome, & d'un temps auquel lon ostera & tollira aux gens d'Eglise & Clergé, leur biens temporels: tellement qu'on ne leur laissera que leur vivre & habit necessaire. Item, aussi est faicte mention des souverains Evesques & Papes, qui apres regneront & gouverneneront l'Eglise: & specialement d'un Pape, qui sera appellé Pasteur Angelique, & d'un Roy de France, nommé Charles Sainct homme. Item, au temps du grand & dernier Antechrist, apres sa mort, jusques au dernier jour du jugement, & en la fin du monde & quand ce doit estre, De nouveau a esté adjousté vers la fin une Prophetie, laquelle demonstre ce qui est advenu depuis le Roy François premier jusques à present*. Paris: Pour Antoine Hoüic, n.d. [Lyons, France: Benoist Rigaud, 1565].

Thou, Jacques Auguste de. *Histoire universelle de Jacques-Auguste de Thou*. 16 vols. London [*recte* Paris]: n.p., 1734.

———. *Historiarum sui temporis tomi sex.* London: Samuel Barclay, 1733.
Vair, Guillaume du. *Les Œuvres du Sr du Vair Premier President au Parlement de Provence. Comprises en cinq parties.* Rouen, France: Jean Osmont, 1614; facs. rpt. Hildesheim, Germany: Georg Olms Verlag, 1973.
Vigor, Simon. *Simonis Vigorii in magno consilio Regio consiliarii Opera omnia.* 4 vols. Paris: Petrus Aubonyus and Jacobus Villery, 1618.

SECONDARY LITERATURE

Abecassis, Jack I. "'Le Maire et Montaigne ont tousjours esté deux, d'une separation bien claire': Public Necessity and Private Freedom in Montaigne." *Modern Language Notes* 110 (1995): 1067–89.
Armstrong, Megan. "Spiritual Reform, Mendicant Autonomy, and State Formation: French Franciscan Disputes before the Parlement of Paris, 1500–1600." *French Historical Studies* 25 (2002): 505–30.
Aubert, Félix. *Histoire du parlement de Paris de l'origine à François Ier (1250–1515).* 2 vols. Paris: Picard, 1894.
Aulotte, Robert. "'Ce ne peut estre malice, c'est pour le plus malheur': Réflexions sur l'attitude d'esprit de Montaigne face au problème de 'l'obéissance du Magistrat' et de la 'manutention des polices.'" In Michel Dassonville, ed., *Ronsard et Montaigne: Ecrivains engagés?* (Lexington, Ky.: French Forum Publishers, 1989), 117–23.
Balmas, Enea. "La religion de du Bellay." In *Du Bellay: Actes du Colloque International d'Angers du 26 au 29 mai 1989*, 2 vols. (Angers, France: Presses de l'Universite d'Angers, 1990), 1:59–74.
Balsamo, Jean. "Les origines Parisiennes du *Tesoro politico* (1589)." *Bibliothèque d'humanisme et renaissance* 57 (1995): 7–23.
Barbiche, Bernard. "L'exploitation politique d'un complot: Henri IV, le Saint-Siège et la conspiration de Biron (1602)." In *Complots et conjurations dans l'Europe moderne. Actes du colloque . . . Rome, 30 septembre–2 octobre 1993* (Rome: Ecole Française de Rome, 1996), 271–88.
Baumgartner, Frederic J. *Change and Continuity in the French Episcopate: The Bishops and the Wars of Religion, 1547–1610.* Durham, N.C.: Duke University Press, 1986.
———. *Louis XII.* New York: St. Martin's Press, 1994.
———. "Louis XII's Gallican Crisis of 1510–13." In Adrianna Bakos, ed., *Politics, Ideology and Law in Early Modern Europe: Essays in Honor of J. H. M. Salmon* (Rochester, N.Y.: University of Rochester Press, 1994), 55–72.
Beame, Edmond M. "The Politiques and the Historians." *Journal of the History of Ideas* 54 (1993): 355–79.
Becker, Michael K. "Episcopal Unrest: Gallicanism in the 1625 Assembly of the Clergy." *Church History* 43 (1974): 65–77.
Bell, David. *Lawyers and Citizens: The Making of a Political Elite in Old Regime France.* Oxford, U.K.: Oxford University Press, 1994.
Benedict, Philip. *Rouen during the Wars of Religion.* Cambridge, U.K.: Cambridge University Press, 1981.

Benson, Robert L. *The Bishop-elect: A Study in Medieval Ecclesiastical Office*. Princeton, N.J.: Princeton University Press, 1968.

Bergin, Joseph. *Cardinal de la Rochefoucauld: Leadership and Reform in the French Church*. New Haven, Conn.: Yale University Press, 1987.

———. *The Making of the French Episcopacy, 1589–1641*. New Haven, Conn.: Yale University Press, 1996.

———. "'Pour avoir un évêque à son souhait': Le recrutement de l'épiscopat au temps d'Henri IV et de Louis XIII." *Revue d'histoire de l'église de France* 81 (1995): 413–31.

Bettison, Christopher. "The Politiques and the Politique Party: A Reappraisal." In Keith Cameron, ed., *From Valois to Bourbon: Dynasty, State and Society in Early Modern France*. (Exeter, U.K.: Exeter University Press, 1989), 35–50.

Birely, Robert. *The Counter-Reformation Prince: Anti-Machiavellianism or Catholic Statecraft in Early Modern Europe*. Chapel Hill: University of North Carolina Press, 1990.

Black, Antony J. *Monarchy and Community: Political Ideas in the Later Conciliar Controversy, 1430–1450*. Cambridge, U.K.: Cambridge University Press, 1970.

Blet, Pierre. "L'Article du Tiers aux etats généraux de 1614." *Revue d'histoire moderne et contemporaine* 2 (1955): 81–106.

———. *Le clergé de France et la monarchie: Etudes sur les Assemblées Générales du Clergé de 1615 à 1666*. 2 vols. Rome: Librairie Editrice de l'Université Grégorienne, 1959.

———. "Jésuites et libertés Gallicanes en 1611." *Archivum historicum societatis Jesu* 24 (1955): 165–83.

———. "Le nonce en France au XVIIe siècle: Ambasadeur et délégué apostolique." *Revue d'histoire diplomatique* 88 (1974): 223–58.

Bloch, Marc. *Les rois thaumaturges: Etude sur le caractère surnaturel attribué à la puissance royale, particulièrement en France et en Angleterre*. Strasbourg, France: Librairie Istra, 1924.

Boucher, Jaqueline. "L'insertion sociale de Laurent Bouchel, avocat au Parlement de Paris, 1559–1629." In *Lyon et l'Europe. Hommes et sociétés: Mélanges d'histoire offerts à Richard Gascon* (Lyons, France: Presses Universitaires de Lyon, 1980), 83–99.

Bouwsma, William. "Gallicanism and the Nature of Christendom." In Anthony Molho and John A. Tedeschi, eds., *Renaissance Studies in Honor of Hans Baron* (Florence, Italy: G. C. Sansoni, 1971), 811–30.

———. "Lawyers in Early Modern Culture." *American Historical Review* 78 (1973): 303–27.

———. *Venice and the Defense of Republican Liberty: Renaissance Values in the Age of the Counter Reformation*. Berkeley and Los Angeles: University of California Press, 1968.

Britnell, Jennifer. "The Antipapalism of Jean Lemaire de Belges' *Traité de la Difference des Schismes et des Conciles*." *Sixteenth Century Journal* 24 (1993): 783–800.

Brives-Cazes, Emile. *La Chambre de Justice de Guyenne en 1583–1584*. Bordeaux, France: G. Gounilhou, 1874.

———. *Le Parlement de Bordeaux et la Chambre de Justice de Guyenne en 1582*. Bordeaux, France: G. Gounilhou, 1866.

Brown, D. Catherine. *Pastor and Laity in the Theology of Jean Gerson*. Cambridge, U.K.: Cambridge University Press, 1987.

Brown, Elizabeth A. R. "Jean du Tillet et les archives de France." *Histoire et archives* 2 (1997): 29–63.

———. "La notion de la légitimité et la prophétie à la cour de Phillippe Auguste." In Robert-Henri Bautier, ed., *La France de Phillippe Auguse: Le temps des mutations. Actes du Colloque internationale (Paris, 29 septembre–4 octobre 1980)* (Paris: Editions du C.N.R.S., 1982), 77–110.

Brown, Elizabeth A. R., and Richard C. Famiglietti. *The "Lit de Justice": Semantics, Ceremonial and the Parlement of Paris*. Simaringen, Germany: Jan Thorbecke Verlag, 1994.

Brown, Frieda S. *Religious and Political Conservatism in the* Essais *of Montaigne*. Geneva: Droz, 1963.

Burns, J. H. "Conciliarism, Papalism and Power, 1511–1518." In Diana Wood, ed., *The Church and Sovereignty: Essays in Honor of Michael Wilks*, Studies in Church History Subsidia 9 (Oxford, U.K.: Basil Blackwell for the Ecclesiastical History Society, 1991), 409–28.

———. *Lordship, Kingship, and Empire: The Idea of Monarchy, 1400–1525*. Oxford, U.K.: Clarendon Press, 1992.

Burr, David. *The Spiritual Franciscans: From Protest to Persecution after Saint Francis*. University Park: Pennsylvania State University Press, 2002.

Cameron, Keith, ed. *Montaigne and His Age*. Exeter, U.K.: University of Exeter Press, 1981.

Campbell, Gerard J. "The Protest of St. Louis." *Traditio* 15 (1959): 405–18.

Céard, Jean. *La nature et les prodiges: L'insolite au XVIe siècle, en France*. Geneva: Droz, 1977.

Chauviré, Roger. *Jean Bodin auteur de la République*. Paris: Honoré Champion, 1914.

Châtelain, Jean-Marc. "Heros togatus: Culture cicéronienne et gloire de la robe dans la France d'Henri IV." *Journal des savants* (1991): 263–87.

Church, William Farr. *Constitutional Thought in Sixteenth-Century France: A Study in the History of Ideas*. Cambridge, Mass.: Harvard University Press, 1941.

———. "The Decline of the French Jurists as Political Theorists, 1660–1789." *French Historical Studies* 5 (1967): 1–40.

———. *Richelieu and Reason of State*. Princeton, N.J.: Princeton University Press, 1972.

Coleman, Janet. "The Dominican Political Theory of John of Paris in Its Context." In Diana Wood, ed., *The Church and Sovereignty c. 590–1918: Essays in Honour of Michael Wilks*, Studies in Church History Subsidia 9 (Oxford, U.K.: Basil Blackwell, 1991), 187–223.

———."Property and Poverty." In J. H. Burns, ed., *The Cambridge History of Medieval Political Thought* (Cambridge, U.K.: Cambridge University Press, 1988), 607–48.

———. "The Two Jurisdictions: Theological and Legal Justifications of Church Property in the Thirteenth Century." *Studies in Church History* 24 (1987): 75–110.

Compagnon, André. *Nous, Michel de Montaigne*. Paris: Seuil, 1980.

Congar, Yves. "Aspects ecclésiologiques de la querelle entre mendiants et séculiers dans la seconde moitié du XIIIe siècle et le début du XIVe." *Archives d'histoire doctrinale et littéraire du moyen âge* 28 (1961): 34–151.

Crawford, Katherine B. "The Politics of Promiscuity: Masculinity and Heroic Representation at the Court of Henry IV." *French Historical Studies* 26 (2003): 225–52.

Cremer, Albert. "Bürger am Hof. Versuch und Scheitern am Beispiel der Richter am

Pariser Parlament 1560–1610." In *Mentalitäten und Lebensverhältnisse: Beispeile au der Sozialgeschichte der Neuzeit. Rudolf Vierhaus zum 60. Geburtstag* (Göttingen, Germany: Vandenhoek und Ruprecht, 1982), 191–204.

Crouzet, Denis. *Les guerriers de Dieu: La violence au temps des troubles de religion (vers 1525–vers 1610).* 2 vols. Paris: Champ Vallon, 1990.

Crowley, Weldon S. "Erastianism in England to 1640." *Journal of Church and State* 32 (1990): 549–66.

Dawson, John. *The Oracles of the Law.* Ann Arbor: University of Michigan Law School, 1967.

Defaux, Gérard. *Le curieux, le glorieux et la sagesse du monde dans la première moitié du XVIe siècle: L'exemple de Panurge (Ulysse, Demosthene, Empedocle).* Lexington, Ky.: French Forum Publishers, 1982.

Delatour, Jerôme, and Thierry Sarmant. "La charge de Bibliothécaire du Roy au XVIIe et XVIIIe siècles." *Bibliothèque de l'Ecole des Chartes* 152 (1994): 462–502.

Demante, Gabriel. "Histoire de la publication des livres de Pierre Dupuy sur les libertés de l'Eglise gallicane." *Bibliothèque de l'Ecole des Chartes* 5 (1843–1844): 585–606.

Denault, Gerard. "The Legitimation of the Parlement of Paris and the Estates General of France, 1560–1614." Ph.D. dissertation, Washington University, 1975.

Denton, Jeffrey. *Philip the Fair and the Ecclesiastical Assemblies of 1294–1295.* Proceedings of the American Philosophical Society 81, no. 1. Philadelphia: American Philosophical Society, 1991.

———. "Taxation and the Conflict between Philip the Fair and Boniface VIII." *French History* 11 (1997): 241–64.

Desan, Phillipe. *La naissance de la méthode (Machiavel, la Ramée, Bodin, Montaigne, Descartes).* Paris: A. G. Nizet, 1987.

———. *Penser l'histoire à la Renaissance.* Caen, France: Paradigme, 1993.

Descimon, Robert, and Elie Barnavie. *La Sainte Ligue, le juge et la potence: L'assassinat du président Brisson (15 novembre 1591).* Paris: Hachette, 1985.

Dewald, Jonathan. "The 'Perfect Magistrate': Parlementaires and Crime in Sixteenth-Century Rouen." *Archiv für Reformationsgeschichte* 67 (1976): 284–300.

Dickinson, Gladys. *Du Bellay in Rome.* Leiden, The Netherlands: E. J. Brill, 1960.

Diefendorf, Barbara. "Give Us Back Our Children: Patriarchal Authority and Parental Consent to Religious Vocations in Early Counter-Reformation France." *Journal of Modern History* 68 (1996): 265–307.

———. *Paris City Councillors in the Sixteenth Century: The Politics of Patrimony.* Princeton, N.J.: Princeton University Press, 1983.

Dillay, Madeleine. "Conclusions du procureur général au Parlement de Paris relatives à la vérification et à l'enregistrement des lettres patentes." *Revue historique de droit français et étranger* 33 (1955): 255–66.

Donckel, E. "Die Prophezeiung des Telesforus." *Archivum franciscanum historicum* 26 (1933): 29–104.

Douarche, Aristide. *De tyrranicido apud scriptores decimi sexti seculi.* Paris: Hachette, 1888.

———. *L'Université de Paris et les Jésuites (XVIe et XVIIe siècles).* Paris: Hachette, 1888.

Doucet, Roger. *Etude sur le gouvernement de François Ier dans ses rapports avec le parlement de Paris.* 2 vols. Paris: Honoré Champion, 1921.

———. *Les institutions de France au XVIe siècle.* Paris: A. et P. Picard, 1948.

Doyle, William. *Jansenism: Catholic Resistance to Authority from the Reformation to the French Revolution.* New York: St. Martin's Press, 2000.

———. *Venality: The Sale of Offices in Eighteenth-Century France.* Oxford, U.K.: Clarendon Press, 1996.

Dreano, Maturin. *La religion de Montaigne.* Rev. ed. Paris: Librairie A.-G. Nizet, 1969.

Dubois, Claude-Gilbert. *La conception de l'histoire en France au XVIe siècle (1560–1610).* Paris: A. G. Nizet, 1977.

Dubruel, Marc. "Gallicanisme." In *Dictionnaire de théologie catholique,* vol. 6.1, cols. 1096–1137. Paris: Letouzey et Arnoë, 1947.

———. "La querelle de la Régale: Soixante ans de procès au Conseil du Roi (1616–1673)." *Bulletin de littérature ecclésiastique,* n.s., 18 (1917): 68–92, 119–228.

Dufournet, Jean. "Le prince et ses conseillers d'après Phillipe de Commynes." In J. Dufournet, A. Fiorato, and A. Redondo, eds., *Le pouvoir monarchique et ses supports idéologiques aux XIVe–XVIIe siècles* (Paris: Publications de la Sorbonne Nouvelle, 1990), 9–26.

Engster, Dan. "The Montaignian Moment." *Journal of the History of Ideas* 59 (1998): 625–50.

Erbe, Michael. *François Bauduin (1520–1573): Biographie eines Humanisten.* Gütersloh, Germany: Gütersloher Verlagshaus Gerd Mohn, 1978.

Evennett, H. Outram. *The Cardinal of Lorraine and the Council of Trent: A Study in the Counter-Reformation.* Cambridge, U.K.: Cambridge University Press, 1930.

Farge, James K. *Orthodoxy and Reform in Early Reformation France: The Faculty of Theology of Paris, 1500–1543.* Leiden, The Netherlands: E. J. Brill, 1985.

———. *Le parti conservateur au XVIe siècle: Université et parlement de Paris à l'époque de la renaissance et de la réforme.* Paris: Collège de France, 1992.

Favier, Jean. *Les finances pontificales à l'époque du grand schisme d'Occident, 1378–1409.* Bibliothèque des écoles françaises d'Athènes et de Rome 211. Paris: E. Boccard, 1966.

Figgis, John Neville. *The Divine Right of Kings.* 2nd ed. Introduction by Geoffroy Elton. New York: Harper & Row, 1965 [1896].

Filhol, René. *Le Premier Président Christofle de Thou et la réformation des coustumes.* Paris: Librairie du Recueil Sirey, 1937.

Foucault, Michel. *Les mots et les choses: Une archéologie des sciences humaines.* Paris: N.R.F./Gallimard, 1966.

Franklin, Julian H. *Jean Bodin and the Sixteenth-Century Revolution in the Methodology of Law and History.* New York: Columbia University Press, 1963.

Fumaroli, Marc. *L'age de l'éloquence: Rhétorique et «res literaria» de la renaissance au seuil de l'époque classique.* Geneva: Droz, 1980; facs. rpt. Paris: Albin Michel, 1995.

———. *La diplomatie de l'ésprit: De Montaigne à la Fontaine.* Paris: Hermann, 1994.

———. "Hiéroglyphes et lettres: La «sagesse mystérieuse des anciens» au XVIIe siècle." *XVIIe siècle* 158 (1988): 7–20.

———. "Temps de croissance et temps de corruption: Les deux Antiquités dans l'érudition jésuite française du XVIIe siècle." *XVIIe siècle* 32 (1981): 149–68.

Gadoffre, Gilbert. *Du Bellay et le sacré*. Paris: N.R.F./Gallimard, 1971.
Galpern, A. N. *Religions of the People in Sixteenth-Century Champagne*. Cambridge, Mass.: Harvard University Press, 1976.
Gaudemet, Jean. "L'appel au concile." *Nouvelle revue historique de droit français et étranger* 67 (1989): 469–78.
Génestal, Robert. *Les origines de l'appel comme d'abus*. Paris: Presses Universitaires de France, 1951.
Giesey, Ralph. "The Juristic Basis of Dynastic Right to the French Throne." *Transactions of the American Philosophical Society* 51 (1961): 64–150.
———. *The Royal Funerary Ceremony in Renaissance France*. Geneva: Droz, 1960.
———. "When and Why Hotman Wrote the *Francogallia*." *Bibliothèque d'humanisme et renaissance* 29 (1967): 581–611.
Gilbert, Felix. *Machiavelli and Guicciardini: Politics and History in Sixteenth-Century Florence*. Princeton, N.J.: Princeton University Press, 1965.
Gilmore, Myron P. *Argument from Roman Law in Political Thought, 1200–1600*. Cambridge, Mass.: Harvard University Press, 1941.
Golden, Richard M. *The Godly Rebellion: Parisian Curés and the Religious Fronde, 1652–1662*. Chapel Hill: University of North Carolina Press, 1981.
Goldmann, Lucien. *Le Dieu caché: Étude sur la vision tragique dans les* Pensées *de Pascal et dans le théâtre de Racine*. Paris: Gallimard, 1959.
Grafton, Anthony. *Defenders of the Text: Traditions of Scholarship in an Age of Science, 1450–1800*. Cambridge, Mass.: Harvard University Press, 1991.
———. "The Footnote from de Thou to Ranke." *History and Theory* 33 (1994): 53–76.
Greengrass, Mark. *France in the Age of Henry IV: The Struggle for Stability*. 2nd ed. London: Longman, 1994.
Grosley, Pierre-Jean. *Vie de Pierre Pithou*. 2 vols. Paris: Guillaume Cavelier, 1756.
Guilhermoz, Paul. *Enquêtes et procès: Étude sur la procédure et le fonctionnement du Parlement au XIVe siècle. Suivie du Style de la Chambre des Enquêtes, du Style des commissaires du Parlement et de plusieurs autres textes et documents*. Paris: Alphonse Picard, 1892.
Hampton, Timothy. *Literature and Nation in the Sixteenth Century: Inventing Renaissance France*. Ithaca, N.Y.: Cornell University Press, 2001.
———. *Writing from History: The Rhetoric of Exemplarity in Renaissance Literature*. Ithaca, N.Y.: Cornell University Press, 1990.
Hanley, Sarah. "Engendering the State: Family Formation and State Building in Early Modern France." *French Historical Studies* 16 (1989): 4–27.
———. *The Lit de justice of the Kings of France: Consititutional Ideology in Legend, Ritual, and Discourse*. Princeton, N.J.: Princeton University Press, 1983.
———. "Social Sites of the Political Practice in France: Lawsuits, Civil Rights and the Separation of Powers in Domestic and State Government, 1500–1800." *American Historical Review* 102 (1997): 27–52.
Hanotaux, Gabriel. *Histoire du Cardinal Richelieu*, Vol. 1: *La jeunesse de Richelieu (1585–1614)*. Rev. ed. Paris: Librairie Plon, 1932.
Hayden, J. Michael. *France and the Estates General of 1614*. Cambridge, U.K.: Cambridge University Press, 1974.

Headley, John M., ed. *San Carlo Borromeo: Catholic Reform and Ecclesiastical Politics in the Second Half of the Sixteenth Century.* Washington, D.C.: Folger Library Books, 1988.
Henshall, Nicholas. *The Myth of Absolutism: Change and Continuity in Early Modern European Monarchy.* London: Longman, 1992.
Hermann, Rudolf. *Die Probleme der Exkommunikation bei Luther und Thomas Erastus.* Berlin: Alfred Topelmann, 1955.
Hexter, J. H. *The Vision of Politics on the Eve of the Reformation.* New York: Basic Books, 1973.
Hildesheimer, Françoise. "De la conservation à l'impression: Les archives du clergé de France." *Histoire et archives* 8 (2000): 59–99.
———. *Richelieu: Une certaine idée de l'état.* N.p.: Publisud, 1985.
———. "Le *Testament politique* de Richelieu ou le règne terrestre de la raison." *Annuaire-bulletin de la Société de l'Histoire de France* (1994): 17–34.
Hirschman, Albert O. *The Passions and the Interests: Political Arguments for Capitalism before Its Triumph.* Princeton, N.J.: Princeton University Press, 1977.
Holt, Mack. "Putting Religion Back in the Wars of Religion." *French Historical Studies* 18 (1993): 524–51.
Hudon, William. "Religion and Society in Early Modern Italy: Old Questions, New Insights." *American Historical Review* 101 (1996): 783–804.
Huppert, George. *The Idea of Perfect History: Historical Erudition and Historical Philosophy in Renaissance France.* Urbana: University of Illinois Press, 1970.
———. *Les Bourgeois Gentilshommes: An Essay on the Definition of Elites in Renaissance France.* Chicago: University of Chicago Press, 1977.
Izbicki, Thomas. "Cajetan's Attack on Parallels between Church and State." *Cristianesimo nella storia* 20 (1999): 81–89.
———. *Protector of the Faith: Cardinal Johhanes de Turrecremata and the Defense of the Institutional Church.* Washington, D.C.: The Catholic University of America Press, 1981.
Jackson, Richard. *Vive le roi!: A History of the French Coronation from Charles V to Charles X.* Chapel Hill: University of North Carolina Press, 1984.
Jacques, Emile. *Phillippe Cospeau: Un ami-ennemi de Richelieu, 1571–1646.* Paris: Beauchesne, 1989.
Jouhaud, Christian. *La main de Richelieu; ou, Le pouvoir cardinal.* Paris: Gallimard, 1991.
Kaiser, Colin. "Les cours souveraines au XVIe siècle: Morale et Contre-Réforme." *Annales: Economies, sociétés, civilisations* 37 (1982): 15–31.
Kaminsky, Howard. *Simon de Cramaud and the Great Schism.* New Brunswick, N.J.: Rutgers University Press, 1983.
Kantorowicz, Ernst. *The King's Two Bodies: A Study in Medieval Political Theology.* Princeton, N.J.: Princeton University Press, 1957.
———. "Mysteries of State: An Absolutist Concept and Its Late Mediaeval Origins." *Harvard Theological Review* 48 (1955): 65–91.
Kelley, Donald. "Civil Science in the Renaissance: The Problem of Interpretation." In Anthony Pagden, ed., *The Languages of Political Theory in Early-Modern Europe* (Cambridge, U.K.: Cambridge University Press, 1987).
———. "Fides Historiæ: Charles Dumoulin and the Gallican View of History." *Traditio* 22 (1966): 347–402.

———. *Foundations of Modern Historical Scholarship: Language, Law and History in the French Renaissance.* New York: Columbia University Press, 1970.

———. "*Historia integra:* François Baudouin and His Conception of History." *Journal of the History of Ideas* 25 (1964): 35–57.

Kerckhove, Martinien van de. "La notion de juridiction chez les décrétistes et les premiers décrétalistes (1140–1250)." *Etudes franciscaines* 49 (1937): 420–55.

Kilroy, Gerard. "Eternal Glory: Edmund Campion's Virgilian Epic." *Times Literary Supplement*, 8 March 2002, pp. 13–14.

Kitchens, James H. III. "Judicial *Commissaires* and the Parlement of Paris: The Case of the Chambre de l'Arsenal." *French Historical Studies* 12 (1982): 323–50.

Knecht, R. J. "The Concordat of 1516: A Reassessment." In Henry J. Cohn, ed., *Government in Reformation Europe, 1520–1560* (London: Macmillan, 1971), 91–112.

Ladner, Gerhard. *The Idea of Reform: Its Impact on Christian Thought and Action in the Age of the Fathers.* 2nd ed. New York: Harper Torchbooks, 1967.

Lambert, Malcolm. *Franciscan Poverty: The Doctrine of the Absolute Poverty of Christ and the Apostles in the Franciscan Order, 1210–1323.* 2nd ed. St. Bonaventure, N.Y.: Franciscan Institute, 1998.

———. *Medieval Heresy: Popular Movements from Bogomil to Hus.* New York: Holmes & Meier, 1976.

la Rochefoucauld, Gabriel de. *Un homme d'église et d'état au commencement du XVIIe siècle: Le Cardinal François de la Rochefoucauld.* Paris: Plon, 1926.

Lauro, Agostino. *Il giurisdizionalismo pregiannoniano nel Regno di Napoli: Problema e bibliografia (1563–1723).* Rome: Edizioni di storia e letteratura, 1974.

Laursen, John Christian. *The Politics of Skepticism in the Ancients, Montaigne, Hume, and Kant.* Leiden, The Netherlands: E. J. Brill, 1992.

Lebigre, Arlette. *La justice du roi: La vie judiciaire dans l'ancienne France.* Paris: Albin Michel, 1988.

le Goff, Jacques. *Saint Louis.* Paris: Gallimard, 1996.

Lebrun, François, et al. *La diocèse d'Angers.* Paris: Beauchesne, 1981.

Levack, Brian P. *The Civil Lawyers in England, 1603–1641: A Political Study.* Oxford, U.K.: Clarendon Press, 1973.

Little, Lester K. "Pride Goes before Avarice: Social Change and the Vices in Latin Christendom." *American Historical Review* 76 (1971): 16–49.

———. *Religious Poverty and the Profit Economy in Medieval Europe.* Ithaca, N.Y.: Cornell University Press, 1978.

Loupès, Phillipe. *Chapitres et chanoines de Guyenne aux XVIIe et XVIIIe siècles.* Paris: Editions de l'Ecole des Hautes Etudes en Sciences Sociales, 1985.

Maclean, Ian. "The Place of Interpretation: Montaigne and the Humanist Jurists on Words, Intention and Meaning." In Grahame Castor and Terence Cave, eds., *Neo-Latin and the Vernacular in Renaissance France* (Oxford, U.K.: Clarendon Press, 1984), 252–72.

Magnaudet-Barthe, Anne. "Edmond Richer et la réforme de l'Université de Paris (1594–1610)." In *Positions des thèses soutenues par les élèves de la promotion de 1983 pour le diplôme d'archiviste paléographe* (Paris: Ecole des Chartes, 1983), 143–50.

Malettke, Klaus. "Pierre Pithou als Historiker." In August Buck, ed., *Humanismus und Historiographie* (Weinheim: VCH Verlag, 1991), 89–103.

Mandrou, Robert. *Magistrats et sorciers en France au XVIIe siècle: Une analyse de psychologie historique*. 2nd ed. Paris: Editions du Seuil, 1980.

Marin, Louis. "The Body-of-Power and Incarnation at Port Royal and in Pascal; or, Of the Figurability of the Political Absolute." In *Fragments for a History of the Human Body* (New York: Zone, 1989), vol. 5, pt. 3, 421–47.

———. *Le portrait du roi*. Paris: Editions du Minuit, 1981.

Martimort, Aimé-Georges. *Le gallicanisme de Bossuet*. Paris: Editions du Cerf, 1953.

Martin, Olivier. *L'Assemblée de Vincennes de 1329 et ses conséquences: Étude sur les conflits entre la juridiction laïque et la juridiction ecclésiastique au XIVe siècle*. Paris: Alphonse Picard, 1909.

Martin, Victor. *Le gallicanisme et la réforme catholique: Essai historique sur l'introduction en France des décrets du concile de Trente (1563–1615)*. Paris: Alphonse Picard, 1919; facs. rpt., Geneva: Slatkine-Megariotis Reprints, 1975.

———. "La reprise des relations diplomatiques entre la France et le Saint-Siège, en 1595." *Revue des sciences religieuses* 1–2 (1921–1922): 338–378, 233–270.

———. *Les origines du Gallicanisme*. 2 vols. Paris: Bloud & Gay, 1939; facs. rpt. Geneva: Slatkine-Megariotis Reprints, 1968.

Martini, Giuseppe. "La politica finanziaria dei Papi in Francia intorno alla metà del secolo XIII." *Nuova rivista storica* 65 (1981): 209–82.

Mastellone, Salvo. *La reggenza di Maria de'Medici*. Messina, Italy: Casa Editrice G. D'Anna, 1962.

Maugis, Edouard. *Histoire du Parlement de Paris de l'avènement des rois Valois à la mort d'Henri IV*. 3 vols. Paris: A. Picard, 1913–1916; facs. rpt. Geneva: Slatkine-Megariotis Reprints, 1977.

McGowan, Margaret M. *The Vision of Rome in Late Renaissance France*. New Haven, Conn.: Yale University Press, 2000.

Menache, Sophia. "A Propaganda Campaign in the Reign of Philip the Fair, 1302–1303." *French History* 4 (1990): 427–54.

Merrick, Jeffrey. *The Desacralization of the French Monarchy in the Eighteenth Century*. Baton Rouge: Louisiana State University Press, 1990.

Meyer, C. A. "L'avocat du roi d'Espagne, Jean Bouchard; le Parlement de Paris, Guillaume Briçonnet et Clément Marot." *Bulletin de la société de l'histoire du protestantisme français* 137 (1991): 7–24.

Millet, Hélène. "Du conseil au concile (1395–1408): Recherche sur la nature des Assemblées du clergé en France pendant le Grand Schisme d'occident." *Journal des savants* (1985): 137–59.

Minnich, Nelson H. "Concepts of Reform Proposed at the Fifth Lateran Council." *Archivum historiæ pontificiæ* 7 (1969): 163–251.

Miskimin, Harry A. *Money and Power in Fifteenth-Century France*. New Haven, Conn.: Yale University Press, 1984.

Momigliano, Arnoldo. *The Classical Foundations of Modern Historiography*. Berkeley and Los Angeles: University of California Press, 1990.

Monter, E. William. *Judging the French Reformation: Heresy Trials by Sixteenth-Century Parlements.* Cambridge, Mass.: Harvard University Press, 1999.

Morrall, John B. *Gerson and the Great Schism.* Manchester, U.K.: Manchester University Press, 1960.

Morrissey, Robert. *Charlemagne and France: A Thousand Years of Mythology.* Translated by Catherine Tihanyi. South Bend, Ind.: University of Notre Dame Press, 2003.

Mousnier, Roland. *L'assasinat d'Henri IV: Le problème du tyrannicide et l'affermissement de la monarchie absolue.* Paris: N.R.F./Gallimard, 1964.

———. *Institutions de la France sous la monarchie absolue, 1598–1789.* 2 vols. Paris: Presses Universitaires de France, 1980.

———. *La plume, la faucille et le marteau: Institutions et société en France, du Moyen Age à la Révolution.* Paris: Presses Universitaires de France, 1970.

———. "Sully et le Conseil d'état et des finances: La lutte entre Bellièvre et Sully." *Revue historique* 192 (1941): 68–86.

Nelles, Paul. "The Public Library and Late Humanist Scholarship." Ph.D. dissertation, Johns Hopkins University, 1994.

Nelson, Eric W. "Defining the Fundamental Laws of France: The Proposed First Article of the Third Estate at the French Estates General of 1614." *English Historical Review* 115 (2000): 1216–30.

———. *The Monarchy and the Jesuits: Political Authority and Catholic Renewal in France, 1590–1615.* Aldershot, U.K.: Ashgate, forthcoming.

Neto, José R. Maia. "Academic Skepticism in Early Modern Philosophy." *Journal of the History of Ideas* 58 (1997): 199–220.

Oakley, Francis. "Almain and Major: Conciliar Theory on the Eve of the Reformation." *American Historical Review* 70 (1965): 673–90.

———. "Bronze-Age Conciliarism: Edmond Richer's Encounters with Cajetan and Bellarmine." *History of Political Thought* 20 (1999): 65–86.

———. "Complexities of Context: Gerson, Bellarmine, Sarpi, Richer, and the Venetian Interdict of 1606–1607." *Catholic Historical Review* 82 (1996): 368–96.

———. "Conciliarism in the Sixteenth Century: Jacques Almain Again." *Archiv für Reformationsgeschichte* 68 (1977): 111–32.

Obermann, Heiko. *The Harvest of Medieval Theology: Gabriel Biel and Late Medieval Nominalism.* Cambridge, Mass.: Harvard University Press, 1963.

Olivier-Martin, François. *Histoire du droit français des origines à la Révolution.* Paris: Doman Montchrestien, 1948.

———. *Les lois du roi.* Paris: Editions Loysel, 1988.

———. *Le régime des cultes en France du Concordat de 1516 au Concordat de 1801.* Paris: Editions Loysel, 1988.

O'Malley, John. "Giles of Viterbo: A Reformer's Thought on Renaissance Rome." *Renaissance Quarterly* 20 (1967): 1–11.

———. *Giles of Viterbo on Church and Reform: A Study in Renaissance Thought.* Leiden, The Netherlands: E. J. Brill, 1968.

———. *Trent and All That: Renaming Catholicism in the Early Modern Era.* Cambridge, Mass.: Harvard University Press, 2000.

Ong, Walter. *Ramus, Method and the Decay of Dialogue: From the Art of Discourse to the Art of Reason*. Cambridge, Mass.: Harvard University Press, 1958.

Orcibal, Jean. *Jean Duvergier de Hauranne abbé de Saint-Cyran et son temps (1581–1638). Les origines du Jansénisme*. Vol. 2. Paris: J. Vrin, 1947.

Ozment, Steven. *The Age of Reform (1250–1550): An Intellectual and Religious History of Late Medieval and Reformation Europe*. New Haven, Conn.: Yale University Press, 1980.

Palanque, Jean-Remy, et al. *Le diocèse d'Aix-en-Provence*. Paris: Beauchesne, 1975.

Parker, Geoffrey, ed. *The Thirty Years' War*. London: Routledge & Kegan Paul, 1984.

Parsons, Jotham. "Money and Sovereignty in Early Modern France." *Journal of the History of Ideas* 62 (2001): 59–79.

———. "The Political Vision of Antoine Loisel." *Sixteenth Century Journal* 27 (1996): 453–76.

———. "The Roman Censors in the Renaissance Political Imagination." *History of Political Thought* 22 (2001): 565–86.

Pascoe, Louis. *Jean Gerson: Principles of Church Reform*. Leiden, The Netherlands: E. J. Brill, 1973.

Pearl, Jonathan L. *The Crime of Crimes: Demonology and Politics in France, 1560–1620*. Waterloo, Ontario, Canada: Wilfred Laurier University Press, 1999.

Pennington, Kenneth. *The Prince and the Law, 1200–1600: Sovereignty and Rights in the Western Legal Tradition*. Berkeley and Los Angeles: University of California Press, 1993.

Perrens, François-Tommy. *L'Eglise et l'état en France sous le règne de Henri IV et la régence de Marie de Médicis*. 2 vols. Paris: A. Durand et Pedone-Lauriel, 1872; facs. rpt. Geneva: Mégariotis Reprints, 1978.

Perrone, Sean T. "Assemblies of the Clergy in Early Modern Europe." *Parliaments, Estates and Representation* 22 (2002): 45–56.

Perrot, Ernest. *Les cas royaux: Origine et développement de la théorie aux XIIIe et XIVe siècles*. Paris: A. Rousseau, 1910.

Pintard, René. *Le libertinage érudit dans la première moitié du XVIIe siècle*. 2 vols. Paris: Boivin et Cie., 1943.

Pocock, J. G. A. *The Ancient Constitution and the Feudal Law*. Cambridge, U.K.: Cambridge University Press, 1987.

———. *The Machiavellian Moment: Florentine Political Thought and the Atlantic Republican Tradition*. Princeton, N.J.: Princeton University Press, 1975.

Popkin, Richard H. *The History of Scepticism from Erasmus to Spinoza*. Berkeley and Los Angeles: University of California Press, 1979.

Powis, Jonathan. "Gallican Liberties and the Politics of Later Sixteenth-Century France." *Historical Journal* 26 (1983): 515–30.

Pratt, Kenneth J. "Rome as Eternal." *Journal of the History of Ideas* 26 (1965): 25–44.

Prodi, Paolo. *The Papal Prince, One Body and Two Souls: The Papal Monarchy in Early Modern Europe*. Translated by Susan Haskins. Cambridge, U.K.: Cambridge University Press, 1987.

Pujol, Pierre Edouard. *Edmond Richer: Etude historique et critique sur la rénovation du gallicanisme au commencement du XVIIe siècle*. 2 vols. Paris: T. Olmer, 1876.

Quillet, Jeannine. *La philosophie politique du Songe du Vergier (1378): Sources doctrinales.* Paris: J. Vrin, 1977.
Radouant, René. *Guillaume du Vair: L'homme et l'orateur jusqu'à la fin des troubles de la Ligue (1556–1596).* Paris: Société française d'imprimerie et de librairie, n.d. [c. 1908].
Ranke, Leopold von. *Franzöische Geschichte vornehmlich in sechszenten und seibzehnten Jahrhunderts.* 6 vols. Stuttgart, Germany: J. G. Cotta'scher Verlag, 1852.
Ranum, Orest. *Artisans of Glory: Writers and Historical Thought in Seventeenth-Century France.* Chapel Hill: University of North Carolina Press, 1980.

———. *Richelieu and the Councillors of Louis XIII: A Study of the Secretaries of State and Superintendents of Finance in the Ministry of Richelieu, 1635–1642.* Oxford, U.K.: Clarendon Press, 1963.
Reeves, Marjorie. *The Influence of Prophecy in the Later Middle Ages: A Study in Joachimism.* Oxford, U.K.: Clarendon Press, 1969.
Remer, Gary. "Rhetoric and the Erasmian Defence of Toleration." *History of Political Thought* 10 (1989): 377–403.
Renaudet, Augustin. *Préréforme et humanisme à Paris pendant les premières guerres de religion (1494–1517).* Paris: Honoré Champion, 1916; facs. rpt. Geneva: Slatkine, 1981.
Reulos, Michel. *Etude sur l'ésprit, les sources et la méthode des* Institutes Coutumières *d'Antoine Loisel.* Paris: Librarie du Recueil Sirey, 1935.

———. "Le Décret de Gratien chez les humanistes, les gallicans et les réformés français du XVIème siècle." *Studia Gratiana* 2 (1954): 677–96.

———. "L'humanisme juridique dans le *De orbis terræ concordia.*" In *Guillaume Postel: 1581–1981, Actes du Colloque International d'Avranches* (Paris: Guy Trédaniel, Editions de la Mainsnie, 1981), 199–206.
Revel, Jacques. "La royauté sacrée: Eléments pour un débat." In A. Boureau and C. S. Ingerflon, eds., *La royauté sacrée dans le monde chrétien (Colloque de Royaumont, mars 1989)* (Paris: Editions de l'Ecole des Hautes Etudes en Sciences Sociales, 1992), 7–17.
Richet, Denis, and Roger Chartier, eds. *Représentation et vouloir politiques: Autour des Etats généraux de 1614.* Paris: Editions de l'Ecole des Hautes Etudes en Sciences Sociales, 1982.
Richet, Denis. *De la réforme à la Révolution: Études sur la France moderne.* Paris: Aubier, 1991.
Roelker, Nancy Lyman. *One King, One Faith: The Parlement of Paris and the Religious Reformations of the Sixteenth Century.* Edited by Barbara Diefendorf. Berkeley and Los Angeles: University of California Press, 1996.

———. *Queen of Navarre: Jeanne d'Albret, 1528–1572.* Cambridge, Mass.: Harvard University Press, 1968.
Romier, Lucien. "La crise gallicane de 1551." *Revue historique* 108–109 (1911): 225–50, 27–55.

———. *Le royaume de Catherine de Médicis: La France à la veille des Guerres de Religion.* 2 vols. Paris: Perrin et Cie., 1925.
Rosa, Susan. "Seventeenth-Century Catholic Polemic and the Rise of Cultural Rationalism: An Example from the Empire." *Journal of the History of Ideas* 57 (1996): 87–107.
Rose, Paul. *Bodin and the Great God of Nature: The Moral and Religious World of a Judaiser.* Geneva: Droz, 1980.

Rowland, Ingrid D. *The Culture of the High Renaissance: Ancients and Moderns in Sixteenth-Century Rome*. Cambridge, U.K.: Cambridge University Press, 1998.
Rummel, Erika. *The Confessionalization of Humanism in Reformation Germany*. Oxford, U.K.: Oxford University Press, 2000.
Sahlins, Peter. *Boundaries: The Making of France and Spain in the Pyrenees*. Berkeley and Los Angeles: University of California Press, 1989.
Salmon, J. H. M. "Clovis and Constantine: The Uses of History in Sixteenth-Century Gallicanism." *Journal of Ecclesiastical History* 41 (1990): 584–605.
———. "The Legacy of Jean Bodin: Absolutism, Populism or Constitutionalism?" *History of Political Thought* 17 (1996): 500–522.
———. "Protestant Jurists and Theologians in Early Modern France: The Family of Cappel." In Roman Schnur, ed., *Die Rolle der Juristen bei der Entstehung des modernen Staates* (Berlin: Dunker & Humblot, 1986), 357–79.
———. *Renaissance and Revolt: Essays in the Intellectual and Social History of Early Modern France*. Cambridge, U.K.: Cambridge University Press, 1987.
Sawyer, Jeffrey. *Printed Poison: Pamphlet Propaganda, Faction Politics, and the Public Sphere in Early Seventeenth-Century France*. Berkeley and Los Angeles: University of California Press, 1990.
Schiffman, Zachary. "Estienne Pasquier and the Problem of Historical Relativism." *Sixteenth Century Journal* 18 (1987): 505–17.
Schnur, Roman. *Die französischen Juristen im konfessionellen Bürgerkieg des 16. Jahrhunderts: Ein Beitrag zur Entstehungsgeschichte des modernen Staates*. Berlin: Dunker & Humblot, 1962.
Screech, M. A. *Clément Marot: A Renaissance Poet Discovers the Gospel. Lutheranism, Fabrism and Calvinism in the Royal Courts of France and of Navarre and in the Ducal Court of Ferrara*. Leiden, The Netherlands: E. J. Brill, 1994.
———. *L'evangélisme de Rabelais: Aspects de la satire relgieuse au XVIe siècle*. Etudes Rabelaisiennes 2. Geneva: Droz, 1959.
Serbat, Louis. *Les Assemblées du Clergé de France: Origines, organisation, dévelopement 1561–1615*. Paris: Honoré Champion, 1906.
Skinner, Quentin. *The Foundations of Modern Political Thought*. 2 vols. Cambridge, U.K.: Cambridge University Press, 1978.
Soman, Albert. "Book Censorship in France, 1598–1607." Ph.D. dissertation, Harvard University, 1968.
———. "Press, Pulpit and Censorship in France before Richelieu." *Proceedings of the American Philosophical Society* 120 (1976): 439–63.
Somerville, J. P. "The Royal Supremacy and Episcopacy 'Jure Divino,' 1603–1640." *Journal of Ecclesiastical History* 34 (1983): 548–58.
Starobinski, Jean. "'To Preserve and Continue': Remarks on Montaigne's Conservatism." Translated by R. Scott Walker. *Diogenes* 118 (1982): 103–20.
Stegmann, André, ed. *Pouvoir et institutions en Europe au XVIème siècle: 27e Colloque International d'Etudes Humanistes, Tours*. Paris: J. Vrin, 1987.
Strauss, Gerald. "Ideas of *Reformatio* and *Renovatio* from the Middle Ages to the Reformation." In Thomas A. Brady Jr., Heiko A. Oberman, and James D. Tracy, eds.,

Bibliography 311

Handbook of European History, 1400–1600, 2 vols. (Leiden, The Netherlands: E. J. Brill, 1994–1995), 2:1–30.

Streuver, Nancy. "Pasquier's *Recherches de la France:* The Exemplarity of His Medieval Sources." *History and Theory* 27 (1988): 51–59.

———. *Theory as Practice: Ethical Inquiry in the Renaissance.* Chicago: University of Chicago Press, 1992.

Sutto, Claude. "Tradition et innovation, réalisme et utopie: L'idée gallicane à la fin du XVIe et au début du XVIIe siècles." *Renaissance and Reformation/Renaissance et réforme*, n.s., 8 (1984): 278–97.

Tallon, Alain. *Conscience nationale et sentiment religieux en France au XVIe siècle: Essai sur la vision gallicane du monde.* Paris: Presses Universitaires de France, 2002.

———. "Le Diocèse au Concile de Trente: Cellule close ou éspace ouverte?" In Gérald Chaix, ed., *Le Diocèse: Espaces, représentations, pouvoirs (France, XVe–XXe siècle)* (Paris: Les Editions du Cerf, 2002), 17–31.

———. *La France et le Concile de Trente (1518–1563).* Rome: Ecole française de Rome, 1997.

Thireau, Jean-Louis. *Charles du Moulin (1500–1566): Étude sur les sources, la méthode, les idées politiques et économiques d'un juriste de la Renaissance.* Geneva: Droz, 1980.

Thomas, Jules. *Le Concordat de 1516: Ses origines, son histoire au XVIe siècle.* 3 vols. Paris: A. Picard, 1910.

Thomson, John A. F. *Popes and Princes, 1417–1517: Politics and Polity in the Late Medieval Church.* London: George Allen & Unwin, 1980.

Thouzellier, Christine. "La place du *De periculis* de Guillaume de Saint-Amour dans les polémiques universitaires du XIIIe siècle." *Revue historique* 156 (1927): 69–83.

Tierney, Brian. *Foundations of the Conciliar Theory: The Contribution of the Medieval Canonists from Gratian to the Great Schism.* Cambridge, U.K.: Cambridge University Press, 1955.

———. "'The Prince is not Bound by Laws': Accursius and the Origins of the Modern State." *Comparative Studies in Society and History* 5 (1963): 378–400.

Tournon, André. "Le magistrat, le pouvoir et la loi." In *Les écrivains et la politique dans le sud-ouest de la France autour des années 1580: Actes du Colloque de Bordeaux 6–7 novembre 1981* (Bordeaux, France: Presses Universitaires de Bordeaux, 1981), 67–87.

Trani, C. "Le Grand Conseil pendant la Ligue." *Revue historique de droit français et étranger* 43 (1965): 458–63.

Trémault, A. de. "Biographie de Louis Servin." *Extrait du Bulletin de la Société Archéologique, Littéraire et Scientifique du Vendômois.* Vendôme, France: Typographie Lemercier et fils, 1871.

Tucker, George Hugo. *The Poet's Odyssey: Joachim du Bellay and the Antiquitez de Rome.* Oxford, U.K.: Clarendon Press, 1990.

Turchetti, Mario. *Tyrannie et tyrannicide de l'antiquité à nos jours.* Paris: Presses Universitaires de France, 2001.

Ubald d'Alençon, F. "Une page de l'histoire de Paris: Le Parlement et les immunités religieuses en 1599." *Etudes franciscaines* 9 (1903): 607–12.

Ullmann, Walter. "The Development of the Medieval Idea of Sovereignty." *English Historical Review* 64 (1949): 1–33.

---. "Juristic Obstacles to the Emergence of the Idea of the State in the Middle Ages." *Annali di storia del diritto* 13 (1969): 43–64.
---. *Principles of Government and Politics in the Middle Ages*. New York: Barnes and Noble, 1961.
Urbain, Charles. *Nicolas Coeffeteau dominicain, évêque de Marseille, un des fondateurs de la prose française (1574–1623)*. Paris: Thorin et fils, 1893.
Valois, Noël. *Histoire de la Pragmatique Sanction de Bourges sous Charles VII*. Archives de l'histoire religieuse de France. Paris: Alphonse Picard et fils, 1906.
---. *La France et le grand schisme d'occident*. 4 vols. Paris: Alphonse Picard et fils, 1896–1902.
van Kley, Dale. "Church, State and the Ideological Origins of the French Revolution: The Debate over the General Assembly of the Gallican Clergy in 1765." *Journal of Modern History* 51 (1979): 629–66.
---. *The Jansenists and the Expulsion of the Jesuits from France*. New Haven, Conn.: Yale University Press, 1975.
---. *The Religious Origins of the French Revolution: From Calvin to the Civil Constitution, 1560–1791*. New Haven, Conn.: Yale University Press, 1996.
Venard, Marc. "Une réforme gallicane?: Le projet de concile nationale de 1551." *Revue d'histoire de l'église de France* 47 (1981): 201–25.
Vodola, Elizabeth. *Excommunication in the Middle Ages*. Berkeley and Los Angeles: University of California Press, 1986.
Waele, Michel de. "De Paris à Tours: La crise d'identité des magistrats parisiens de 1589 à 1594." *Revue historique* 299 (1998): 549–77.
---. "Image de force, perception de faiblesse: La clémence d'Henri IV." *Renaissance and Reformation/Renaissance et réforme* 17 (1993): 51–60.
Walker, D. P. *The Ancient Theology: Studies in Christian Platonism from the Fifteenth to the Eighteenth Century*. Ithaca, N.Y.: Cornell University Press, 1972.
---. *Unclean Spirits: Possession and Exorcism in France and England in the Late Sixteenth and Early Seventeenth Centuries*. Philadelphia: University of Pennsylvania Press, 1981.
Wanegffelen, Thierry. *Une difficile fidélité: Catholiques malgré le concile en France, XVIe–XVIIe siècles*. Paris: Presses Universitaires de France, 1999.
---. *Ni Rome ni Genève: Des fidèles entre deux chaires en France au XVIe siècle*. Bibliothèque littéraire de la Renaissance, Series 3, Vol. 36. Paris: Honoré Champion, 1997.
Wells, Charlotte C. *Law and Citizenship in Early Modern France*. Baltimore: Johns Hopkins University Press, 1995.
Wilks, Michael. "*Reformatio regni*: Wyclif and Hus as Leaders of Religious Protest Movements." *Studies in Church History* 9 (1972): 109–30.
Wolfe, Michael, ed. *Changing Identities in Early Modern France*. Durham, N.C.: Duke University Press, 1997.
---. *The Conversion of Henry IV: Power, Politics and Religious Belief in Early Modern France*. Cambridge, Mass: Harvard University Press, 1993.
---. "Piety and Political Allegiance: The Duc de Nevers and the Protestant Henry IV, 1589–93." *French History* 2 (1988): 1–21.

Yates, Frances A. *The Art of Memory*. Chicago: University of Chicago Press, 1966.
———. *Astræa: The Imperial Theme in the Sixteenth Century*. London: Routledge & Kegan Paul, 1975.
———. *Giordano Bruno and the Hermetic Tradition*. Chicago: University of Chicago Press, 1964.
Yunck, John A. *The Lineage of Lady Meed: The Development of Mediaeval Venality Satire*. University of Notre Dame Publications in Mediaeval Studies 17. South Bend, Ind.: University of Notre Dame Press, 1963.
Zeller, Gaston. *Les institutions de la France au XVIe siècle*. Paris: Presses Universitaires de France, 1948.

Index

absolutism. *See* political theory, absolutist
administration: civil, 67, 74, 89, 115, 202, 243–44;
    ecclesiastical, 11, 26, 33, 49, 52, 115, 120, 157–59,
    206, 232, 235–36, 243–44, 261, 263
Almain, John, 32–33,
Anglican church, 134, 138, 157, 201, 206, 224. *See
    also* HenryVIII, King of England; reform,
    Protestant
apostles, 12, 14, 16, 19, 22, 30–32, 44, 49, 154,
    156–57, 167, 211, 236; canons of the, 20, 23,
    210–11. *See also* papacy, authority of; poverty,
    apostolic
appeals: Act in Restraint of, 138; *comme d'abus*, 117,
    128, 138–39, 146–47, 188, 191–92, 214, 217,
    220–22, 232, 251, 272; to Rome, 34–35, 188–89,
    192, 199, 220; from French courts, 146, 160,
    187–88, 192, 198, 211; from popes, 117, 128.
Aquinas, Thomas, O.P. (Saint), 1, 148, 236
Aristotle, 54, 79–80, 91
Arnauld, Antoine, 100, 124, 160, 259
assassination, 123, 174, 197, 199–200, 255–57. *See
    also* tyrannicide
assemblies of the clergy. *See* clergy, assemblies of
Augustine of Hippo (Saint), 14, 168
Augustinian Hermits. *See* Egidio of Viterbo
avarice, 8, 14–15, 17, 20, 23, 29, 36–37, 41, 55, 94,
    157, 207, 215. *See also* poverty, apostolic
Avignon, 7–8, 19, 142, 192

Balsac d'Entragues, Charlotte Marie de, 187–90
Balsac d'Entragues, Henriette de, 188, 219

Basel, Council of. *See* Council, Church, of
    Basel
Bassompiere, François de, 187–90, 222
Baumgartner, Frederic, 185–86
Belgium. *See* Netherlands
Bellarmine, Robert, S.J. (Saint), 201, 242
Bellay, Eustache du (bishop of Paris), 113
Bellay, Jean (Cardinal) du, 38, 41, 44, 82, 84
Bellay, Joachim du, 44–50, 53, 62, 83, 112
Bellièvre, Pomponne de, 135, 189, 216, 226, 229
benefices, 12, 13, 19, 34–36, 39–40, 121–22, 130, 138,
    143, 158, 198, 207, 217, 232, 233–36, 258. *See also
    conseil de conscience*; *régale*
Bergin, Joseph, 243, 248
Bible. *See* Scripture
Bignon, Jerôme, 99, 142, 147, 166
Biondo, Flavio, 43
bishops, 4, 21–22, 25, 33, 36, 41, 82, 97, 107, 111,
    118, 121–22, 140–43, 146, 149, 151, 153, 157, 159,
    170, 185, 189, 194, 199, 200, 204–7, 209–12,
    214–15, 222, 224, 229–41, 248, 250–51, 272, 275,
    277. *See also* apostles; clergy; *conseil de conscience*;
    papacy; Richelieu
Blet, Pierre, S.J., 272
Bochard, Jean, 35–36
Bodin, Jean, 90–91, 124, 133, 135, 145, 172–73, 178,
    173
Boëtie, Etienne de la, 72, 75, 85, 109–10, 122
BonifaceVIII, Pope, 7, 15, 18–19, 147, 170
Bonnefoy, Jean, 160
Bordeaux. *See* Guyenne

315

Borromeo, Carlo (Cardinal) (Saint) (archbishop of Milan), 116, 205, 241, 275
Bouchel, Laurent, 100, 102–4, 130, 168, 195, 197–98, 202, 213, 215, 217, 223
Bouchet, Jean, 28–29
Bouju, Theophraste, 153–54
Bourdin, Gilles, 99, 119, 126–27, 129, 195, 219. *See also* Pithou, Pierre, *Les libertez de l'eglise gallicane*
Bouwsma, William, 52, 162–63
breviaries, 76, 160, 208, 214–17, 241, 251
Brossier, Marthe, 198–99, 242
Brulart, Noel, 39, 99
Budé, Guillaume, 37, 57–58, 65, 86, 102–3, 145
bulls, papal, 116–17, 126, 128, 172, 173, 180, 195, 231; *In cæna domini*, 112, 127, 191–92, 220; *Unam sanctam*, 24, 147; *Unigenitus*, 278
Bureau de Jurisdiction, 278–79, 283–84. *See also* clergy, assemblies of; jurisdiction
Byzantine Empire, 31, 158. *See also* Rome, empire

Cajetan, Tomasso de Vio, O.P., 32–33, 103
Calvin, John, 65, 238; Calvinism, 2, 107, 110, 111, 162, 165, 253. *See also* Huguenots; reform, Protestant
Campion, Edmond, S.J. (Saint), 43
canons, capitular, 21, 41, 121, 125, 159, 185, 193–94, 198, 204–7, 209–12, 214–15, 217, 218–20, 234, 248
Capetian dynasty, 114–15, 169
Cappel, Jacques, 38–41, 99, 126, 129, 130
Capuchins. *See* Franciscans
Carmelites, 195, 218
Carolingian dynasty, 26, 82–83, 89, 169, 207, 214, 235
Casaubon, Isaac, 253
Catherine de Medicis, Queen of France, 51, 106–7, 116, 195
Catholic Church. *See* bishops; bulls, papal; canons, capitular; Carmelites; Council, Church; clergy; diplomacy, Franco-papal; Dominicans; episcopacy; Franciscans; Gallican church; legates, papal; mendicant orders; papacy; reform; Society of Jesus
Cavaillon, diocese of, 142–43
chapters. *See* canons, capitular
Charlemagne, Emperor, 28, 50, 114, 116, 173. *See also* Carolingian dynasty
Charles V, Holy Roman Emperor, 24, 47, 88

Charles VI, King of France, 19–20, 23
Charles VIII, King of France, 24
Charles IX, King of France, 50, 116, 121, 141
Christ, 22, 32–33, 36, 59, 74, 147, 149, 154, 157, 159, 166, 168, 206, 221, 222, 236, 268, 278. *See also* Holy Spirit
Christendom, 14–15, 17, 22, 29, 31, 32, 111, 114, 149, 168, 178, 183, 235, 253–54
Church, William Farr, 2, 269–70
Cicero, Marcus Tullius, 38, 43–44, 53, 63, 76, 86–87, 144, 189, 276
civil wars. *See* Wars of Religion
Clement VIII, Pope, 135, 206, 220, 233, 239–40
clergy, 16, 18, 29–33, 41, 91, 178, 211; assemblies of, 10–11, 26–27, 33, 40, 83, 107, 120–21, 186, 189, 205, 211–12, 214–16, 223–24, 227–38, 245–52, 267–73, 274–84; French, 3–4, 11, 21–23, 96–97, 106–7, 132–33, 136, 185–86. *See also* bishops; Bureau de Jurisdiction; canons, capitular; Council, Church; estates; Estates General; jurisdiction, ecclesiastical; mendicant orders; papacy; sacraments
Coeffeteau, Nicolas, O.P., 202–3, 255
collation. *See* benefices
Colloquy of Poissy (1561), 37, 106–7, 109, 130, 227
conciliarism. *See* Council, Church, authority of
Concordat of Bologna (1516), 9, 25, 33–36, 39, 40, 42, 108, 128, 147, 174, 185, 188, 233
Concordat of 1801. *See* Napoleon (I) Bonaparte
Condé, Henri (II) de Bourbon, Prince de, 98, 117, 182, 222
confessionalization, 37, 42, 45–46, 106, 111, 247. *See also* Calvin, John; Colloquy of Poissy (1561); Luther, Martin; reform, Catholic
conseil de conscience, 6, 248, 268, 272
Constantine I, Roman Emperor, 16–17, 22, 31
Contarini, Gasparo (Cardinal), 79–80
Coquille, Guy, 100, 111, 125, 130, 156, 158
Cordeliers. *See* Franciscans
Cospeau, Phillipe (bishop of Aire), 267–68, 277
Council, Church: authority of, 5, 11, 17, 23–25, 32–34, 111, 115, 148–55, 159, 202–4, 206; of Basel, 20, 23, 35, 206, 241; of Constance, 23, 27, 150, 203, 261; Fifth Lateran, 30–31, 33, 35–36; Fourth Lateran, 213; national, 156, 169, 211, 236, 271; of Pisa (1511–1513), 27–30, 32–33; of Trent, 12, 27, 38–39, 51, 96, 98, 107–8, 110, 118–19, 121, 123, 132, 149, 205–7, 214, 223, 228, 238, 267, 272–73, 275–76. *See also* clergy, assemblies of;

Gallican church; papacy; reform; schism, Great Western
council, royal: *d'état*, 40, 189, 204, 208, 216, 233, 265, 276; *privé*, 146, 188, 192, 211, 221, 264. *See also conseil de conscience*; Grand Conseil
counsel, 77, 80–95, 101, 114–16, 128, 165, 174, 186, 212, 231, 240, 249–50, 258, 265, 271–72, 282
Counter-Reformation. *See* reform, Catholic
Cour des Monnaies, 100, 125, 155. *See also* Fauchet, Claude
crusade, 29, 168
Cuignières, Pierre de, 39
Cujas, Jacques, 81, 145–46
Cusanus, Nicolas, 62, 70
custom, 8, 36, 56, 63–77, 81, 89–90, 95, 101, 110, 114, 158, 179, 186, 196, 198, 211, 215, 224–25, 235–36, 244, 258, 273, 280–81, 283; in law, 65, 69–70, 127, 225. *See also* history; law; skepticism

De la puissance royalle et sacerdotale, 119–21, 158, 176, 236, 252
dioceses. *See* bishops; canons, capitular; clergy
Dionysius the pseudo-Aeropagite, 151
diplomacy, 3, 92, 142, 187, 201, 252, 261; Franco-papal, 13, 39, 45, 51, 116–17, 125, 135, 183–84, 188, 196, 199, 202–3, 214, 220, 238, 239–40, 246, 275–76. *See also* Gallican crisis (1551); legates, papal
Dominicans, 15–16, 29, 32, 195, 202–4. *See also* mendicant orders
Doucet, Roger, 34
dueling, 187, 191, 268–70, 272
Dumoulin, Charles, 40, 42–43, 100, 107–8, 113, 155–56, 278
Dupuy, Pierre, 34, 98–100, 127, 130–31, 134, 181, 184, 189, 277, 281
Duval, André, 154, 198, 204

Edict of Nantes (1598), 93, 227, 243
Egidio of Viterbo, 30–31
election of prelates, 33–35, 41, 50, 154, 158, 159, 194, 236, 248–49, 258, 262. *See also* Concordat of Bologna (1516); Pragmatic Sanction of Bourges (1483)
empire, 53, 54, 58, 60, 137–38, 223. *See also* Byzantine Empire; Holy Roman Empire; Persian Empire; Rome, empire
Enlightenment, 10, 283–84
Erasmus, Desiderius, 37, 44, 63, 93, 107–8, 162

Erastianism, 138, 165
Estampes, Léonore d' (bishop of Chartres), 275–77
estates, 49, 63, 94, 132, 190, 225–26, 229–31. *See also* clergy, French; nobility
Estates General, 111, 154, 186, 231, 245; of 1484, 21; of 1560, 50–51; of 1576–1577, 121, 227; of 1588, 257; of 1593, 128, 142, 154, 257, 231; of 1614–1615, 3, 98, 131, 180, 182, 189, 193, 201, 213, 219, 222, 231, 248–49, 257–67, 274, 276; of 1789, 10, 279
Estates of Provence, 189
Evangelicism. *See* reform, evangelical
excommunication, 18, 97, 117–17, 145, 148, 191–92, 196, 205, 212, 217, 220–22, 246; of kings of France, 26, 128, 168–84, 197, 232, 246, 255–56, 259. *See also* appeals, *comme d'abus*; jurisdiction, ecclesiastical

Faye d'Espesses, Charles, 4, 100, 126, 130
Faye d'Espesses, Jacques, 4, 99, 110–11, 119
Flacius Illyricus, Marcus, 45
Florence, 24, 44, 46, 70, 196
Franciscans, 15–17, 22, 29, 161, 195–98, 213, 218, 257. *See also* mendicant orders
François I, King of France, 12, 25, 33–36, 57–58, 82
François II, King of France, 50
Frederick II, Holy Roman Emperor, 18
Froger, George, 179–80
Fumaroli, Marc, 90

Gallican Articles (1682), 277
Gallican church 4, 8–9, 11, 18–21, 23, 25–27, 32–34, 38, 40, 49, 82–84, 95, 129, 141, 147, 164, 194–95, 211, 223, 233, 236, 238, 242, 246, 281–82; liberties of, 3–5, 9–13, 15, 27, 34, 41, 97–99, 115, 119, 123–24, 126–31, 156–57, 165–66, 186, 193, 210–12, 219, 222, 227, 283. *See also* clergy, French; Leschassier, Jacques; Pithou, Pierre; *Les libertez de l'eglise gallicane*
Gallican Crisis (1551), 39–43, 106, 118, 157
Gallicanism: definitions of, 3–13, 126–28, 210–11; ecclesiastical, 6, 15–18, 21–24, 26–27, 133–36, 275–78; medieval, 14–25, 28. 55, 146–47; opposition to, 6, 23, 134, 154, 185–99, 202–26, 228–54, 260–64, 275–82; royal, 6, 18–20, 24–29, 39–43, 277; treatises on, 119–22, 125–31, 133–35, 175–78, 209–12. *See also* Concordat of

Bologna (1516); Gallican Articles (1682); Gallican church, liberties of; Pragmatic Sanction of Bourges (1438)
Genebrard, Gilbert, 123–24
gens du roi: avocat général, 11, 38, 97, 108, 110, 125, 129, 133, 139, 159–60, 172, 192, 252, 259; corporate body, 97–106, 119, 126, 128–29, 131, 192, 199, 200, 230–31, 234, 240, 281; *procureur général*, 39, 118, 129, 131, 133–34, 140, 153, 165, 192, 195–96, 198, 208, 212, 234, 246
Germany. *See* Holy Roman Empire
Gerson, Jean, 17, 32, 150–54, 155, 158, 162, 166, 171, 184, 263
Godefroy, Denis, 152, 156–57
Godefroy, Théodore, 98–100
Gousté, Claude, 130
Grand Conseil, 100, 134, 154, 209, 212, 232, 234, 235
Gregory VII, Pope, 169–71
Guesle, François de la (archbishop of Tours), 207, 247–48
Guesle, Jacques de la, 52, 80, 99, 130, 146, 165–68, 175, 183, 197, 211, 234
Guillaume de Pierre Godin, 22
Guise, Charles de (Cardinal de Lorraine), 49, 107, 118, 157, 173,
Guise, Henri, Duc de, 123, 200
Guyenne, 59, 64, 218–19, 242, 259. *See also* Loisel, Antoine; Montaigne, Michel de; Sourdis, François de (archbishop of Bordeaux)

Hampton, Timothy, 67, 137
Hapsburg family, 28–29, 92, 111, 140, 201, 253. *See also* Charles V, Holy Roman Emperor; Holy Roman Empire; Netherlands; Philip II, King of Spain; Philip III, King of Spain; Spain
Harlay, Achille de, 59, 105–6, 164, 181, 240
Harlay, François de (archbishop of Rouen), 242
Hennequin family, 188, 205
Henri II, King of France, 39–42, 82, 106, 140, 173
Henri III, King of France, 96, 110, 119, 123, 157, 174, 200, 213, 233
Henri IV, King of France, 4, 10, 91–94, 96–97, 105, 108, 117, 119, 123–28, 131–35, 152, 164, 167, 171–72, 174, 183–84, 187–88, 190, 194, 196–99, 200–205, 208, 213, 216–17, 218, 220–21, 225, 229–33, 241–43, 246, 249, 252, 255–56, 262, 273, 282
Henry IV, Holy Roman Emperor, 169–70

Henry VIII, King of England, 157, 176. *See also* Anglican church
Hermann, bishop of Metz, 169
historicism, 1, 9–10, 12–13, 28, 38–43, 45–49, 52–56, 63, 77–95, 98–99, 111, 113–16, 125–28, 130–31, 135, 154–60, 167, 174, 178–79, 181, 186, 210–12, 231, 273, 280, 282. *See also* humanism; political thought
Holy Roman Empire, 7, 37, 92, 169–71, 253. *See also* Hapsburg family; Netherlands
Holy Spirit, 17, 164, 250, 258. *See also* Christ
Hotman, Antoine, 41, 99, 101, 130, 133–35, 142
Hotman, François, 69, 72, 84, 89
Huguenots, 92, 116, 118–19, 132, 190, 195, 199, 204, 227–28, 241. *See also* Edict of Nantes (1598)
humanism, 2–4, 25, 28, 37–51, 53–56, 62–63, 85–89, 91–94, 108–9, 128, 131, 162–63, 205, 224, 261, 279, 283; among French jurists, 9, 38, 61, 77, 81, 96, 102, 160, 168, 280–81; Italian, 28, 43–45, 58. *See also* Aristotle; Cicero, Marcus Tullius; historicism; political thought; Plato; reform, evangelical
Hurault de l'Hospital, Paul (archbishop of Aix-en-Provence), 188–94, 204, 205, 249, 251, 261

ideology, 3–4, 6–10, 21–25, 39, 43, 69, 75, 77, 79, 81, 94, 96, 101–2, 105–6, 108, 118–19, 123, 131–32, 143–44, 152, 164–66, 168–69, 185–87, 189–90, 196, 216–19, 224–25, 232–33, 247, 267, 273, 280–83. *See also* Gallicanism
imperium, 145–46, 160, 162, 167. *See also* jurisdiction
interdict, 26, 172, 212. *See also* Venice, Interdict affair (1607)
Italy, 5, 7, 12, 24, 26, 39, 43–49, 56, 112, 119, 138, 152, 196, 198, 205, 208–9, 213, 224–25, 241, 254, 280. *See also* Florence; humanism, Italian; Rome; Venice

Jacob, Florentin, 165, 196–97, 200, 202
Jacobins. *See* Dominicans
James I, King of England, 181–82, 200, 201, 253–55, 262–63
Jansenism, 132, 152, 160, 268, 274–75, 277, 279, 281. *See also* bulls, papal, *Unigenitus*
Jean de Paris (Jean Quidort), O.P., 15–16, 21–22, 120, 170–71
Jeanne d'Albret, Queen of Navarre, 116–17, 140, 195
Jesuits. *See* Society of Jesus

INDEX   319

Jesus. *See* Christ
Joachim of Fiore. *See* prophecy
Julius II, Pope, 26, 30–31
Julius III, Pope, 39, 46
Jupiter, intimate relations with Ganymede of, 46, 261
jurisdiction, 7, 72, 74, 127–28, 136, 137–62, 168–84; criminal, 192; defined, 139, 143–51, 155–56; ecclesiastical, 5, 10, 13, 21–25, 32, 43, 83, 97, 108, 116, 118, 120–21, 125, 132, 192–94, 201–25, 228–41, 246, 250–52, 255, 263, 266, 268–69, 271–72, 274–75, 278–83; relation to sacramental order, 148–54, 161–62, 166, 190, 210, 217; secular, 18, 33, 53, 83, 134, 185–86, 203–4, 223, 231–32, 239, 261; territoriality of, 139–43, 155–59. *See also* appeals; Bureau de Jurisdiction; bulls, papal; canons, capitular; Concordat of Bologna (1516); Council, Church, authority of; excommunication; *imperium*; Pragmatic Sanction of Bourges (1438); sacraments
jurisdictionalism, 10, 106, 138–39, 185
jurisprudence, 60, 73, 77, 80, 82, 101, 120, 134, 137, 145, 205, 208
justice, 12, 57–68, 71–74, 77, 79, 85, 87, 101, 103–4, 151–54, 193, 220–21, 243, 247, 266, 269

Kelley, Donald, 42
Kermadec, François de, 263

Lanier de l'Effretier, Guy, 100, 133–34
law, 58, 62, 67–69, 72, 79–80, 209; canon, 5, 10, 12, 23–24, 58, 82, 101, 108, 121, 140–41, 144–48, 158, 161–62, 167, 172–74, 177, 188, 197, 203, 206, 209–11, 220, 228, 233, 236–37, 241, 248, 261, 267; common, 8, 23, 34, 41, 69, 127; divine, 12, 149, 156, 161, 173, 236, 275; French, 69, 81, 137–38, 144, 146–47, 186, 196, 259–61, 274; natural, 40, 53, 62, 65–66, 70–71, 236, 243–44, 283; Roman, 57, 61, 69, 80, 103–4, 114, 120, 144–46, 147, 149, 156, 160, 206, 211. *See also* apostles, canons of the; Councils, Church; custom, in law; duelling; jurisdiction; jurisprudence
League, Holy Catholic, 76, 93, 105, 119, 123, 128, 132–33, 135, 142, 165, 174, 197–99, 208, 213, 216, 230–34, 242, 253, 273, 281. *See also* Estates General, of 1593
legates, papal, 127, 142, 213, 216, 232, 237, 239–40. *See also* diplomacy, Franco-papal
Lemaire de Belges, Jean, 27–29, 41, 42, 83, 201

Leo X, Pope, 33–34
Leroy, Louis, 68–71
Leschassier, Jacques, 4, 100, 156, 166, 201–2, 208–12, 218, 259
l'Estoile, Pierre de, 100, 111, 130
l'Hospital, Michel de, 49, 77, 107, 109, 118
Loisel, Antoine, 59–65, 72, 75, 99–102, 109, 119–23, 128–30, 204, 259
Lorraine. *See* Guise
Louis "The Bold," Emperor, 28
Louis "The Fat," Emperor, 246
Louis IX (Saint), King of France, 18–19, 57, 115
Louis XI, King of France, 20–21, 33, 69
Louis XII, King of France, 24–27, 33, 40, 277
Louis XIII, King of France, 10, 12, 101, 125, 179, 223, 264, 268, 274, 282
Louis XIV, King of France, 121, 227, 232, 248, 254, 272, 274, 277
Louis XV, King of France, 6, 279, 282
Louis XVI, King of France, 282
Luther, Martin, 28, 36–37, 114, 165, 167, 237; Lutheranism, 139. *See also* reform, Protestant
Lyons, 27, 53, 217, 238, 259

Machiavelli, Niccolò, 39, 44, 54–56, 70, 84, 86–87, 167, 244. *See also* Pocock, J. G. A.
Maistre, Gilles le, 99
Major, John, 149
Marca, Pierre de (bishop of Couserans), 224
Marie de Medicis, Queen of France, 188, 222, 252, 254
Marion, Simon, 99, 159–60
Marsiglio of Padua, 28, 122, 161, 170
Martin, Victor, 23, 108
Masselin, Jean, 21
Maugis, Edouard, 132, 232
Mazarin, Jules (Cardinal), 6, 146, 194, 268
mendicant orders, 16, 18, 22, 113, 148–49, 195–96, 207. *See also* Dominicans; Franciscans
Mesnil, Baptiste du, 11–12, 99, 108, 113, 116–18, 129–30, 140–41, 143, 159
Milletot, Benigne, 100, 130
Miron, Charles (bishop of Angers), 212–17, 251
Molé, Mathieu, 97–101, 131, 189, 259, 274–75, 281
monarchy, theories of, 3, 10, 24–25, 29, 32–33, 57–61, 71–72, 76, 89–90, 103–4, 114–16, 135, 153, 167–84, 189, 193, 225, 245–52, 267, 269–73. *See also* absolutism; political theory; Salic Law; tyrannicide

Monluc, Jean de (bishop of Valence), 107–8, 110, 118
Montaigne, Michel de, 53, 63–75, 78, 109–10, 112, 119, 124, 135, 179, 191

Nancel, Pierre de, 100, 255–56
Napoleon (I) Bonaparte, 1, 5
Navarre, 140–43. *See also* Henri IV, King of France; Jeanne d'Albret, Queen of Navarre
Neoplatonism. *See* Plato
Netherlands, 28, 92, 110, 268–69
Nevers, Ludovic de Gonzague, Duc de, 91, 125, 135, 230
nominalism, 17, 66, 69–70, 236
nuncios, papal. *See* diplomacy, Franco-papal

Ockham, William of, O.F.M., 17, 236. *See also* nominalism
Optatus Milevitanus, 8, 166, 235
Orleans, 25, 259. *See also* Estates General, of 1560.
Ossat, Arnaud (Cardinal) d', 220, 242. *See also* diplomacy, Franco-papal

Paige, Louis-Adrien le, 281
papacy: authority of, 7–8, 21–22, 110, 171, 176, 180, 195, 200; corruption and reform of, 12, 17, 22, 37, 45–49, 111–12, 117, 215; nature of, 4–5, 157–58, 237; relations with French church, 5, 11, 37, 40, 42, 146, 216, 219–21, 230–32, 238; relations with French courts, 9, 20–21, 34–36, 147, 188–89; relations with French monarchy, 8, 18–20, 26, 39–43, 50–51, 54, 116, 142, 168–84, 221, 239, 253–54. *See also* bulls, papal; Council, Church; diplomacy, Franco-papal; excommunication, of French kings; legates, papal; reform, Catholic; reform, Christian
parlements, 6, 34, 58, 89–90, 101, 109, 110, 114–15, 126, 139, 153, 193, 199, 212, 219, 225, 228, 229, 239, 250, 252, 266, 281–82; of Aix-en-Provence, 142, 190–94, 250–51, 279; of Bordeaux, 218–23; of Dijon, 100, 198; of Paris, 20–21, 33–36, 38–39, 40, 42, 51, 59, 76, 82, 89, 91–93, 97–106, 108, 113–14, 118–21, 125, 128–32, 134, 139, 142, 153, 160, 163–64, 173–74, 179, 188, 190, 195–200, 202–4, 209, 210, 213–17, 229, 230–32, 234–34, 238, 239–40, 243, 246, 249, 251, 259, 263–64, 269, 276–77, 281; of Rennes, 275; of Rouen, 188; of Toulouse, 197–98, 205, 223. *See also gens du roi*; Trésor des Chartes

Parma. *See* Gallican Crisis (1551)
parquet. See gens du roi
Pasquier, Estienne, 81, 99–100, 182, 207, 281; anti-Jesuit writings, 108, 112–14, 129–30, 194, 278; *Pourparlers,* 62–63, 65–66, 68, 84–90; *Recherches de la France,* 89, 114–18, 120, 141, 157, 166–67, 173, 175–76, 178, 230, 234
paulette. See venal officeholding
Peleus, Julien, 137, 139, 160, 162
penitent confraternities, 198
Pepin ("The Short"), King of the Franks, 7, 28, 30, 115–16. *See also* Carolingian dynasty
Pericard, François de (bishop of Avranches), 252
Perron, Jacques Davy (Cardinal) du, 134–35, 154, 184, 201–4, 241–42, 254, 261–63, 267
Persian Empire: Achæmenid, 60; Safavid, 27.
Philip II ("Augustus"), King of France. 1, 114
Philip II, King of Macedon, 73
Philip II, King of Spain, 124, 271
Philip III, King of Spain, 142
Philip IV ("The Fair"), King of France, 7, 15, 18–20, 25, 26, 40, 42, 147, 170
Piard, Antoine, 175–78, 181
Pithou, Pierre, 64, 90–91, 100, 102, 119, 124–25, 134, 156, 163, 234, 271; *Les Libertez de l'Eglise gallicane,* 5, 52, 126–30, 172, 176, 191, 219. *See also* Bourdin, Pierre
Pius V, Pope, 140
Plato, 30, 38, 60–61, 80, 87, 151
Plutarch, 53
Pocock, J. G. A., 49, 54
police. See administration
political theory: absolutist, 83, 104, 114, 127, 135–36, 145, 176, 179, 247–49, 265, 267–68, 273, 282; medieval, 24, 56–57, 70; of erudite Gallicans, 52–56, 75–76, 81–95, 101–6, 210–12, 214–15, 230–32, 235, 259–60; of French prelates, 107–8, 222–25, 236–38, 243–52, 260–73, 276–84; republican, 8–9, 15, 38, 41, 49, 54–56, 58, 60, 70, 79–80, 85–90, 94–95, 104, 113–14, 138, 143, 157, 166–67, 189, 207, 235, 248, 258, 281, 284. *See also* Bodin, Jean; Budé, Guillaume; Contarini, Gasparo (Cardinal); Council, Church, authority of; Enlightenment; Montaigne, Michel de; papacy, authority of; Pasquier, Estienne; Richelieu, Armand-Jean du Plessis (Cardinal) de (bishop of Luçon); Stoicism; Seyssel, Claude de
politique party, 75, 85, 118–19, 122, 171, 190

Popilinière, Lancelot Voisin de la, 77–78, 87
poverty, apostolic, 14, 16–17, 19, 29–30, 49
Pragmatic Sanction of Bourges (1438), 20–21, 24, 27, 29, 33–35, 42, 50–51, 82, 123, 129, 174, 223
privilege, 11, 22, 40, 123, 141, 160, 161, 172–73, 180, 195, 220, 228–29, 231. *See also* Gallican church, liberties of; jurisdiction
prophecy, 16–17, 24, 28–31, 38, 49–50, 54–55, 57, 60, 82–83, 123, 199, 254
Protest of Saint Louis, 18–19
Protestantism. *See* Anglican church; Calvin, John; Huguenots; Luther, Martin; Poissy, Colloquy of; reform, Protestant
Pyrrhonism. *See* skepticism

Rabelais, François, 37, 40, 45
Raemond, Florimond de, 219
Rambouillet, Claude d'Angennes de (bishop of Le Mans), 134–35, 183–84, 237, 246, 267
reform: Catholic, 2, 4, 6, 107–8, 132, 197–98, 198, 204–6, 213–16, 218–19, 224–25, 233, 239, 241–42, 246–47, 260, 280, 282; Christian, 8–9, 12, 14–18, 25, 27–39, 44, 47, 49–51, 82–83, 94, 114, 168, 215, 280; evangelical, 35, 37, 44, 81, 88, 106–7, 109–11, 155, 162–63; political, 43–44, 48, 56, 69, 83, 89, 257–59, 269–73, 272; monastic, 115, 213, 218; Protestant, 4, 9, 11, 25, 35, 37, 45, 51, 56, 75, 82, 138, 241–42. *See also* Anglican church; Borromeo, Carlo (Saint); Calvin, John; Concordat of 1515; Council, Church; Erasmus, Desiderius; Gerson, Jean; Gregory VII, Pope; Luther, Martin
régale, 121–22, 127
remonstrances and orations: by clergy, 229, 238, 245–52, 261–63, 265–69; by magistrates, 20–21, 34–36, 53–54, 58–62, 82, 105–6, 129, 165–67, 192–94, 230. *See also* Cicero, Marcus Tullius
republicanism. *See* political theory, republican
Revolution, French. *See* Estates General, of 1789
Richelieu, Alphonse de (archbishop of Lyons), 217
Richelieu, Armand-Jean du Plessis (Cardinal) de (bishop of Luçon), 6, 10, 104, 157, 202, 205, 222, 241, 253, 264–72, 276, 282
Richer, Edmond, 147, 149, 152–54, 161, 166, 179–81, 201–3, 206–7, 216, 226, 238, 240, 242, 277
Roche Flavin, Bernard de la, 102–3, 252
Rochefoucauld, Alexandre de la, 198–99, 208

Rochefoucauld, François (Cardinal) de la (bishop of Clermont-en-Auvergne), 198–99, 208, 241–45, 276–77
Roelker, Nancy Lyman, 111, 130, 226
Rome: city and diocese, 21, 30, 43–49, 53, 62, 116, 122, 174, 190–91, 242; empire, 31, 43, 47, 49, 74, 140, 144, 155–56, 158–60, 168; republic, 56, 87, 144. *See also* Byzantine Empire; Holy Roman Empire; papacy
Rouen, 21, 242. *See also* parlements, of Rouen
Rousseau, Jean-Jaques, 1, 79, 284
Roze, Guillaume (bishop of Senlis), 208–12, 218

sacraments, 22, 36, 109, 121, 144, 148–52, 155, 161–66, 178, 182, 210–12, 274, 278–79; baptism, 158; confirmation, 109; eucharist, 107, 109–10, 151; orders, 110, 148, 158; penance, 148, 255–56, 271; matrimony, 158. *See also* clergy; jurisdiction; excommunication
Salic law, 76, 128–29, 154
Salmon, J. H. M., 225, 273
Salvian of Marseille, 124–25, 215
Sarpi, Paolo, 201, 209, 211
Satyre menipée de la vertu du catholicon d'espagne, 124, 130, 171
Savonarola, Girolamo, O.P., 24, 54
schism, 29, 30, 38–39, 41, 148, 193, 197, 216, 263–64; Great Western, 7, 19, 23–26, 126, 129, 150, 280
Scripture, 11–12, 52–53, 59, 138, 154, 162–65, 215, 223–24, 236, 241, 260
secularization 2–3, 138, 280–81. *See also* state, French, development of
Séguier, Antoine, 53–54, 56, 99, 125, 172, 176, 183; family of, 2
Servin, Louis, 43, 76, 99–101, 104–6, 125–26, 128, 131, 133, 156, 158–60, 163–64, 173, 181, 198, 201, 207–8, 213–18, 250–52, 256, 259, 263–64, 269, 277
Seyssel, Claude de, 58, 114, 245
simony, 23, 28, 29, 35, 36, 41, 109, 258
Sirmond, Jacques, S.J., 156, 199, 271
skepticism, 62–65, 70, 154, 224, 280, 282–83
Skinner, Quentin, 165
Society of Jesus, 12, 85, 96, 108, 112–14, 115, 129, 132, 149, 181, 194–98, 200, 202, 213, 218, 255, 257, 268, 271, 275, 276, 278–79, 283. *See also* Pasquier, Estienne, anti-Jesuit writings
Solon, 53–54, 120

Sourdis, François (Cardinal) de (archbishop of Bordeaux), 205, 208, 218–25, 241–42, 264
Spain, 12, 24, 124, 128, 140–43. *See also* Hapsburg family; Netherlands
state, French, development of 2–4, 57, 69, 97–98, 140, 189–90, 214, 225–26, 257–58, 266, 269–73, 277–84. *See also* political theory
Stoicism, 64, 66, 86, 125, 164. *See also* Ciciero, Marcus Tullius
Suarez, Francisco, S.J., 101, 173, 201, 257
Sully, Maximilien de Béthune, Duc de, 134, 189, 221, 253

Tallon, Alain, 5, 149, 201. *See also* Council, Church, of Trent
Tanquerel, Jean, 194–95
taxes and revenue: French, 7, 18, 104, 227, 229, 257, 271; papal, 5, 7, 18–21, 34–36, 39, 42. *See also régale*
Telesphorus of Costenza, 29–30
Thomas à Becket (Saint) (archbishop of Canterbury), 252
Thou, Christophle de, 108, 110
Thou, Jacques-Auguste de, 91–95, 99, 117, 119–20, 163–64, 199, 253
Tillet, Jean du, 40–41, 43, 82–84, 88, 91–92, 94, 98–100, 117–18, 126, 129–30, 141, 158, 168, 207, 209–10. *See also* Trésor des Chartes
Tours, 25, 27, 198. *See also* Estates General, of 1484; parlements, of Paris

Trent, Council of. *See* Council, Church, of Trent
Trésor des Chartes, 39–41, 98–99, 101
tyrannicide, 173, 180, 199–200, 203, 242, 253, 256–57, 259–60, 263, 276. *See also* assassination; Council, Church, of Constance

ultramontanism. *See* Gallicanism, opposition to
University of Paris, 22–23, 35, 85, 108, 112–15, 159, 164, 171; Faculty of Theology, 23, 32, 42, 113, 115, 147, 149, 152–53, 164–67, 179, 194–202, 204, 214–16, 226, 240. *See also* Almain, John; mendicant orders; Pasquier, Estienne; Richer, Edmond; Society of Jesus

Vair, Guillaume du, 128, 142–43, 159
venal officeholding, 100, 193, 257–58, 281
Venice, 26–27, 29, 44, 79–80, 87, 143, 250; Interdict affair (1607), 201, 208–9, 216, 238, 254
Versoris, Pierre, 113
Villars, Jerôme de (bishop of Vienne), 248–49
Villeroy, Nicolas de Neufville de, 135, 203, 252–53
Vincent Ferrer, O.P. (Saint), 29
Voltaire (François-Marie Arouet), 278

Waldensians, 16–17, 21
War of the League of Cambrai. *See* Venice
Wars of Religion, 9, 49, 53, 71–72, 81, 96–97, 109, 116–18, 122–33, 164, 169, 185, 190, 194, 196, 199, 205, 213, 221, 227–28, 232, 254, 273

The Church in the Republic: Gallicanism & Political Ideology in Renaissance France was designed and composed in Centaur with Requiem display type by Kachergis Book Design, Pittsboro, North Carolina; and printed on 60-pound Nature's Natural and bound by Thomson-Shore, Dexter, Michigan.

www.ingramcontent.com/pod-product-compliance
Lightning Source LLC
Chambersburg PA
CBHW020913020526
44107CB00075B/1668